Augsburg College
George Sverdrup Library
Minneapolis, Minnesota 55404

MORALE IN THE CIVIL SERVICE

One of the hundred Ledger Sections at Records Branch, Ministry of Pensions and National Insurance, Newcastle. (See chapter 5.)

MORALE
IN THE CIVIL SERVICE

*A STUDY OF
THE DESK WORKER*

NIGEL WALKER

*Reader in Criminology, University of Oxford
and formerly an Assistant Secretary in the British Civil Service*

EDINBURGH
AT THE UNIVERSITY PRESS

© 1961 N. D. Walker
Edinburgh University Press

Agents

THOMAS NELSON AND SONS LTD
Parkside Works Edinburgh 9
36 Park Street London W1
312 Flinders Street Melbourne C1
302-304 Barclays Bank Building
Commissioner and Kruis Streets Johannesburg

THOMAS NELSON AND SONS (CANADA) LTD
91-93 Wellington Street West Toronto 1

SOCIÉTÉ FRANÇAISE D'ÉDITIONS NELSON
97 rue Monge Paris 5

Printed in Great Britain
by T. & A. CONSTABLE LTD, Hopetoun Street
Printers to the University of Edinburgh

TO MY WIFE

FOREWORD

To think both usefully and objectively about the members of any large organisation one must both belong to it and not belong to it. I achieved this mystical state through the co-operation of two enlightened employers. Nuffield College at Oxford awarded me a Research Fellowship for one year, and the Scottish Home Department granted me the necessary sabbatical leave. Readers may feel—as I sometimes did myself—that I could have chosen a more profitable subject: but I certainly could not have found a better place in which to study it. My thanks to those who helped me in specific ways are recorded below and elsewhere. The Warden and Fellows of Nuffield College are not collectively mentioned there because it is impossible to describe in a sentence the extent of my indebtedness to them. Their interest in what I was trying to do was so genuine that it survived three terms of my company; and they will find many of their ideas and suggestions developed in these chapters.

As for my fellow bureaucrats, some of what follows may seem to them not so much objective as disloyal. This is probably inevitable in a survey of this kind, which would serve no purpose by powdering small blemishes. Nevertheless, this book is neither a sermon on the iniquities of the British Civil Service nor a hymn in praise of its perfection. It is intended to be a factual study of the psychological aspects of being a bureaucrat in a modern democracy.

N. D. W.

October 1960

ACKNOWLEDGMENTS

I wish to record my gratitude to:

Mr. J. T. Baldry, Mr. D. E. Baptiste, Mr. A. Hibbs and Dr. C. W. Long of the Post Office, for their co-operation in my investigation of their sick-leave records.

Miss O. B. Bertie of Nuffield College Library, for securing me access to many publications.

Mr. Hugh Clegg of Nuffield College, for advice on many points.

The Controller of Her Majesty's Stationery Office, for permission to reproduce the Crown copyright material in this book.

Mrs. Perry Curtis, for her assistance in handling the questionnaires described in Chapter 7.

The Institute of Experimental Psychology at Oxford, for making me free of their library and seminars.

Mr. P. G. Gray of the Social Survey Division of the Central Office of Information, for advice in the design of my questionnaire.

Mr. John Handyside of the National Institute of Industrial Psychology, for advice and for access to the results of his own work in measuring job-satisfaction.

Miss E. M. Harris, Information and Publications Officer of the Institute of Personnel Management, for her assistance in finding a Company to submit to my questionnaire.

Mr. J. H. McCarthy, Mr. W. H. Watling, Mr. R. G. Eayres and the staff of Records Branch in the Newcastle Office of the Ministry of Pensions and National Insurance, for their interest and help in the investigation described in Chapter 5.

The Establishment Officers and their Divisions, and the Personnel Officers and their Departments, in the anonymous Ministries and Companies who submitted to my questionnaire.

Mr. Graham Pyatt, then of Nuffield College, for guidance in statistical technique.

The secretarial staff of Nuffield College, for typing many of the documents involved in this survey.

The Institute of Statistics, and particularly the Acting Director, Mr. K. J. C. Knowles, for lending me the services of Mrs. Smith to punch Hollerith cards; and to Mrs. Smith herself.

The Theoretical Physics Division of the Atomic Energy Research Establishment, for the services of their Hollerith 555 Calculator and for the many hours of work which Mr. J. E. Hailstone and Mr. C. W. Jackson devoted to planning and carrying out the tabulation described in Chapter 7, and to advising me on the interpretation of the results.

The Treasury's Central Staff Records Division, for the information which they extracted on sick leave, retirements and other subjects.

The Treasury's Training and Education Division, for allowing me to attend sessions of their training courses and supplying other information on which Chapter 2.2 is based.

The Treasury Welfare Adviser, for much of the information and introductions on which Chapter 2.1 is based.

CONTENTS

1 Introduction	1
2 Two Positive Approaches	15
3 A Dilemma: The Uses of Dismissal	34
4 A Conceptual Question: What is 'Morale'?	57
5 A Practical Study: The Office as a Factory	64
6 A Search for an Index: Turnover and Sick Leave	108
7 Two Ministries and Two Companies: Arranging a Questionnaire	143
8 Two Ministries and Two Companies: Results of the Questionnaire	161
9 Some Reflections	248
Appendixes	269
Index	295

1
INTRODUCTION

1.1. THE NEED TO CONSIDER THE SERVICE'S 'MORALE'

The idea of studying the *morale* of the British Civil Service might suggest that its efficiency was so low as to justify any sort of remedy, however desperate and far-fetched. This is certainly not the assumption upon which my project was based. But it can safely be said of any organisation that it is never as efficient as it could be. However high you raise the pay, however attractive you make the jobs to the sort of recruits you want, whatever mechanical and other devices you introduce to save human labour, you will not by these means alone extract from your organisation the highest quality or greatest output of work of which it is capable.

This characteristic is probably not peculiar to very large groups of men; but it was the behaviour of very large groups that first drew attention to it. Good leaders of armies have known for centuries that the efficiency of their troops and their success in battle depended not only on the standard of their pay, feeding, health, training and equipment but also on something which was much less easy to define or measure. This elusive factor could cause well-fed, healthy, trained and well-armed men to be routed by ill-armed, half-starved, diseased and undisciplined irregulars.

It was not until the last fifty years that the operation of this factor was detected in other types of organisation. The first scientific studies of it were probably those carried out by industrial consultants in the U.S.A. who were looking for ways to increase the productivity of factory workers. They found that while this could be raised by obvious measures such as greater mechanisation, better working conditions, time-and-motion studies and incentive payments of various kinds, it also depended on the workers' attitude to the management and to their immediate supervisors, on the value which other people seemed to attach to their work, and on other such pyschological factors. This may seem obvious enough nowadays to anyone acquainted with human beings, but the impersonal attitude of the nineteenth century towards industrial labour had to a great extent obscured it, and it was not until the nineteen-thirties that the work of Elton Mayo in the United States reminded industrial managers of this possibility. His famous 'Hawthorne experiment', in which the physical conditions under which a team of girls worked were first improved in various successive ways and then finally restored to their original state, seemed to show that the girls' output improved not only when conditions were being improved but also when they were being changed again for the worse; and the inference drawn from it was that they worked harder mainly because they felt that an interest was being taken in them. Whether the experiment really did justify this—or any other—inference is a question that has been debated fiercely ever since.[1] The historical point of the Hawthorne experiment, however, is not what it really proved, but what a great many people thought it proved; and there is no doubt that it began the swing away from the nineteenth-century tendency to treat the worker as nothing more than a machine of a rather unreliable kind. From the nineteen-thirties onward there was an expanding market for psychological theories about the handling of manual workers. Some of these theories swung the pendulum so far in the other direction that they underestimated the importance of physical conditions of work and material rewards for it; but to be carried too far is the inevitable fate of any new idea.

The 1939-45 war reminded us that the problem of 'morale' had first been encountered in military campaigns. The long spells of comfortable inactivity, alternating with periods of acute danger or hardship, made it difficult even for the best of commanders to maintain the 'morale' of their forces. Unlike the 1914-18 war, the last one coined many expressive phrases for what the psychologists would call 'low job satisfaction': men became 'browned-off', 'cheesed-off', 'depot types' who 'had had it all', and were given to 'binding'. Conscious efforts of many kinds were made to fight against this endemic condition. Army commanders issued homilies, major-generals summoned colonels, colonels returned to harry company commanders, who complained about the quality of junior officers. Subalterns took the men for cross-country runs, made them listen to lectures on Heraldry, French Wines and Positivism, and allowed them to play football and housey-housey. To do them justice, many military, naval and air-force commanders still preserved, by some sort of tradition, the art of keeping troops in good heart, and could do by instinct what the industrialists had to learn. Later in the war, however, scientists began to be imported to study the problem under the complex strains of modern combat, and Doctors of Philosophy became heirs to the secret of Caesar and Napoleon. One of the largest customers for this sort of investigation has been the U.S. Office of Naval Research, whose interest has survived the war and has caused it to commission a great deal of work by the Institute for Social Research of the University of Michigan.

Very little of this psychological attention, however, has been paid so far to a third great sub-species of civilised man, the office worker. He

[1] Although most popular works on occupational psychology ignore the controversy and give only Mayo's conclusions, or their own interpretation of them. For a review of the controversy, see H. A. Landsberger's *Hawthorne Revisited* (1958).

does not perform in such large groups as soldiers or factory workers, and—until recently at least—has been less prone than the craftsman or unskilled labourer to join unions through which he can express his grievances. His output and its quality are not so easy to measure as those of the factory, and there is a temptation to assume that because it is the product of the intellect it is less subject to the influence of moods and other irrational forces than is the work of his hands. This assumption may or may not be correct. It is true that it is very rare for the white-collar man in this country to down tools out of strong dissatisfaction in the same way as a miner will.[1] But even if he stays on the job he may very well be so disturbed that he is incapable of doing any useful brain-work; whereas it is quite possible to perform fairly skilled manual tasks in a highly emotional state. The very difficulty of measuring losses in output or quality from this cause suggests that these might be quite considerable without being suspected. All that is certain is that we do not know.

The Home Civil Service is by far the largest homogeneous organisation of office workers in Britain, and probably consumes a higher proportion of our intelligent manpower than the civil service of any other country in the world. Although it has recently had some difficulty in recruiting enough staff of the right quality for almost every one of its classes,[2] it has tried not to reduce its standards of quality to any appreciable degree as a result. It is therefore important both as the biggest single user of the country's intelligent manpower and as the obvious field for the study of the British black-coated worker in the mass.

From the point of view of those who have already entered the service it is safe to say that it is a benevolent employer. Its buildings, while not as luxurious as some provided by private companies, compare very well with the typical office. A good deal of attention is paid by the Ministry of Works to lighting, heating, ventilation and sanitation; first-aid rooms and canteens for lunch and tea are provided. Offices themselves are adequate, if not always impressive. Civil servants of ranks above Principal and its equivalents have rooms to themselves and personal shorthand-typists who also do other secretarial duties. Principals, Assistant Principals, Senior and Higher Executive Officers usually share

---

[1] Probably because a strike is regarded as 'working-class behaviour' by the essentially middle-class office worker. In France, it bears no such stigma and school-teachers, university staffs and civil servants strike with a will.

[2] The Royal Commission on the Civil Service, 1953-55, paragraphs 398-404, 469, 482, 510, 538, 580, 595-6. Subsequent reports of the Civil Service Commissioners suggest that there has been a slight improvement—for example in recruitment to the Executive Class—which must no doubt be attributable in part to the recommendations of the Royal Commission. But some of the improvement has been in classes which did not benefit spectacularly from the recommendations, and this may be due simply to a slackening demand for such recruits from other office organisations which had been competing strongly in the decade after the end of the war.

a room with another officer of approximately the same rank. Officers of lower rank are usually grouped in larger rooms according to the subjects on which they are working. Their conditions of work are not, of course, perfect. Overcrowding seldom if ever nowadays reaches the point at which it is likely to affect health, but is quite often enough to be an inconvenience, and even a hindrance to efficiency. There is seldom enough properly designed space for keeping the sort of papers and reference books which they must have by them, and it is difficult to get the best out of a talk with a visitor when there are several other people in the room, some of whom may be telephoning or interviewing visitors of their own. Probably the least satisfactory accommodation for junior officers is in the small offices which have been improvised here and there out of large dwelling-houses. But standards of accommodation are steadily improving, and it is difficult to argue that they have a serious effect on individual efficiency, although the splitting-up of large Ministries among half a dozen buildings probably lowers their organisational efficiency.

The service's pension scheme is of course one of the envies of other office workers, and its sick-leave scheme, which we shall be examining, is more generous than that of any large private concern in this country. Its allowances of leave are less generous than those of schools or university teachers (not all of whom, however, are idle for all their vacations), but as generous as those of most office concerns, and more generous than many. Promotion prospects vary greatly from one grade to another, from one Ministry to another, and from one decade to another. Some people have been lucky enough to enter or be in an expanding Department at the right level and the right age; others have an understandable feeling that they have been unlucky in their choice of Ministry. But only a frustrated careerist will argue that promotions in the service are determined to any appreciable degree by favouritism or improper influence. Indeed, the chief criticism that is made of the service's methods of promotion is that they still give a great deal too much of weight to seniority; to the extent to which this is true it is likely to remove more grievances than it creates.[1]

It is difficult to say anything on the subject of civil service pay which would not at once be challenged. Between the Royal Commissions[2]

---

[1] I very much doubt whether any promotions above the rank of Assistant Secretary—or its equivalent—are nowadays influenced appreciably by seniority. If it were difficult to choose between two men on merit, the senior might be chosen, particularly if the other had been only a short time in his present rank; but if the senior were nearing sixty the younger man might be chosen. For lower ranks the principle can probably be described as 'taking the most senior man who is clearly fit to promote', and in practice this usually means that quite a few senior men and women are passed over. We shall see in Chapter 8, however, what different types of civil servant do feel about the promotion system.

[2] The Tomlin Commission of 1931 and the Priestley Commission of 1953-55.

which are appointed once in a generation to deal with the subject, Governments have relied mainly on the civil servants in the Treasury to advise them on the claims and arguments that are put forward by the organisations that represent the various grades. The Treasury officers are understandably concerned neither to favour nor to appear to favour demands from which they themselves may directly or indirectly benefit, and in consequence fight a rearguard action with skill and real determination. Moreover, the Government have had to consider the civil servants' pay claims in the light of their anti-inflationary policy of discouraging pay claims in general. The result has been that at least until the Priestley Commission had its effect the civil service was a less generous employer in this respect than it was in such matters as superannuation and sick leave. The effect of this, in combination with the pressure of rising prices upon civil servants' incomes, has been to produce a good deal of dissatisfaction in the post-war years.

Some of this dissatisfaction was no doubt justified; for the increases proposed by the Priestley Commission showed that it regarded most, if not all, of the grades concerned as underpaid to varying extents. But this has now been remedied,[1] at least for the time being; and the principles formulated by the Commission should make it less likely that civil service pay will in the future fall so far behind as it has done in the past. In particular, the establishment of the Civil Service Pay Research Unit, independent both of the Treasury and of the staff organisations, to search outside the service for jobs comparable to those within it, and ascertain their pay and conditions of service, has simplified and quickened negotiations between the two sides.

Any grievances about pay which are still to be found in the service can probably be divided into three kinds. There are a few anomalies and disagreements, affecting some comparatively small classes of officers—usually professional or technical—which have still to be cleared up. There is a mild resentment, which lingers on as an after-effect of ten years of hard fighting with the Treasury, and which cannot be immediately abolished by any rational argument. There may also be a third kind of grievance. It has been suggested[2] that, at least in industry, an incessant series of pay-claims which is not abated by any increases that are conceded is a symptom of the workers' feeling that their job is not being valued highly enough by the community. One example might be the

---

[1] The Civil Service Pay Research Unit has not so far published any comparison between the pay of equivalent posts in the civil service and elsewhere. But the Pilkington Commission on doctors' and dentists' remuneration has published an analysis of the salaries of a wide range of professions, including the Administrative Class of the civil service, from which it can be seen that while this group does not attain the princely rewards earned by a few industrialists, actuaries or medical consultants, it compares reasonably well with the great majority of all the professions (Cmnd. 939, H.M.S.O. 1960).

[2] For example, by J. A. C. Brown, *The Social Psychology of Industry* (1954).

British miners, who certainly feel that the unpleasantness and danger of their work is not appreciated, and who have equally certainly been very persistent in their demands for better pay. The post-war civil servant too has been very much preoccupied with his pay packet; and this preoccupation has coincided with the post-war decline in the prestige of the service. In contrast, university staffs, who have certainly been no better paid than the administrators who were their contemporaries at school and college,[1] seem to be less concerned with pay, but since the war have probably enjoyed a higher status in public estimation than ever before. It is possible—I do not feel justified in putting it more strongly—that these three occupations are all examples of a displaced reaction to the status awarded to them by the community.

However this may be, my point in these brief references to pay, promotion and other conditions of work is that the stage has been reached at which they no longer offer much scope for improvements which will add to the efficiency of the service. This does not, of course, mean that the Government of the day should not continue to behave as a reasonably benevolent employer for moral reasons unconnected with expediency. Nor, from the point of view of pure expediency, can the Government afford to let pay fall behind again, or to allow other conditions of work to be worse than those of the ordinary 'good employer' of office staff. My argument is simply that if efficiency is to be increased much further, it will not be by raising pay beyond what is needed to keep pace with other white-collar workers; nor by giving the clerical officer more and more space to work in; nor is there much prospect of improving the chances of promotion. It is therefore imperative to consider whether it is possible to increase the efficiency of the service by attention to that elusive, intangible factor which, until it can be discussed more fully,[2] I must call *morale*.

1.2. THE SERVICE'S PRESENT ATTITUDE TO 'MORALE'

In the hubbub of lip-service that is paid to 'human relations in industry', 'man-management', 'human engineering', and other gods with strange names, the voice of the civil servant is a silent, or at most a still small one. I think that there are two reasons for this, one of which may be fairly sound. In the first place, there is a tendency in the service to assume that the interaction between people who are working together in an office unit is purely of an intellectual kind, and to ignore the possibilities of emotional distortions of this process. The transactions of one man at a desk are supposed to be determined wholly by rational information, questions, principles and instructions to which he reacts with unemotional logic; his reactions will be imperfect or inappropriate only in so

---

[1] See the Pilkington Commission's report (*loc. cit.*), pp. 297, 311.
[2] As it is in Chapter 4.

far as these communications or the information to which he has access are ambiguous or incomplete. Nobody denies that his enjoyment of, and efficiency at, his work is affected by irrelevant factors, such as his attitude towards the ultimate purpose of what he is doing, and his liking for or dislike of his superiors, immediate or remote, his colleagues, subordinates and any outsiders with whom he has to deal. But the extent to which these factors can make him prompt or dilatory, obtuse or understanding, defeatist or resourceful, sound or wrong-headed in judgment —factors to which we give full weight when we are thinking of the work of novelists, professional footballers, clergymen, actors and politicians —is belittled in the case of the man at the desk because, unlike them, he is supposed to work with nothing but his intellect.

The other reason for the civil service's cautious attitude to the problems of *morale* is a better one. In the market of new ideas the bureaucrat is a hesitant customer, buying only what has proved its worth, and preferring to watch others risk their money on untried inventions. This does not mean that the service is behind other large organisations in every aspect of personnel management. The Whitley machinery for consultation and negotiation between 'management' and 'employees' has now worked continuously for thirty years, much longer than any comparable arrangement for other large groups of office workers in this country. As we shall see, there are still large private firms who have no machinery for consulting their office staffs. But very little credit for the innovation could be claimed by the Treasury officials or Ministers of the day, who were yielding to strong pressure from the staff associations, fortified with the recommendations of the Rt. Hon. J. H. Whitley's Committee.

The possibility, therefore, that the work of occupational psychologists might have a bearing on the efficiency of the civil service is one which the service itself has not hastened to explore. Psychologists *are* to be found in the service, and there are about 70 of them. As a recruiting pamphlet says:

> Psychologists are employed in the Admiralty, War Office, Air Ministry, the Ministry of Supply, the Ministry of Labour and National Service, the Prison Commission and the Civil Service Commission. The work in the three defence departments and the Ministry of Supply relates mainly to members of the armed forces; that in the Ministry of Labour and National Service to workers in need of physical restoration and vocational guidance; that in the Prison Commission to the prison and Borstal population; and in the Civil Service Commission it consists mainly of the construction of tests for recruitment to civil service posts, mostly in the lower grades, and of 'following-up' results....

But there is no psychologist whose job it is to investigate or advise upon the psychological aspects of the training or management of the men at the desks of Whitehall. The Organisation and Methods Division of the Treasury, which is most directly interested in the efficiency of the service, and has sired small but useful replicas of itself in all the major Ministries, neither employs nor consults psychologists. This is less surprising at a second glance, because O & M (to use the affectionate service abbreviation) concentrates upon causes of efficiency or inefficiency that can be manipulated fairly easily—in fact, upon organisation and methods. 'O & M advises on organisation—the relationship between parts of the work and between those engaged on it—and the methods and procedures employed in doing the work, with the expressed object of promoting efficiency at all levels.'[1] This definition makes a curtsey in the direction of occupational psychology when it refers to the relationship between those engaged on the same work; and the same publication makes a short reference to 'slack leadership' and 'lack of drive in managers or supervisors' as possible causes of inefficiency.[2] But the possibility that the work may be intrinsically boring and monotonous, or that it could be made more interesting by some measure or other, is not discussed. Indeed, I have only once come across an O & M proposal which appealed to the argument that by reorganising work so as to give more operations to each individual his interest could be kept at a higher level; and even here the argument was used only as a secondary one, since the main justification for the proposal was a saving in staff. As I have said, however, O & M's concentration upon factors that are comparatively easy to manipulate is neither surprising nor deplorable; there is so much scope for constant overhauling of procedures, forms, chains of responsibility and so forth, and these overhauls yield such tangible and immediate results, that O & M are no doubt justified in paying most attention to them.

What is more, however bright the horizon may be for occupational psychology, its present achievements are not yet very impressive. Perhaps the most convincing demonstrations of its worth have been in vocational guidance—that is, in advising people on the jobs that are best suited to their interests and abilities—and in the selection of the people who are best suited for certain jobs. As we have already seen, the Civil Service Commission already employ psychologists to devise tests for would-be entrants.[3]

[1] 'The Practice of O and M', H.M.S.O., 1954, p. 1.
[2] Ibid., p. 41.
[3] Since I was concerned with the psychological effect of civil service work upon those whom the Commission admitted, I discussed with one of their psychologists the extent to which they have regard to the personalities of candidates. The paper-and-pencil tests which they devise for different grades are tests of intellectual ability, and not of temperament. All likely candidates for the Clerical, Executive and Administrative classes are interviewed, with the singular exception of Open Competition candidates for the Clerical Class between sixteen and twenty years of age. But with one important exception these interviews are conducted by boards of laymen. These interviewers are experienced, but are concerned more with gaining information about the candidates' background, history and achievements than with detecting their psychological weaknesses. The important exception is the series of interviews which

But when it comes to giving advice on the conditions under which the selected entrants to the civil service spend the rest of their working lives, the occupational psychologist would have to be cautious. Most research into problems of civilian morale has been carried out among manual workers in North American industry. Some of it, like other research in the behavioural sciences, has produced contradictory conclusions; and even when the conclusions are clear it is often unsafe to assume that they would be true of factory workers in Britain, whose attitudes and traditions are in many ways so different from those of United States labour, particularly where the relationship between management and employee is concerned. Still less could it be assumed that what is true of the factory worker is true of the office worker. There are many factories, for example, in this country where the workers show dissatisfaction with their jobs by simply staying away for a day, or even longer; but this, for various reasons which I shall be discussing, is not the office worker's way. So that to apply the conclusions of psychologists about factory workers in the United States to civil servants in Britain would be doubly unjustifiable, unless something could be done to check the assumption that the two species will react in the same way.

Let me illustrate this. It has been found possible to increase the efficiency of manual workers by imbuing them with the spirit of competition. This was demonstrated, for example, by an experiment among the stokers (or 'firemen', as they were called) of the boilers in a United States electricity generating plant in 1932. '. . . It was decided that, in addition to what the firemen knew as to the efficiency of each battery of six boilers, data were needed as to the actual operation of the separate boilers stoked by different men. As a result, instruments were installed to provide each man with information as to what was expected of his own boiler and precisely how efficiently or inefficiently it was working. "For the first time", according to Bingham (the research worker), "the men really knew when they were being successful in their work. A new spirit spread among them. A fresh pride replaced the old indifference. Graphic daily and weekly records for each boiler were posted. Rivalry sprang up, competition between the three eight-hour shifts. . . ." [1]

It might be safe to assume that the same spirit of rivalry could be

are the main hurdle in the Method II test for entry to the Administrative Class, and which include a private interview with a psychologist who is primarily interested in weaknesses of this kind. This seems to have the effect of eliminating a small percentage (less than 5 per cent.) of candidates who would otherwise be suitable; and the conditions under which the other tests are performed are also such that some candidates' weaknesses show up by handicapping them. The result is that from the evidence which the Commission get by following-up successful candidates and by studying cases of resignation Method II is found to admit a smaller proportion of those who later resign or are diagnosed as failures than does Method I, in which the only interview is with a board of laymen.

[1] Morris S. Viteles, *Motivation and Morale in Industry*, p. 144.

instilled into British office workers if their efficiency at their tasks could be measured and compared. An attempt was made to do just this in the Records Branch of the Ministry of Pensions and National Insurance at Newcastle,[1] where teams of clerical officers deal with claims for benefit from the insured population. Their output and accuracy are subject to continual review, and at one time their 'management' made a practice of announcing comparative figures over the loudspeaker system, so that sections knew which of them had done better than others. But the spiritual rebirth which had regenerated the American stokers was not repeated in Newcastle. The sections regarded the announcements as simply a device for getting more work out of them, which indeed it was; and instead of being stimulated they were merely resentful. It is easy, of course, to think of explanations of the two different reactions. In 1932 the American stokers were probably working under the threat of losing their jobs; there were plenty of unemployed men to take the place of the hindmost, and they may have seen these measuring instruments as a means of weeding out the least efficient. The Newcastle clerical officers were not in the same danger; as we shall see in Chapter 5, the output of individuals was not known by the management, and with the exception of temporary clerks it would have been very difficult in any case to dismiss them without serious trouble with the Civil Service Clerical Association. However this may be, the point of these two stories at the moment is simply that conclusions and methods cannot safely be borrowed from industry here or in the United States and applied unhesitatingly to British civil servants.

There are therefore few maxims which O & M Division, or any other Division of the Treasury, could safely adopt ready-made from the occupational psychologists. This does not mean that the Treasury is totally unreceptive to such ideas. The last two 'Heads of the Civil Service', Lord Bridges and Sir Norman Brook, both addressed encyclicals to the various Ministries of the service in which they showed their awareness of the problem of *morale*. In June 1957, for example, Sir Norman Brook wrote that 'we need in the service a better concept of leadership', and pointed out that 'a sense of participation', particularly in large units, is a very powerful motive for good work. The Treasury Medical Adviser, Dr. Chieseman, and his Deputy, Dr. Long,[2] with whom I discussed my project, were convinced of the importance of the civil servant's attitude to his work as a factor that influenced his health; and they had of course first-hand experience of this in the case of retirements on medical grounds and temporary breakdowns under stress. It was encouraging, too, to find that outside the Treasury almost every Establishment Officer[3] with whom I had to deal considered my

[1] Whose work and organisation is described in Chapter 5.
[2] Who is also medical adviser to the Post Office.
[3] With the exception recorded in Chapter 7.

investigation well worth making, and seemed particularly willing to assist it.

There are one or two instances in which the initiative of individual psychologists has prompted them to study *morale*, or something like it, among certain specialised grades in the service. In 1948 and 1949 two investigations of Typing Pools were carried out, the first by Mr. R. G. Stansfield, now of the Department of Scientific and Industrial Research, and the second by three investigators, Mr. Stansfield, Mr. E. Anstey (now a Principal in the Home Office) and Mr. A. H. J. Baines (now a Statistician in the Ministry of Agriculture, Fisheries and Food). Seven years later, a brief reference to the main results of these investigations was made in a Treasury booklet 'Typing Work in Government Departments', which was issued by O & M Division to Departments in 1956; since the reports themselves can be found only in files, I have included brief summaries of them in Appendix A.

In 1950-52 a post-graduate student from the U.S.A., Dr. N. F. Kristy, with the co-operation of the Civil Service Commission and the Post Office, carried out a study of the 'Criteria of Occupational Success among Post Office Counter-clerks', which was described in his Ph.D. thesis submitted to the University of London. His thesis reposes unpublished in the University's library, and I learned of it only through a reference in Michael Argyle's *Scientific Study of Social Behaviour* (1957).

A few years later, a Ministry asked the National Institute of Industrial Psychology to study the extent to which the training courses for supervisors of teams for certain type of staff succeeded in their object. The results of the study were the subject of a report to that Ministry in 1958 by Messrs. John D. Handyside and John Crowther, of the N.I.I.P., and are summarised in Chapter 2.

In 1956 a symposium on 'The Direction of Research Establishments' was convened at the National Physical Laboratory at Teddington, and at it a number of papers were read which had an interesting bearing on *morale* among scientific workers in Government (and other) research laboratories. The papers, with summaries of the discussions on them, were published by H.M.S.O. in 1957.

Two things are worth noting about these studies. In the first place, I learned about each one from a different source, and there was no single person or branch in the service who had been able to tell me about them all. Indeed it took me so much trouble to unearth the reports themselves that I have thought it worth while to summarise them either in the following chapters or in Appendix A.

In the second place, they deal with very specialised work. None of them is concerned with the work of the main 'Treasury Classes' which provide the non-industrial, non-specialist, non-professional staff of every sizeable Government Department; that is, with the Administrative, Executive and Clerical grades. Admittedly these workers are so diverse in age, social origin, status and type of work that the difficulties of establishing any general facts about them are great—just how great, the rest of this book will show. But the very fact that these grades pervade the service, and play so important a part in the decisions and day-to-day work of every Ministry, makes their efficiency, and any factor that may affect it, of prime importance. Yet a glance at the studies I have listed showed how unlikely it was that a study of the morale of the Administrative, Executive and Clerical grades would ever be commissioned by the service itself. This encouraged me to concentrate upon them; in the rest of this book I shall have a little to say about other types of civil servant, but chiefly for the light which comparison with them throws upon these three classes.

In order to spare myself and my readers the constant repetition of the long-winded phrase 'the Administrative, General Executive and General Clerical Classes', I shall refer to them as 'the desk classes'. I hope that this will not be regarded as an undignified title; it was chosen because it draws a graphic and, I think, genuine distinction between the nature of their work and that of doctors, lawyers, architects, engineers, scientists, inspectors, typists, messengers and cleaners. Many of these other kinds of civil servant have desks, and some of them use them; but the symbols of their skills are the consulting-room, the court, the drawing-board, the slide-rule, the travel-stained Morris, the Olivetti, the glass-panelled cubby-hole and the mop. It is the shadowy figure behind the desk, whose rank may be anything from Clerical Assistant to Permanent Secretary, that is my subject.[1] In the chapters that follow I shall first describe and discuss how the civil service attempts, with as much success as can be expected in this imperfect world, to tackle at least two of the aspects of *morale*. Then I shall deal with one aspect which it is popularly believed to neglect—the elimination of the unsatisfactory employee. By this stage it will be clear that the whole concept of *morale* needs to be thought about with care; and Chapter 4 is a brief analysis of it. Chapter 5 describes the results of an attempt to measure the collective efficiency of groups of office workers engaged on repetitive tasks in a factory-like situation, and to identify some of the psychological factors which affect their efficiency. Chapter 6 shows the difficulties of finding a satisfactory indirect index of attitude to work where office workers are concerned. These difficulties were so great that I resorted to a direct measuring instrument, in the form of a questionnaire; and the results are described in Chapters 7 and 8. My concluding reflections are the subject of Chapter 9.

Anyone who is abnormal enough to study his fellow office workers instead of merely working with them must resist at least one dangerous temptation. This is the desire to draw on his own experience of them,

[1] Readers who find the titles, abbreviations and inter-relationships of the grades unfamiliar should consult Figure 1.01.

FIGURE 1.01

The Desk Classes in an imaginary Ministry

THE MINISTER[1]
his Private Secretary (P.S.)—a
Principal: and staff—"the Private
Office".[2]

THE PARLIAMENTARY SECRETARY[1]
his P.S.—an Assistant Principal
(A.P.)[2]

THE PERMANENT SECRETARY
his P.S.—an Assistant Principal (A.P.) and clerical staff

2 DEPUTY SECRETARIES
each with a Personal Assistant (P.A.)[3] and responsible for
Administrative and Executive departments of the
two kinds illustrated below

an ADMINISTRATIVE Department	an EXECUTIVE Department
2 UNDER-SECRETARIES each with a P.A.[3] and	1 *PRINCIPAL EXECUTIVE OFFICER* (P.E.O.) with a P.A.[3] and
2 ASSISTANT SECRETARIES each with a P.A.[3] and	2 *SENIOR CHIEF EXECUTIVE OFFICERS* (S.C.E.O.) each with a P.A.[3] and
2 PRINCIPALS (or 1 PRINCIPAL and 1 *SENIOR EXECUTIVE OFFICER*) (S.E.O.) sometimes with an ASSISTANT PRINCIPAL (A.P.)[4] understudying one of them[5] each with	2 *CHIEF EXECUTIVE OFFICERS* (C.E.O.) each with 2 *SENIOR EXECUTIVE OFFICERS* (S.E.O.) each with several
2 *HIGHER EXECUTIVE OFFICERS* (H.E.O.). and each with	*HIGHER EXECUTIVE OFFICERS* (H.E.O.) each with several
2 *EXECUTIVE OFFICERS* (E.O.)[4] each with	*EXECUTIVE OFFICERS* (E.O.)[4] each with several
2 CLERICAL OFFICERS (C.O.)[4] each with, or sharing	CLERICAL OFFICERS (C.O.)[4] assisted by
a CLERICAL ASSISTANT (C.A.)[4]	CLERICAL ASSISTANTS (C.A.)[4]

NOT SHOWN are legal, accounting, and other professional, scientific, inspecting and technical staff, or typing, telephone, messenger, paper-keeping and servicing staff

[1] Not civil servants
[2] These are civil servants, but some Ministers also retain personal secretaries to handle private and constituency correspondence
[3] P.A.s are usually Clerical Officers with shorthand-typing qualifications and the grade of C.O.-Sec.
[4] These are "entry grades", to which appointments are made by competitive examination, although all but the A.P. grade are also supplied by promotion from below
[5] This may or may not involve responsibility for part of the Branch and its work

which merely results in the voicing of prejudice and not in the formulation of scientific statements. A single person's vicissitudes and feelings may be material for an entertaining autobiography, but they do not justify the general propositions that are of practical value. Even if one can combine introspection with observations of the behaviour of other human beings, what one's colleagues say or do in the presence of one person is not good evidence of their behaviour at other times, and still less of their inward thoughts. Even Establishment or Welfare Officers, whose work involves them in listening to the troubles of a fairly wide cross-section of individuals in their Ministries, cannot be sure that it is representative, since it consists of people whose difficulties are sufficiently acute or unusual to bring them to the specialist's door. In any case, since the task of the specialist is to find a cure for each case, he cannot act as a detached observer; the more intractable the trouble is, the stronger will be the temptation to dismiss it as the fault of the individuals concerned, or to take up some other emotional attitude towards them.

Thus the problem is not only what to study but how to study it, and especially how to study it without the distortions which arise from participation. Part of the solution in my case was clearly to study Ministries to which I was a stranger. In doing so, however, I had also to rely as little as possible on the impressions of a single informant, such as an Establishment Officer or Welfare Officer; this would merely have led me to offer the reader a second-hand impression of another organisation instead of a first-hand one of my own. Information of this kind must either be supported by fact or confirmed by several independent informants. Yet even beliefs which are shared by quite a lot of members of the same organisation may be largely or wholly myths. In most large private companies, for example, you will be told the story of the man who is earning less than one of his subordinates although neither of them know this. Folk-lore of this kind is always interesting as a phenomenon to be explained; but it must not be mistaken for fact.

My desire to avoid 'impressionism' must excuse some of the apparently roundabout methods described in the later chapters of this book. If they occasionally seem merely to confirm what we already know, this is at least a reassurance that the instruments we are using are reliable.

2

TWO POSITIVE APPROACHES

Chapter 1 may have given the impression that the attitude of the Treasury and other Departments to *morale* is merely one of enthusiastic contemplation. There are, on the contrary, two important aspects of the subject with which the service makes a conscious and determined effort to cope. One of these is the damaging effect which private difficulties, outside the working situation, can have on the quality of an individual's work. The chief instrument for dealing with this factor is the Departmental Welfare Officer, whose work I shall describe in the first part of this chapter. In the second half I shall discuss the way in which the service attempts to improve the standard of supervision on the job.

2.1. WELFARE OFFICERS[1]

During the 1939-45 war the transfer of thousands of industrial and office workers from one part of the country to another, coupled with the effects of the evacuation and later of the bombing of the cities, created domestic difficulties for a great part of the labour force. Lodgings were hard to find, and the separation of workers from their families caused anxieties and estrangements, with serious effects upon efficiency at work. Following the example of industry, some Ministries gave one or two of their officers the task of trying to alleviate these difficulties among their own staffs. Billets were found, and hostels were provided to house men and women from other parts of Britain; these hostels were often directly supervised by these 'Welfare Officers', as they came to be called. Staff with other domestic difficulties were also encouraged to seek their help. Officers whose work suddenly began to deteriorate for no obvious reasons were tactfully interviewed, and often confessed to private problems and stresses which the Welfare Officer could sometimes help to relieve.

The practice of designating one or more of their own staff as Departmental Welfare Officers spread fairly rapidly among the large war-time Ministries; and in 1943, after a series of conferences jointly arranged by the Treasury and the Industrial Welfare Society had emphasised the need to plan and co-ordinate the work of Welfare Officers, a Treasury Welfare Adviser was appointed. The first occupant of this post, Miss R. Culhane, has held it ever since. Her duties are to advise the Treasury, other Departments and their Welfare Officers on anything affecting the

---

[1] There are one or two Departments—in particular the Post Office—to which some of the statements in this section do not apply, since their welfare organisations have grown up in special circumstances.

welfare of non-industrial civil servants. This means that she has not only to keep in touch with the senior Welfare Officers in all the major Departments, but also to be aware of developments in the policies of good employers in private industry. I found her keenly interested in the subject of *morale*. Through her, I was able to get some idea of the way in which this institution had grown and also introductions to the senior Welfare Officers in one or two large Ministries, who were equally interested and helpful.

Although the Welfare Officer was a war-time innovation in the non-industrial civil service, he[1] has proved so valuable that he has been retained as a permanent feature of Departmental organisation. Every Ministry of substantial size has at least one full-time Welfare Officer, and the large Ministries have several assistants working under a senior. In small Departments and in some out-stations of larger ones, the job is sometimes combined with other duties, such as that of training officer. Welfare Officers with assistants are usually Senior Executive Officers; Assistant Welfare Officers and single officers are usually of lower Executive grades. The Treasury Welfare Adviser is a Principal.

Departmental Welfare Officers still include a number who were recruited during the war from among industrial personnel officers. Some of these, and some later recruits to this work, have university qualifications in the social sciences, or have previously engaged in voluntary welfare work. The present method of appointment, however, is not to advertise these posts to applicants from outside the service, but to invite applications from officers of suitable grades in the Department with a vacancy; some Ministries make a point of inviting applications from other Ministries as well. The final selection is made by an interviewing board, on which the Treasury Welfare Adviser is often invited to sit, especially where the post to be filled is a senior one.

Thus unlike most of his industrial counterparts the Departmental Welfare Officer is not as a rule recruited from among professionally trained specialists, but is someone who had enough vocation for this work to apply for the vacancy, and enough aptitude to impress a selection board. He has usually entered the service as an Executive or Clerical Officer, and, like all desk workers in the service, has performed a variety of the jobs allotted to these grades. As for training, his Department is encouraged to send him to the Treasury's three-week course for Welfare Officers, which includes lectures and discussions on the social services, case-work, human relations and the medical aspects of his work. He may also be able to squeeze in part-time attendance at classes provided, for example, by extra-mural departments of universities. But none of

---

[1] Although I use the conventional 'he', the great majority of Welfare Officers are women. Women are on the whole more likely to be successful at this work, not so much because their own sex have more personal problems to confide as because they are the natural confidantes for both sexes.

this training is compulsory and none of it is followed by an examination. Like all non-specialist members of the desk classes, the Welfare Officer is liable to be transferred to other work. The Treasury's advice to other Departments is that 'while there are objections in many cases to keeping staff in welfare posts as a life career, continuity is highly desirable, and five years is suggested as a normal absolute minimum tenure, after a trial period of, say, six months'.

The difference between the methods of recruitment in industry and in the service does not necessarily mean that the latter's are inferior. They certainly have disadvantages. Women—and men—sometimes apply for these posts simply because they offer the 'human interest' which their present jobs too often lack. Whether this is their motive or not, applicants may well have no personal experience of this kind of work, unless they have been employed in other Establishment duties, which may or may not be a recommendation. A great deal of their job involves helping people to make use of the various social services—such as Legal Aid or the local authorities' Home Helps; and they have to pick up the necessary 'know-how' from hand-books or colleagues. But a more serious disadvantage may be the fact that the Welfare Officer is known to many of the people who might need his services. If you have worked with Miss Smith in the Registry for a couple of years before she is made a Welfare Officer you hesitate to confide your private difficulties to her, however much you trust her discretion; and your hesitation is increased by the thought that in another year or two she may be your colleague or your superior in some other Branch. Even if she is not personally known to her 'clients', it is a fact well-known to most social workers that people talk more freely about personal problems to the right kind of 'outsider' than to someone whom they regard as 'one of themselves'. Moreover, the mere quality of being a specialist, with experience and qualifications from elsewhere, often gives a consultant—in almost any field—an ability to inspire confidence in his client which is quite unrelated to the practical value of his advice; this may be dangerous in some fields, but in social work, where the removing of the client's anxiety or distress is often half the battle, it can be very useful.

But it is too easy to exaggerate these weaknesses of the system, and to overlook its advantages. The fact that the recruits have usually belonged to the Ministry's staff means that the board which selects them knows their careers and characteristics far better than an industrial personnel officer can get to know an applicant from outside the firm through a perusal of his references and an hour's interview. The newly appointed Welfare Officer begins his job with a knowledge of the service that can be got only by working in it; he knows what it is like to be one of its employees, through the personal experience which many industrial personnel officers lack. He may not know as much as a trained social worker about the best way to manipulate the social services, but he certainly knows far more about the best ways of manipulating the inner machinery of his Ministry—for example, in order to get someone transferred from one local office to another. And if the Ministry is a large one, the chances of his being personally known to people who might have wanted to consult him are smaller.

In almost all Departments the Welfare Officer is part of the Establishment Division. This is both logical and convenient, since much of his work must consist of consultation with other branches of this Division about such matters as the possibility of getting special leave for someone with domestic troubles, or a transfer to another office for someone who is failing to 'get on' with a colleague or superior. At the same time, if the Welfare Officer is to be someone in whom the staff can confide, it must be a firm[1] rule that he does not pass on information without the permission of his informant. In the Departments whose Welfare Officer I spoke to it was a first principle that his files were open to no one but the Welfare Officers, and certainly not to other officers in the Establishment Division.

This is a good illustration of a principle which the civil service was probably the first organisation in this country to adopt, and which it has, I think, carried further than most other large organisations. This is that responsibility for the personal careers and affairs of individual officers is kept as far as possible out of the hands of their superiors in the hierarchy for the handling of business. Apart from instructing, directing and supervising his subordinates in the jobs they have to do, a superior has as little say as possible in their careers. It is true that he reports on them annually[2]; but his reports must be countersigned by the man above him, so that he cannot be too arbitrary or prejudiced in his verdict. In any case, by the time the subject of the report comes to be considered for promotion, the merry-go-round of transfers will have ensured that he has been reported on by several superiors. It is therefore very difficult for one man's opinion to make or mar the career of another, and freedom from the need to curry favour with one's boss is one of the healthiest features of this system. What I have said, of course, applies with more accuracy to the lower and middle levels; the nearer a man gets to the top, the fewer the people under whom he can serve, the less weight is attached to formal reports—if any are rendered —and the more scope there is for the operation of individual prefer-

[1] It must also be a well-known rule. I have talked with officers in some of these Departments who did not realise how strictly the Welfare files are insulated. But in a system which recruits Welfare Officers from among the staff and usually returns them in the fulness of time to ordinary Departmental duties, it is obviously not quite true to say that 'only the Welfare Officer will ever know'.

[2] At the higher levels annual reports are not rendered. Sometimes the justification is that the qualities required of senior officers are too ineffable to be reduced to black and white; sometimes it is that the officers are so few that those responsible for promoting them should be able to know their worth without this formality.

ences; but discussion of what the various levels feel about the system must wait until Chapter 8.

Almost the only way in which a superior can interfere with much effect in a subordinate's private life is in the matter of leave; the subordinate must use his allowance in such a way that the work of the Branch is not disorganised by his absence. Even in this, however, the superior's power is limited; he would seldom stop a man's leave indefinitely. Everything else—pay, transfers, promotion, sick pay, special leave, retirement pension—are handled by the Establishment Division. This insulation of personal affairs from the chain of command for the conduct of business is to a greater or lesser extent a feature of most large organisations, and in addition to the advantage which I have just mentioned it brings the other benefit of specialisation. But it is carried further in the civil service than in any other organisation I know.

The job of the Welfare Officer extends this principle by yet another logical step, and emphasises that even within the sphere of personnel management there are certain affairs that are best handled by someone who has no connection either with the conduct of business or with promotion and discipline. It means that a man's superior is relieved as much as possible not only of power to affect his career but also of the duty—and the right—to concern himself with his private affairs.

On the whole this is probably for the best. The Welfare Officer is more likely than a man's superior officer to receive the sort of confidence that may be necessary. Even if the client's troubles have nothing to do with his relations with his superior—and of course they often have—the Welfare Officer is better qualified to listen and advise. Nor should we pay too much attention to people who assert that superiors must take a close interest in the personal affairs of their staff, and who deplore any system which relieves them of this necessity. Officers in the armed forces used to be taught—perhaps still are—that if they are to be effective leaders they must know as much as possible about their men's 'background' and 'family lives'. This may be good advice for the barracks, the airfield or even the shop floor; but it is certainly not advisable in the office. Time and again in discussions with Clerical Officers, Executive Officers and administrators I led the conversation round to the question whether their superior took enough personal interest in them. In almost every case their reaction was that he had more sense. Women were particularly quick to resent any attempt by their boss, especially if he were a man, to know more than was officially necessary about them; and men showed the same attitude in a milder form. The Englishman's determination to keep his private affairs to himself seems to be intensified in his office life; a year or two[1] in a job is not enough to let him form close

---

[1] Indeed, ten years may not be enough; my study of the Newcastle C.O.s suggested that there may be something about office life that discourages the formation of friendships, except perhaps among unmarried women.

friendships, and if he has to answer personal questions in every Branch to which he is posted too many people are going to know far too much about him. The Welfare Officer is an excellent solution of the difficulty that arises when private affairs begin to have an adverse effect on official life.

Let us consider his job in a little more detail. The Treasury's definition of it in Estacode[1] begins

> The main object of the work of a welfare officer is to develop close personal contact with staff as individuals and to deal with questions of staff well-being which, in a large organisation, are in danger of being overlooked unless someone is specially charged with considering them; and it is essential that this work should be carried out with sympathetic understanding. . . .

There follows a long list of duties which the Treasury considers suitable for Welfare Officers. In this, as in so many other questions of organisation, the Treasury is speaking only as an adviser and not as a director, and it is open to Departments to adopt or modify this list; but in most cases it probably represents what the Welfare Officer is supposed to do. I say 'supposed', because in practice he finds that certain activities make great and almost exclusive demands on his time, and yield more tangible results than others, which recede into the background of his thoughts. For my part, I shall discuss only those duties which seem to me of real importance from the point of view of *morale*.

The Welfare Officer—or one of his assistants—interviews all staff soon after their arrival in the Ministry, partly in order to find out whether the new entrant has any problems, such as lodgings, and partly to let him or her know about the amenities and services which are available in the Ministry. Most important of these is commonly the canteen, where meals can be got more quickly and cheaply than they usually can in pubs and cafés outside. There are often hostels or lists of good private lodgings for young and junior staff who have been posted from the other end of the country; and there are probably clubs for various recreations where the new entrant can find other civil servants with similar interests. Some of these amenities often owe their existence to the encouragement of the Welfare Officer or one of his predecessors; if so, he usually tries to launch them without remaining at the helm himself: it is obviously better for the clubs to have their own separate vitality.

The greatest part of his time, however, is spent in sorting out the personal and private difficulties of members of the staff who consult him on their own initiative or who are persuaded to do so by colleagues or superiors who have noticed that something is wrong. Among cases

---

[1] The loose-leaf manual of rules and advice for Establishment Divisions which is issued and kept up to date by the Treasury.

of which I was told (anonymously) by Welfare Officers were:
1. a woman suffering from an unfortunate love-affair, who also got on rather badly with her colleagues at work. The Welfare Officer was able to have her transferred to another job in another part of England;
2. a man whose ill-dressed, unkempt appearance had caused complaints from his colleagues, who felt that they were disgraced by it. He was given tactful advice;
3. a man whose wife had died very suddenly was visited and given advice on how to care for his young family;
4. a woman who had become depressed and convinced of her incompetence at her job was interviewed; at least part of the cause turned out to be her difficulty in understanding the dialect spoken by her senior officer;
5. a woman was helped to solve a housing problem;
6. a young and ambitious woman who resented the low status of her job was told how to take part-time training which would qualify her for more interesting work.

The typical problem, however, which recurs again and again, is the working woman who is having difficulty in coping with a job as well as with a sick husband, mother or other dependent. These problems are naturally hard to solve, and many of the Welfare Officers' files are not short stories in which everyone lives happily ever after, but lengthy chronicles of recurrent crises: 'Mrs. B has had to stay away from work again, as her home help has stopped coming and the children are on holiday. Spoke to the local authority, who promised to do what they could. Told Mrs. B that she could not rely indefinitely on the home help, and she said she was hoping that her sister would come over from Holyhead for a month to help.'[1] We shall see in Chapter 6 that the uncertified 'sick leave' of married women is probably affected by such crises.

Most of the Welfare Officer's problems are thus what the professional social worker would call 'case-work'. Occasionally he is called in because a whole office is complaining about the lavatories, the ventilation, or the behaviour of some individual or group. But these cases are the exceptions. Most of the case-work is concerned with real and practical difficulties to which some sort of active solution must be found or improvised if the client is to be an efficient worker. Quite often, however, the real trouble lies in the personality of the client, who may, for example, want a transfer out of a branch where he fails to get on with his colleagues, but may in fact be the sort of man who will always manage to get on badly with his fellow-workers or his boss. Some Welfare Officers learn to recognise these types fairly quickly, after wasting a little time in trying to find them a congenial branch. One or two also knew that in

[1] Fictitious.

TABLE 2.01

Consultations with the Welfare Officers in the Large and the Small Ministry

(Based on replies to question 45 of the questionnaire described in Chapter 7)

Grade	Subject of Consultation	
	'A problem in my work'	'A private problem'
	%[2]	%[2]
Administrative[1] (up to Asst. Secy.)	3·4	3·4
Executive above H.E.O.[1]	7·4	5·3
H.E.O. & E.O.:		
men	3·5	12·4
women	8·6	17·2
C.O., C.A. & C.O. (Sec.):		
men	5·7	15·3
women	7·8	20·2

TABLE 2.02

Consultations with the Personnel Departments of the North and South Firms

Level	Subject of Consultation	
	'A problem in my work'	'A private problem'
	%[2]	%[2]
Upper[1]	24·1	10·4
Middle—men	14·3	15·3
women	10·3	17·9
Lower —men	22·4	13·2
women	11·6	4·6

[1] The figures for these levels include no women: see Chapter 7.
[2] The figures are percentages of respondents at the levels listed.

TWO POSITIVE APPROACHES

some cases they were simply faced with someone who was trying to adjust himself to his job—or to some private situation—and that the way in which they could help most was simply to listen to him. But most Welfare Officers clearly felt more at home with cases in which they could look for—and usually find—some active solution, even if it were only temporary.

It would be a mistake, however, to assume that the Welfare Officer's work is confined to domestic problems or to the lower levels of civil servant. In the questionnaire which I issued to grades from Clerical Assistant up to Assistant Secretary in two Ministries, and to corresponding levels in two large firms in central London, I included a question:

Have you ever consulted one of the personnel officers ('Welfare Officers' in the civil service) about a personal problem?

        No..............................
        Yes, on a problem in my work..........
        Yes, on a private problem.............

The results are summarised in Table 2.01, and show the quite substantial extent to which the senior officers have made use of the Welfare Officers, not only over private matters but also over matters connected with work. It is true, however, that the lower grades make markedly more use of this service, and that in the grades of H.E.O., E.O., C.O. and C.A., where there are enough women among the respondents for a comparison, they seem to consult the Welfare Officer more often than do the men.

Respondents who had consulted the Welfare Officer were asked in the next question whether the result was helpful, with the following result:

TABLE 2.03

Subject of Consultation	Reply to 'Was the result helpful?'		
	'No'	'Hard to say'	'Yes'
	%	%	%
'A problem in my work' . . .	12·0	16·0	72·0
'A private problem' . . .	25·0	11·5	63·5

The percentages of cases in which the result was judged helpful by the respondent himself seemed to me very creditable indeed, especially when I considered the almost intractable difficulties of some of the cases whose files I had been shown in confidence (by another Ministry).

I have shown in Table 2.02 the percentages for the two firms who co-operated in the questionnaire. These are not strictly comparable with the replies from the civil servants, since the Personnel Departments of the firms corresponded more closely to the whole Establishment Division of a Ministry than to the Welfare Branch; and very little emphasis was placed on 'welfare' as a distinct function of personnel officers. This probably explains why the percentages for consultations over problems at work are larger in most cases than consultations about private problems, especially in the case of men at the managerial upper level. The percentage of women at the lower level who consult the Personnel Department over private problems is strikingly low, particularly when they are compared with their counterparts in the civil service, who are the most frequent consulters of this kind; the explanation of this may be that the civil service recruits its clerical class from all over the country, and that the young girl who enters a Ministry at this level is quite likely to have difficulty in finding suitable lodgings, whereas the firms probably recruit young girls who are able to travel from home to work.

Another kind of case-work which takes up a lot of the Welfare Officer's time is the visiting of civil servants who are absent on sick leave. Sometimes these visits enable him to uncover problems which he can help the invalid to solve; he may be able to arrange for the children to be looked after while their mother is confined to bed, and he may be able to get the invalid into a convalescent home and so assist in her recovery. Often, however, he is the mute with the bowstring, and has the unhappy task of breaking to an invalid the news that the Treasury Medical Advisers have advised his Department that he must retire, often before he has qualified for more than a fraction of his full pension. This is a gloomy message to have to carry, and the Welfare Officers disliked it; but they appreciated that it was better to have it brought by someone whom the invalid knew and could discuss it with, than delivered in a letter, however humanely drafted.

There is a third kind of duty, however, in connection with sick leave, which is not altogether consistent with the Welfare Officer's rôle of confidant and helper. All the Ministries whose Welfare Officers I met rely on them to pay special attention to cases in which a civil servant takes an abnormally high amount of sick leave.[1] Usually the cause is genuine ill-health. Sometimes it is simply a lack of some facility—such as transport for an arthritic—which the Welfare Officer can help to remedy. Occasionally, however, his visits do disclose that the civil servant has been staying away from work longer, or oftener, than he need; the result is his immediate return. The service's sick-leave rules are so benevolent that some check on malingering is clearly justified, although, as we shall see in Chapter 6, abuse seems to be extremely rare. Whether the Welfare Officer in fact reports malingerers or merely frightens them himself, one or two cases of this kind can prejudice him in the eyes of the staff: in at least one Department whose welfare arrange-

[1] The sick-leave rules, and the question whether they are abused on any substantial scale, are discussed in Chapter 6.

ments I discussed I found that many of the staff regarded him as a 'snooper' of the Establishment Division, and overlooked the helpful side of his work. Welfare Officers are extremely conscious that they must at all costs avoid this impression. Their normal practice is to send the invalid a postcard to say that they will be in his neighbourhood in, say, two days' time, and will call on him. Usually the illness is found to be genuine, but very occasionally the invalid returns to work before the visit. In either event the same practical result is achieved at the cost of less suspicion: the malingerers are identified, the others are not antagonised. It is obviously economical in staff to use the Welfare Officer for all kinds of sick visiting; but every effort must surely be made to see that it does not destroy his value as a confidant.

It was especially interesting to see that one item in the Treasury's list of 'duties suitable for allocation to welfare officers' was the 'study of sick records, absenteeism and labour wastage from welfare aspect, and interviews with voluntary leavers'. This is clearly an attempt to keep an eye on what are regarded in industry as symptoms of *morale*. I shall be discussing in Chapter 6 the extent to which these statistics are of any value as indices in the civil service; it is enough to say here that their value is very limited. It was therefore interesting to find that the Welfare Officers to whom I talked did not seem to regard this as an important part of their duties; and some clearly did not trouble about it. Their interest in sick leave was in the people they had to visit, and not in statistics. As we shall see, the study of sick leave from the point of view of *morale* is a far from easy business, and so far as I know Chapter 6 is the first attempt to discuss its fundamental difficulties. But in any case, the statistics kept by most Departments are exceedingly simple, not to say crude, and make few of the necessary distinctions. Even the Newcastle Central Office of the Ministry of Pensions and National Insurance, which produces detailed and useful morbidity statistics for the whole of the insured population, is unable to furnish much that is of use for this purpose about their own staff. There are exceptions: the Post Office, for example, have excellent records of sick leave which go back into the nineteenth century, and the Health Departments, as one might expect, study the sickness of their own staffs fairly thoroughly. But in most Ministries the Welfare Officer has neither the material nor the expertise necessary to diagnose low *morale* from an examination of sickness records; and not surprisingly he does not try.

This brief section on the Departmental Welfare Officer is not an exhaustive description, nor an attempt to pass judgment on him. My object has been to show that the effect which private troubles can have on the civil servant's efficiency has for some time been recognised by the service, which has found an effective tool for handling it. Like other kinds of tool, this one is constantly being improved; but it has already shown that it can do its job. One important conclusion that we can draw is that in dealing with the private and domestic causes of low *morale* there is not very much that the service has to learn; we can confine ourselves to the forces that operate at work, or more precisely in what sociologists would call 'the office situation'. It is true that the Welfare Officer is occasionally concerned with this aspect, too; but his intervention, as we have seen, is limited very largely to case-work with individuals whose troubles have become acute, and it is, as it were, the sub-clinical, endemic form of low *morale*—if it exists—that I am concerned with.

2.2. MANAGEMENT TRAINING

The other positive and conscious attack upon an aspect of *morale* is the training of civil servants in the management of subordinates. So far as the desk grades are concerned, the possession of this skill counts for very little either in the selection of new entrants or in the promotion of serving officers. This is not surprising: in selecting young entrants it is hardly possible to predict which of them will develop a skill they have not yet had to exercise. At most it may be possible to spot one or two whose personalities make it unlikely that they will be good leaders or supervisors. As for promotion, neither those who report annually on an officer nor those who sit on the board that interviews him can have any real notion of his way of handling his subordinates, while the subordinates themselves, who could speak from first-hand experience, are not asked to report on their superior.[1]

Nor is it safe to assume that officers selected or promoted for other good qualities, such as intelligence, industry, power of self-expression and all the other virtues in the annual report forms, are more likely to possess this particular skill. The Assheton Committee, which made its recommendations on the training of civil servants in 1944, had some insight into this difficulty:

> Brilliance on individual work is no guarantee of ability to supervise other people. It is therefore very necessary that every officer who occupies, or is to occupy, a position in which he has staff working under him should be assisted to understand the nature of supervisory duties. The first essential is, of course, that those called upon to fill such posts should be fitted for them by temperament and inclination.[2] It is desirable from the training point of view that, wherever possible, an officer should be tried in a supervisory post before being promoted to it.[3] Apart from this, however, special steps ought to be taken to give the prospective or newly appointed supervisor some guidance on the handling of subordinates. The basic principles of staff supervision are already being taught by some Departments and firms, and we think that such instruction ought to be generally adopted. . . .

---

[1] It would be interesting to be able to compare copies of the same form of report, one filled in by a man's immediate superior, others by his immediate subordinates.

[2] As I have suggested, this is easier to recommend than to ensure.

[3] I have never come across any examples of this recommendation in practice; it might create more problems than it solved.

As a result of the Committee's recommendations, a certain amount of education in the management of people is now included in the training courses for the main desk grades. Departments in which Executive Officers have to supervise work by large sections of clerical staff—as they may have to do in the Ministry of Pensions and National Insurance or the Inland Revenue—run courses for these officers in which the chief subject is the technique of supervision. Most Departments hold courses for the higher grades of the Executive Class, which may also be attended by Principals. These courses are on the wider subject of 'the conduct of public business', but they include sessions on 'management of personnel', (It is perhaps worth noting that clerical workers are 'supervised', but higher grades are 'managed').

For Assistant Principals and Principals the Treasury Training and Education Division runs periodic courses at the two appropriate levels; and for Assistant Secretaries and senior Scientific and Professional staff there are training conferences run by the same Division. All these courses include a certain amount of training in management.

My impression, however, is that the higher the grade for which the course is designed, the less the attention paid to 'supervision' or 'management' as such, and the more it becomes lost in the subject called 'organisation'. However this may be, there are no courses of training at all for Under Secretaries and higher ranks. I am not sure whether this is because they are too few, too busy or too advanced in their careers to be subjected to training. Certainly most Under Secretaries—apart from those who are Establishment Officers—are protected from the day-to-day problems of personnel by the Assistant Secretaries under them. But this does not mean that they have no effect upon *morale*. Indeed, just as 'supervision' of clerical workers is dignified as the 'management' of Branches and Divisions, so there is a kind of 'management' which, when it reaches the most senior officers, can be glorified by the name of 'leadership'. Is 'leadership' an incommunicable gift? This is not the assumption underlying Sir Norman Brook's statement that 'we need in the service a better concept of leadership'.

I would, however, have some sympathy with the argument that we do not yet know enough about the real ingredients of leadership, particularly in large office organisations, to make it worth the attempt to instil it by formal training or memoranda. This is not in any sense a criticism of the training techniques employed by the Treasury's Training and Education Division or by the Departmental training officers. Indeed, these techniques seemed to me to be extremely up-to-date, imaginative and stimulating, and it is worth a short digression to make this clear.

The methods of instruction employed by the Training and Education Division in their own courses, and demonstrated to Departmental instructors, for use in dealing with such difficult subjects as 'management and supervision', are based on the principle that lectures, however good, and however well supported by visual aids, questions and the rest of the stock-in-trade of orthodox expository teaching, are unlikely to have much effect upon mature students.

One of the skills of an instructor in the Civil Service must be to capture the concentration of his students. This task is not always easy; in many fields of work, instructors are dealing with groups of mature people who do not have a strongly felt and compelling motive to learn. For instance, the course may deal with supervision or management. . . . The listeners may consider themselves already to be satisfactory supervisors or good managers. . . . If the instructor is to make any impression on them, he must arouse their interest, stimulate their thoughts and keep them thinking actively and purposefully about the subject. Some students may be open-minded, receptive and co-operative—the apple of the hard-working instructor's eye; but others may be more sophisticated, and more ready to question any apparent oversimplification of ideas, any 'steering' by an instructor to predetermined conclusions. . . . In these general fields of study there is a danger of an instructor uttering pious platitudes which will fall on deaf ears and leave minds closed. . . .
Apart from the danger of boring the listener, there is also the danger of dealing with this subject in terms so broad that they fail to make any contact with the everyday realities of people's jobs. . . . The Civil Service instructor must always try to bridge the gap between the apparent artificiality of the training centre room and the reality of the job itself. . . .[1]

Instead, instructors use what has come to be known as the 'case-study' and 'rôle-playing'. The case-studies are disguised but realistic descriptions of management problems, set in the background of an anonymous or imaginary Department, and compiled from genuine instances of personnel problems that have occurred in the civil service. They are presented in the form of narratives and character-sketches; and several of those I have seen are prepared with such pains and skill that the situations and personalities are as alive as any in 'The Small Back Room' or 'The New Men'.

The subtlety and complexity of the crises in these case-studies must obviously be suited to the rank and experience of the students. One that is now quite well known, 'The Inter-planetary Research Establishment',[2] which was designed for a training conference of Assistant Secretaries and senior scientific and professional staff, provides material for several two-hour sessions of discussion. The chief virtue of the technique as the Training and Education Division employ it is that they do not make the mistake of producing an official solution to any of the problems. The students can be relied upon to tear to pieces any suggestions that are

[1] From 'The Use of Case-study in the British Civil Service', by Avice Turnbull, a tutor in the Training and Education Division of the Treasury (in the journal *Public Administration* for summer 1957). The whole article is worth reading for those who would like to see a concrete example of a case-study.
[2] It is summarised in an article by Miss Avice Turnbull and Mr. Z. M. T. Tarkowski in the journal *Public Administration* for autumn 1959. Another good example, at a lower level, is to be found in Miss Turnbull's article quoted above.

really stupid; and the rival solutions expounded by the administrators and the scientists is an object-lesson to the others of the differences in their ways of thinking.

These case-studies are sometimes made even more vivid by 'rôle-playing'—that is by making two or more students, with or without an instructor, take the part of some of the characters. From the narrative given to them at the start of the course they have all grasped the situation and the sort of people with whom they are supposed to deal. The next step may be for one of the students, not acting, but dealing with the situation as he thinks best, to have a talk with another student, or someone brought in from outside, who acts the part of a subordinate or a member of the public. This interview is acted in front of the rest of the students, who discuss it later. Even dignified middle-aged bureaucrats can be got to play this game without too much self-consciousness. Other ways in which the case is brought to life are the use of real 'personal files' with names and locations altered to obviate recognition, tape recordings of interviews or models to illustrate problems in which office layout plays a part.

These methods obviously involve much more ingenuity, pains and thought than the old-fashioned method of the pundit-lecture. Quite apart from the possibility—to which Miss A. Turnbull has drawn attention —that lectures in broad terms may make no impression, there is also the danger that if they do make an impression it may be a misleading one. As I hope I shall make clear in the course of this book, we really know very little about 'what makes people tick' in offices, let alone in the special kind of office of which Whitehall is composed. It is a situation in which the more a man knows the less he says. So that the Treasury's Training and Education Division is doubly justified in concentrating upon less didactic methods.

What is not so clear is just how effective even the best techniques are in improving people as 'supervisors', 'managers' or 'leaders' of men. How much has been scientifically proved on this subject?

It is of course almost entirely irrelevant to ask the students themselves such questions as 'How much have you enjoyed this course?' or 'What lessons have you learned from it?' If the intention of the course were to impart factual information the second question might yield relevant answers; the first would not do so in any circumstances, but is often asked. If the course were intended to alter people's attitudes rather than their knowledge, both kinds of reply could easily be misleading. It is possible to ask questions which, taken together, will reveal a certain amount about a supervisor's attitudes—for example, whether he is sympathetic to the difficulties of his subordinates, and whether he thinks a 'tough' line or a 'soft' one is the best tactic in dealing with them. If enough supervisors are subject to the same training, it is possible to test the attitudes of a random half of them in this way before they begin, and the rest after the course; where a difference is observed, there is a certain probability, depending on the size of the sample and the extent of the difference, that it is due to the training.

Even under conditions as favourable as this there is the possibility of two serious fallacies. One is to assume that apparent changes in attitude will be maintained by the trainee after his return to work. At the worst, he may merely have learned to profess what he now knows to be the officially approved attitude, without really being in sympathy with it. Or he may depart with genuinely good resolutions, only to find them wearing off under the friction of every-day contact with his subordinates. After all, only long-term psychotherapy or conditioning can bring about drastic changes in personality; and an intellectual acceptance of a method of supervision is not the same thing, particularly if the method goes against the supervisor's natural grain.

The other fallacy is of course to assume not only that all the respondents' answers reveal a genuine and lasting attitude but also that we know what sort of changes in attitude result in more effective supervision. The National Institute of Industrial Psychology, for example, devised an 'attitude test' which probably discriminated well between 'enlightened' and 'old school' supervisors; but as Handyside says[1]

'... it has not yet been possible to demonstrate directly that supervisors who express views in marked disagreement with those of the human relations trainers are regarded as inconsiderate or incompetent by the people they actually supervise. Nor has it yet been possible to compare performance on the attitude scales with supervisory effectiveness determined by an adequate criterion.

A second difficulty about the use of attitude measures of this kind is that they tend to be unreliable in the sense that the same individual obtains relatively variable scores when tested at different times or on different versions of the test. . . .' (p. 99).

With these reservations, it is interesting to consider the results of the only investigation on these lines that has been carried out in the British Civil Service. This was a study of some of the effects of training courses upon supervisors of certain teams of staff whose work brought them into frequent contact with members of the public. The study was financed by the Medical Research Council, and undertaken in 1956 by John D. Handyside and John Crowther, of the National Institute of Industrial Psychology.

The aim of the experiment was confined to discovering how far the courses were effective in changing the attitudes of the supervisors concerned, on the assumption that changed opinion is a necessary, but not sufficient, condition for improved supervisory behaviour. The population of supervisors was divided into two groups by selecting alternate courses at each of the six training centres and administering the same

[1] In his very clear and interesting paper 'The Effectiveness of Supervisory Training' in the *Journal of the Institute of Personnel Management* for June 1956.

paper-and-pencil 'survey of Supervisor's opinion' to each group, the only difference being that one group gave their answers before being 'exposed' to the course, while the others gave them on the last day of the course, when its effects were no doubt at a maximum. It was explained and demonstrated how replies would be treated anonymously, and the instructors never saw the replies.

The main results were these. In their attitudes to the members of the public with which they dealt the male supervisors showed no significant improvement,[1] while the women did. Neither the men nor the women showed a significant improvement in their attitude to the 'management'; indeed, there was a slight but not quite significant *deterioration* in the women's attitude, a phenomenon which has been noticed in some other studies of this kind. Both men and women, however, showed a significant improvement in their attitude to their subordinates and to training. Neither sex showed any significant improvement in their satisfaction with their jobs. Even those changes that were significant were small in comparison with the pre-existing range of differences between individuals.[2]

As Handyside is the first to admit, however, 'improvement in expressed opinions may not be associated with on-the-job behaviour' and the most that can be said is that 'if expressed opinion does not change it is highly unlikely that overt behaviour will do so. Thus changed opinion can be regarded as a necessary, but not sufficient, condition for improved supervisory behaviour.' His findings therefore mean merely that so far as attitudes to subordinates (and training) are concerned, there was nothing to suggest that the supervisors had not changed in the direction intended by the instructors, and that therefore if the instructors really knew what made a good supervisor there was a certain probability that these men and women had become better supervisors. But in certain other respects it was unlikely that their attitudes had changed enough to make any difference to their behaviour on the job.

In other words, the only satisfactory test of the efficacy of training in supervision is one which measures changes in the actual factors that good supervision is supposed to influence; that is, presumably, the attitudes not of the supervisors but of the subordinates, and the efficiency of the working unit. But this sort of test is even less easy to devise. So far, only three studies of this kind have been reported, two in United States industries, and one in a London factory (again by Handyside).[3]

[1] 'Improvement' of course meant 'change in the direction intended by the instructors'.

[2] Incidentally, there were some interesting differences between the sexes. Men showed more favourable attitudes to both higher management and subordinates, and more job-satisfaction.

[3] Summaries and discussions of the results of the three industrial experiments will be found in Handyside's paper cited above.

The two studies in the U.S.A. 'have two findings in common—first, that the formal courses in human relations that were studied were having little general effect as far as the subordinates of the foremen could see, and second that the behaviour of the foreman's own boss was a very important variable in the situation. Unfortunately, neither of these studies included any production indices, so it is impossible to say whether the training courses led to an increase in productivity, as they might well have done, by making the foremen more conscious of their responsibilities for production, planning etc.' (Handyside, *loc. cit.*).

Handyside summarises his own results among supervisors in a London factory as follows:

> There are certain clear similarities between the results of this British experiment and those of the American studies. . . . Again it appears to be the case that subordinates were unable to see any improvement in human relations skills of supervisors who had attended a training course. Again the crucial character of the behaviour of senior management is emphasised. One new factor, however, has appeared: despite the absence of an improvement on the 'satisfaction' measures there does appear to have been an improvement in 'efficiency'! It is plausible to argue, particularly when one knows the intimate details of the experimental situation, that this improvement was probably attributable to increased co-operation between the supervisors and the production planning department, for it was certainly the case that before the training programme the supervisors knew very little about the way in which this department worked, and that consequently they were unable to co-operate very intelligently with its personnel.

Among foremen in industry, then, the results of investigation of the actual effects of supervision upon their subordinates suggest that training has very little effect. What are we to conclude about the efficacy of training in supervision, management and leadership in the desk grades of the civil service?

We must not of course jump to the conclusion that it is useless. There are two very real possibilities. One is that desk workers benefit more from courses of instruction than do foremen in factories; this is after all probable, since it is their job to assimilate facts and rules from written and oral communications. The other possibility is that the training techniques used by civil service instructors are better than those used in the foremen's courses. After all, I have just described one case in which training techniques certainly produced some (though not all) of the intended changes in the attitudes of supervisors. We have also seen how up to date and imaginative are the case-study and rôle-playing techniques used to train the desk grades in supervision and management.

At the same time, the evidence for the success of supervisor-training in other occupations shows how little it is wise to assume that we know about supervising office workers. Some of the attitudes of the office workers at Newcastle and in the two Ministries' London headquarters, which I shall be describing in later chapters, are not only relevant but rather different from what one would expect. There is a need for rigorous experiments among desk workers in this field, on the lines of Handyside's experiments; and at least one place where conditions are as favourable for such work as they ever are in real life is the Records Branch at Benton which I shall describe in Chapter 5.

3

A DILEMMA:
THE USES OF DISMISSAL

In the previous chapter I discussed two aspects of *morale* to which the service undoubtedly pays attention. I now want to consider one which it is popularly believed to neglect.

In almost every organisation of full-time workers the most obvious incentive to work hard and efficiently is the fear of losing the job. There are of course certain conditions under which this fear is too remote to be effective. Among prisoners and military conscripts, for example, it disappears altogether. A shortage of skilled labour may deter an employer from sacking an idle craftsman, who may, in any case, know that he can find a similar job with ease. Or the employees may be organised into unions that can use the counter-threat of withdrawing their members from work in order to protect individuals against dismissal.

In the non-industrial civil service, however, none of these special conditions is present to an effective extent. Civil servants are not undergoing forced labour. Any shortage of manpower for desk jobs is merely relative. Although competition to enter the clerical, executive and administrative classes is no longer as keen as it was before the war, it is still healthy; and though individual departments may sometimes complain that they are not getting enough new Assistant Principals or Executive Officers this has not yet been used as an argument for not dismissing the unsuitable. The third condition—the organisation of employees into unions—is certainly present; the civil service unions are more comprehensive in membership and powerful in negotiation than any other unions of office workers in Britain. But it is very difficult to argue that they exert any effective pressure to prevent dismissal of the unsuitable employee. It is true that someone given notice of dismissal may—and often does—seek the help of the Departmental representative of his Association. But these representatives are responsible officials, who will want to be satisfied that there is a *prima facie* likelihood of a genuine injustice before they will arouse their Association on the member's behalf. Their relations with the Departmental Establishment Divisions are such that their first step is usually to discuss the case with one of the Establishment Officers, and only if he failed to satisfy them that no injustice was being done would they bring their Association into official action.[1]

[1] Dismissals of this kind must of course be carefully distinguished from dismissals of redundant staff, a matter in which the staff associations are extremely active.

There is therefore no obvious reason why the threat of dismissal should not be an effective incentive in the non-industrial civil service. In practice, how effective is it? Let us consider separately the various forms of dismissal, beginning with the least drastic.

3.1. NORMAL RETIREMENT

For the established[1] civil servant in the desk classes, normal retirement is possible at any age after his sixtieth birthday. So long as he has at least ten years' service behind him, he may then leave the service and until his death draw a pension proportionate to his service and his retiring salary.[2] Another possibility is for him to be 'disestablished'—that is, to retire formally—but to be employed in the same or a lower grade. His new grade may be one or more steps below his former one, and an Executive may well find himself re-employed as a Clerical Officer: but he is unlikely to suffer financially.[3]

Complete retirement may be the result of the civil servant's own decision. If he has strong interests outside his work—perhaps even another post awaiting him—or feels his strength or enthusiasm waning, he may come to the conclusion that he should be content with the pension he has earned and go. The decision, on the other hand, may be taken by his Department, who may for some time have regarded him as not very satisfactory but not sufficiently unsatisfactory to justify more severe measures, of the kind which I shall describe in 3.2. Reversion to a lower grade, however, which means loss of status, responsibility and perhaps interest,[4] is seldom his choice; it is almost always a compromise offered by his Department. The reason may be that they do not consider him quite capable of continuing to fill his present post, but are aware that complete retirement would impose unusual hardship on him—for example, because he has not enough service behind him to have earned a substantial pension, or because he is still supporting a young family. The compromise may, however, have nothing to do with his standard of efficiency; if his Ministry is contracting or reorganising itself, there may be a surplus of staff in his grade; or he may, on the other hand, be

---

[1] As distinct from 'unestablished' officers, who may qualify for a gratuity but not for a pension. They may be unestablished for various reasons—method or age of entry into the service, or the nature of the post.

[2] More precisely, he will receive
  (i) a *pension* of *one* eightieth for every year of service of his average annual salary for his last three years of service, up to a maximum of forty-five eightieths, of which only forty can be earned by service before the age of sixty; and
  (ii) a *lump sum* of *three* eightieths for every year of service of his average annual salary for his last three years of service.

[3] If he is to be re-employed as a disestablished civil servant, he receives the lump sum and as much of his pension as will not, together with his new salary, exceed his former salary.

[4] But not often a financial loss, for the reasons given.

reverted to enable someone in the grade below to be promoted at an age when he is still capable of adapting himself to higher duties.

In 1957, 260 members of the Executive Class were downgraded on reaching sixty to levels varying from Clerical Assistant to junior Executive grades. A further 171 between sixty and sixty-five were downgraded to similar levels, while five men over sixty-five became Clerical Officers or Clerical Assistants. In contrast, in the same year no Administrators were downgraded on reaching sixty, and only two were downgraded to the Executive Class at ages between sixty and sixty-five. The ratio of Administrators to Executives in this age-group was about 1:14, and the great disparity between the incidence of downgrading is almost certainly due to the existence in many large Departments of agreements between official and staff sides to downgrade Executives at sixty or later ages, in the interests of promotion.[1]

Until recently, most Departments insisted on complete retirement (or in some cases reversion) by the age of sixty-five, irrespective of the individual's standard of efficiency, and many still do. The Treasury's advice now, however, to Departments is that the general aim should be 'maximum retention'—that is to say 'to employ all fit and willing officers of all grades for as long as is possible'.[2] It is left to Departments themselves to determine what is an acceptable standard of efficiency and to measure individuals against it. The Treasury recognises that 'the higher the grade the lower the age at which officers are likely to be retired'.[2] Departments which are contracting in size may have stricter views as to what is acceptable when the alternative is to discharge younger men simply because they are redundant. They may be influenced in the other direction by difficulties in finding satisfactory replacements, and so tolerate a specialist even though he shows plain signs of declining in health or slowing down in output. Nevertheless, from the age of sixty onward each civil servant's position is examined critically at frequent intervals.

Table 3.01 facing shows the net result of this system for the year 1957. Since it was not possible to distinguish between voluntary and compulsory retirements it must simply—but safely—be assumed that the bulk of the retirements in the first year after sixty took place at the individual's choice, but that an increasing fraction were compulsory, until at the upper end of the scale there were few voluntary retirements. The very high percentage of Executives who appear to retire at sixty,

[1] It is possible that Administrators are more likely to choose complete retirement in preference to the loss of status involved in downgrading; but this cannot account for more than a fraction of the difference.

The figures for the General Clerical Class are not given, partly because the scope for downgrading is obviously limited in their case, partly because for technical reasons it was not possible to be sure that they were comprehensive.

[2] From Estacode, the Treasury's manual of guidance for Departments on matters of staff management.

THE USES OF DISMISSAL 37

however, includes a substantial number who did so simply to revert to a lower grade; without them the percentage would be about 26 per cent. The table shows that many Departments still regard sixty-five as a normal upper limit, for there is a noticeable 'hump' in the percentages at this point. At the same time, a good third of the General Clerical Class are kept after that age, either because they are difficult to replace or because many were late entrants to the service who have not yet earned a pension on which they could retire without hardship.

TABLE 3.01

Staff Group	(N)[1]	Percentages retiring on attaining the age of						Mean Ages on Retirement years
		60 %	61 %	62 %	63 %	64 %	65 %	66+ %	
Administrative	(139)	22	18	18	17	10	12	4	62·3
General Executive	(1743)	41	14	10	7	7	16	5	62·0
General Clerical	(2292)	12	6	5	7	8	28	34	64·7

In practice there are thus three reasons for normal retirement: the wish of the individual, a decision by his Department in the interests of promotion, or a decision by his Department on the grounds that he is no longer satisfactory. In the first two types of case the result may sometimes be the removal of men and women who are better than their successors, even after the latter have learned the job. Indeed, there are senior civil servants who believe that this is increasingly frequent, and that each new generation of recruits is progressively less satisfactory than their predecessors, although there is general agreement that this decline was not apparent when they themselves entered the service. Apart from such cases, however, there are many jobs in the service—and particularly in the Clerical and Clerical Assistant grades, as we shall see in Chapter 5—where there is not much scope for variations in quality, and where the decline in efficiency that accompanies advancing age must take the form of pure slowing down. We shall be studying a good example in Chapter 5; and another instance is registry work. Here efficiency can be measured very largely in units of work such as the number of files dealt with; and the hard-headed taxpayer might well argue that from his point of view what mattered was the ratio between the work done and the cost of paying for it to be done. If so, he might point out, three elderly men might between them be able to do the work of two younger men; and it is cheaper to pay them full salaries for doing so than to pay them half their salaries for doing nothing and pay two full salaries to their replacements.[2] But this is a dangerous argument. The

[1] N=total number to which the percentages refer.
[2] The economics of the choice are not really, of course, so simple; but the principle is.

three slow men are probably setting a bad example to their juniors, who form a low estimate of the acceptable speed of working. In any case, as soon as the argument is applied to a level of work at which there is scope for variation in quality, it breaks down. An old man who is unable to solve new problems—or even recognise their existence—may not only slow down his own work; he may dislocate the organisation of a whole office, or even make mistakes—of commission or omission—that will interfere with a public service.

The dilemma posed by the elderly civil servant has become more, not less, acute; for the desk classes have been slowly ageing. We shall see[1] that the average age of the desk workers in two Ministries was about ten years more than in two private Companies. Like the population as a whole, the service is yielding to the ageing process by slowly advancing the age at which it insists upon complete retirement. From the narrowest economic point of view, the shorter the time for which a civil servant draws his pension the better, and as his expectation of life increases so should the age of retirement. From the point of view of the elderly civil servant himself, it is also a welcome tendency; he probably dreads having nothing to do even more than living on half-pay. From the point of view of the younger civil servant, the tendency not only means a longer wait until he can hope for promotion to a job for which he may have been fit and ready long ago; it also means that consciously or unconsciously he has to adapt his speed of work and ways of thought to those of his elders, and accept a standard of efficiency for which they are the yardstick. This dilemma faces not only the Establishment Division of every Department, but also every officer who has to report— usually every year—upon the fitness for retention of any subordinate who is over sixty. There is often a direct conflict between humanity and expediency, and, rightly or wrongly, the bias of the service is in favour of humanity.

3.2. RETIREMENT BEFORE THE NORMAL AGE

A number of men and women, however, leave the service each year before they attain the age of normal retirement. Some do so voluntarily —the men because they have found a better-paid or more congenial job; the women usually to get married or to devote themselves to marriage. Some have to be discharged as redundant, some because of persistent ill-health; a few are dismissed for misconduct. I shall deal briefly with these cases, before coming to the most important of all—those discharged or demoted for inefficiency.

A civil servant may be discharged at any time without notice, without pension and without the necessity for justifying this action. In practice, there are only two kinds of case in which he is not given a pension or gratuity in proportion to his service:

[1] In Chapter 7.1.

(i) if his career has been very short; almost all such cases are failures during probation, which I shall explain later;
(ii) if the reason for his discharge is misconduct.

As for justification, in practice he is discharged only for one of the reasons considered below.

Redundancy, Misconduct, Ill-health

Now and again the contraction of a Ministry or one of its subdivisions or the complete abolition of an office, removes the need for one or more civil servants. Where it is possible to absorb them into vacancies created by retirements elsewhere, this is done: but sometimes—and particularly if they are specialists—this is impossible, and they have to be declared redundant. Many precautions are taken to ensure not only that the choice of those to be declared redundant is as fair as possible, but also that they have time to find other jobs, and, if they want it, the help of the Ministry of Labour and National Service. They receive as compensation the pension or gratuity for which their service qualifies them. There is no attempt to select the less efficient for discharge: the staff associations, who are especially vigilant over redundancies, would argue that this would be an abuse, and that inefficiency should be dealt with by the proper procedures.

Occasionally a civil servant is found either to have behaved with such impropriety or such indiscretion in his official work, or else to have been convicted of a sufficiently grave criminal offence unconnected with his work, to make it inadvisable to retain him in the service. In such circumstances he is dismissed forthwith, usually without a pension. In the four years 1954-57 this befell 2 Administrators, 17 Executives, 86 Clerical Officers and 33 Clerical Assistants. Expressed as rates per 1,000 per annum of the total number to whom this might have happened,[1] these show a remarkable uniformity:

Administrators	0·20
Executives	0·13
Clerical Officers	0·21
Clerical Assistants	0·25

The Executives seem to be slightly superior in virtue or subtlety to the other desk classes: but the rates are too low to be a firm foundation for

[1] Since the periods covered by the statistics which the Treasury were able to give me varied from one year (1957) to eleven years (mid-1949 to mid-1959), and since the numbers at risk in the desk classes vary so enormously, this is the only sound basis of comparison. During the years 1954-57, from which most of the statistics are taken, the numbers in each class were more or less steady at the following levels:

Administrative	2,500 (including 190 women)
General Executive	36,000 (including 7,500 women)
General Clerical	78,000 (including 28,000 women)
Clerical Assistant	33,700 (including 19,700 women)

any criminological hypotheses. We are not, in any case, concerned with the somewhat specialised kind of inefficiency which they represent.

A civil servant whose health makes it doubtful whether he will ever be restored to full efficiency is examined by one or more of the Treasury's Medical Advisers. If they are satisfied that he is permanently incapacitated he will be retired forthwith, whatever his age, and awarded the pension (or gratuity), if any, for which the length of his service qualifies him, with the concession that if he has more than 10 but less than 20 years' service he may be treated as if he had 20 years. Since the reason for discharging the physically or mentally unfit is that they are unable to work with full efficiency there are sometimes 'borderline cases' in which it would be hard to say how much of the individual's inefficiency is due to his physical or mental health, and how much to a chronic or progressive inability to cope with his responsibilities; this exit thus makes possible the compulsory discharge of some of the less efficient. Over the four years 1954-57 the rates of discharge on grounds of ill-health for the main desk classes were:

Administrative class	1·5	
General Executive class	3·1	per 1,000 per annum
General Clerical class	3·1	
Clerical Assistants	6·9	

Voluntary Resignation or Early Retirement

Before the age of fifty, a civil servant who resigns voluntarily is not normally eligible for a pension, although women who resign to get married receive a 'dowry'. In 1954-57 roughly five women in every thousand in the desk classes resigned voluntarily, and while a few must have done so on getting other jobs, we can assume that the great majority were about to marry, or, having married earlier, now wanted to devote themselves wholly to their homes, as usually happens with the arrival of the first child. The resigning men, on the other hand, must have intended to take up other jobs. After the age of fifty, voluntary *retirement* is now possible: the Superannuation Act of 1949 allows civil servants over fifty but under normal retiring age to resign and claim a proportionate pension when they reach that age, although the Treasury may accept compassionate arguments for immediate payment. This concession, which assumes that the civil servant will find some source of income to bridge a gap of anything up to nine years, is intended primarily for the man who is attracted by some job outside the service, but will take it only if he does not forfeit the pension he has earned by two or three decades in the service. Together, resignation and voluntary retirement among men[1] in the years 1954-57 occurred at the following rates per 1,000 per annum:

[1] The table excludes women because a high but unknown percentage of their resignations and retirements are due to marriage, as has already been explained.

Administrative Class . . 6·1 (29% in their fifties)
General Executive Class . 2·9 (17% in their fifties)
General Clerical Class . 13·4 (2% in their fifties)
Clerical Assistant Class . 3·9 (7% in their fifties)

The obvious feature of this table is the rate for the General Clerical Class, which is twice the rate for the administrators, three times the rate for the Clerical Assistants, and more than four times the rate for the Executives. Most of it consists of resignations in the first few years of the Clerical Officer's career; and we shall give it more consideration in Chapter 6. Meanwhile, the point is worth making that nobody knows whether these losses from any of the desk classes are removing the better or the worse men. It is arguable that the retirements after fifty are most unlikely to be removing any unsatisfactory ones, since it is the exceptional rather than the below average who can change horses in middle age; at best, this arrangement is getting rid of a few misfits with good qualities; at worst, it is taking the best. But the retirements are greatly outnumbered by the resignations in the twenties, thirties and forties, and about these only hard facts will tell us whether on the whole they are a good riddance or an unfortunate loss.

Inefficiency

It is however the possibility of discharge for inefficiency to which we must devote the closest attention, not only as a direct means of raising efficiency by replacing the less with the more efficient, but also as an incentive to the intermediate category to be more efficient. The position here can be fully appreciated only by a brief glance back into the nineteenth century.

Not only could any civil servant be discharged at pleasure by the Crown without legal remedy or right to a pension: the original Superannuation Acts[1] which regularised the payment of pensions to civil servants did not in fact provide for the payment of a pension to one dismissed for inefficiency. But this was the period during which Departments were trying to rid themselves of the incapables who had secured posts before the Northcote-Trevelyan reforms. Strange as it may seem nowadays, these reforms were not popular with all politicians, and one of the practices which helped to get rid of the 'passenger' without a fuss was the award of a pension. For many years after 1857 the Treasury paid these pensions without statutory authority, protecting themselves by the annual Appropriation Acts; but by the eighteen-eighties Parliament was getting restive about this practice, and it was criticised by successive Committees of Public Accounts. The Treasury were forced to introduce a Bill to regularise these pensions, and the result is Section 2 of the Superannuation Act of 1887.

[1] Of 1834 and 1859.

The explanatory memorandum which prefaced the Bill had a difficult piece of advocacy to perform. It had to establish that there was a need to pension off an appreciable number of men, while at the same time avoiding the admission that they should have been got rid of long ago. The result was the following paragraph:

> Men able to discharge their accustomed duties are not infrequently found inefficient to superintend or carry out reforms for which opportunities in a great public service from time to time arise. As a matter of experience, heads of offices will not turn such men adrift, and either medical certificates of impaired health, unsatisfactory in their nature, are pressed upon the Treasury, or proposals are made to the Treasury for re-organisation of office by which the inefficient men too often obtain, under the existing Pension Acts, pension in excess of the ordinary superannuation scale, or the reform is imperfectly carried out or postponed.

Section 2 allows the Treasury, if they think the special circumstances justify it, to grant a 'retiring allowance', not greater than the pension he has earned, to a civil servant who is 'removed from his office on the ground of his inability to discharge efficiently the duties of his office'. But if they do this, they must lay before Parliament a minute setting forth not only the amount of the allowance but also the reasons for it. This procedure thus involved a very public disgrace for the officer named in the minute. Whatever the immediate effect of this section upon the rate of discharge of the inefficient, this publicity has in the long run acted less as a safeguard against abuse than as a discouragement from its proper use. This can be read between the lines of the speech with which Mr. Glenvil Hall, as Financial Secretary to the Treasury, moved the Second Reading of the Superannuation Bill of 1949:

> What this clause (34) does is to facilitate compulsory retirement on proportionate pension of civil servants who, having reached the age of 50, are no longer fully efficient. The Crown has of course the right to discharge any civil servant without notice and without pension, and nothing in this provision derogates from that power. That plainly is not the way to deal with relative inefficiency. Section 2 of the Superannuation Act, 1887 gives power to retire on proportionate pension any civil servant who is unable—and here I quote—'on account of inability to discharge efficiently the duties of his office'. This procedure however requires the laying of a minute before Parliament, giving the name of the individual concerned and the reasons for his discharge—a not altogether humane way of treating an individual who has really done nothing criminal, and who has failed to live up to expectations through a variety of causes like sickness. It has therefore been thought that we should introduce this provision into this measure in order that a civil servant, after the age of 50, can be pensioned with a proportionate pension on a certificate from his Minister that his retirement is desirable in the interests of efficiency . . .' (the rest of this part of his speech is concerned with the other sub-clause, dealing with voluntary retirement).

Since 1949 it has thus been possible to discharge some civil servants without the laying of a minute before Parliament, but on the certificate of their Minister. The new provision, however, applied only to civil servants of the age of fifty or more; to get rid of a younger one it was

THE USES OF DISMISSAL   43

still necessary either to use the nineteenth-century procedure or to discharge him without any allowance whatsoever. The use which has been made of these two procedures since 1949 can be seen from the two tables overleaf which were supplied to me by the Treasury. It is noticeable that the use of the 1887 Act still continues, although in practice limited to men and women under the age of fifty, and therefore too young to be eligible for compulsory retirement under the 1949 Act.

Lesser Penalties

Since we are considering the threat of dismissal partly in its rôle of an incentive, we must also take notice of two lesser penalties which can be inflicted in the interest either of discipline or of efficiency.[1] An increment of pay, whether future or already earned, may be ordered by the head of the department to be forfeited, and can be restored if the officer's efficiency improves. A heavier penalty is downgrading. We have seen that this can take place after the age of sixty with little or no reflection on a man's efficiency. When it takes place before that age it is almost always the result of a decision that he is not equal to the duties of his grade; very occasionally he himself asks to revert to his former grade. In 1957, in the whole of the Administrative, General Executive and General Clerical Classes, this happened to only twelve Clerical Officers, six members of the Executive grades, and no administrators.

Responsibility for Dismissal

In theory, the responsibility for dismissing a civil servant rests with the Minister of his Department. This was made clear as recently as 1954 by the then Home Secretary.[2]

> The position of the civil servant is that he is wholly and directly responsible to his Minister. It is worth stating again that he holds his office 'at pleasure' and can be dismissed at any time by the Minister; and that power is none the less real because it is seldom used. The only exception relates to a small number of senior posts, like permanent secretary, deputy secretary and principal financial officer, where, since 1920, it has been necessary for the Minister to consult the Prime Minister, as he does on appointment.

---

[1] In addition to these there are: (iii) formal reprimand; (iv) a fine or restitution for loss or damage; (v) suspension with loss of pay. But these are reserved for one or more distinct actions of a reprehensible kind, and are not used against chronic inefficiency.

[2] In the debate on Crichel Down on 20th July 1954. Unfortunately for our present purpose this debate was concerned almost entirely with the relationship between Ministers and civil servants when, as the Home Secretary put it, 'action has been taken by a civil servant of which the Minister disapproves and has no prior knowledge, and the conduct of the official is reprehensible': this is something rather more than inefficiency, or at least a very special form of it. But some of the general statements by the Home Secretary and Mr. Herbert Morrison are relevant to the problem of inefficiency.

TABLE 3.02

Compulsory Retirements under Section 34 (1) of the 1949 Act and Section 2 of the 1887 Act, from 1949 up to and including 2nd quarter 1959

(Figures in brackets show the administrators included in the total)

Year	1949 Act	1887 Act
1949 (½ year)	4	–
1950	19 (4)	–
1951	20 (4)	–
1952	16 (2)	1
1953	17 (1)	–
1954	14	–
1955	10	2
1956	16	2
1957	19	2
1958	16 (1)	1
1959 (½ year)	4 (1)	2
Totals for 10 years	155 (13)	10

TABLE 3.03

Grades of Civil Servants compulsorily retired under Section 34 (1) during the eleven years from mid-1949 to mid-1959 (retirements under Section 2 of the 1887 Act are not included)

Grade	Nos.
Under Secretary	1
Principal Assistant Secretary	1
Assistant Secretary	5
Principal	6
Senior Chief Executive Officer	1
Chief Executive Officer	2
Senior Executive Officer	8
Higher Executive Officer	24
Executive Officer	22
Departmental Executive	4
Higher Clerical Officer	1
Clerical Officer	34
Departmental Clerical	3
Sub-Clerical	7
Typing Grades	1
Inspectorate	1
Messengers, Cleaners, Police, etc.	7
Minor and Manipulative (Post Office)	2
Professional, Scientific and Technical	21
Others	4
	155

In practice, however, it is almost impossible for the Minister to act in such a matter without the agreement of his senior civil servants. Two ex-Ministers testified publicly to this at the time of the debates on Crichel Down:

> One of the very first things my Permanent Secretary thought fit to teach me was, 'Whatever you may think of me or any other civil servant here, you cannot sack us. . . .'[1]
>
> Theoretically it is now possible to retire an officer, with a pension, at any time after the age of fifty. On one occasion I tried to do this. I roused against myself all the camaraderie of the civil service, and every obstacle was put in my way. Eventually a compromise solution was evolved. I can honestly say that this was the only time I was thwarted by my officials.[2]

Mr. Strauss's account is clearly less dramatised than the other: but both emphasise that civil servants regard dismissal as a matter for decision by them rather than by Ministers. The Treasury are almost explicit on this point in Estacode:

> Discipline is a matter for the head of the department and derives from two responsibilities. First is the general responsibility to Parliament, and second is the responsibility of the Accounting Officer to the Public Accounts Committee.[3] It follows that heads of departments must have disciplinary powers over agents employed under them, for unless they have the powers to admonish, reprimand, penalise and in the last resort dismiss those agents, they cannot in any real sense be responsible for the conduct of business in their departments.

Whether it is desirable that the Minister should be as powerless as this is a debatable question. Civil servants would argue that he cannot, but they can, assess the difficulties of the task which the officer in question is trying to perform, or compare his performance not only with that of others in similar circumstances but also with his performance in other posts in which he may have been quite competent. On the other hand, we must seriously consider the argument that the 'camaraderie' of which Mr. Strauss wrote does operate to prevent civil servants from being as objective as they should. We shall see in later chapters that it is certainly a phenomenon which occurs in the civil service. For the moment, let us analyse in rather more detail the respective parts played by civil servants at different levels in the decision to dismiss an officer.

Probation and After

Everyone appointed to a permanent post in one of the desk classes— or in the professional and scientific classes—is on probation for at least a year if he is a Clerical Officer or Assistant and usually two years if he has entered a higher grade. The intention of the probation scheme is

[1] Quoted by C. A. Campbell in *The Civil Service in Britain* (1954), p. 360.
[2] Mr. G. R. Strauss, ex-Minister of Supply in a letter to the *New Statesman and Nation* for November 1954.
[3] Strictly speaking, the first is a responsibility of the Minister; but the second does belong to the permanent head, as Accounting Officer.

that if he seems to fall short of the necessary standard, he should be warned as early as possible, and certainly not less than six months before his probation expires. When it does, his superiors will have to recommend whether his appointment should be confirmed or terminated; or whether he should continue on probation for a little longer. This procedure is not altogether a formality, for in the six years 1954-59 ten new Clerical Officers, five new members of the higher professional and scientific grades, and 33 new junior scientific and technical officers were discharged for inefficiency. In the Administrative and General Executive Classes, however, there were no failures during probation in these years: either selection was more successful, or the procedure less effective.

After he has survived his probation, and until he has reached a certain rank[1], he will be the subject of an annual report, on a comprehensive form which requires the officers for whom he works to assess separately all his official qualities, from 'output' to 'responsibility', usually by assigning to each, one of five values. The reporting officer must conclude by assessing not only his fitness for promotion but also his overall performance of his present duties, again using a five-point scale ranging from 'outstanding' to 'unsatisfactory'. Many civil service management courses include lectures and practical exercises in reporting on staff, chiefly in order that standards should be as uniform as possible.

The reporting officer must observe two important rules. He must not consult the ratings awarded by any other reporting officers of earlier years; and if he awards the lowest rating for overall performance he must tell the subject of the report, so that the latter can put his side of the case to the Establishment Division. There are three exceptions to the second rule, two of them obvious and the third interesting. He need not tell the man that he is rated 'unsatisfactory' if this is merely the result of inexperience because he has served less than a year in this grade; nor need he do so if it is likely to have a bad effect on his health. The third exception is 'where it is clear that no useful purpose can be served by repeated notifications to an officer of a failing in certain respects. Such an officer will normally have been notified on at least one occasion of the defect, and he should be advised of the proposal to discontinue future notifications to the same effect.'[2] The implication is that even the repeated award of the lowest rating will not necessarily lead to downgrading or dismissal.

[1] Which varies from one Ministry to another. But Assistant Secretaries and Chief Executive Officers (and their professional equivalents) are not subject to annual reports; where Principals are, these reports usually take the form of short essays and not report forms. Table 3.03, however, shows that grades which are not the subject of annual reports are still at risk of dismissal.

[2] From the Whitley Council agreement of June 1938, quoted in pp. 183-4 of the C.S.C.A. compendium.

The next stage is the countersigning of the report—whether good or bad—by the officer above the reporting officer. He can add comments of his own, which may tone down or increase the severity of the report, although neither he nor anyone else can tell the reporting officer to alter his ratings. When the report reaches the Establishment Division it is examined, and any 'unsatisfactory' rating would lead to a comparison with previous years' reports, and especially any from a different branch, where the reporting officer and probably the nature of the work were different.

More often, however, it is not the annual report which leads to serious consideration of dismissal or some less drastic step, but a special report, prompted by some particular sin of commission or omission, or by the exhausted patience of a superior officer who has to carry the additional burden. However this may be, the Establishment Division will first consider the possibility that the individual would prove more satisfactory in another type of work or under another superior; and if this is the first report of its kind he will probably be transferred elsewhere. If reports on him continue to be unfavourable, the Establishment Officer will have to propose to the Head of Department that he should be deprived of one or more increments of salary, or downgraded or, in the last resort, retired. The individual himself will be given the opportunity of stating his case, and if compulsory retirement is in question the Head of Department takes the advice of a board of senior officers of his own Department, to whom the individual may state his case in person, with the assistance, if he wishes, of a friend or colleague.

I hope that I have demonstrated the inaccuracy of the popular belief that civil servants can be moribund, idle or dishonest with complete impunity. I have certainly shown how many safeguards for the individual are built into the procedure for detecting and dealing with inefficiency of the kind that does not amount to impropriety, is not accompanied by persistent ill-health and does not show itself until after probation. What I have not yet attempted to answer is the question 'Are the penalties used often enough?', which must be approached in rather a different way.

3.3. TOO MANY OR TOO FEW?

The difficulty of giving a straight answer to this question is recognised not only by civil servants themselves but also by the Ministers whom they have served. Herbert Morrison summed up his attitude to this problem in his chapter on the relations between Ministers and civil servants:

> There are arguments both ways about the greater use of the power to dismiss. The argument for the quality of mercy is, I think, that if dismissals on grounds of nefficiency were noticeable in numbers, or considered to be ruthless, the morale of

the service might suffer and civil servants develop a habit of 'looking over their shoulders'; and that it might result in the resignation even of able people to take up appointments outside owing to a feeling of insecurity. Finally, the man who is distinctly below average and, perhaps, inefficient at 55, has very likely given many years of good service in the past; and it is often by no means altogether his own fault that he is no longer efficient, since he may have been kept on too long in the same job or have suffered in other ways; and generally the staffs of most Departments would prefer to suffer themselves through having to work harder to carry their 'below average colleagues' rather than see them pushed out at great personal hardship. There is an *esprit de corps* in the service which in itself is desirable although it may lead to excessive sympathy. For dismissal it can be argued that the public service cannot afford to carry the inefficient and that inefficient work should not be tolerated; that dismissals on such grounds from time to time may provide an incentive to the staff to be on their toes. An extreme view on either side would, I think, be wrong, but I am disposed to the view that rather more dismissals on grounds of inefficiency would be good for the morale, the spirit and the liveliness of the service.[1]

Before discussing the question 'Is dismissal used often enough?' we should, if possible, formulate it more precisely. 'Often enough' to do what? To get rid of the inefficient? This answer is based on the assumption, which is quite common, that 'inefficiency' is an affliction from which most people are free and with which only a few are cursed, perhaps in varying degrees, much as most of the population are free from tuberculosis while a small percentage suffer from it. This is, however, only one of three possibilities, and the least probable of them. A less naïve hypothesis is that like any machine everyone is to some extent inefficient, but that there is a definite group of people who are markedly less efficient than the ordinary run: this is theoretically improbable and there is no empirical evidence for it. What is most probable is that inefficiency is distributed in the same way as height or intelligence; that is, that there is a mean level of efficiency which is also the most frequently encountered, and that instances of higher or lower efficiency become progressively rarer at about the same rate the further they are from this mean in either direction.[2] If so, the question is not whether we have succeeded in eliminating all those who are infected with inefficiency, but at what level we should draw the line; that is, what degree of inefficiency should be tolerated. But what is to be the sign that we have drawn the line in the right place?

The extent or intensity of public criticism—even if it could be accurately measured in some way—would not be a reliable index. The low esteem in which the general public hold the desk-working civil servant is certainly a social phenomenon that deserves attention, for it seems to occur in all countries with a well-developed bureaucracy. Without

[1] *Government and Parliament* (1955), pp. 334-5.
[2] In Chapter 8 we shall be considering the efficiency ratings in the annual reports of about 1,000 civil servants. Although these are a crude measure for scientific purposes, the ratings were distributed in a symmetrical pattern that is consistent with, even if it is not strong confirmation of, a 'normal' distribution of efficiency in the population.

arguing that low efficiency is never a contributory cause, we must recognise that some other factors are more largely responsible. An economic and social policy that appears to frustrate the activities of the individual and of non-Governmental organisations is bound to focus attention on the way in which the bureaucrat implements this policy; and resentment of his prohibitions may take the form of criticism of his competence. For this and other reasons public criticism is so chronic that it can serve only as a danger signal in those extreme cases in which the execution of policy is so cumbrous, indiscriminate or paradoxical that it provokes an outcry.

It is in fact very hard to see what sort of external symptom could serve as an indication that the service is tolerating too great a degree of inefficiency. But is it not possible to find some internal indication, some symptom apparent to those within the service, that they should be dismissing or demoting more of their own number? For example, can we not rely on the experienced noses of senior civil servants themselves to smell out a dangerous patch of incompetence among their subordinates?

One difficulty about this suggestion is that the degree of efficiency which they will regard as tolerable will depend not only on their own but also on the general level of the Department's. Even among civil servants themselves certain Ministries have a reputation for tardiness, lack of co-ordination between the left and right hands, or inability to give a straight answer. The senior officer who has spent his career in one of these has a lower standard of efficiency; and even one who is imported from a brisker and more competent Department will soon have to fit his tempo and his tune to the rest of the band.

Let us suppose, however, that a civil servant is dissatisfied with the performance of one of his subordinates. His first difficulty will be to convince himself that he is justified. There are a great many possibilities that must be excluded before he can act with confidence. He must be sure that the subordinate is not overworked through understaffing or the illness of a colleague or assistant; and that he has not been assigned to work requiring specialised abilities which not all members of his level need to possess—such as numerical intelligence. If he has to take decisions it is necessary to make certain that he has had clear statements of the principles on which he should take them and the limits of his discretion. His age must be taken into account: to put an Executive Officer fresh from school in charge of a roomful of elderly Clerical Officers may lead to friction. Some other jobs, however, demand the constitution of youth; an elderly Principal is not usually able to stand the pace of life as a Minister's Private Secretary, although his experience and stability may make him more competent than a younger man in other kinds of post.

At the higher levels, where it is correspondingly important to be able to anticipate trouble and take sound decisions for which no rules can be laid down, it is not easy to pick out those mistakes which should have been avoided. An error of judgment is, after all, simply a choice which in the light of present information seems inferior to an alternative; it is not a fact of nature. Moreover, it is a commonplace that there are some situations in which there is no right answer—only solutions of varying degrees of awkwardness. Thirdly, the oftener a man takes a decision or initiates some action, the greater the chances that one of his decisions will be less than perfect; it is the men who avoid the responsibility of deciding and turn a blind eye to the need for action of some sort whose records are cleanest. Mistakes in judgment are dangerously subjective grounds for labelling a man unsatisfactory.

Even when the superior is himself convinced, there is still the question whether he can face the unpleasant task of convincing others. Since the code of the service is that a superior to whom unsatisfactory work is submitted by a subordinate must remedy its defects before he lets it go further, he may be the only person to appreciate just how negligent or stupid his subordinate is. His efforts to convince those who have to be convinced may draw upon himself the suspicion of being too hard to please, or prejudiced against this individual, or even 'inhumane'. The officer who countersigns an adverse report will feel that he should find something to say in favour of the unfortunate subject, while the Establishment Officer will be tempted to point to a less unfavourable verdict from a less honest reporting officer, or to find extenuating circumstances.

The result is that, as we shall see later in Chapters 5 and 8, office workers are very reluctant to be critical of their colleagues. The adverse reports that set the machinery of dismissal or downgrading in motion must, in the nature of things, be signed by men and women for whom the subject has worked for some time. The longer this association has lasted, the more difficult it is to condemn with confidence. The more one knows about a man's history and domestic life, the more excuses one can find for his unsatisfactoriness and the more pretexts for hoping that he will improve. We shall see in Chapter 8.2 how rare an adverse report is in practice.

What is more, the effects of long association are not all as logical. As we shall see, working together seems to produce among the desk classes a certain cohesiveness, which manifests itself in a reluctance to criticise colleagues or subordinates. The replies of the civil servants and other office workers to my questionnaire showed how they hesitated to use any critical phrases about their colleagues or subordinates. This cohesiveness—or 'camaraderie'—has its virtues. It encourages civil servants to co-operate; to help each other out of difficulties; to protest collectively against injustice to an individual; and to rebut criticism of a colleague by an outsider (although they may privately agree with it).

THE USES OF DISMISSAL 51

Does this product of close association also make them over-indulgent in dealing with incompetence?

We seem to be in a position in which we can neither define nor detect the *optimum* rate of dismissal. Is there another approach? In such situations the logical course is to consider whether it is possible to define upper and lower *limits* beyond which the rate should not rise or sink.

Obviously the upper limit is reached when we are getting rid of such a high percentage that we cannot replace them by people who are better. Is the civil service anywhere near this limit? Recruitment to the desk classes has certainly been less easy than before the war, and I have heard from one Establishment Officer or another, complaints that he is not getting enough new C.O.s, E.O.s or A.P.s. The difficulty of recruiting clerical staff who are willing to work in London is a current problem, and probably accounts for the retention of so many beyond the age of sixty-five. In the higher grades, however, gaps can always be filled by promotion. In many Departments C.O.s have to wait for twelve years before they can be considered for normal promotion, while E.O.s may have to wait for eight years or more: and so on. With the possible exception of the Clerical and Sub-clerical Classes, the service does not seem to be near the upper limit to the rate of dismissal or demotion.

The lower limit is less easy to decide upon. To rely upon public outcry would be theoretically possible, but in practice too damaging to the service's reputation: a danger signal can itself be too dangerous. Is there an alternative? So far we have considered dismissal simply as a means of getting rid of the less efficient: but as I pointed out at the beginning of this chapter it can also have another function. The possibility of it can be an incentive. For want of a better criterion, should the lower limit be defined as the point at which the rate of dismissal is so remote a possibility that it is no longer serving as an incentive?

The first objection that is likely to be raised to this definition is that it sets the limit so low that it could never be reached in practice; we shall see whether this is really so improbable. Another is that to function as an incentive to efficiency the rate of dismissal must be known (or appear) to the employee to be appreciable, whereas out of the consideration for the dismissed employee Departments are extremely discreet about the fact of dismissal. The Treasury's advice to Departments is that they should 'take all possible steps to ensure that, so far as the conduct of the necessary official business is concerned, the knowledge that a man's retirement is compulsory is confined strictly to those whose duties make it essential for them to know the facts'. It is not, of course, possible to conceal the compulsory nature of the retirement when it takes place under the 1887 Act procedure, since this involves naming the civil servant in a minute which is laid before Parliament; and the Treasury's advice therefore applies only to compulsory retirement of men or women between fifty and sixty. Sometimes, however, the civil servant is offered and accepts the alternative of 'voluntary' resignation. The practical effect of this discretion is to avoid increasing the difficulty which he will have in finding another job; but to many people the stigma of dismissal is equally important. There can be little doubt that this practice prevents the small numbers of dismissals which do occur from acting as a stimulus to efficiency. The compromise of publishing annual totals of dismissals for inefficiency without naming individuals, and thus combining humanity with the interests of the service, has not been adopted. Most of the figures in this chapter are published here for the first time.

A third and very practical query is whether it is feasible to take any measurements to show when dismissal is or is not regarded by employees as a genuine possibility. The questionnaire which is described in Chapters 7 and 8 therefore included two questions on this subject. The respondents—who represented between 63 and 75 per cent. of those who received the questionnaire—had a choice between four descriptions of the way in which they thought that 'incompetent people' were dealt with in their Ministry or Company. The first two choices were intended to represent a fairly strict policy, the third one of leniency tempered with some common sense, and the fourth a policy of complete toleration. The result can be seen in Table 3.04A. Nearly half of the Companies' staffs thought that incompetents were 'given a chance and then got rid of' or even 'got rid of quickly', whereas only a sixth of the civil servants subscribed to either of these beliefs. Nor was this the belief of the lower grades only: the administrators and the professionals were the most disillusioned of all.

My next question asked the respondents to say whether they approved of their employer's policy as they visualised it. One-sixth of the private office workers and one-fifth of the civil servants sat on the fence, and replied 'hard to say'; but of the rest only 42 per cent. of the Ministries' staffs, as compared with 66 per cent. of the Companies', approved. Table 3.04B shows in more detail what they approved or disapproved of. For example, only a handful attributed but disapproved of a tough policy, just as very few attributed and approved of a policy of complete toleration. Most interesting of all, however, is the very large number—two-thirds of the civil servants and one-third of the other office workers—who believed that incompetents were 'put where they did least harm'. What was interesting about them was that they were so evenly divided between approval, disapproval and inability to make up their minds—the last a sure sign of conflicting feelings.

As I shall explain in Chapter 8.2, I was able to distinguish between the replies of the more efficient and the less efficient halves of my civil service respondents, and comparison with their replies tended to confirm that their beliefs on this subject had nothing to do with their own efficiency. Among the more efficient—numbering 480—only 14·7 per

TABLE 3.04

Replies of Civil Servants and Private Office Employees to Questions 41 and 42 of Questionnaire GG 59, dealing with their organisation's way of treating incompetent people

A. What they believed

Question 41: 'Incompetent people are	Private Office-Workers	Civil Servants					
		All Grades	Admin.	S.E.O. etc.[1]	H.E.O. & E.O.	Clerical[2]	Professional
	%	%	%	%	%	%	%
got rid of quickly	4·2	1·3	—	1·1	0·9	2·5	—
given a chance and then got rid of	43·2	15·8	7·7	18·7	14·4	20·4	8·4
put where they do least harm	33·1	63·5	73·6	68·8	64·5	55·9	72·3
allowed to stay wherever they are.'	19·5	19·4	18·7	11·4	20·2	21·2	19·3
N (=100%)	624	1,067	91	96	430	367	83

[1] i.e., all members of the Executive Class above the rank of H.E.O.
[2] i.e., Clerical Officers, C.O. Secretaries and Clerical Assistants.

B. What they thought of what they believed

Question 41: 'Incompetent people are	Question 42: 'Do you approve of this?' (private office workers are in parentheses)			
	'Yes'	'No'	'Hard to say'	
	%[1]	%[1]	%[1]	N (=100%)
got rid of quickly	64·2 (88·5)	7·2 (7·7)	28·6 (3·8)	14 (26)
given a chance and then got rid of	91·1 (94·1)	1·8 (0·7)	7·1 (5·2)	169 (270)
put where they do least harm	28·7 (34·0)	45·7 (35·9)	25·6 (30·1)	677 (206)
allowed to stay on wherever they are'	0·5 (0·8)	91·3 (82·8)	8·2 (16·4)	207 (122)

[1] Percentages are of those who chose each of the four replies to Question 41.

cent. attributed one of the two tougher policies to their Ministries, whereas among the less efficient 500 the percentage who did so was 20·0; if these beliefs were having any effect upon efficiency, the difference ought to be in the opposite direction.[1]

The point of Table 3.04, of course, is not that it allows us to compare the actual policies of these Ministries and Companies. In fact, several members of the desk classes in these Ministries *had* been retired compulsorily since the 1949 Act. What the table does show is that the civil servants at all levels had a low opinion of their Ministries' handling of this problem; and also, in case it should be alleged that all office workers feel like this, that it is possible for private desk workers both to attribute a stricter policy to their employers and to approve of it. In sum, if the lower limit to the rate of dismissal is defined as the point where it ceases to operate as an incentive, then there is some evidence that among the desk classes the rate may be near that limit.

It is sometimes argued, however, that while higher rates may be found in other office organisations, these are usually small concerns, and that among organisations of a size comparable to the civil service it would be found that the desk worker's job was more or less as secure as the civil servant's. It would, therefore, not be a complete waste of time to compare the rate of dismissal of a large industrial concern. I purposely avoided a nationalised concern or other public undertaking because I argued that there was a strong possibility that they imitated the policy of the civil service in this as in other conditions of service; and I therefore deliberately chose a type of organisation with a completely different tradition.

The organisation which gave me information was one of the largest with headquarters in this country. It consisted of a group of companies with a uniform personnel policy; and its 'management class', which was distributed among these, totalled well over 1,000—a number not out of scale with the 2,300 administrators whose compulsory retirements we have been considering. I would of course have liked to compare wastage at all levels, but this would have imposed too much on the helpfulness of the industrial concern; and in any case the levels I was able to compare are those at which competence is most necessary. The figures for the 'management class' covered a recent seven-year period during which an expansion was taking place; the civil service was contracting during the early half of the ten-year period for which I had information, but this ought if anything to have increased its rate of dismissal.

[1] This is an instance where a negative conclusion can be drawn from the absence of the expected difference although a positive one could hardly be based on its presence alone. It may be argued that what the difference does show is that beliefs about dismissal policy could never be an incentive; but this would be unjustified, since all we have evidence of here is the situation when dismissal rates are at a low level.

THE USES OF DISMISSAL

The two groups in which I was interested were those who resigned voluntarily and those who resigned at the request of the organisation. In the 'management class' the first group averaged 16 per 1,000 per annum, compared with about 6 per 1,000 per annum for the Administrative Class for the four years 1954-57. It was explained to me that while a number of the resigning managers had no doubt found better jobs on their own initiative, others had been given hints that their prospects in the organisation were so poor that they would do well to look elsewhere. The group who resigned at the express request of the organisation, on the other hand, averaged 5 per 1,000 per annum. The 13 Administrators who were compulsorily retired from the civil service in the ten years from 1949 to 1959 represent a rate of about one-half per 1,000 per annum.

An obvious query is whether this industrial organisation was as careful in selecting entrants to their 'management class' as the civil service is in admitting men and women to the Administrative Class. Roughly half of the Administrative Class consists of promoted members of the Executive and other Classes; the other half are university graduates, or men and women of similar education, who have entered through one of the competitive examinations or tests: a few have been allowed to enter in special circumstances from other careers. All these methods of entry serve as fairly effective filters for the elimination of the grossly incompetent, although the academic type of examination which at one time was the only filter for direct entrants is a test of intellect rather than of efficiency in the ordering of business.

Some 16 per cent. of the managers in the industrial organisation had been recruited direct from outside, no doubt because they had proved their competence in other concerns. The rest had been promoted from below. Some of these were, like the Assistant Principals who furnish about half of the Administrative Class, university graduates, who had been through 'a careful selection procedure by a senior board, comprising a group of senior managers from a rota and the collaboration of psychologist advisers'; after which they had served a training period of about three years before being appointed to managerial posts. Whether this procedure is as thorough as Methods I or II in the civil service is difficult to say; certainly competition for entry into this concern cannot be as intense. But this procedure had supplied only a small percentage of the managers who formed the population for the wastage figures I have been quoting. Altogether, I do not think that we can conclude with any confidence that the selection of the industrial managers for the tasks which they had to perform competently was such as to yield a much higher risk of wastage.

Let me sum up the argument as far as it has gone. The rate at which civil servants—and particularly administrators—are got rid of for inefficiency is markedly lower than any other form of premature retirement. The problem of what the rate should be is not the problem of identifying a few abnormal officers but one of determining the level at which to draw the line. It is difficult to see how any objective index can be found to help in determining this level; but at the same time the practice of leaving it to the judgment of individual officers has its dangers. The fact that a large percentage of the desk grades in two Ministries regarded their Ministry's handling of the problem of the incompetent as too lenient suggests at least one conclusion: that if the rate of dismissal falls to the level at which it is regarded as too low by the employees themselves, then it is certainly failing in one purpose, which must be to act as a stimulus to efficiency in those who are not dismissed. Comparison of the annual rate of voluntary and forced resignations in the Administrative Class of the service and in the Management Class of a very large industrial concern shows that the former is very much below the latter.

I have left to the last the argument—referred to, for example, in the quotation from Herbert Morrison—that an increase in the dismissal-rate might, when it became common knowledge in the service, damage 'morale' in such a way as to do more harm than good to efficiency. The assumption that the rate is so high that any increase would produce some undesirable reaction among employees is, as we have seen, rather less probable than the converse—that it is so low that it is having an effect of a kind which nobody could call desirable. But there is a more interesting implication in this argument. This is that there is in organisations such as the civil service something quite distinct from efficiency which must be fostered with care because otherwise it may produce some unwanted result. I have deliberately postponed discussion of the nature of *morale*, and kept the word itself in italics, until I had explored at least one issue in which it can, and probably does, affect our practical thinking. If the next chapter succeeds in clarifying the notion of *morale* it will, I think, show that any appeal to it in an issue of the kind we have been considering is misconceived.

4

A CONCEPTUAL QUESTION: WHAT *IS* 'MORALE'?

The two theories about the nature of morale are not difficult to state. One is that there is such a thing; the other is that there isn't. Perhaps these statements should be amplified a little before we decide between them. Until recently those who have thought about 'morale'—whether they were commanders or psychologists—have assumed that it was something which really existed, and which operated as a single force upon human beings. They thought of bad 'morale' as something like hunger, which shows itself in symptoms such as pain in the stomach, lack of physical strength, unscrupulous methods of getting food and so on. In much the same way bad morale was supposed to manifest itself in several different ways—for example, in absenteeism, strikes, high labour turnover, a high rate of accidents, and grumbling about minor inconveniences.

This theory—which I shall call 'the condition-with-symptoms theory' —is seldom stated in this explicit form. Probably because the notion has such a long and respectable history, investigators who make use of it have tended to assume either that everyone knows what is meant by it, or that everyone will agree with their definition of it.

When investigators began to define the word, it soon became obvious that everyone did *not* agree on what they meant by it. In the first place, some of them treated morale as something which belonged to an individual, whereas some regarded it as a property of groups. For example:

1. 'The term *morale* refers to a condition of physical and emotional well-being in the individual that makes it possible for him to work and live hopefully and effectively, feeling that he shares the basic purposes of the groups of which he is a member; and that makes it possible for him to perform his tasks with energy, enthusiasm and self-discipline, sustained by a conviction that, in spite of obstacles and conflict, his personal and social ideas are worth pursuing.'[1]
2. '*Morale* is obedience to an internal, personal authority (obedience to a sense of duty, it is sometimes called), which arises out of an ideal or value common to the group, the end sought by the group being defined by the ideal or value.'[2]
3. 'As the term is used ordinarily by the employer, labourer and psychologist alike, it refers to a feeling of "togetherness". There is a sense of identification with and

---

[1] Examples 1 and 4 were among the definitions emerging from the Conference on Psychological Factors in Morale held in 1940 under the auspices of the Division of Anthropology, National Research Council (U.S.A.).

[2] T. T. Paterson, *Morale in War*, p. 99, which is influenced by F. C. Bartlett, as the context makes clear.

interest in the elements of one's job, working conditions, fellow-workers, supervisors, employers, and the company. The more a worker possesses such feelings, the higher his morale.'[1]

4. 'Morale refers to the condition of a group where there are clear and fixed group goals (purposes) that are felt to be important and integrated with individual goals; where there is confidence in the attainment of these goals; and, subordinately, confidence in the means of attainment, in the leader, associates, and finally in oneself; where group actions are integrate and co-operative; and where aggression and hostility are expressed against the forces frustrating the group rather than toward other individuals within the group.'

Definitions 1-3 differ from definition 4 in one important respect. If we imagine a squad of factory hands—called, let us say, Henry James, Walter Pater and Ronald Firbank—then the first three definitions would allow us to talk about James's 'morale', Pater's 'morale' and Firbank's 'morale', but not about the 'morale' of the whole squad, whereas the fourth definition would make it sense to refer only to the 'morale' of the whole trio. This is not simply a matter of verbal usage, because definitions 1-3 would allow us to say that James's morale was 'good' or 'high', but that Firbank's was 'bad' or 'low', whereas the fourth definition would make this nonsense.

On the other hand, it is noticeable that none of the 'individualist' definitions go so far as to exclude all mention of the group to which the individual belongs, while the 'group-property' definitions use such phrases as 'individual goals' and 'confidence in oneself'. There are, however, usages of 'morale' which would allow us to talk about the 'morale' of a man on a desert island[2] or in solitary confinement; and attempts have been made to describe situations in which the efficiency and cohesiveness of a group was extremely high although the individuals of which it was composed were each disgruntled and discouraged.[3] Such extreme definitions, however, are somewhat forced, and tend to be found in fiction rather than in psychological case-histories.[4] They serve, on the whole, to emphasise that morale is usually thought of in terms which include references both to the individual and the group.

The other common feature of the definitions which we have so far considered is that all treat morale as if it were what I have called 'a condition with symptoms'. The 'condition' (as definitions 1 and 4 actually call it) is not one which can itself be measured; you cannot measure 'physical and emotional well-being' (definition 1) or 'obedience to an internal, personal authority' (definition 2). It is regarded, however, as manifesting itself in, or causing, behaviour which is to some extent measurable. This behaviour takes the form of high or low productivity,

---

[1] A. B. Blankenship, cit. M. S. Viteles, *Morale and Motivation in Industry*, p. 284.
[2] The unabridged version of *Robinson Crusoe* contains numerous passages dealing with what might be summed up as Crusoe's 'morale'.
[3] See, for example, Herman Wouk's novel *The Caine Mutiny*.
[4] A distinction at least of degree, if not of kind.

frequency or infrequency of absences, complaints, strikes, quarrels within the group, and so forth.

This theory is, of course, a comforting and optimistic one for the investigator. He is like the doctor who wants to cure a patient's cough, lack of appetite, fever and night-sweats, and knows that he is dealing with several symptoms of one disorder, tuberculosis, which he can tackle by direct methods. If absenteeism, low productivity, complaints and inefficiency are all symptoms of a real disorder called 'low morale', then perhaps this can be treated by some direct method, and so at one stroke remove the underlying cause of all these inconveniences?

As I have said, however, there is also the theory that there is no such thing as morale. According to this theory it is a mistake to assume that there is any single cause underlying all these kinds of industrial behaviour. Even if it were firmly established that there is a very close connection of some sort between them (and, as we shall see, it is not), is there any point in assuming that there exists yet another factor to which they are all linked? Only if you can either measure or manipulate that factor separately. We have just seen how unlikely it is, from the very definitions of the factor which are offered to us, that it will prove measurable; but what about manipulation? If we could show that all the measurable factors could be moved up or down by doing something to the workers that had no obvious connection with any one of these factors, we would have some justification for thinking that we were altering some hidden condition that was causally connected with them, just as a doctor is justified in assuming that he is dealing with a bacillary infection if he succeeds in curing earache by injecting an antibiotic into the thigh. But in order to be sure that one is manipulating something one must be able to measure what one is doing, even if it is only in a rough and ready way; and one is then dealing merely with one more measurable factor. If so, the argument concludes, is there any point in the notion of morale as an unobservable, unmeasurable condition underlying the behavioural symptoms of members of a group?

Investigators who take this view sometimes resort to defining morale instead as a combination of a number of measurable factors. These 'composite definitions', as I shall call them, usually include two, three or even all of the following four concepts:

Productivity or Efficiency

One or other of these factors usually figures in these combinations. 'Productivity' is of course chosen where the employees are producing something that can be measured, such as a raw or processed material: 'efficiency' where they are performing a service of some sort, such as dealing with enquiries by telephone, interview or correspondence. It is worth noting, however, that not all definitions of morale include one or other of these factors: some investigators appear to use the term in a sense in which it is possible, at least theoretically, for morale to rise or fall in an organisation without being accompanied by any corresponding fluctuation in productivity or efficiency.

Job-satisfaction

This, too, appears in most composite definitions. It is the technical term for the extent to which the employee likes his job (as distinct from his attitude towards his employers, supervisors and colleagues). Unlike such things as output or absenteeism, it cannot be measured by counting products or hours worked, but has to be estimated by some sort of communication with the employee himself. This communication may take the form of an interview; but most investigators feel that an interviewer's impression of the job-satisfaction of someone to whom he has talked, even if he attempts to quantify it, is subject to too many distortions from the way in which interviewer and interviewee react to one another; and they prefer to rely on a written questionnaire in which the employee takes his choice from a number of carefully chosen phrases representing various degrees of satisfaction or dissatisfaction with the job. An example will be found in my questionnaire in Appendix B. When large enough numbers of employees answer this sort of question it is possible to compare the job-satisfaction of one group with that of another.

Pride in the Working Group

This is the term invented by Katz, Maccoby and Morse (see Appendix A) for the 'degree of feeling of attachment to and satisfaction with the accomplishment of the immediate or secondary work group of which the employee is a member'—in other words, the attitude that makes a man maintain that his Section (the immediate working group) or his Company are 'better' than the one next door. Under the rather unfashionable name of *esprit de corps* this is a factor that has been recognised for a much longer time in military groups, who go to great lengths to foster it. An attempt to measure it in some office workers will be found in my questionnaire in Appendix B.

Cohesiveness

This is 'the extent to which members of the group like one another',[1] although more precise definitions have been offered. It can be measured by observing the extent to which they associate with each other at times like lunch-breaks, and to which, by discussion and agreement, they form common attitudes on questions such as speed of working. Sometimes it is measured by questionnaires asking members to identify those with whom they prefer to work as colleagues, and similar questions; groups

---

[1] M. Argyle, *The Scientific Study of Social Behaviour.*

whose members tend to select members of other groups are rated low for cohesiveness. An attempt to measure it in some office workers will be found in my questionnaire in Appendix B.

Cohesiveness is thus quite distinct from pride in the working group. Nor should it be confused with 'co-operativeness'. Co-operativeness is the extent to which the members of the group assist each other at the tasks which they, or the group as a whole, are given. No doubt this depends to a certain extent on the members' attitude toward one another; but it also depends very much on the nature of the task and on the attitude of the supervisor towards co-operation. For purely mechanical reasons it is virtually impossible to collaborate with another human being in assembling the parts of a wrist-watch, however cohesive the collaborators may be; again, in any work in which the supervisors encourage a competitive spirit co-operation is bound to suffer. Co-operativeness is not therefore easy to measure in its 'pure' state.

The most ambitious composite definition of morale would include all these factors. 'High morale' would be that a state of a group in which its output is above average, its members score high on job-satisfaction questionnaires and evince considerable pride in their group and cohesiveness, and 'low morale' the state in which they produce less than other comparable groups, claim to dislike their jobs, show little *esprit de corps*, and would on the whole prefer to work with members of other groups. Unfortunately, this sort of composite definition assumes that there is a straightforward and positive relationship between these four factors, an assumption which has been found to be mistaken. High output is not necessarily associated with high job-satisfaction; people who enjoy their work are not always the hardest workers.[1] The most that can be said is that low job-satisfaction probably produces high labour turnover and absenteeism, which themselves damage collective efficiency through loss of the time of trained or partly trained workers. Nor are the most cohesive groups always those with the best output; a cohesive group will sometimes agree, explicitly or tacitly, to work at a certain pace which may be slower than the maximum which they are capable of. On the other hand, cohesive groups have higher job-satisfaction. Pride in the working group has been found in one study of office workers[2] to be associated with high productivity *in the groups*; what it does to the individual nobody seems to have asked.

There is of course no point in going to the other extreme and defining morale merely as one of these four factors; and it begins to be doubtful whether enough is known about the relationship between any two of them, let alone any trio, to make any composite definition safe. The only pair between which most of the evidence points to a positive association

[1] See for example the summary of Kristy's study in Appendix A.
[2] In the Prudential Insurance Company, U.S.A.—see Appendix A.

is cohesiveness and job-satisfaction; but this is getting so far from the ordinary man's idea of morale that to use it in this sense would achieve little but misunderstanding. Like 'the weather' the word 'morale' is best relegated nowadays to the rôle of a label for a field of study, which is concerned with factors of the sort I have mentioned. To use it as a name for any one of them is otiose; to use it to refer to any combination is at best obscure and at worst assumes relationships which may not exist; and, as we saw earlier, to use it as a name for something which is none of these things but in some ways underlies them all—a sort of personnel manager's Holy Ghost—is almost certainly mistaken. In the rest of my chapters I shall use the word as seldom as possible, and then only to mean 'the sort of factors I have discussed in Chapter 4'.

At this point the employer—any employer—is entitled to ask, 'In that case, what should be the aims of a personnel policy? What am I trying to do, with my attention to welfare, labour turnover, absenteeism, my relations with employees and so on?' The answer, out of all the enormous literature on the subject, is that there are only two factors which qualify as ultimate objectives. 'Cohesiveness' is studied only because from the employer's angle it may increase or reduce efficiency[1] and from the employee's angle it may strengthen his hand in his dealings with his employer. 'Pride in the work group' is similarly a means to an end, and not an end in itself. The reduction of absenteeism and labour turnover have some point in themselves, because, whatever obscure condition they are symptoms of, they certainly reduce efficiency simply through loss of trained labour. But the main aim of an employer is bound to be efficiency, both individual and collective.

The other factor that must clearly be considered as an end in itself is the employee's enjoyment of his job. To him—if it is not overshadowed by purely economic thoughts—it is probably paramount. Is there any strong reason why it should not also be the objective of the employer? Nobody has succeeded in demonstrating that to enjoy your work makes you worse at it; and it may even have two or three tangible advantages from the employer's point of view. It will probably make you less likely to take a day off: we shall see that this applies to civil servants too. It may well make you less likely to look for another job, and so waste the time and money that has been spent on teaching you your job (or allowing you to learn it yourself): we shall see that this may be true of clerical officers. The time may even be at hand when competition for recruits to certain occupations—including office work—is so intense that enjoyment of the work may be a deciding factor; for all we know it is already the deciding factor with the literate school-leaver who is thinking of an office job.

All this, however, tends merely to show that attention to job-satis-

[1] 'Productivity' should of course be understood as included in the term 'efficiency' as a special form of it.

faction can be justified—if it is not too costly—on grounds of expediency. We have reached the stage, however, when the best kind of employer is no longer the man who is simply not short-sighted or oppressive in his treatment of his employees, but is what is called 'the good employer'. This notion is used in ways which seem to me to imply that he initiates measures which make his employees' working hours pleasanter even if they cannot be shown to produce any tangible advantage from the point of view of efficiency, and indeed even if he is out-of-pocket as a result. If so, job-satisfaction will no doubt qualify as an end in itself.

In other words, if we are faced with the allegation that some step—such as an increase in the rate of dismissal for inefficiency—will damage morale, we need not become involved in any intricate argument about factors known only to occupational psychologists. All that need be asked are two questions—'How will it affect individual or collective efficiency?' and 'How will it affect the employees' enjoyment of their jobs?'

5

A PRACTICAL STUDY:
THE OFFICE AS A FACTORY

Clearly one question to be answered at an early stage of my enquiry was whether there was any possibility of directly measuring efficiency in office work, and particularly in the kind of office work which is done in the civil service. The question was one which had not, so far as I could discover, been adequately investigated. The Treasury's Organisation and Methods Division, who had the closest interest in such problems, knew of no studies of this subject. The reason was no doubt that in the circumstances of most large offices this is unlikely to be a fruitful field for research. Efficiency in offices is the ratio between the service given and the cost, in men and machines, of giving it; and the only purpose of measuring it can be to compare one kind of organisation, or one part of an organisation, with another. But in most cases the mere existence of more than one organisation, or part of an organisation, means that they are performing different services, or performing the same one in a different way; and the first pre-requisite of a comparison is lacking. This is certainly the obstacle to any such comparison among Whitehall Departments.[1]

There are some situations, however, in which the service given by an office is largely represented by a measurable or countable product, usually in the form of a document. If the nature and number of the operations leading to its production do not vary too much from office to office or from week to week, the document can be treated as a uniform unit of production, and the 'output' of two or more offices can be compared in much the same way as the output of a bicycle factory. This

---

[1] I say 'Whitehall Departments' deliberately, because a few of them have counterparts in Scotland whose functions are so similar that foreigners have difficulty in understanding, and Scots in explaining, the need for their separate existence. Thus the naïve investigator might be tempted to compare the efficiency of the Ministry of Education with that of the Scottish Education Department, for example by calculating the ratio of staffs who are providing roughly the same services for English and Scottish 'customers', and comparing this with the ratio of English and Scottish customers. He would find that the Scottish Education Department had relatively more staff, at any rate of the senior non-professional grades. He would be rash to conclude, however, that the Ministry of Education is more efficient. It is more likely that at the higher levels at any rate
    (i) the smaller the country the larger the proportion of civil servants to population required to provide a similar service;
and/or
    (ii) size apart, devolution makes greater demands on the time of civil servants.

THE OFFICE AS A FACTORY 65

is what one would expect in theory; and this is what investigators of efficiency in offices live in unquenchable hope of finding, like bridge-players hoping that some day they will hold an all-spade hand. Very occasionally one hears stories of both phenomena. The investigators at the New Jersey offices of the Prudential Insurance Company of the U.S.A. seem to have found a situation so nearly of this kind that they were able to distinguish groups of girls with high productivity from groups with low productivity by some process which involved counting insurance claims dealt with; their report (which is dealt with more fully in Appendix A) is not as explicit about the exact basis of comparison as one would like, but it was sufficient to make me wonder whether something of the sort could not be found in the British Civil Service.

5.1. THE NEWCASTLE CENTRAL OFFICE

One likely choice for my purpose was the Records Branch of the Central Office at Newcastle of the Ministry of Pensions and National Insurance. The whole of the Central Office is of great interest because so much of its work is carried out by officers of one grade—the Clerical Officer Grade—working together in large teams of uniform size upon very similar tasks, under higher grades whose part in the work is not to carry it out—except in unusually complicated cases—but to plan and supervise it, and solve the problems of personnel management and organisation which it throws up. It is the largest example of this sort of establishment in Britain, and perhaps in Western Europe. It was therefore very likely that this office would offer an opportunity of comparing the output of similar teams of office workers doing similar tasks, on a scale which would be impossible among the comparatively small clerical sections of Whitehall Ministries, each of them engaged on work which varied widely from desk to desk and from week to week. It was also probable that Newcastle would provide the best possible illustration of the effects upon office workers of a repetitive and impersonal job performed in circumstances which would emphasise to the worker the enormous number of others who were doing exactly the same thing.[1]

My proposals for studying part of the Newcastle Office were received with interest and helpfulness by its Controller and his Establishment Officer; and later I encountered the same welcome attitude among the local representatives of the staff associations whose members were affected by my proposed study—the Society of Civil Servants (whose members

[1] I considered as an alternative choice the Savings Bank Departments of the Post Office. Not only were these smaller, however, and more scattered, but important parts of them had been the subject of an Organisation and Methods survey of which the results were under consideration, and which would have interfered with the attitude of the staff to my investigation.

are the Executive Class) and the Civil Service Clerical Association (whose members at Newcastle are the Clerical Officers, Clerical Assistants and Machine Operators, and whom I shall refer to as the 'C.S.C.A.'). One of the difficulties that I had expected to have to surmount was resistance on the part of official and staff sides to investigations by an outsider that might conceivably upset the people who were the subject of them,[1] and would certainly involve extra work in providing me with information. But this particular snag I never encountered at Newcastle, although it was not the first occasion on which they had been troubled by research workers.

Most of the Newcastle Central Office is spread over one enormous site in the suburb of the city called Benton. Unlike the typical London Department, it has neither a stately Carolean façade nor the requisitioned glory of a modern business building, but is housed in long, low blocks of single-storied brick, very like the war-time hospitals to whose architectural period they belong. It is, I think, its appearance and not its way of life that has led some of its neighbours to refer to it as 'the holiday camp'. Strictly speaking, its style is pre-Butlin: it was built under the restrictions of severe economy just after the war, as a temporary cradle for the Ministry that was about to be born. The blocks are distinguishable only by their numerals—at least to the stranger, who finds his way about at first by using as landmarks the chimneys of the boiler-houses or the hangar-like bulks of the canteens. But the buildings —within the limitations imposed by their cost and function—are well designed, and comfortably spaced, with wide and well-kept lawns and pavemented roads separating them from one another.

Records Branch, in which I was most directly interested, occupies a series of these huge blocks, interconnected by its main corridor—a square tunnel of painted brick—which runs straight down a slight incline until it disappears into obscurity four hundred yards away. Branching off it on either side, like wards in a hospital, are the 'spurs'— the large rooms in which the sections of Clerical Officers work. These are well-spaced, with pleasant strips of grass separating them from each other; and the large windows give plenty of natural light. Artificial illumination, which gave rise to complaints at first, now consists of strip lighting, and is satisfactory. The boiler-houses provide central heating, and the only physical discomfort about which most of the Clerical Officers are agreed is the ventilation, which has to be managed through the swinging steel windows, and is the subject of the usual schism between those who like fresh air and those who dislike draughts and flying papers. Each of the 16 blocks has a cafeteria, where staff can get cups of tea or coffee at lunch-time, and eat their own sandwiches or the cafeteria's buns and biscuits. There are two huge canteens on the site,

[1] An objection which was raised, and quite understandably, in at least one private firm to my proposed Questionnaire: see Chapter 7.

THE OFFICE AS A FACTORY

where you can eat a meal, served by a waitress at a table, for a couple of shillings or so, and have coffee in a roomy lounge. Apart from their size, these are very much the sort of amenities to be found in most large Ministries. But the site has others. There is a post office, and seven first-aid rooms with a State-registered Nurse and assistants. Private enterprise is represented by two banks and two hairdressers. These are rather more than luxuries, because of the distances which most of the staff have to travel from their homes to get to the site. Their trains or buses leave before the shops are open, and get them home too late for shopping at the end of the day. Benton itself has a few shops, where some shopping can be done during the short lunch-break; but the centre of Newcastle is out of reach. These facilities on the site therefore save considerable trouble for the staff and reduce the requests for an 'extended lunch-break', which waste official time.

Transporting nearly seven thousand civil servants to and from Benton at the peak hours of 9 a.m. and 5.30 p.m. would be too great a strain for the Newcastle buses and trains. So the working day begins at 8.15 a.m., and ends at 4.30 p.m., with a 45-minute lunch-break. This makes it possible for special services to be run right on to the site, where fleets of buses can be seen waiting at half-past four to take the staff back to the widely scattered towns and villages from which they are recruited; many of them spend as much of each day in the bus as their London colleagues do in the electric train.

One of the main reasons for choosing Newcastle as the location for the Central Office was the fact that this was an area where the high unemployment of the nineteen-thirties showed signs of persisting into the post-war period, and where new employers of labour were therefore needed. A nucleus of experienced clerical staff (and of course of senior officers) had to be imported when the office was set up, soon after the end of the war; but most of the staff soon consisted of locally recruited temporary clerks. Some of these had worked before in other kinds of offices; but for many this was their first try at clerical work. Some of these newcomers, of course, were young men and girls who had just left school, but others were adults from the shipyards, the shop counter, the factory bench or the mines. Selection tests were used to eliminate those whose abilities were too limited; some who were accepted found the work uncongenial and left. It was inevitable that the first few years should have been unsettled, with fairly high wastage and several reorganisations; but the Ministry managed to confine dismissals to individuals whom poor conduct or ill-health made obviously unsuitable for the work. Later, many of the temporary clerks who had proved themselves satisfactory were established as Clerical Officers ('C.O.s') or Clerical Assistants ('C.A.s'). By the time of my visits the growing pains of the office had long ago ceased, and recruitment and wastage had settled down to balanced levels.

Staff relations, too, had settled down after an early period of wary skirmishing. From the start the C.S.C.A. had recruited members vigorously among the new clerical workers, and later, when punched-card methods were introduced on an increasing scale, among the machine operators. By the time of my visit they had a membership of nearly 80 per cent. of the eligible staff, well above the C.S.C.A.'s national average. They had engaged in many stern fights with the 'official side' over the grading of jobs, the methods of supervision and the physical conditions: I was told, for example, that they had introduced their own photometer into the C.O.'s rooms in a successful effort to convince the Ministry of Works of the inadequacy of the lighting. The local branch of the C.S.C.A. ran a monthly magazine, with the pointed title of *Headway*, entirely for their members on the site. Its contents were of course chiefly matters of official concern to the local branch, such as the appointment of office-bearers, the current pay negotiations, and the chronic dissatisfaction with the prospects of promotion for Clerical Officers. But it also contained comments and jokes about daily life in the various branches which gave me useful indications of some of the other aspects about which the C.O.s had views. These comments showed, for example, that C.O.s found the canteen prices, low though they were, heavy on their pockets. By the time of my visit, however, the local branch were conducting their negotiations with the official side with no more than the usual sharp but good-natured criticism that is exchanged in most Departments. The C.O.s to whom I talked were grateful to their branch of the association for their efforts in the early days, although some of the younger ones knew of them only by hearsay, and consequently felt less deeply on the subject. Many, however, seemed to regard the main function of their branch nowadays as being to seek remedies for the grievances of individuals rather than the betterment of the position of the whole grade.[1] I myself found the office-bearers of the local branch extremely co-operative. They naturally hoped that my investigation would lead to some improvement in the organisation or conditions of the work, so that I had to be careful not to give any inadvertent encouragement to these hopes, and to emphasise that I did not expect to be able to suggest solutions to problems, but would be content if I managed to describe them.

Both the formulated criticisms of the C.S.C.A. and the vaguer dissatisfactions of the C.O.s in general seemed to me to be sympathetically understood by the official side, even when they could not yet see any way of meeting them. One peculiarity of the Benton Office is probably relevant here. The senior staff consisted entirely of officers of the Executive Class, of grades ranging from Executive Officer to Principal

---

[1] I do not of course mean that they were uninterested in the campaign of their National Executive Committee for better pay, etc.; I am referring only to their attitude towards their *local* branch.

Executive Officer. The Administrative Class was not represented in this hierarchy—although the Controller ranks as an Under-Secretary—but the administrators in the London headquarters of the Ministry were of course in close touch with Benton in matters of policy. The organisation thus resembled large parts of the Inland Revenue Department, where great volumes of work involved in carrying out settled policy are organised and supervised by members of the Executive Class, and the few administrators are concerned instead with such matters as possible changes in the statutes, or major innovations in procedure. The importance of this from the point of view of staff relations at Benton is that the great majority of the senior officers there have done clerical work themselves or, as Executive Officers, have been the immediate supervisors of C.O.s, sitting in the same large room and in continuous contact with them throughout the day's work. Many members of the Administrative Class, of course, are promoted Executive Officers, and some are promoted Clerical Officers; these have the benefit of the same first-hand or second-hand acquaintance with the C.O.'s life. But the direct entrants to the Administrative Class have what is at best a third-hand acquaintance with it, and in some cases not even that. It is not easy for them to know which of their decisions are going to be troublesome to junior staff, or to distinguish between complaints that are warnings of long-term problems and those that are merely part of adjustment to some new condition. No doubt differences in economic and social background contribute to this; but in this respect the three desk classes now diverge much less than they did between the wars. The chief cause of the handicap is more probably nothing more than the fact that the Assistant Principal has not spent some of the formative years of his career sitting at a desk in a large room full of men and women of all ages, carrying out a repetitive task amidst the distractions and irritations caused by their idiosyncrasies. Many administrators are only too aware of this gap in their experience, and their awareness sometimes prevents them from handling staff with the confidence and sureness of touch which can smooth over minor awkwardnesses, and which members of the Executive Class soon acquire.[1]

I was therefore inclined to think that the atmosphere of staff relations at Benton, which can be described as healthily bracing, owed something

---

[1] I do not mean, however, to give the impression that staff relations at Benton were any more 'democratic' than in the ordinary Whitehall Department. Indeed, there were one or two small privileges for senior officers—such as the use of special lavatories—that I had not seen in Whitehall. The junior staff to whom I talked did not make any reference to these; and I do not think that delicacy would have discouraged them if they had felt resentment. I came across one mild joke about this privilege in *Headway* (the C.S.C.A. magazine which I have mentioned). Small concessions to status of this kind are very common in industry (though very rare in the civil service), and it may well be that on Tyneside they were simply accepted as natural.

to the fact that the management was composed almost entirely of the Executive Class. In 1948, when the office was still in its difficult early period, Dr. Buzzard, of the Medical Research Council's Unit of Applied Psychology at Cambridge, made a survey of some aspects of the office, which led him to make some recommendations for the keeping of better sickness records, the improvement of methods of selection, further research on such matters as heating, lighting and rest pauses, and the investigation of the running of the hostels in which many of the staff then lived (but which are no longer needed). He found, however, 'an enthusiastic atmosphere among the senior staff and a live appreciation of the problem of morale'. My impression, ten years later, was that the senior officers had not lost interest in this problem, as indeed their helpfulness towards my proposed study showed.

Records Branch

After I had been given a brief explanation of the work of the various branches into which the office is divided, I came to the conclusion that Records Branch was the one which it would be most profitable to study closely. It was by far the largest branch, employing more than half of the 3,374 C.O.s. It was organised into 100 teams of 16 men and women each, and each of these teams,[1] which were known as Ledger Sections, performed exactly the same tasks on one-hundredth of the insured population. No other branch was organised with quite the same uniformity, and in no other branch did the work consist of so few, and so uniform, operations. Nor was any other branch so unpopular with the C.O.s, as the rate of requests for transfer to other branches demonstrated. The most popular branches clearly were the small ones, where, rightly or wrongly, the C.O.s believed that the work would be more interesting and that the chances of being 'noticed' and promoted would be greater.

The function of Records Branch is to act as an enormous memory for all the local offices throughout the country which receive claims for sickness and unemployment and other National Insurance benefits. Before each claim is paid they must verify that the claimant fulfils certain conditions—for example, that he has paid the necessary number of weekly contributions. Every claim therefore means an enquiry which has to be answered by consulting a record sheet for the claimant; and the procedure for handling these enquiries has been streamlined to what seems the practicable limit short of mechanisation.[2] The enquiries arrive

---

[1] With the exception of Statistics Sections, which were Ledger Sections that also performed special tasks in extracting statistics for their cross-section of the population: these sections had additional staff.

[2] Some readers are bound to ask why this process cannot be mechanised. Many of the processes in the Benton office have been; the country's pension books, for ex-

in the form of cards, which are mechanically sorted and despatched to the right Ledger Section (according to the last two figures of the claimant's number) by pneumatic tube. These 'shuttle cards' are taken by a Clerical Assistant to the desk of the right C.O. (according to the third last figure of the number) who has the ledger for this block of the population; he turns up the record sheet of the claimant and enters on the card the record of the claimant's contributions. Each C.O. shares his 'line' of the population with a 'partner', who sits next to him, and they check each other's cards before they are returned to the local office via the pneumatic tube and the despatch room. Every shuttle card—unless there is something very odd about it—must be dealt with on the day of arrival. This process, together with correspondence, occupies most of the morning. Lunch-time is fixed for the whole section by a timetable, so as to spread the load on the canteens and cafeterias. Three-quarters of an hour later the C.O.s must be back at their desks.

Just before or after lunch (according to the volume of shuttle cards and the earliness or lateness of the section's lunch-hour) begins the second main process, known as 'card-posting'. It is not necessary for the ordinary reader to have more than a superficial grasp of the Ledger Sections' work, so I shall content myself with a brief explanation.

Practically everyone who has left school but has not yet begun to draw his pension has an insurance card, on to which stamps are stuck each week to show that his contributions have been paid. Every twelve months this card has to be replaced by a new one, and the old one is returned to Records Branch, where the details on it are 'posted' into the individual's ledger. In order to 'stagger' this work over the year, there are four 'contribution years', each ending in a different quarter, and the insured population's cards are divided up between these four contribution years. The Ledger Sections of Records Branch thus receive about six million cards for posting each quarter. Ideally, these cards would be evenly divided between each of the one hundred sections; but for reasons which are not worth expounding here each section has two consecutive quarters in which large batches have to be posted, and two consecutive quarters in which the batches are smaller. These batches are called the 'heavy and the light staggers'; a heavy stagger should be completed in nine weeks, a light one in seven weeks.

ample, are issued, with individual names and numbers, by a battery of specially modified Hollerith machines. If a way could have been seen of giving the same service to the public by a mechanised Records Branch, it would have been adopted; but there are great difficulties which have still to be overcome. For example, any member of the twenty-four million insured people in the country may give rise to a claim on any week-day in the year, so that any mechanical system would have to allow for some quick means of access at random to any part of its 'memory'. These problems will, of course, be solved eventually, but it seems likely that human beings will have to do the work of Records Branch for some time to come.

F

Originally this work was done by sections consisting of 4 C.O.s and 20 C.A.s each under an Executive Officer (E.O.). It soon became apparent, however, that the work was more complicated than had been foreseen, and was in the main more suited to C.O.s. Although the operations as I have described them sound simple, there are in practice so many different kinds of insured workers, and so many curious vicissitudes which complicate their records, that the indexed manual of guidance which each clerical worker now has on his desk is nearly two inches thick. During the first thirteen weeks in Records Branch each C.O. has to be treated as a trainee, with periods of instruction alternating with practical work; and it may be a year or two before he is able to equal the average speed of his experienced colleagues. The C.S.C.A. argued that most of the work should be regarded as 'C.O. work', and by stages the ratio of 20 C.A.s to 4 C.O.s was altered until it became 2:20. Reductions in the work, streamlining of procedures and experience of the speed at which trained C.O.s could perform it led the official side to reduce the number of C.O.s to 18, and recently to 16. By taking advantage of normal wastage these reductions were achieved without dismissing any staff. They were, however, very much resented by some of the older C.O.s, who felt that they were being gradually forced to work faster and faster. The C.S.C.A. protested vigorously at each reduction, but the official side were able to point to the fact that the sections were showing no signs of failing to get through their allotted work. I shall return later to this important bone of contention.

One effect of the change in organisation, however, was that a situation in which C.A.s had to do some work that was agreed to be C.O.s' work was replaced by one in which some of the C.O.s' work was really too simple for them. The two C.A.s in each section were able to do the work of answering the telephone, distributing shuttle cards and correspondence to the right desks, and partially sorting out the thousands of cards that came in at the beginning of each quarter; but this still left the C.O.s with a lot of rather mechanical sorting and handling to do before they could get down to what they regarded as their real job. By the time of my visit many of the C.O.s, some of whom indirectly owed their rank as C.O. to the upgrading of their work, had begun to resent the amount of C.A. work that was involved in it. This resentment was expressed even by those who had personally benefited from the upgrading, and also by those who got no particular satisfaction out of the work that they accepted as proper to a C.O.; and it was clearly a question of status that was in their minds. In this case the notion may have been consciously connected with the steady pressure of the Clerical Class for higher pay; but, as we shall see from Chapter 8, status is in any case something of which office workers are very much aware.

THE OFFICE AS A FACTORY 73

At the time of my visits, then, each Ledger Section consisted of 16 C.O.s and 2 C.A.s, working under the supervision of an Executive Officer. Usually about 9 of the C.O.s were men, and 7 were women. Both sexes ranged in age from school-leavers to men and women in their early sixties, although girls were beginning to predominate among the young C.O.s, and the proportion of men increased with age. A remarkably high percentage of the C.O.s were married women in their twenties and thirties, whose earnings were helping to save for the purchase of a house or the birth of the first child. The Executive Officers were also of all kinds, from the elderly promoted C.O. to the young man or woman in the late teens or early twenties who had just entered the service.

In the typical room, two such sections sat, one down each side, with their E.O.s at one end, divided by a long line of cabinets holding contribution cards. Each pair of C.O.s sat at a specially designed desk, which had recesses for their ledgers and allowed them to hand their cards to each other for checking. The desks stretched down the long rooms in parallel rows, thirty-four inches apart. Although the C.O.s appreciated the design of this new furniture, the very uniformity of this layout, and the carefully measured spaces allotted to them, seemed to them to emphasise their insignificance as one of sixteen hundred identically treated souls.

The impression given by one of these 'spurs' was very different from the noise and bustle of a section in Whitehall. There, colleagues from other sections come in and out, picking their way through the irregular pattern of desks, to find a file or discuss something with a C.O. at his desk; people talk or shout to one another across the room. At least one, and often two or three telephone conversations are in progress, and sometimes a typewriter is clattering away in a corner. By contrast, the rooms at Benton were quiet, with much less movement of people to and fro. There is only one telephone for each section, and most of the calls are taken by one of the C.A.s. Personal visits from one section to another are seldom necessary. Pneumatic tubes deliver the shuttle cards and take them away again. Sometimes a C.O. walks up the room to consult the E.O. or a colleague; and now and again the E.O. moves round the desks. About twice a week, a loudspeaker system, installed in every room, broadcasts some announcement, such as an advance warning of a new procedure, or more often an announcement of some activity of the Sports and Social Club. But for the most part the C.O. sits undisturbed, taking a new shuttle card from his tray, looking up the information in the ledgers at his desk, and passing it across to his partner to be checked. In Whitehall the E.O. sometimes has to intervene to put a stop to conversations that are wasting time; here many of the C.O.s themselves not only resent the sound of others wasting their time but also find conversations within their range of hearing an irritating distraction. (Men seemed to find this more distracting than women did, and usually referred to 'the chattering of the girls').

Comparing Productivity

These conditions seemed very favourable for the sort of study that I had in mind. There was hardly any variation in the physical environment or the amenities enjoyed by the different sections[1]; on paper at least the size of each section was the same, although their actual strength fluctuated a little as the result of sick leave, annual leave and the proportion of trainees allotted to them. There was no difference in the nature of the tasks which they performed. My first hope was that under these conditions, which were almost as favourable as those of a laboratory, I would be able to obtain figures of output for individuals, and would thus be able to compare men with women, the young with the middle-aged and elderly, and newcomers to the work with those who had been doing it for years. Every day, for example, the total of cards posted by each C.O. was added up; and this information would have been very interesting. Unfortunately this was just what the Ministry could not give me. In the early days of Records Branch the E.O. of each section had been in the habit of counting the output of individuals in order to report the section's daily progress. But for reasons which I shall be discussing later in this chapter the C.S.C.A. made such strong protests against 'individual counts' that the official side, after some understandable resistance, had to make a concession. In future the daily individual counts would be carried out not by the E.O. but by the senior C.O. of each section, who would report the sum of all the 16 C.O.s' totals, but not any individual's total, to the E.O., for transmission at the end of the week to the H.E.O. in charge of that group of sections. The only circumstance in which an E.O. could take an individual count was in a case in which he was considering whether he should make an adverse report on a C.O., and in that exceedingly rare event[2] he would give formal notice of an individual count. This practice had been in force for about ten years, and I was told that any attempt to obtain the

---

[1] The only exceptions were those rooms where, because of a temporary shortage of space, three instead of two sections had had to be housed: to get three sections in it had been necessary to reduce the space between desks from 2 ft. 10 in. to about 2 ft. 8 in., a measure which was resented by many of the C.O.s, who felt that it emphasised the impersonality of the way in which they were regarded by the Ministry.

[2] In view of what I have said about dismissals in Chapter 3.2, I was interested to find that dismissals of clerical staff solely on the grounds of inefficiency were extremely rare in Records Branch, although not completely unheard of. There had, however, been considerable numbers of discharges of staff with poor sickness records, which, as we have seen, is often regarded as a humane way of getting rid of staff who are inefficient in other respects. There was however a feeling among senior officers to whom I spoke that with a staff of this enormous size it was possible to carry a few 'lame ducks' who were honestly doing their best.

THE OFFICE AS A FACTORY 75

result of individual counts would arouse the worst suspicions of my investigation.[1]

I therefore turned to the possibility of comparing the output of the sections, to see whether there were any marked differences. For example, each section's weekly total of cards posted was recorded, and card-posting was the task which seemed to be regarded as the main activity of the sections. It was the task to which they settled down when they had dealt with the day's intake of shuttle cards and the day's correspondence. Here again, however, there were snags.

While efforts were made to equalise, so far as possible, the volume of card-posting work borne by all the sections on a 'heavy stagger' and those on a 'light stagger', the time left to each one for this work varied each day from section to section, because they could not settle down to it until they had completed the two other tasks of dealing with the shuttle-cards and their correspondence. In spite of this, however, it might well have been possible to arrive at a rough but serviceable numerical measure of the 'productivity' of different sections by dividing the number of cards posted in a quarter by the number of man-days worked in each section. Unfortunately there seems to be another, and rather interesting, factor at work which would have made this kind of calculation useless. The sections know that the card-posting must be completed by a certain date, and that if it seemed unlikely to be completed by that date either another section would have to help them or they would have to work overtime; neither of these measures were popular. They therefore took some interest in the weekly totals of cards which they had posted, and in the number which remained. Moreover, they could see the incoming cards piling up in their trays. The effect of this upon their output is demonstrated by Table 5.01, where column (3) shows how the Ledger Sections seem to regulate their rate of card-posting so that it takes more or less the allotted nine weeks to complete the task.[2] Output rises until a peak is reached in the fourth or fifth week,

---

[1] I also discussed with the Ministry's Survey Section whether they had figures that would enable me to make comparisons between individuals. Their job is to time the operations involved in such tasks as card-posting or dealing with shuttle cards, in order to determine the complements necessary for the different kinds of sections. They are allowed to time C.O.s at work, and could therefore provide the sort of figures that I wanted—in theory. Here again, however, the C.S.C.A. have intervened to protect their members, and the Survey Officers are debarred from recording the details such as the name, sex or age of individuals whom they time. In any case, I was doubtful how valuable their timings would have been, in view of several factors. The subjects who were being timed were artificially protected from the ordinary disturbances. More important, people who are being timed—at least over short periods—tend to work faster or slower than their normal speed, according to whether their dominant motive is pride in their performance or fear of a reduction in staff. The Survey staff assume that the speeds shown by their calculations are too fast by 15 per cent., and this allowance is deducted in determining complements.

[2] In the first of the two quarters chosen, a few sections took ten weeks.

with a rate at which the cards remaining would be finished a week or more before the end of the period. It then falls sharply, until the cycle is completed just on time, or a little after. In other words, the sections' output seemed to be regulated by one overriding consideration—the speed necessary to finish on time.

TABLE 5.01

Cards Received and Posted by Records Branch in Two Quarters of 1958-59

Week Ending Friday	Cards Received		Cards Posted		Balance on hand
	Weekly Total	Cumulative Total	Weekly Total	Cumulative Total	
	(1)	(2)	(3)	(4)	(5)
Sept. 5	642,045	642,045			
12	1,594,004	2,236,049			
19	1,816,935	4,052,984			
26	950,167	5,003,151			
Oct. 3	313,627	5,316,778	574,942	574,942	4,741,836
10	261,521	5,578,299	750,896	1,325,838	4,252,461
17	98,180	5,676,479	734,941	2,060,779	3,615,700
24	90,353	5,766,832	639,519	2,700,298	3,066,534
31	61,072	5,827,904	755,418	3,455,716	2,372,188
Nov. 7	29,948	5,857,852	694,362	4,150,078	1,707,774
14	20,601	5,878,453	578,117	4,728,195	1,150,258
21	15,730	5,894,183	381,141	5,109,336	784,847
28	15,209	5,909,392	190,108	5,299,444	609,948
Dec. 5	—	5,909,392	(609,948[1])	5,909,392	—
Dec. 5	644,956	644,956			
12	1,767,729	2,412,685			
19	1,582,798	3,995,483			
26	53,049	4,048,532			
Jan. 2	135,979	4,184,511			
9	1,333,522	5,518,033	503,231	503,231	5,014,802
16	169,426	5,687,459	692,732	1,195,963	4,491,496
23	87,397	5,774,856	677,543	1,873,506	3,901,350
30	54,266	5,829,122	827,408	2,700,914	3,128,208
Feb. 6	35,271	5,864,393	802,832	3,503,746	2,360,647
13	23,491	5,887,884	679,065	4,182,811	1,705,073
20	17,611	5,905,495	512,412	4,695,223	1,210,272
27	14,201	5,919,696	391,456	5,086,679	833,017
Mar. 6	—	5,919,696	(833,017[1])	5,919,696	

[1] These figures for the final weeks of each cycle must be ignored, as they are calculated so as to balance the totals.

This phenomenon is not confined to Newcastle or to the civil service. I have noticed it in universities, where no matter how much time a student is given to write an essay, or a senior member to compose a lecture, a review or a book, the work will tend to be completed slightly —or more than slightly—late. There are many people who seem to be able to work in top gear only when they are in arrears. Stansfield, who studied typing pools,[1] observed that in some pools the typists always had a day or two's arrears, which usually stayed at this level, and neither increased nor decreased; in other words, they were working at exactly the rate at which new work was coming in, and a short burst of extra speed would have brought them up to date; but their pace seemed to be governed by the amount of work which they saw in their in-trays.

This is a digression, however; the point of the phenomenon in this case was that I could not use the numbers of cards posted as a quantitative comparison of the output of different sections.

The impossibility of using figures of cards posted did not, of course, mean that it was impossible to say whether one section was more 'productive' than another. In conversation with the Senior Executive Officers ('S.E.O.s') in charge of about 30 Ledger Sections each I gathered that they were fairly confident of their ability to identify the 'good' and 'bad' sections; and they thought that the Higher Executive Officers ('H.E.O.s') under them, each of whom has charge of six sections, could separate the sheep from the goats among their smaller flocks. Their judgments would, it was true, be open to the objection that, for the very reasons I have been discussing, they could not be based on a sound quantitative measure of output. They might also be biased by some of the very factors I wanted to study, such as the supervisory techniques of the E.O.'s: for example, an officer might unwittingly be influenced to classify one section as a 'good' one because he himself approved of the way in which it was run, without having any real evidence that this way of running it did in fact make it any better. But bias of this kind could be greatly reduced by two expedients. Both the H.E.O.s and the S.E.O.s could be asked to make independent assessment of the sections under them, and the extent to which these assessments agreed could then be examined. Secondly, these assessments could be compared with the annual reports on the E.O.s, which were filled in by the S.E.O. (and countersigned by the C.E.O.), to see whether there was a suspiciously high correspondence between their rating of the E.O. and their assessment of his section.

The Ministry agreed quite readily to this suggestion; and in March 1959 the S.E.O.s and H.E.O.s received a note explaining what they were supposed to do. In effect, they were asked to place each of the sections under them into one of five categories—

[1] See Appendix A.

A   Well above average
B   Somewhat above average
C   Average   } in productivity and efficiency.
D   Somewhat below average
E   Well below average

They were asked

(i) not to discuss their assessment with anyone else (but were allowed to consult any of their own written records);
(ii) to make it on the basis of their sections' work in *recent* months;
(iii) to make allowances for sections which had suffered abnormal handicaps from sick leave, but not for any other factor;

and they were assured that their assessment would not reflect on the merits of the E.O. or any other individual in any section, but would be used solely for the purpose of this piece of research.

The results were rather interesting in themselves, and are summarised below. The most obvious feature of them is the refusal of both S.E.O.s and H. E. O.s to classify any section as 'E'. This is probably due to the disinclination of people who answer most kinds of questionnaires of this form to make any use of the most critical of the possible choices (see, for example, Chapter 7 on the preparation of my questionnaire for office workers). The same disinclination is found in civil servants' annual reports on their subordinates, and the reason is not simply that the subordinate has to be informed if he is given an 'E' rating, for it happens in the U.S.A. as well, where the subordinate is informed of whatever rating he is given.[1] Only one section was classified 'A' by any H.E.O., but five were put in this category by the S.E.O.s, who showed a general tendency to rate their sections more highly than did the H.E.O.s ; this may be an instance of greater familiarity breeding a slightly lower opinion.

TABLE 5.02

Ratings of the performance of Ledger Sections by Senior and Higher Executive Officers

Ratings	A	B	C	D	E	Total
by S.E.O.s	5	21	53	21	—	100
by H.E.O.s	1	17	63	19	—	100
Agreements	1	9	42	12	—	64[2]

[1] See P. M. Blau, whose work is summarised in Appendix A.

[2] Since both S.E.O.s and H.E.O.s had to distribute their sections among a limited number of categories—in theory five, in practice four—and since their preferences for certain categories are known, it is possible to calculate the percentage of agreements which could be expected even if they were merely assigning the sections at random in these proportions: it would be 41 per cent. The percentage of actual agreements is very much greater—64 per cent.

I then proceeded to study more closely the 23 sections[1] which both the S.E.O. and the H.E.O. had placed above or below the average. The Establishment and Organisation Division (which I shall call E.O.D., as everyone at Benton does) compared the ratings given to these sections with the ratings given to their E.O.s in charge of them by the same S.E.O.s. These ratings were also in the form of an A, B, C, D or E classification, although as I have said the E classification is hardly ever used in practice. For obvious reasons I cannot give the results of the comparison in detail, but it satisfied me that there was less correspondence between the rating awarded to any given section and the rating awarded to its E.O. than was to be expected if the S.E.O. had been influenced by his opinion of the E.O. in making his rating of the section. The extent of the agreement between the H.E.O.s' and the S.E.O.s' ratings of the sections, and the extent of the disagreements between these and the personal ratings of the E.O.s in charge of the sections thus enabled me to be fairly confident that in the case at least of the 23 'A', 'B' and 'D' sections I was dealing with a genuine difference in performance and not with mere idiosyncrasies in the judgment of the H.E.O.s and S.E.O.s.

There was only one unfortunate thing about my batch of 23 ABD sections (as I shall call these that were classified as above or below the average). The 11 AB sections were found to include four that had more than the usual complement of 16 C.O.s. One of these was a 'statistics section', which had to do some special work in addition to the normal work of a Ledger Section; these Statistics Sections (of which there are two) provide certain statistics from a 2 per cent. sample of the insured population and have several extra C.O.s over and above the normal complement of 16. The other three sections had only one or two more than the normal complement, simply because the Branch as a whole had one or two C.O.s over and above its strict complement. I thought it safest, however, to confine my comparisons to the 7 AB sections and the 12 D sections which had normal complements, in case the mere difference in complements had been responsible for any difference in performance.

5.2. THE CLERICAL OFFICERS

There were a number of possibilities that could be investigated by a simple statistical study of information on paper. For example, were young C.O.s better at this work than older ones, or vice versa? Were women better than men, as they are sometimes said to be when the work is detailed and repetitive? Did performance deteriorate after they

[1] That is, the 22 about whose classification there was complete agreement, plus one which was classified as above average by both S.E.O. and H.E.O., but was placed in category 'A' by the S.E.O. and in category 'B' by the H.E.O. (remember that S.E.O.s tended to be more generous with their 'A's).

had been engaged on this sort of work for a long time? The Ministry therefore provided me with the sex and age of each C.O. in these sections, with the method by which they had entered the grade of C.O. (for example, by promotion or open competition) the number of months for which they had been in Records Branch (which I shall call 'branch-months') and the months for which they had been in their present section (which I shall call 'section-months').

I would also have liked to have information about the amount of sick leave, both certified and uncertified, which had been taken by the members of the ABD sections over the last six or twelve months, but unfortunately the Ministry's records were not kept in a form that made this possible. It seemed a pity that the Ministry, who provide excellent analyses of morbidity for the population as a whole by means of a punched-card sample of claims for sickness benefit, should not do this for their own staff, but it was a deficiency that had to be accepted.[1] I therefore had to be content to compare the AB sections with the D sections in respect of their sex composition, the C.O.s' method of entry, and the three factors in which time was involved—age, time spent on the same kind of work, and time spent in the same working group. The result was to make it highly probable that the most important of all these factors was the last.

Sex

Of the 304 C.O.s in the 19 ABD sections, 171 were men and 133 were women. Therefore it was to be expected that the typical composition of a section would be 9 men and 7 women. This was by far the commonest pattern; it occurred in 7 of the 19 sections:

TABLE 5.03

Sex Pattern		Frequency	
Men	Women	A or B	D Sections
11	5	–	2
10	6	2	2
9	7	2	5
8	8	2	2
7	9	1	1

The table shows a slight tendency for the AB sections to have more women (a mean number of 7·3 per section) than the D ones (with a mean of 6·8); but this is not nearly large enough to be significant. This does not, of course, disprove the hypothesis that women are better than men

---

[1] In my chapter on sick leave I shall be discussing the doubtful value of various kinds of sick-leave statistics as indirect indices of attitudes to work.

THE OFFICE AS A FACTORY 81

at this sort of work; all it means is that the variations in the sex pattern of these 19 sections are not enough to give much support to such a hypothesis. In order to test it by this method it would probably be necessary to make up a number of sections entirely of men and others entirely of women; an experiment which is hardly worth considering, because it would inevitably give rise to feelings among the C.O.s that would interfere with their performance and render any comparison fallacious.

Method of Entry

Here again no significant differences could be found between the AB and the D sections. At different periods in the last twelve years the Ministry, like most Departments, had recruited C.O.s in many different ways. They had established Temporary Clerks; promoted Clerical Assistants and others; admitted successful candidates in the Reconstruction Competitions that followed the end of the 1939-45 war, in the Open Competitions and in the Limited Competitions for candidates from lower grades; and—in the last two years—they had admitted boys and girls who had secured a certain number of passes in the General Certificate of Education (Ordinary Level) and had been successful in an interview. Not only were these differences in the method of entry into the grade of C.O. represented among both the AB and the D sections in proportions that did not differ greatly, but they were also complicated by the fact that at different dates different methods had been the most common, so that, for example, a C.O. who had entered through the Reconstruction examination was likely to have been in Records Branch much longer than one who had entered as a GCE (O) candidate. As with the two sexes, therefore, there may be differences in the performance of C.O.s from different methods of entry, but the composition of the ABD sections was not such as to confirm this.

Time Factors

There remained three more factors about which I had information—the clerical officers' ages, the length of time for which they had been doing this work (measured in 'branch-months') and the length of time for which they had been doing it in that particular section (measured in 'section-months'). There was obviously bound to be a certain amount of interdependence between these three 'time factors'; the younger a clerical officer was, the less likely he was to have spent a long time in the branch, and the less time he had spent in the branch the less time he was likely to have spent in any given section. Table 5.04 shows how these factors differed in the AB and in the D sections, and Figure 5.05 demonstrates visually how the individual sections were distributed with regard to them (the numbers used to distinguish the various sections have been disguised by others, chosen at random).

TABLE 5.04

Comparison of Ages, Branch-months and Section-months of the Clerical Officers

Section's Rating	Mean Ages in Years			Mean Branch-months			Mean Section-months		
	Men	Women	Both	Men	Women	Both	Men	Women	Both
AB	41·2	35·5	38·6	79·6	70·4	75·4	66·4	58·3	62·7
D	41·5	34·1	38·3	82·6	59·7	72·8	57·9	48·9	54·0
Difference (AB−D)	−0·3	+1·4	+0·3	−3·0	+10·7[1]	+2·6	+8·5	+9·4	+8·7[2]

What do the Table 5.04 and the Figure 5.05 show in practical terms? In the first place, it is commonly believed in the Ministry that age has an effect upon output in this work. This is usually expressed by saying 'the best C.O.s are in their thirties and forties; before that they tend to be fast but slapdash; and in their fifties they begin to slow down a bit'. Consider this belief in the light of the facts. The mean ages of the sections range from just over thirty-four to just under forty-four—quite a wide range. Both AB and D sections are distributed over this range, with only one difference: those with the highest and with the lowest mean age belong to the D group, and the AB group are distributed over a narrower range, from just under thirty-seven to just over forty-one. But most of the D sections are also within this range. In other words, this is *consistent* with a belief in the inferiority of young and elderly C.O.s, but is *not strong support* for it. Table 5.04 shows how little difference there is between the mean ages of the AB sections C.O.s and the mean ages of the others. To get more conclusive evidence on this point we should have to resort to one of two methods, both of them objectionable. One would be to obtain the result of the counts of the day's output of individual C.O.s which are made by senior C.O.s; as I have explained, the C.S.C.A. would have the strongest objection to this. The other method would be to make up sections consisting wholly of men and women of different age-groups; but it would be a long time before these sections settled down and resumed their normal speed of working after the upsetting effect of this reallocation. For the Ministry, the main consideration must be whether such an experiment, if it succeeded in establishing a relationship between age and efficiency, could be followed by any positive action to make use of it. I found it difficult to see how it could be, and I decided that there was little justification for trying to persuade them to try either of these methods.

A more practical question is what effect the time spent by the C.O.s

[1] Although *apparently* the largest, this difference is significant only at about the ·15 level.

[2] CR=1·89, which is significant practically at the ·05 level.

THE OFFICE AS A FACTORY 83

FIGURE 5.05 *Mean Branch-months and Section-months of the ABD Sections*

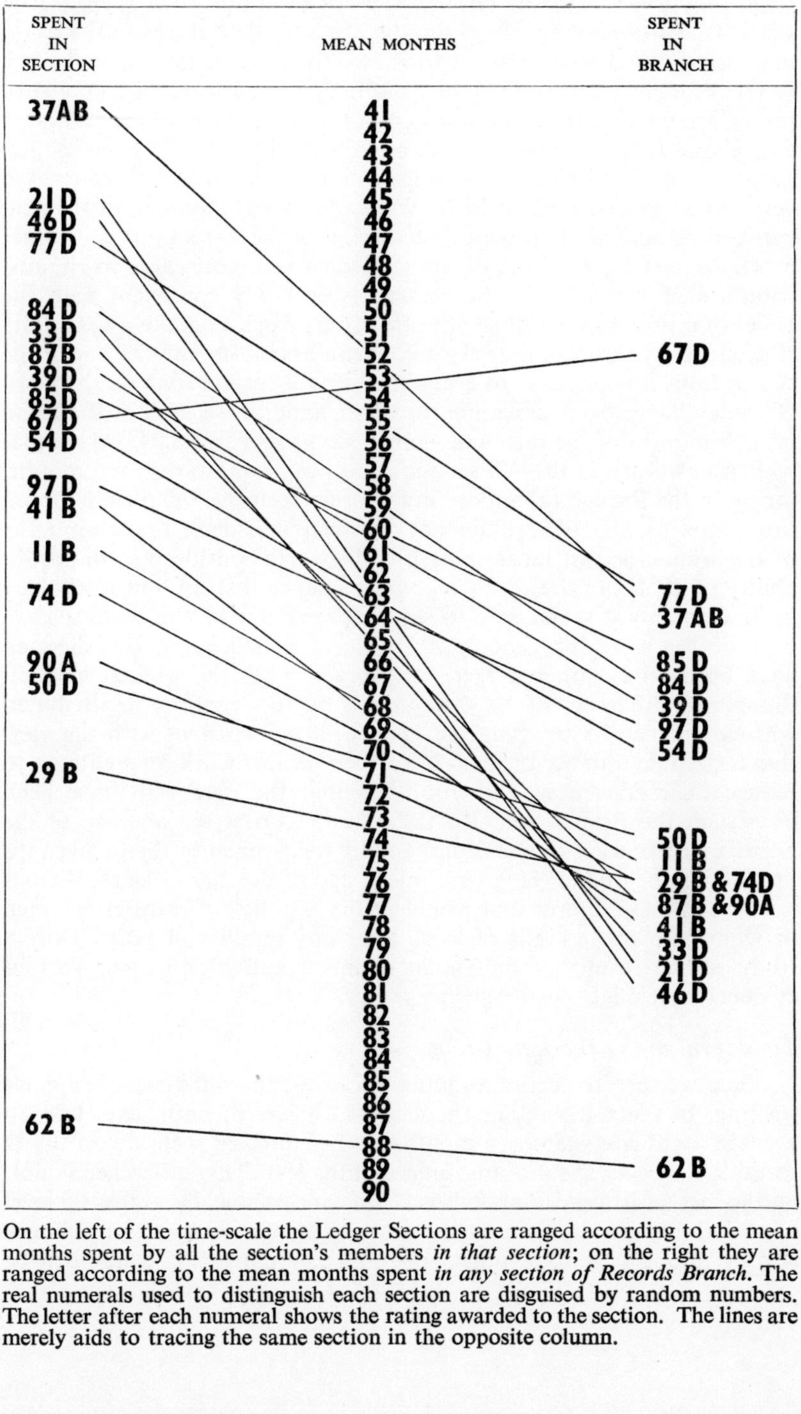

SPENT IN SECTION	MEAN MONTHS	SPENT IN BRANCH
37AB	41 42 43 44	
21D 46D 77D	45 46 47 48 49	
84D 33D 87B 39D 85D 67D 54D	50 51 52 53 54 55 56	67D
97D 41B	57 58 59 60	
11B	61 62	
74D	63 64 65	77D 37AB
90A 50D	66 67 68 69 70	85D 84D 39D 97D 54D
29B	71 72 73 74 75 76 77 78 79 80 81 82 83 84 85 86	50D 11B 29B & 74D 87B & 90A 41B 33D 21D 46D
62B	87 88 89 90	62B

On the left of the time-scale the Ledger Sections are ranged according to the mean months spent by all the section's members *in that section*; on the right they are ranged according to the mean months spent *in any section of Records Branch*. The real numerals used to distinguish each section are disguised by random numbers. The letter after each numeral shows the rating awarded to the section. The lines are merely aids to tracing the same section in the opposite column.

on this work had upon the efficiency of the sections. Some of them had spent only a month or two in the Branch; but others had spent eleven years. It was commonly alleged in the Ministry that although the training period lasted six months it took two to three years of actual work in the Branch before a C.O. became fully versed in all the details of procedure which had to be followed in the more unusual cases. Figure 5.05 shows that the mean branch-months of the C.O.s in each section ranged from 52 to 89. With two exceptions, the AB sections clustered very closely round a mean of 76, while the D sections were distributed between 52 and 82. This wide distribution of the D sections is a rather more marked form of the difference which was noticeable in the distribution of mean ages. The pattern is certainly consistent with the belief that it takes a number of years at this work to make a C.O. fully efficient; but in view of the very high mean branch-months of one of the AB sections it is not easy to argue that after a certain time on the work efficiency begins to decline. On the other hand, if we look at the mean branch-months of the men and women C.O.s in Table 5.04, we see that while the women in the AB sections had been, on average, ten months longer in the Branch than those in the other sections, the men had been three months *less*! The difference between the mean branch-months of the women is just large enough to be worth considering; the probability of its being the result of purely chance distribution is about 1 in 7. Certainly it seems safe to say that very few of the women have been on the work long enough to *reduce* their efficiency. But the men have been on it rather longer, on average, than the women, and although the difference of −3·0 months is far too small to be attributed with confidence to anything but chance, it is *consistent* with the view that a sizeable number of them have been on this work long enough to reduce their efficiency. The trouble is that the men who have been longest in the Branch are also the oldest, so that the absence of the positive difference which is found among the women of the two groups may simply be due to the greater mean age of the men. Clearly there is nothing in these figures that would justify a policy of transferring men or women to other kinds of work after any number of years. Only a study of the results of individual counts could produce the sort of evidence that might justify such a policy.

Time spent in the Working Group

When we turn to section-months, however, the differences are more striking. In the AB sections the clerical officers of both sexes had on average spent five years two months in their present sections; in the D sections they had spent about nine months less. This difference is not, on the face of it, very large, but is significant practically at the ·05 level of probability; in other words, the probability of its occurring by chance is only about 1 in 20. Notice, too, that in Figure 5·05 a line can be drawn at the mean section-months of all 304 C.O.s (whether in AB or in D sections) and will then separate the AB and the D sections, with the exception of two AB sections which overlap the D sections, and two D sections which overlap the AB sections. It is also reassuring that very much the same difference is found among both men and women if they are considered separately. Where age and branch-months are concerned, there is a tendency for the men in the AB and in the D sections to differ in the opposite direction from the women. This may be the operation of pure chance, or it may be that with men the effect of a factor such as age or time spent on the same kind of work, though it exists, is so much less than with women that the method of comparison by sections reveals it only among the women. It is worth pointing out that even where section-months are concerned the difference is slightly greater among the women than among the men. Here we do seem to have a firm basis for conclusions of practical importance. With the exceptions I have mentioned, the D sections are those whose members have spent less than six years together, while the members of the AB ones tend to have spent more than this time together. In some way the time spent in working together seems to have increased the collective output and efficiency of these groups.

The Interviews

In my talks, therefore, with the E.O.s and C.O.s I paid particular attention to any information that seemed to be relevant to the question why the time which the C.O.s had spent in a particular section should be important to its productivity. These talks were interviews of half an hour to which each E.O. or C.O. was invited separately. The talks with the E.O.s were preceded by a meeting at which the Establishment Officer, office-bearers of the staff side and I were present, and to which all the E.O.s from the 19 ABD sections were invited. We explained the rough purpose of my investigation, emphasised that it was not being carried out on behalf of the Ministry, that the anonymity of anything said would be carefully respected and that it could have no effect upon the future of any individual. After one or two questions had been asked and answered, I proceeded with the interviews, and found the E.O.s very ready to talk frankly about the features of their job which they liked or disliked. I had argued that we should make no secret of the fact that the sections had been selected as being above or below average, and this did not arouse as much anxiety or resentment as I had thought it might. All the E.O.s of the AB sections seemed to know that their sections were regarded as good, and most of those in charge of D sections seemed to suspect that their sections were not. Only two of the latter seemed to be anxious about the possibility that this reflected on their own merits, and only one of these two was seriously upset; even this E.O. seemed to become more reassured during the interview, and our talk was no less profitable than the others. In my 58 interviews with the E.O.s and C.O.s I tried to make sure that the same topics were covered each time, though not necessarily in the same order. So far as possible I tried to let each topic come up naturally in the course of conversation; but to make sure that I did not forget the important ones I used a stereotyped form as an *aide-mémoire*. I also tried to avoid questions of a form which indicated the sort of answer I expected, and in any case to note down as far as possible the key phrases which the E.O. or C.O. actually used in his remarks.

The talks with the C.O.s, which took place about six weeks after those with the E.O.s, were arranged by issuing a public circular in the Branch, explaining my project very roughly and giving the same assurances as we had given orally to the E.O.s. During my previous visit I had explained to the C.S.C.A. that I would like to talk to at least one male and one female C.O. from each of these sections, and they had urged that this method of issuing a circular was most likely to reassure people. The C.S.C.A. representatives, who were extremely interested, raised no objection; and I was able to say in the circular that my interviews had the full support of the staff side. The C.O.s whom I selected each received an invitation to be interviewed at a set time; but it was also made clear that they could decline by simply returning a slip of paper attached to the invitation. In the event, 6 out of the 19 women and 2 out of the 19 men did decline. Where this happened I first chose another name from the list for that section, and then, if I had another refusal, asked for a volunteer; in both cases in which I had to do this a volunteer was forthcoming. It was interesting to note that four refusals came from a D section, but that the other four came from the section which both the S.E.O. and the H.E.O. had agreed to rate as 'A'. I was of course unable to make direct contact with those who had declined, but I asked those who did come from the same section whether they had any idea of the reason for the refusals. Some suggested that it was simply dislike of being interviewed and questioned, and said that they knew C.O.s who dreaded the interview boards for possible promotion (although it was the hope of practically every C.O. to be asked to appear before such a board). Others thought that there were certain questions which the declining C.O.s were afraid of being asked, although they could not—or would not—say exactly what they might be; and since the eight refusals came from only two sections it seems very likely that this was the reason. As for the nature of the questions which they were afraid of being asked, I can only make a guess, based on what I noticed about those who did come for interview.

For the most part they talked fairly freely, although it would be ridiculous to assume that they had no reservations. But at certain points their replies seemed to become more stereotyped than usual, and it seemed to me that these were points at which they felt they were in danger of criticising, or appearing to criticise, the others in their section. This feeling extended even to their remarks about their E.O., who worked in the same room with them; but did not seem to operate when they were talking about their H.E.O. It was at its most acute, however, when they were talking about the person with whom they shared a desk.

The relationship between the pairs of C.O.s who shared a desk, and therefore a 'line' of ledgers (i.e. a block of the population distinguished by the antepenultimate numeral in their insurance numbers), involved close and continuous contact throughout the working day, every day of the week, every week of the year, sometimes for several years. The pair checked each other's shuttle cards, helped each other when one fell behind with his or her card-posting, and dealt with the other's correspondence and cards when they were away. Any difference in attitude to the work, or in manner of working, could quickly give rise to intense irritation on one or both sides. A young girl who liked to converse as she worked might get on very well with another of the same mind, but would soon antagonise a middle-aged man who liked peace in which to concentrate. Sometimes one C.O. liked to work at a steady pace throughout the day, but the other liked to get through the work in fast spurts, and leave a little time for conversation, newspaper reading or other extra-curricular activities. These incompatibilities between partners were, of course, not altogether rational; often it seemed more probable that a difference in attitude towards conversation was the excuse that covered irritations and antipathies for which the C.O.s could not really account. Situations of this kind were most frequent and acute where one or both partners were women in middle or later life. Young women in their teens and twenties got on well with each other and with the rest of the section; and some of the older women had the same happy faculty. But it was noticeable that when the story of one of these incompatibilities was elicited, at least one, and sometimes both, of the parties turned out to be a woman past her middle thirties.

When this situation had arisen, one of the partners eventually asked the E.O. to be 'moved up the room' (this was the euphemism for changing partners). The inevitability of these incompatibilities, and the need for breaking up such a situation in the interests of the work, had long been recognised in the Branch, and the E.O.—if he was sensible—would do his best to arrange some new combination. But most E.O.s wisely made a practice of asking one of the other C.O.s whether they were willing to work with the partner whom he proposed to put with them; and if one of the incompatible pair had a reputation for being difficult to work with he might not find the new combinations easy to arrange. If he were fortunate he would find a C.O., probably a placid man in middle age, who was able to get on with—or to ignore—most kinds of human imperfection; and the problem would be solved for the time being. If he were unlucky he might have on his hands a C.O. with whom he tried to combine a series of his other C.O.s, to be faced each time with a request for a move up the room; and at last he would have to ask his H.E.O. whether the difficult C.O. could be moved to another section. Since this usually achieved no more than the shifting of the problem to another room, the H.E.O. was not always willing to do this. The C.O.s themselves disliked being moved to another section in the Branch, although many of them would have welcomed a transfer to completely different work. But often this proved the only solution, unsatisfactory though it might be.

I noticed, however, that while the E.O.s were fairly ready to discuss this problem of management with me, the C.O.s themselves were not anxious to mention it. When I led them on to the subject of their colleagues in the section, their first reply was, 'Oh, they're all right: yes, quite nice.' Later, when I showed that I knew how difficult it could sometimes be to work with someone in this way, they would tell me of their own experience with an incompatible partner. Most often this would be a partner whom they had had in the past; their present partner was usually 'all right: yes, quite nice to work with'. Probably, of course, this was so; since the C.O.s I had invited to talk to me were those whose records showed that they had seen a good deal of service in one, or if possible more, sections in the Branch, the chances were that they had by now found a partner with whom they could work. But my impression was that even if they had not they would have been reluctant to criticise their present partner. The same reluctance was evident in talking about the other C.O.s in their section; these were usually 'all right: quite nice to work with', and it was not until they had talked their way through this phase that they would hint that there were one or two whose attitude to the work they disapproved of. (I shall explain later what they did disapprove of.) Even when they were talking about the E.O. they were anxious to make it clear that they had no fault to find with him or her. I found it best to ask them what qualities they thought a really good E.O. should possess. On this subject they were very ready to discourse, and sooner or later it would become clear how close to or how far from their ideal their own E.O. was. The E.O.s, too, showed some of the same hesitation in discussing any personal shortcomings of their C.O.s, although I do not think that either they or the C.O.s can have been restrained by any fear that what they said would be repeated in detail: there were other subjects on which they spoke with much less restraint.

This feeling in those whom I interviewed suggested very strongly that the eight C.O.s from the two sections who had declined to be interviewed were motivated by nothing more mysterious than the same feeling in a stronger form, and were simply anxious to avoid discussing their sections with an outsider. This seemed to be consistent not only with the attitude of those who did consent to be interviewed but also with one other fact. The two sections from which they came had both a

THE OFFICE AS A FACTORY

high average of section-months among their members: in other words, most of them had been together a long time. Their averages were not the highest, but were both well over the mean for all the ABD sections.

Another question that interested me was this: if the length of time for which the members of the section have been together is important to their productivity, what sort of relationship does develop between the C.O.s with time? It seems to include a dislike of discussing their colleagues with an outsider. Did it also include personal friendships with them? There was no doubt at all about the answer to this. So far as men were concerned, their personal friends, with whom they spent any leisure outside working hours which their family ties allowed them, were not drawn from their section, and these friendships were not formed as a result of contacts at work in the office. With the women, the answer was not quite so simple. Young women in their teens and twenties formed friendships with each other in the section which extended to activities outside office hours. But these were not usually friendships with their partners at the desk so much as the formation of a companionable group among the three or four young women in the section. Often these groups persisted after the women had married, as so many did without giving up their work in the section. Sometimes, but not by any means always, they included the older women in the section, who did not seem to make friendships of this kind on their own. Their activities seemed to take the form of organised outings or of sociable evenings spent by invitation at the house of one or other of the group. These groups, where they existed, were very much valued by the women, particularly the older ones. Finally, quite a number of marriages took place between young men and women in the same section; but almost any kind of situation serves as an opportunity for this sort of relationship.

There was thus no general tendency to form close friendships with the people with whom they worked, even with their partners at the same desk. Indeed, these partners were often of different ages and sexes; a middle-aged woman might find a man or girl in their early twenties a congenial partner. The older C.O.s, of course, enjoyed being given a trainee as a partner; it slowed them up, but it gave the work more interest, and they enjoyed, I think, the feeling that they had a skill which they could teach to someone. Nor was this feeling unjustified, for the variety of instructions, many times amended, which they had to remember (if they were to avoid the time-consuming labour of looking them up) was impressive; and it was many months—or even a year or two—before they could boast that they could work for a whole afternoon without opening the manual.

That their feeling was one of attachment to the group rather than to a single partner was demonstrated by the fact that they did not mind being moved up the room nearly so much as they minded being moved from one section to another. A move of this kind was the last resort; as one woman said, when telling me the story of how she had failed to get on with a colleague, 'I felt so bad I actually asked to be moved to another section.' The E.O.s and H.E.O.s were well aware of this dislike of changing sections, and tried to avoid it except when there was no other solution.

Cohesiveness?

All this may be an example of what occupational psychologists call 'cohesiveness', which has been defined as 'the force acting on the members to remain in the group'. I do not like to assert too confidently that it is, because Argyle with his usual directness and simplicity says that this property of the group is just 'the extent to which the members . . . like one another',[1] and that the factor contributing most to it is 'mutual compatibility of the group members. This may occur by chance, by natural mobility, or by deliberate agreement. If people are allowed to be with those they like, or to choose which group they join, the groups will become more cohesive.'[2] None of these factors is present to any great extent in the Ledger Sections, for the C.O.s have no opportunity to choose the section whose members they like best (it is hard to see how they could, unless they happened to have a friend in a section). The most we can say is that as time goes on the process of separating the more incompatible of the pairs will have led to a situation in which relatively few C.O.s are working with people whom they dislike. This in itself is hardly enough to explain the difference in performance between the AB and the D sections. Nor can I find any indication that occupational psychologists have investigated the effect of pure lapse of time upon 'cohesiveness', far less tried to suggest what the causal connection between the two might be.

It seems, for example, that cohesive groups enjoy their work more: and I learned with interest that the section with the highest average of section-months had had no requests from its members for a transfer out of the Branch (i.e. to work of a completely different kind) for several years, although such requests, as we have seen, were extremely frequent. Cohesive groups may also have more than average output; and if sheer weight of section-months can increase cohesiveness this would be consistent with the situation in Records Branch. But apparently cohesiveness may also produce lower than average output; the suggestion is that in such cases the members of the group come to some sort of agreement, which may be explicit or unspoken, to the effect that a certain rate of working is all that it is fair to expect of them, and that anyone who works faster is letting the others down. It is, of course, extremely difficult to be sure that this is really what is happening in any given case; workers who have an agreement of this sort may very well not voice it

[1] *The Scientific Study of Social Behaviour*, p. 124.   [2] *Ibid.*

amongst themselves, and are most unlikely to expound it to a visiting research worker.

Nevertheless, I had to consider the possibility that cohesiveness was operating in both ways among the Ledger Sections. If it were, this would explain, for example, why one section was below average although most of its members had been with it for as long as most of the members of the AB sections. Part of my talks with the C.O.s was therefore directed to finding out whether there was any widespread notion of a certain rate of working as a fair one. I therefore asked each C.O. how many cards he or she posted in an afternoon. They all began by explaining to me that this would depend very much on the number of difficult cards that were included in the afternoon's work (cards for 'juveniles', for example, gave them more trouble) and upon whether they had to stop posting in order to deal with an afternoon batch of shuttle cards. But almost all after a little thought gave either the figure of 150 or a range of which 150 was the upper end—for example, '130 to 150'. On the other hand, many added, 'But I know people who can post much more —300, for example.' Most of them agree that if they were racing to catch up with their schedule they could post more—say 200; but none of them felt that they could keep this up, and none of them claimed that they themselves could achieve 300. I must make the point here, however, that as I had invited C.O.s who had been some time in the Branch they included very few young ones, and it was the young ones who were said to be capable of these feats. I must also emphasise that they mentioned these feats with admiration rather than disapproval (although one or two wondered whether the extremely fast C.O.s were as careful to avoid mistakes): and that I did not notice any difference between the estimates of the C.O.s from the AB and the D sections.

I did learn, however, from my conversations with the senior officers in Records Branch that at one time in the past, after the survey officers had timed the card-posting operation, it had been said by the official side that C.O.s should be able to post 50 an hour; and one or two of the C.O.s did use this hourly figure. The 'afternoon' is roughly a three-hour period, and it is very possible that the figure of 150 was so frequently quoted merely because it was literally a quotation—from the survey officers. In other words, my impression was that the C.O.s with whom I talked were not consciously or deliberately limiting their output, but that there was a widespread notion that a speed of 50 cards in an hour was one that could be kept up without strain by the average man or woman, and that it was the exceptional C.O., young and fit or a little slapdash, who could keep up a higher rate.

'Helping Out'

I do not think, therefore, that cohesiveness was operating to produce deliberate setting of speeds. The difference which I did observe between the AB and the D sections, and which is obviously connected with something like cohesiveness, was in the extent to which the members 'helped out'. The pair on a particular line may fall behind with their work for one of several reasons. One of the pair may have been off ill, or on leave. One may be a trainee. One or both may be slower than average. Sometimes the operation of pure chance has the effect that one 'line' incurs substantially more shuttle cards than the rest. In these circumstances, if the section is to finish its card-posting on schedule, the other C.O.s' help is needed. The way in which the 'lines' are permanently divided up between the pairs means that the C.O.s naturally come to regard their own line as their work, and someone else's line as his work; when they have dealt with their own shuttle cards and correspondence for the day, and posted enough cards in their own ledgers to keep up with, or get a little ahead of, the card-posting schedule, there is an understandable tendency to feel that they have done their bit for the day and to spend the last half-hour in some more enjoyable way, such as conversation. Conflicting with this tendency is the awareness that the sections as a whole must keep up to schedule, and that if this is to be managed the weaker—or unluckier—brethren must be helped. In my talks with the C.O.s and E.O.s I noticed that those from the AB sections spoke of 'helping out' as something that took place as a matter of course, and seemed to be accepted by the C.O.s without question, whereas those from the D sections tended to speak of it as something which the C.O.s had to be told by the E.O. to do. Quite a few of those from the D sections spoke of the unwillingness of some of the others in their sections to 'help out', and C.O.s who had served in other sections sometimes spoke of the differences in attitude to this practice. I was particularly interested to learn from one C.O. in a D section that until recently there had been no systematic 'helping out' in that section. The E.O., who seemed to be efficient and liked by the section, was nevertheless very young, had not been long in charge, and had not yet instituted any system for helping out. This year, however, the C.O.s themselves had decided at a meeting that there must be some organised helping out, and a system was now in force. This may, of course, have been an example of skilful handling of the section by an E.O. who felt that a decision taken by them was more likely to be carried out willingly.

However this may be, I thought it possible that this section was undergoing the process which transformed a D section into a B one. It seemed to me that one C.O. in a section that was recognised to be one of the best summed up the situation rather well by saying, 'but we work together so well that we'd get through the work even if the E.O. weren't there'.[1]

One other point seems worth making. Earlier, when describing my

[1] This was not a criticism of the E.O., who was clearly regarded as likeable and competent.

efforts to find a source of figures which would enable me to compare the output of individual C.O.s of different sexes, ages and experience of the work, I explained that 'individual counts' were strongly opposed by the C.S.C.A. It is tempting to jump to the conclusion that this is an unhealthy symptom. But this may be over-simplifying the issue. If the phenomenon we have just been considering is a symptom of what has been called 'cohesiveness' among the C.O.s of the sections, is it not possible that the determination to protect the less able members of their teams against what is regarded as a means of discrimination and pressure is another symptom of the same thing? If so, and if 'cohesiveness' is desirable in the interests of efficiency, is this 'protectiveness' really unhealthy? The issue resolves itself into the question 'Would the sections be more efficient if they were less cohesive and less protective to their members?' I am by no means certain that they would; but this is the point at which logical argument can take us no farther, and only speculation is left.

The Work Itself

I did not, however, concentrate entirely on topics connected with the C.O.s' attitude to their colleagues. Their feelings about the work itself and about the way in which they were supervised were also extremely interesting. In the course of the interview I asked the neutral question, 'What is the work itself like?' and noted the aspects which they mentioned without prompting. I also asked them what qualities they thought that a C.O. required, and noted their answers.

Quite a variety of qualities was offered as desirable in a Ledger Section C.O. Placidity, patience and a sense of humour were suggested as antidotes against the monotony. Conscientiousness, a good memory and ability to keep one's head at times of stress were needed to guard against mistakes. One or two of the replies showed that some C.O.s had a low opinion of the quality of the work. 'All you need is a small mind.' 'It's a disadvantage to be capable of too much—you feel the monotony.' 'It's C.A. work.' Others, on the other hand, had speed in the forefront of their thoughts. 'You need to be young and quick' was said by quite a few who were no longer young. Only one woman and one man thought that women were better at the work than men; and nobody thought the opposite.

As for the work itself, there were two features which most of the C.O.s mentioned with dislike. One was of course, the monotony. As one of them put it, 'You know that you'll be doing the same thing next week, next month and next year.' Another said, 'You feel there isn't much point in getting through the cards, because next quarter it'll start all over again.' The problem of this monotony is something of which both the official and staff sides are very conscious, and from time to time there have been discussions of how it can be dealt with; no solution has been found, and indeed it is hard to see what form the solution could take so long as this work has to be done by human beings. It is true that the work is not quite as lacking in variety as it might be; each day there are three different tasks to be dealt with—shuttle cards, correspondence and card-posting. In some sections the sequence is more varied than this, and they may begin the day with an hour's card-posting, until the bulk of shuttles has arrived; some sections change over the work in the afternoon as well. But there is a limit to the amount of variety that can be contrived in this way.

The other feature, which was stressed even more by practically every one of the C.O.s was what they called 'the pressure'. Almost every officer in charge of a section or group of sections in Records Branch spends a good deal of his time in scrutinising the figures that show what progress is being made with the big task of card-posting. S.E.O.s compare the performances of the sections under their different H.E.O.s: the H.E.O.s keep 'league tables' in which the E.O.s can see how their sections are keeping up with or falling behind the group: the E.O.s are not allowed to compare individual C.O.s any longer, but as one or two of the C.O.s put it, 'they can still breathe down our necks'. In the minds of the C.O.s this pressure was linked up with the way in which the complements of the sections had been reduced in successive stages from 24 C.O.s and C.A.s to 16 C.O.s and 2 C.A.s. Some of these reductions had accompanied changes in the nature and volume of the work, but the most recent one, in 1957, had, they felt, merely relied on them to work at extra speed to see that the Branch did not fail to do its work. The C.O.s also pointed out that another objective of which they were being constantly reminded was the keeping of mistakes to the minimum. A special section, called the audit section, scrutinised a sample of their work for mistakes, and abnormally high percentages of a particular kind of error were brought to the attention of the E.O. Moreover, a C.O. whose mistake resulted in an overpayment of insurance benefit to a claimant was sent for and personally reprimanded by the H.E.O. The C.O.s felt that the insistence on speed was inconsistent with the desire to keep down errors. It was this feeling of pressure that had been partly if not wholly, responsible for the protest against 'individual counts' ten years before. The C.O.s had apparently felt that E.O.s who were trying to 'apply the whip' to their section were using the counts as the occasion for comparing one C.O. with his neighbour, although, the C.O.s argued, the E.O. could have no idea how many difficult cases the C.O. might have had in his tray that day. The C.O.s also felt that some of their older colleagues were going as fast as they could, and that to compare them with a younger and faster man or woman was unreasonable.

Another measure which was resented by the C.O.s (and also by some of the E.O.s) was any attempt to introduce a 'spirit of competition' between the sections. At one time comparisons between the output of different sections had been read out over the loudspeaker system. This had been regarded, however, as an indirect but still very crude lever for increasing 'the pressure'. It still survived in the form of 'league tables' kept by one or two H.E.O.s for the sections under their command, but comparisons were no longer broadcast.

One question that is bound to occur to anyone with experience of factory workers is whether this attitude of the Benton C.O.s is the same phenomenon as the resistance of the man at the bench to 'timing' him at work. It is usually assumed that the reason for this is that the stopwatch is a means of reducing the pay-packet of those workers who are paid in proportion to their output. This may be so; but the C.O.s at Benton were not paid any more or less according to the number of cards they posted. It is possible that their objection to the counts sprang from the industrial background and traditions to which many of them were accustomed. But there was no doubt that the basic objection to it was dislike of 'pressure', and this made me wonder whether the same might not be true of other work situations in which a repetitive task is being performed and in which the worker feels that the speed which suits him is not the speed that suits the management.

The feeling of pressure had of course been intensified by the reductions in the complements of sections. The C.O.s could not argue that a complement of 16 was too small for the job at normal times, since the Branch as a whole was coping with its work without overtime. What they said was that the complement left nothing in reserve to cope with the inevitable sick leave and annual leave; as soon as one or two members of the section were away, the strain began to be felt. The argument that even so 'the work got done' merely exacerbated their resentment, since they point out that it got done simply because they produced the extra turn of speed that the situation demanded.

I was interested to see whether any of the C.O.s believed that the 'pressure' had any effect upon health. As we shall see in Chapter 6, there is a small and fairly uniform percentage of office workers who think that their work affects either their physical or their mental health. I found no trace, however, of this belief among the 38 C.O.s. Since I was able to make no comparison between the sick leave of Sections or Branches, I could not verify whether there was in fact any abnormality in the incidence of illness among the Ledger Sections.

It was difficult for me, who had not worked in the Branch, to be sure how necessary the feeling of pressure was; in other words, how much slower the C.O.s would work if it were not there. My talks with the E.O.s confirmed that the pressure was a very real thing; but I found it difficult to be certain how great was the danger of falling behind at normal times. The shuttle cards had to be dealt with on the day of receipt, and it was only when there was a winter epidemic of influenza that any special steps, such as overtime, had to be taken to see that this was done. As Table 5.01 showed, there was not much risk of a failure to complete card-posting within the nine or ten weeks allowed; most sections, even on the 'heavy staggers', had time in hand, and as their peaks showed had a reserve of speed to call upon if things went wrong. If a section were suddenly hit by an unusual amount of sick leave—for example at a time when annual leave was also at its peak—it could easily get into difficulties; but the remedy of asking another section to help out, though very unpopular, was always practicable. I was inclined to wonder whether the constant emphasis on speed, with its accompaniments of 'league tables' and what the C.O.s called 'the whips' from the supervisors, were not an inheritance from days when the Branch really had been in difficulties which were no longer a genuine danger.

Valuing the Work

One or two of the C.O.s to whom I talked made the interesting remark that the work was not really monotonous if one took it seriously and tried to avoid mistakes. Certainly there seemed to be a tendency among the C.O.s themselves to put a rather low value on the work, particularly when I considered the amount of training that was required to make them competent at it. One or two even went so far as to describe it as 'thankless'; as they put it, it didn't matter whether you did good work, nobody thanked you for it. This feeling—which was expressed by men as well as women—was no doubt intensified by the knowledge that there were 1,599 other C.O.s doing exactly the same job in the same building: it is very difficult to feel that there is anything specially valuable about one's own work if a large number of other people are doing it too. The C.O.s, too, had the impression that such a low value was placed on Ledger Section work that it was a disadvantage, if one ever succeeded in appearing before a promotion board, to have spent most of one's career in this Branch.[1]

This feeling that a very low value was placed on what they were doing was not accompanied by any belief that what they were doing was in fact unnecessary or trivial. Some of them felt that it was too easy; two of them did raise the fundamental question whether it would not be simpler to enforce the payment of contributions quite independently of the payment of benefits, and so make it unnecessary to consult the records every time a claim had to be met. But with these exceptions the C.O.s seemed to be quite satisfied that what they were doing was essential to the community; what they resented was the fact that the community did not recognise its value.

[1] This is yet another case where the truth or falsity of the belief is not the point; what matters here is that this is what the C.O.s believe. It is one of the reasons why they apply in such large numbers for transfers to other work.

This feeling of 'thanklessness', to use the C.O.s' own phrase, may have had some connection with the value which most of them set on visits from the senior officers. Most (but not all) H.E.O.s visited their half-dozen sections at least once each day. The S.E.O.s had very much larger commands—anything up to 30 sections each; and it was not surprising that their visits were less frequent. But the C.O.s under one S.E.O. spoke with real appreciation of his practice of trying to make a daily round of his sections. Even the former Head of Branch (now retired) had made regular rounds of all his 100 sections, talking to one or two C.O.s here and there.[1] Although for many of them he seems to have personified the 'pressure' which I have just been describing, there is no doubt that these 'rounds' helped to reduce the C.O.s' feeling of being 'lost in the crowd' and of 'doing a job for which you get no credit'.[2] The Controller of the whole Newcastle Office came round the Ledger Sections when visitors were being shown the workings of the Branch, and he toured every inhabited room on the site during Christmas week. All this suggested that the value of personal contacts, even if they had no official function, was appreciated by quite a few of the senior officers. Not by all, however: occasionally, when I was enquiring about the functions of one or other of them the C.O. would say, 'Oh, we never see him'; and this was clearly regarded as a demerit.

It is possible that all these attitudes of the C.O.s—their feeling that the work is monotonous, that it is done under pressure, that accuracy and other standards are sacrificed to speed, that the work is thankless, that they never see some of the men at the top, are all connected. I have already mentioned the C.O.s who said that the work was not really monotonous if one took it seriously and tried to avoid mistakes. It must be difficult, however, to take it seriously if one feels that what is really valued by the men at the top is speed, and that the difficulty of the work is not appreciated. I certainly do not mean that this is the outlook of senior officers—although, as I have said, there is a natural hangover of anxiety about 'keeping up', from the times when this really was not easy. The important thing is that this was what the C.O.s believed.

I must not give the impression, however, that they found their life in Records Branch intolerable. Obviously if they had literally done so they would have left it. As we have seen, a comparatively high percentage did apply for transfers to other C.O. jobs, but in some cases their motive

[1] The new Head of Branch had only recently taken over, and had to spend a great deal of the time since away from Newcastle investigating methods of mechanising the procedure for the forthcoming graduated pensions scheme.

[2] 'Rounds' by senior officers can, of course, have their damaging effect. C.O.s may take the opportunity to raise, directly or indirectly, some sore question on which they do not see eye to eye with their immediate superior; and the senior officer, if he is not very adroit, may be lured into expressing a view without having heard the arguments of the Executive Officer. But this can be avoided without rendering the 'rounds' pointless.

was to improve their chances of promotion. A more interesting symptom was the level of voluntary resignations. Among the C.O.s at Benton (of whom more than half worked in Records Branch) the rate was less than 2 per thousand per annum,[1] which is very much lower than the national rate of about 13 per thousand for the General Clerical Class as a whole which I have quoted in Chapter 3.[2] Over 80 per cent. of the resigners were under twenty-five years of age. The older C.O.s whom I interviewed spoke of the younger C.O.s as having attitudes of which they did not altogether approve; they were irritated by their 'couldn't care less attitude', and by their habit of rushing through the work and then indulging in 'chatter' or horseplay during working hours. Many of the staider C.O.s in their thirties, forties and fifties saw this, pessimistically, as a symptom of a deterioration in the conscientiousness and general outlook of the young since their day. It is possible, however, that the difference was simply that the C.O.s I interviewed—who were deliberately selected from those who had been in the Branch for some years—had adjusted themselves to the requirements of the work, whereas the younger ones were still trying to do so. No doubt some were trying harder than others. But we shall see in Chapter 8 that office workers' liking for their jobs increases a little with time; and I am inclined to think that most of the C.O.s whom I interviewed had undergone some internal process of accommodation to the work. Only one man and two women out of the 38 expressed a definite and emotional dislike of the place; with the exception of one woman (who liked it so much that she couldn't understand the grievances of most of her colleagues), the rest were critical but philosophical.

5.3. THE EXECUTIVE OFFICERS

My interviews with the E.O.s were chiefly directed towards their relationship with the C.O.s, since it was the groups consisting of the latter, with the E.O. as their head, that were the subject of my study.[3] It would for example, have been interesting to cover all the aspects of their work more thoroughly, and to see, for example, whether the Society of Civil Servants (their staff association) played the same rôle as the C.S.C.A. did for the C.O.s. But my time (and theirs) was limited; and in any case

---

[1] For men and women, but excluding women who left simply to get married.

[2] The two rates are not precisely comparable, since the rate in Chapter 3 excludes *all* women, while the rate I have had to give for Benton excludes only women who left to get married. But it is most unlikely that the difference would be greatly reduced if the rates were made strictly comparable.

[3] Strictly speaking, each group also includes the two C.A.s who distribute the incoming cards and answer telephone calls. But I thought it unlikely, from their subordinate position and their small number, that they greatly influenced the rest of the section's attitudes. Life is too short for exploring every avenue, and the man who says he has left no stone unturned is a liar.

the Executive Class at Newcastle was the subject of a study which was being carried out by another research worker.[1]

I therefore paid a good deal of attention to the E.O.'s views on staff management. One-third of the three-week basic training which an E.O. receives when he is sent to Records Branch is devoted to 'staff relations'.[2] This part of the training is largely built up on the technique of case-study and discussion which I have mentioned in Chapter 2. Since this technique is essentially Socratic, and deliberately avoids the handing out of lists of precepts to the students, I could not be sure exactly what influence these courses were having in the E.O.'s attitudes to supervision. But I did notice two things about the E.O.s to whom I talked. One was that they had obviously thought about the problems of managing staff under the conditions I have described. The other was that they did not produce ready-made answers. When you interview nineteen people in quick succession, any common source for their ideas soon reveals itself in the frequency with which you hear the same phrase. As we shall see, the E.O.s in charge of the better sections, and those in charge of the D ones, did have ideas in common, but their way of expressing them was sufficiently varied to make it unlikely that they were simply repeating what they had been told by an instructor.

Before I come, however, to the impressions which I gained from the interviews with the E.O.s, let me deal briefly with the statistical facts about them.

Age and Sex of Supervisors

The ages of the E.O.s ranged from twenty to the early sixties. The E.O.s of the AB sections tended to be younger than those of the D sections, but the difference between their mean ages (39·1 years compared with 44·3 years) was not enough, in the small sample of nineteen, to make it very probable that this factor affected the quality of the sections.[3] It does, however, make it rather unlikely that it is the older men and women who make the better supervisors in this sort of work. There were one or two cases in which the E.O. was markedly younger than most of his or her C.O.s, but these occurred both among the AB and among the D sections; they included the section that was rated A and the section that was rated AB (i.e. A by the S.E.O. and B by the H.E.O.), and were therefore, in all probability, the best of the 100 Ledger Sections. But both in my interviews with the E.O.s and in

---

[1] Mr. C. H. Dodds, of the University of Leeds. His work was not sufficiently far advanced at the time of my investigation to be made available to me.

[2] As an illustration of the importance attached by official and staff sides to promotion procedure, another third of the course is spent on the subject of 'reporting on staff', in an effort to achieve as much uniformity as possible throughout the office. The remaining third is concerned with the job itself.

[3] The critical ratio was only 0·83.

talks with other members of the staff I got the impression that the older C.O.s in a section would often be particularly helpful to a young and inexperienced E.O. As one E.O. put it, 'sometimes *they* supervise *me*'. The senior C.O. in a section, who is recognised semi-officially as a second-in-command,[1] is often a strong support to the young E.O.

Eight of the nineteen were women. Seven out of the eight were in charge of D sections. This distribution suggests that women may not be as good as men at supervising work of this kind.[2] Certainly the female E.O.s were practically unanimous in preferring a different sort of executive job—for example, local office work, in which they dealt with individual problems, often face to face with the member of the public who was concerned. They did not enjoy the supervisory part of their duties, and they preferred to discuss other aspects of their work. This is an understandable attitude, particularly in women; and it is only fair to add that I noticed it in some of the men as well.

Time in Charge and Method of Entry

The periods for which the E.O.s had been in charge of their present sections varied from four months to just over nine years. It was noticeable that most of them fell into two groups—five who had been in their sections for more than four and a half years, and eleven who had spent two years or less with their sections. But these two groups were more or less evenly divided between the AB and the D sections. Indeed my impression was that in quite a number of cases the E.O. himself felt that he or she had not been long enough in charge of the section to have had much effect upon their quality. Several of those in charge of AB sections —and particularly the younger of them—attributed their section's efficiency to their predecessor's qualities as a supervisor; this may have erred in the direction of modesty, but in some cases it seemed to me to fit the facts. In short, it is very unlikely that the length of time for which the E.O.s had been in charge of their sections had much to do with the latter's accuracy or output.

All but three of the E.O.s had reached their present grade by promotion, usually from the grade of C.O. The other three had entered the civil service in this grade, as a result of Open Competitions or one of the competitions for ex-servicemen. No conclusions could be drawn from the distribution of these three between the AB and the D sections.

---

[1] It is the senior C.O. who asks each C.O. for the total of his day's output, and reports the grand total, but not individual totals, to the E.O. This in itself gives him a certain amount of authority. He also takes charge when the E.O. is away for a day or so.

[2] Although they may well, of course, be as good or better at supervising in other kinds of work, or other kinds of teams.

Attitudes

So much for the indisputable facts about the E.O.s of these 19 sections. What follows is based upon my impressions from my interviews with them and with the C.O.s under them.

Like the C.O.s, the E.O.s for the most part knew whether their sections were regarded as better or worse than average. They had no very interesting theories, however, as to what it was that made their section good or bad. When I asked this question, the E.O. in charge of an AB section usually said that he was lucky in having a good lot of C.O.s. The E.O. in charge of a D section, on the other hand, did not say that he had a poor lot; he would usually offer some other explanation—for example, that they had been unlucky enough to have a lot of sick leave recently.[1]

Most of the E.O.'s time seems to be spent in 'checking'. This consists in examining a selection of the cards or other documents already completed by the C.O.s to see whether they contain any errors. It is a task that does not give them any great satisfaction. The part of their job which all of them find interesting is dealing with the out-of-the-ordinary cases which are referred to them by the C.O.s (or occasionally come down from the H.E.O.). Quite a few sections have one or two trainees allotted to them—that is, C.O.s who have just completed the official course of training, but need to work with an experienced officer who can point out their mistakes and show them the way round difficulties. Some E.O.s work with these trainees themselves, perhaps in order to introduce more variety into their own routine, perhaps in order to free all their C.O.s for uninterrupted work. Only one of the E.O.s spontaneously mentioned any other kind of supervisory activity as part of his everyday duties. In fact, however, almost all have to keep an eye on their C.O.s in order to discourage the less conscientious ones from irrelevant conversations or other unofficial pursuits. Quite often they have to reorganise their sub-sections temporarily, in order to fill gaps caused by sickness or leave; but they prefer, if they can, to avoid this by redistributing the work of absent C.O.s among those who are present.

Some studies of supervisors, particularly in the U.S.A., have suggested that supervisors of teams with high productivity are democratic, 'employee-centered', and less authoritarian than supervisors of the less productive teams: a good example is the investigation by Katz, Maccoby and Morse in the Prudential Insurance Company.[2] With this in mind, I tried to elicit the attitude of the E.O.s towards their C.O.s, and toward the supervisory side of their duties.

My interviews certainly did not suggest that the conclusions of the American investigators were applicable to the Ledger Sections at

[1] It was unfortunate that the way in which sick leave records were kept did not allow me to verify this.
[2] Summarised in Appendix A.

Benton.[1] It seemed to me that the E.O.s of the AB sections could be distinguished from the others by rather different qualities. They were, in the first place, more confident of their ability to handle their sections, and they seemed to do so with more firmness. Those in the D sections initiated very few changes in the way their sections worked; if I asked about the origin of some minor peculiarity in their section's way of tackling the work, they would reply, 'Well, that was the way they were doing it when I arrived, so I let them carry on.' The firmer E.O.s would say, 'Well, I didn't like the way they were doing it, so I decided we would do it in this way.' The most interesting answers, however, were given to the question 'What sort of person do you think would be best at your job?' Those in charge of the D sections tended to say, 'Well, someone with tact, sympathy for the C.O.'s difficulties—not too strong a disciplinarian.' The E.O.s of the AB sections, on the other hand, emphasised that 'You must know how to do the job yourself.' 'You must be the same; don't be soft one minute and jump at them the next time.' 'A little aloofness does no harm.'

We must not of course assume too readily that it is the differences between the two kinds of supervisor that are helping to produce the differences between the AB and the D sections. The possibility that there is a causal link working in the other direction must be seriously considered. In other words, being in charge of one of the better sections might quite well help a supervisor to become more confident and firm, and his confidence and firmness might have no effect upon the efficiency of his section. After all, we have just seen that the efficiency of the sections seems to be related to at least one factor that has nothing to do with the E.O.; that is, with the length of time the C.O.s have been working together in that section.

There are two pieces of evidence, however, that favour the straightforward hypothesis. The first is the sex distribution of the E.O.s between the AB and the D sections. We noticed that all but one of the women were in charge of D sections, and that the women seemed to display a greater dislike of the supervisory part of the job than did the men. The qualities of firmness and confidence in a supervisor are those which one would be inclined to associate with men rather than with women, just as women are regarded as possessing the virtues of tact and sympathy in a greater degree than men. It is therefore highly probable that the E.O.s possessed the qualities which they exhibited to me, independently of the kind of section of which they were in charge.

The other piece of evidence is the opinions of the C.O.s themselves.

---

[1] This does not mean of course that the American investigators were mistaken about the office workers whom they studied. As I have pointed out in Chapter 1, this is simply an example that suggests how dangerous it is to assume that what is true of one kind of worker in one country is true of another kind in the same country or the same kind in another country.

I asked each of them for the qualities which made a really good E.O. The answers which I got were remarkably similar to those from the E.O.s of the better sections. Although some C.O.s—usually women—mentioned tact and 'treating people like human beings', both these C.O.s and the rest almost invariably said, 'Well, the E.O. must know the job. He must be fair—not have favourites—but be firm.' By 'knowing the job' they meant knowing the C.O.'s job; one or two of them told me stories about E.O.s (usually, as I have said, about former E.O.s and not their present ones) who had never really familiarised themselves with the intricacies of the instructions which the C.O. had to observe, with the result that C.O.s who asked for a ruling on a doubtful point were sometimes given one that they knew to be wrong; whatever the answer was, it was not that. Their dislike of anything that might be an indication of favouritism was very strong: and extended to any friendship between the E.O. and a C.O. in his section. The E.O.s, too, were well aware that it was dangerous for them to have friends in their own section.

Most surprising, however, is the C.O.'s own desire for a 'firm' E.O. The E.O. had to exercise his authority in two chief ways. First, he had to prevent time-wasting on the job. This might take the form of unnecessary talking, or occasionally of some more boisterous activity among the younger males. The good E.O., apparently, was the one who knew just how much latitude to give; he allowed them some diversion during the short mid-morning break for tea, and perhaps at the end of the day when the card-posting was well up to schedule and nobody needed to be helped out. But if he allowed it at other times he lost the respect of the other C.O.s, and perhaps also of the offender himself. The other main point at which firmness was needed was in time-keeping. The morning started at 8.15 a.m., and the E.O. had a book in which each C.O. had to sign his or her name on arrival. He was supposed to remove it at 8.20, so that anyone who came in later would earn a black mark and would eventually receive a reprimand. Some E.O.s were humanely slow in removing the book; but this did not seem to earn them any real favour with the conscientious majority in their sections. At lunch-time, everyone was allowed a break of 45 minutes. Occasionally a C.O. who needed to buy something out of the ordinary in Newcastle, or who had to attend some clinic or hospital, would ask for what was called 'an extension' of, say, half an hour. Here again the E.O. had to exercise his own discretion, although I heard of—but did not meet—one or two who sheltered behind higher authority. If he granted it too seldom he was disliked; if too often, he lost the respect of his section. Their difficulties were increased by the fact that a C.O. who was very aggrieved by what he considered an unfair decision of this kind might get the C.S.C.A. to take his case up with higher authority, who would probably try to find some compromise that would concede something to the C.O. without completely overturning the E.O.'s decision. These cases were not common, and my impression was that it was the minority of C.O.s who appealed to the C.S.C.A.; but one case of this kind could be very disturbing to the E.O.'s authority.

There were cases in which C.O.s spoke of some past E.O. who had been 'very strict indeed'; yet they almost always added 'but very fair'. It was clear that strictness in itself, so long as it was not accompanied by favouritism or unpredictability, and so long as the C.O.s had some small latitude within which to give occasional rein to their need to relax, or to use their lunch-hour for some purpose other than eating, was not resented. We have already seen, for example, how a section in which the E.O. had not compelled the unwilling members to help out when necessary took matters into their own hands and agreed upon a system to achieve this.

On this point, as on others, I must not give the impression that the Ministry were on the wrong tack. They were conscious of the fact that some E.O.s, though excellent in other ways, might be unsuitable for taking charge of Ledger Sections. One of their principles was to avoid, if possible, giving these sections to young women who had just entered the Executive grade from outside the service.

5.4. COMMENT

My primary purpose in studying Records Branch was to find a situation in which the efficiency of office workers could be measured by counting units of output, and to see what relationship it bore to the psychological conditions under which the work was done. I have shown that in this sort of situation the office worker's tendency to regulate his speed to fit his programme makes measurement of productivity and efficiency difficult, but that there is a rough and ready, yet reliable, way to overcome this and make comparisons between working groups with high and low output. Some of the forces which seemed to be operating among these working groups in this case—such as 'the pressure'—may or may not operate to the same extent elsewhere. Other forces—such as the one which I have tentatively identified with 'cohesiveness'—are probably present in most other groups of office workers, although their effect may not be so clear.

The situation I have just been describing is an example of desk work in which this approximates as closely as possible to the life of the industrial worker; indeed, this was said as a criticism by the desk workers themselves when they referred to Records Branch as 'the factory'. Office work of this kind is by no means confined to Newcastle, which merely offered an example of it on the largest scale and under favourable conditions for studying it. The Savings Bank Division of the Post Office is another example, and smaller 'factories' can be found in the large banks and insurance companies. It is a kind of office work which is

THE OFFICE AS A FACTORY

slowly being replaced by mechanical methods, but so slowly that normal wastage by retirement and resignation is keeping pace with the contraction of clerical jobs. One cannot therefore shrug off the psychological problems of managing such 'factories' with the excuse that they are temporary.

In any case, the situation of the C.O.s in Records Branch illustrates, rather more clearly and acutely than usual, the predicament of many members of the desk grades in the civil service. The physical conditions under which they do their work are cleaner, healthier and less depressing than in many other occupations. The pay and the pension is not glittering: neither is it despicable. Unless they are grossly inefficient or misbehaved, they need not fear dismissal; and only the pathologically ambitious are compelled to curry favour. They are not denied all use of their intelligence or initiative. Many a worker at another kind of desk, or at a factory bench, would consider all this enough and more.

On the other hand, the task is not intrinsically interesting, although it is possible to acquire an interest in almost any kind of work by various mental exercises. Under the present system, it must be done by someone; but the doer has the disturbing feeling that if the system were better it would not be necessary, and that in any case it is work for a machine. It is too repetitive to give the worker a feeling of creating anything: like the man who ploughs the sea-shore he knows that he will have to do the same tomorrow, and there will still be nothing to show for his work.

In a sense it is fair to ask, 'But didn't these people choose this work, and can't they leave it if they dislike it?' The answer, however, is not a simple 'Yes'. They certainly chose to enter the civil service. What determined their choice cannot be known for certain: if they themselves knew once, they have probably forgotten. What is certain is that in choosing they were not selecting a precisely defined task for their desk work. In most cases the newly recruited C.O. can hope to be posted to the locality or to the Ministry of his choice, whichever seems to him to be most important; he will be fortunate if he achieves both. Whether he attains the Ministry he wants or not, he has no say in deciding to which part of it, or to what sort of tasks, he will be assigned.

The picture of the job which the service hangs outside its doors to attract recruits to the Clerical Class is not dishonest, or even seriously misleading. The 'Choice of Careers' pamphlet on the Executive and Clerical Classes contains descriptions of the various types of task on which the C.O. is likely to find himself engaged. In one of these it is not hard to recognise the building we have just left:

'RECORDS'

In Departments or branches where extensive records have to be kept there is a volume of work which, while routine in its nature, needs great accuracy and speed. Susan Wilson works in such an office. She was previously a clerical assistant and became a clerical officer on promotion.

At various times each day she receives enquiry cards from local offices asking for certain information from the central ledgers, for example, about the number of contributions paid by an applicant for benefit or about the date of his entry into insurance. For every card she had to look in the ledger, obtain the information and enter it on the card. The cards are then checked and dispatched.

Sometimes an enquiry has to be sent out to a contributor: Miss Wilson has to check that she gets replies to the forms she sends out, and has to alter or make additional entries in the ledgers when she receives cards bearing arrears of contributions. She gets batches of returned insurance cards and must enter the appropriate details from these into the ledger with complete accuracy. The ledgers are looked out and prepared for her by a clerical assistant, who files the used cards in them. Miss Wilson then checks the name on the card with that on the ledger sheet, copies the details of contributions and credits and completes the cumulative totals. Where appropriate she fills in a notification about contributions in arrears and has it sent to the insured person.

Her work for the day is divided into fairly well-defined periods. Although most of her queries are conducted by the use of stock cards or forms, she sometimes uses the telephone to get information from other sections. The types of queries she handles are very varied and it took her several months to learn about them all.

During the last quarter of an hour each day she makes out a return, under about twelve categories, of the work she has done.[1]

From what I saw of Records Branch at Benton I would find it hard to point to any part of this passage that was misleading. It is true that Miss Wilson will be lucky if she gets her C.A. to file the insurance cards for her during the height of the card-posting; but that is a detail. Nor does the passage say for how many years she had been doing the same thing, or how long ago she applied for a transfer to a local office, where she can meet some of the people whose cards she handles. It is after all a recruiting pamphlet. On the whole, however, it is very honest. It says, 'If you enter the Clerical Class of the civil service, this is one of the jobs that you may find yourself doing.'

As for the argument that those who don't like the job can leave it, there is some truth in this too. We have seen how few C.O.s at Benton do resign. But it is possible to push this argument too far. Office jobs are not particularly easy to come by, especially in the Newcastle area. By the time they are twenty-five many of the men have acquired wives and begotten children, and will hesitate to involve them in a bold decision. As I have pointed out, the great majority of the resigners are under the age of twenty-five.

The senior civil servant on the other hand is both employee and employer; and as employer he is in a dilemma that is just as clear. The work must be done, and done with enough efficiency and accuracy to satisfy the public. Since it cannot yet be done by a machine, it must be done by men and women. For the present at least he finds it possible to recruit these men and women to do the job, without being dishonest about it or offering any special inducements. Once they have been recruited, they find it duller and more irritating than they had expected,

[1] H.M.S.O., *Choice of Careers*, New Series No. 32, pp. 24-5.

and quite a few of them ask whether they cannot be given something more interesting to do: but few of them actually resign.

Thus the Records Branch at Benton provided me not only with an opportunity for objective comparisons between matched groups of office workers, but also with an illustration, as vivid as I was likely to find anywhere, of the psychological situation in which large masses of civil servants find themselves today. It is a situation to which I shall return in my final chapter: but before that there are other questions which I must try to answer.

6

A SEARCH FOR AN INDEX: TURNOVER AND SICK LEAVE

In the previous chapter I tried to demonstrate both the possibilities and the difficulties of studying the attitudes to their jobs of desk workers who were engaged on very similar and very uniform work. But almost ideal situations of the kind which I found at Benton are very exceptional in the civil service, even in the clerical grades. If you take at random two C.O.s sitting side by side in the same section of a Whitehall Ministry, you will probably find that their jobs not only vary in nature from day to day, but are quite different from each other. One may be handling the section's routine correspondence, while the other may be keeping its statistics or its files. And among the higher grades the possibilities of finding any substantial numbers of officers performing comparable tasks is much more remote.

This meant that the technique of interviewing a relatively small sample, which was reliable enough when the people whom I was studying were all engaged on similar and unvarying tasks, would be useless. In order to cancel out the effect of differences in the nature of the jobs, it would be necessary to find some way of ascertaining the attitudes of very much larger numbers, so large, in fact, that interviewing was out of the question. In practice there were two ways of doing this. One was to issue a postal questionnaire; and in Chapters 7 and 8 I shall describe the results of this expedient. The other was to find some easily measurable phenomenon that could safely be regarded as an indirect index of attitudes to the job.

Among industrial workers two such indirect pointers have been found to serve reliably as indications of the extent to which people like or dislike their jobs. These are absenteeism and labour turnover. The higher the workers' rate of voluntary absenteeism or of voluntary resignations, the lower their 'job-satisfaction'. These indices, however, are of little use for measuring the job-satisfaction of non-industrial civil servants. Absenteeism is almost completely useless because, unlike many manual workers, the civil servant cannot simply stay away from work now and again without producing a very sound justification—unless, that is, he is willing to run the risk of some severe penalty.

As for strikes, there has not been one in the desk-classes of the British civil service within living memory. Many civil servants believe incorrectly that they are prohibited by law from striking; in fact it is simply regarded officially as an offence against discipline. In any case, however, to strike or not to strike is a choice which in Britain is usually determined by one's social class. In France, by contrast, many middle-class workers, including civil servants, have gone on strike, real or token, since the war.

TURNOVER

Labour turnover among the desk grades is also extremely low, and with one exception is probably too low to be a significant symptom. The table below shows the number of voluntary resignations per thousand at risk per annum for the four desk classes during the four years 1954-57:

Rates of Voluntary Resignations among Established Members of the Desk Classes from 1954 to 1957

Staff Group	Mean Annual Number of Resignations[1] per 1,000 at risk	
	Men	Women
Administrative	4·3	26·3
General Executive	2·4	16·9
General Clerical	13·0	55·4
Clerical Assistants	3·6[2]	54·3

The rates for women are, of course, very much higher than for men. But the difference is almost certainly due to the fact that most of the women who resigned did so because of marriage: if the women's rates are indices of anything, it is of the nubility of the different groups. It is to the men's rates that we should direct our attention. With one exception these are uniformly low, between 2·4 and 4·3 per 1,000 per annum. The exception is the rate for the C.O.s, which is about four times as high as the average rate for the other three classes.

This phenomenon seemed to have a double importance. In the first place, recruitment to the Clerical Class, particularly for posts in London, had been so difficult in recent years that the Treasury had set up a working party to examine the problem.[3] Any possibility of reducing such losses must therefore be of great interest to the service. Secondly, the reasons for these resignations might help to throw more light on the attitudes of C.O.s to their jobs.

The Treasury were able to provide me with some interesting information about this wastage. The great majority of those who resigned were

[1] Not including voluntary retirements before the normal retiring age: see Chapter 3.
[2] The great majority of male C.A.s during this period were over forty years of age, so that it is not surprising that their resignation rate is so much lower than that of male C.O.s.
[3] See the *Ninety-Third Report of the Civil Service Commissioners*, who were represented on the working party.

twenty-one or twenty-two years of age, after which the rate of resignation declined rapidly and steadily; the pattern (but not the rates) for other desk grades was much the same. The rate was highest among those who had entered by the normal open competition; in other words, those who had served in lower grades before becoming C.O.s were less likely to resign than those who were new to the service.

These facts were consistent with the replies to the questionnaire which I distributed among the desk workers in two Ministries and two Companies in central London, and which is described in Chapters 7 and 8. This showed that men (but not women) in the Clerical Class were much more dissatisfied with their jobs than were respondents from other grades. It also showed, however, that men in the clerical levels of the two Companies were just as dissatisfied in comparison with their seniors and their female colleagues, if not a little more so. What is more, dissatisfaction with one's job, though it occurs at all ages, seems to be at its height among the young, new entrants. It is very probable that this dissatisfaction is closely linked to the high rate of voluntary resignations among young male C.O.s who enter the grade from outside the service.[1]

The Treasury also made the interesting observation that the rate of resignation was highest in the Departments with the smallest complement of male C.O.s:

TABLE 6.01

Resignation Rate of Male C.O.s in 1957[2] (per 1,000)	Number of Departments in Group	Mean Number of Male C.O.s in the Departments in the Group
Less than 10	10	2,295
10-20	10	1,740
20-30	10	217
30-40	9	168
Over 40	8	80

Although the period covered is only one year, the number of resigners was substantial—664. There seems to be some factor at work which encourages resignations in small Departments. This may very well be poorer promotion prospects. We shall see in Chapter 8 how important the chances of promotion and the fairness of the promotion-system are to the desk grades, and how long the C.O.s—at least in the

[1] Many of the resigners must be men who have recently returned to their desks from National Service, which seems to have an unsettling effect in other occupations. It will be interesting to see what effect the abolition of National Service has upon the resignation-rate.

[2] Including the handful who retired voluntarily after the age of fifty but before the normal age of sixty to sixty-five.

two Ministries concerned—had to wait before they became eligible to be considered for promotion. It is probable that in the small Departments, where the vacancies in the Executive Officer grade occurring by promotion, death or retirement are fewer, the prospects of promotion either are or appear to be worse than in larger Ministries.

This is speculation, however, and underlines the need for information about the reasons for these resignations. This is something that only the resigners themselves can supply, and they are in the nature of things less accessible than those who do not resign. It is true that one of the duties listed as suitable for Departmental Welfare Officers[1] is the interviewing of voluntary leavers, and some Welfare Officers do attempt this.[2] But any information which had been collected by individual Departments in this way had not been collated, and may not even have been comparable. There were some grounds for thinking that Departments which insisted upon exercising their right to transfer C.O.s from one part of the country to another had a higher rate of resignation as a result. But this can only be one of many motives for resigning. What is needed is information about the young men who, without an obvious reason like this, resign soon after entering in order to enter other jobs, especially other *clerical* jobs. What is the main consideration? Pay? Promotion? The nature of the work? Physical working conditions? The way in which they are supervised? This is information which it would not be difficult to get by means of a survey using either the Departmental Welfare Officers or trained interviewers, and it seems essential to a proper understanding of the problem.

Among the senior desk classes—the Administrative and Executive grades—voluntary resignations are so few that they are a very insensitive index of job-satisfaction. This is what might be expected. Unlike many manual workers, members of these grades enter them with the intention of making their career in the civil service; and they are much less

[1] See Chapter 2.
[2] For example, the Establishment Division at Benton (see Chapter 5) analysed the 'reasons for leaving' of the 75 male and single female C.O.s who did so in the period January 1957 to June 1958, with this result:

	%
To undertake vocational training	8·0
For other *clerical* jobs	9·3
For *non-clerical* jobs	24·0
Because of travelling difficulties	16·0
Returning to their home area	13·3
Emigrating	12·0
To be married (women only)	17·4

Unfortunately (for my purpose) the resignation rate at Newcastle was well below the national average, perhaps because the difficulty of finding other jobs in the area was greater than in London. Moreover, the analysis raises, but does not answer, the important question, 'Why were the other *clerical* and *non-clerical* jobs more attractive to one-third of the C.O.s?'

'mobile' than the industrial worker. To a great extent (just how great was shown by the replies to Question 47 of my questionnaire) they are attracted to—and presumably kept in—this career by the very security which I have discussed in Chapter 3, and by the prospect of a non-contributory pension at the end of it. Once in, they become increasingly convinced of the difficulty of obtaining a better job outside the service. When one of them succeeds in doing so, it is so unusual as to be a subject of conversation amongst even his remotest acquaintances. In contrast, professional and scientific civil servants move in and out of the service with much more freedom; but they serve only to emphasise the 'immobility' of the desk classes with which we are concerned.

SICK LEAVE AS AN INDEX

So far, then, we have not found a satisfactory universal indirect index of job-satisfaction (to say nothing of efficiency) for the desk classes. But if absenteeism and resignations are too rare among them, there is one form of quantifiable behaviour which certainly is not. This is sick leave. The theory that sick leave can be used as an indirect symptom of 'morale' is becoming popular—I might almost say 'fashionable'—not only among general medical practitioners who are weary of signing certificates of incapacity but also among occupational psychologists who are prevented by some difficulty—such as we have just found in the civil service—from using one of the two tested indices, absenteeism and labour turnover.

I have been unable to find any thorough scientific discussion of this theory, or even a precise statement of it. There is no mention of it in the two comprehensive studies by M. Viteles[1] and M. Argyle[1]; the reason is probably that they were principally concerned with research that has been done among industrial workers, where absenteeism and turnover have been found to be satisfactory indices, and where sick-leave schemes were non-existent or primitive. In 1941-42 T. T. Paterson, who was trying out measures to improve 'morale' at an R.A.F. Fighter Station, compared the incidence of 'nervous conditions', 'gastric upsets (non-infective)' and 'accidents' among women in the Women's Auxiliary Air Force over two periods of six to seven months. During the first period, boredom and dissatisfaction were prevalent; during the second he was taking steps to increase their sense of the usefulness of their work and interest them in the work of the Station. He found a significant improvement in the incidence of these disorders. Like civil servants, the W.A.A.F.s could not without great difficulty go absent or change their jobs; but they could 'go sick'.

In 1951 the anonymous investigators of the Acton Society Trust,

[1] M. Viteles, *Motivation and Morale in Industry* (1953) and M. Argyle, *The Scientific Study of Social Behaviour* (1957).

while studying the relationship between the size of an organisation and the 'morale' of its workers, compared sickness rates among the staffs of one group of factories and one chain of stores belonging to a large retail organisation.[1] They found, among other things,

(i) that stores with high voluntary absenteeism also had high rates of 'short-term' sickness (undefined);
(ii) lower sickness rates in the smaller (as compared with the larger) factories and stores;
(iii) lower rates of certified sickness among workers who were not entitled to sick pay than among workers (of the same kind) who were.

The assumption underlying both these sets of observations is that the incidence of absences attributed to sickness is to some extent affected by the attitude of the worker to his or her work. In its extreme form, no doubt, this relationship may be what is sometimes called 'malingering'—that is, a conscious use of fictitious sickness as an excuse for absence from work. In its milder form, it is simply the fact that a man who is very interested in what he is doing at his work, or believes that he is indispensable and irreplaceable, will sometimes decide to go on working through a bout of influenza or a common cold, while a man who is uninterested and thinks that his job will be done whether he is there or not will take sick leave for an illness of exactly the same severity.

Everyone knows that human nature operates in this way. Unfortunately this *a priori* knowledge is rather stronger than the actual evidence that sick leave can be used as a reliable index of job-satisfaction or of any other subjective attitude to work. Paterson's figures are very small, and subject, as he would be the first to admit, to all sorts of objections. He does not say, for example, why he chose just this rather odd assortment of disorders; or whether the women who were sent to hospital with one of them during the first period, and who were probably therefore more prone to them than the remainder, had all returned to the Station by the beginning of the second period (which followed immediately on the first—and incidentally covered a different half of the year). The Acton Society Trust certainly confirmed that economic motives affect sickness absence; but regard for one's pay is not the same as interest in one's job. Their discovery of a positive correlation between voluntary absenteeism and sick leave conflicts with another study, in a metal fabricating factory[2] which found that low absenteeism (and high job-satisfaction) were accompanied by *high* sickness rates. The different sickness rates for the different sizes of factories are unfortunately open to the objection—so far as can be guessed from the

---

[1] In *Size and Morale* (1953).
[2] Kerr et al., 1952, cited by Argyle, *loc. cit.*

facts given—that these were in different parts of the country; and it has been shown[1] that the incidence of respiratory disorders, which account for so large a part of minor sickness, varies with the air pollution in different parts of Britain: a shop in London is bound to have more respiratory complaints among its shop assistants than one in North Wales.

I must also repeat my warning against the assumption that office workers behave or think in the same way as manual workers (or shop assistants). In short, the theory that sick leave operates as an indirect symptom of job-satisfaction or efficiency is no more than a probability, which justifies investigation. Before it can be relied upon we must do our best to eliminate other plausible explanations of the sick-leave statistics in the civil service. Since I know of no thorough examination of the sickness absences of a large organisation from this point of view, what follows may be of interest to readers outside the civil service from the theoretical as well as the practical standpoint.

Conditions of Sick Leave in the Civil Service

In fact, it is among civil servants that we seem to have the best possible conditions for testing this theory. The rules governing their sick leave are so liberal that motives such as interest in the job have more freedom than in most other salaried occupations to influence their behaviour. Every established non-industrial civil servant[2] whatever his age, seniority or grade, is allowed sick leave on full pay for not more than six months in all during any period of twelve months, and, after his six months on full pay has been exhausted, sick leave on half pay until his total sick leave over any period of four years amounts to twelve months. This rule is subject, of course, to a number of provisos. For example, there must be a reasonable prospect that he will eventually recover and be fit to work again; if not, his Department, with the advice of the Treasury Medical Adviser, must consider whether he should be compelled to retire on medical grounds, with any pension to which he may be entitled.

To qualify for the privilege of sick leave, he must produce at certain intervals a medical certificate of incapacity. But Departments are given discretion—which they all use—to waive this requirement for short absences up to four days in length, provided that the civil servant does not take more than seven days of paid sick leave in this way in any period of twelve months. This not only protects hard-worked general practitioners against a large number of requests for certificates for disorders that do not really call for medical attention; it also helps to reduce the spreading of colds and influenza by civil servants who would

---

[1] By D. D. Reid and A. S. Fairbairn in the *British Journal of Preventive and Social Medicine* for April 1958.

[2] The rules for unestablished or non-industrial staff are less liberal.

otherwise have to be at their desks, exhaling virus at their colleagues, until they could attend their doctor's evening surgery.[1]

Uncertified Sick Leave

It is this allowance of seven days of uncertified illness in a twelve-month that seems to offer most scope for the operation of motives such as lack of interest in the work, and indeed for outright malingering. Since I have found quite a widespread belief that this concession is abused, I shall deal with this subject first. In the form in which it has usually been stated to me, the belief is that civil servants use their seven days of uncertified sick leave as a 'supplement' to their allowance of annual leave. I have been assured of this by people who have never been in the service but who 'know plenty of civil servants who do it'; I have been told by industrial civil servants of the way in which this concession is abused by their non-industrial colleagues; and—most alarming of all—I have been told by one or two civil servants that while they would not stoop to this practice themselves they know of others in their office who do.

As evidence for the truth of this belief, its mere prevalence is worth something, but not very much. We are usually ready, if not eager, to entertain discreditable theories about other groups in the community (or even about our own colleagues, although loyalty forbids that they should be propounded by outsiders). It is certainly not the sort of theory that can be tested by direct questioning. The existence of some malingering was acknowledged by Welfare Officers; and the Post Office produced some indirect evidence pointing to malingering among a sample of 101 employees of various grades whom they had dismissed for dishonesty or generally unsatisfactory conduct.[2] But this evidence —which concerned long-term sick leave, and, in the case of the Post Office, sick leave among a rather unusual group—was no real indication of malingering in the service as a whole.

I could think of only one way of testing the hypothesis. I would

---

[1] Many private firms now waive the demand for a medical certificate for short absences in much the same way: see *Trends in Personnel Practice*, issued by the Office Management Association, 1958. But their allowances of periods of paid sick leave are much less liberal than those of the civil service. In roughly 1 in 4 firms there was no guarantee of sick leave on full pay; it was governed by 'management discretion'. Of the remaining 39 firms who took part in the survey, only 6 promised full pay for as long as six months, and to qualify for this it was necessary to have ten year's service (five years in one case). Allowances of sick leave on half pay were even more restricted in comparison with the civil service.

[2] Over three years nearly 10 per cent. of these 101 men and women had been absent for an annual average of 42 days or more, whereas among their staff as a whole less than 7 per cent. incurred this amount of sick leave in *any one year*, and the percentage whose average for three consecutive years reached this level must have been very much smaller. It is unlikely that there was such a close association between moral and physical infirmity.

suppose that the worst were true, and that a large percentage of civil servants were in the habit of abusing uncertified sick leave in this way. On this assumption, where would one expect to find the heaviest incidence of it? Was this expectation confirmed? If so, was there any other more plausible explanation?

On what I shall call the 'uncharitable hypothesis', we would, I think, expect to find:

(a) that staff groups with smaller allowances of annual leave took more uncertified sick leave; indeed the commonest form in which the hypothesis is stated is that annual leave is 'supplemented' in this way;

(b) that officers who did abuse this concession would do so as near to the limit as they thought prudent; in other words, that there would be a tendency for officers taking 5, 6 or 7 days to be commoner than, on probability, one would expect;

(c) that as civil servants gained experience of the service, and of the extent to which this concession could be abused, their uncertified absences would become more frequent and longer;

(d) that married women, who are subject to more demands from dependants than men or single women, would incur more uncertified sick leave, particularly in the age-groups 25-45, when they probably had the maximum number of children at an age needing maternal care.

Let us see whether any of these predictions are confirmed.

Annual Leave. Before the recommendations of the Priestley Commission altered them, the allowances of annual leave for non-industrial civil servants were:

Administrative Class:	36 days (48 after 10 years' service)
Executive Class (higher grades):	36 days (48 after 15 years' service in a grade eligible for 36)
Executive Class (junior grades):	36 days
Clerical Officers:	24 days
Clerical Assistants:	18 days (21 after 5 years' service)
Shorthand Typists:	21 days (24 after 5 years' service)
Typists:	18 days (21 after 5 years' service).

In practice, the grades which could in theory qualify for 48 days had been restricted during the war to 36 days; this restriction has not been removed. What is more, a large percentage of the Administrative and Executive Classes found themselves unable, during the decade that followed the war, to take even their reduced allowance of 36 days (chiefly because of greater Parliamentary activity). This meant that most Administrators and senior officers in the Executive Class had an unexhausted reserve of at least a day or two at the end of their leave year. Grades with lower allowances, on the other hand, usually managed to exhaust them. Under these circumstances the uncharitable hypothesis would lead us to expect the General Clerical Class to take more uncertified sick leave than the Administrative and Executive Classes, and Clerical Assistants and Typists more than the Clerical Officers.

The table below, which is based on a 3 per cent. random sample[1] covering the eight post-war years before the Priestley Commission's

TABLE 6.02

Mean Days of Uncertified Sick Leave per Man-year during the eight years 1946-53 for the Main Staff Groups
(Based on the 3 per cent. sample)

Staff Group	Mean Days per Man-year		
	Men	Single Women	Married Women
Administrative	0·89	0·71	—
General Executive	1·00	1·34	1·44
General Clerical	1·29	1·73	2·09
Sub-Clerical	1·42	2·09	2·51
Typists	2·38[2]	2·15	2·70

changes, shows that there is a slight tendency in this direction. The lower the grade, the higher the mean amount of uncertified sick leave per man-year. But there are differences between groups whose annual allowances of leave hardly differ—for example, between Administrative and General Executive grades, and between Clerical Assistants and Typists. More important, we shall see later that there is very much the same steady decline in *certified* sick leave as one ascends the grades,

[1] In 1954 it was decided to make a study of the sick-leave behaviour (or 'experience', to use the fashionable term) of different grades and age-groups in the non-industrial civil service. A random sample of about 3 per cent. of the service was compiled by the Treasury, who asked all Departments to extract from their records for the 8 years 1946-53 all absences of established non-industrial staff born on the 19th of every month. The duration of each absence, the diagnosis on the certificate (if any) and the sex, age and grade of the absentee, were punched on Hollerith 80-column cards, each representing one absence (i.e. any period of 1 day or 2 or more consecutive days). Through the courtesy of the Treasury I was given copies of the tables compiled for their purposes, and was able to have one considerable sorting and tabulating operation carried out for mine; I should like to take this opportunity of thanking the staff concerned for their helpfulness in this and other ways. There is still a great deal of useful information which, but for the heavy demands on the time of staff and machines, could have been extracted from the sample: for example, diagnoses have still to be analysed. The information is of such interest to any study of office workers (not merely of civil servants) that I hope that circumstances will allow this to be done before the sample is too out of date.

[2] The sample numbers less than 50.

and that as far as certified sick leave is concerned the differences between the groups are largely removed if we eliminate the differences in the risk of infection from respiratory disorders. In other words, by far the most likely explanation of the differences in table 6.02 is that the lower the grade the greater the risk of catching a cold, largely through working in the same room as a number of other officers.

There is also another small piece of evidence against the hypothesis that allowances of ordinary leave have something to do with uncertified sick leave. One of the questions in my questionnaire asked respondents to place ten potential attractions of their job in rank order. Some of the results of this were interesting—I shall quote one example later in this chapter. But they failed to support the notion that there was a connection between ordinary leave and uncertified sick leave. One of the potential attractions was 'holidays', and 26·0 per cent. of the respondents gave this first or second place out of ten. A comparison of takers of uncertified sick leave with non-takers showed practically no difference between the percentages who gave such a high place to holidays (24·9 per cent. for non-takers, 27·2 for takers). This is not in itself strong evidence; but we shall see later on that the answers to this question are related in at least one way to uncertified sick leave, so that the absence of a positive relationship here is interesting and suggestive.

'Bunching at the Limit'. Is there any sign that takers of uncertified sick leave are going as near as they dare to the permissible maximum of seven days in a twelvemonth? If this were so, we should expect to find what I shall call 'bunching at the limit'. This requires a little explanation. Tables 6.03 and 6.04 show that about half of all civil servants take no uncertified sick leave. If the taking of uncertified sick leave were governed purely by factors such as the actual incidence of infection with colds and so forth, and the recuperative powers of the sufferers, we should expect that the next largest group of civil servants would be those who took only one day off in 365, the next would be those who took two days, and so on in a smoothly declining curve until we reached the smallest group of all—those who took seven days off. If, on the other hand, there were a widespread habit of taking as much uncertified sick leave as one is allowed, the curve would be deformed by a bump somewhere near the seven-day limit—say at five or six days.

To verify the actual distribution from the 3 per cent. sample would have required a considerable sorting operation. But here I was able instead to study the respondents to the questionnaire which I issued to the desk classes in two Ministries in central London.[1] Table 6.03 shows the result. There is no sign here of any bunching towards the seven-day

[1] For a full account of the issue of this questionnaire, and a discussion of the question how representative the respondents were, see Chapter 7.

TURNOVER AND SICK LEAVE

limit, even when the respondents are separated into grades and sexes.[1] The percentages decline smoothly and virtuously from 0 to 7 days.

The only interesting feature of the distribution is the difference between the two Ministries. In the 'Small Ministry' only 41·9 per cent. of the respondents took uncertified sick leave, but in the Large Ministry 50 per cent. did. This difference is too large to be ascribed to chance.[2] Nor can it be due to any differences between the Ministries in the distribution of their respondents among the grades or sexes: for a higher percentage of the Large Ministry's respondents came from the higher grades (see Table 7.02 in Chapter 7), which would lead us to expect a *lower* percentage of takers of uncertified sick leave in the Large Ministry, instead of a higher one; and a lower percentage of their respondents were women, which would also lead us to expect a *lower* percentage of 'takers'. Neither Ministry could discover a reason for this difference: research by the Large Ministry merely suggested that the percentages of 'takers' among these grades was even higher (about 53 per cent.) than among the respondents. I shall return later to this curiosity.

TABLE 6.03

Uncertified Sick Leave of Respondents to Questionnaire G.G. 59 from two Ministries

	N[3]	Days of Uncertified Sick Leave in last convenient Period of Twelve Months							
		None %	1 %	2 %	3 %	4 %	5 %	6 %	7 %
Large Ministry	780	50·0	15·9	14·6	9·4	4·7	3·0	1·8	0·6
Small Ministry	310	58·1	14·7	13·1	5·8	5·3	1·3	1·0	0·7
Civil servants in both	1090	52·3	15·5	14·2	8·4	4·9	2·5	1·6	0·6
Grades (men only). Administrative	90	66·7	11·5	10·3	9·2	2·3	—	—	—
Executive above H.E.O.	90	68·4	8·7	10·9	5·4	1·1	3·3	1·1	1·1
H.E.O. and E.O.	310	52·0	18·7	13·9	8·7	2·6	1·9	1·6	0·6
C.O., C.O. (Sec.) and C.A.	430	48·1	13·5	14·0	12·6	7·7	1·4	2·7	—
Women (H.E.O., E.O., C.O., C.O. (Sec.) and C.A.) Single Women	220	44·5	17·1	17·1	6·8	7·2	5·0	1·4	0·9
Married Women	50	30·2	17·0	28·3	5·6	7·6	5·6	3·8	1·9

[1] The small peaks at 5 days for Executives above H.E.O., and at 4 days for women H.E.O.s and E.O.s are probably chance effects: they are certainly too slight to form the basis for any conclusions.

[2] The probability of its occurring by chance is less than 1 in 50.

[3] Numbers are approximate to nearest 10, they exclude 'spoilt' answers, the numbers of which vary slightly from one question to another.

I

Uncertified Sick Leave and Age. Is it true that officers with more experience of the civil service take uncertified sick leave more frequently, or that their absences are longer? I could not get from the 3 per cent. sample any analysis of such absences by length of service, but what I could get was an analysis by age-groups; and age is of course closely linked with length of service.[1] Table 6.04 shows three things.

TABLE 6.04

Uncertified Sick Leave by Sexes and Age-groups, 1946-1953

(Based on the 3 per cent. sample[2])

Age-Group	Absentees per 1,000			Mean Absences per Absentee			Mean Days of each Absence		
	Men	Single Women	Married Women	Men	Single Women	Married Women	Men	Single Women	Married Women
55-9[1]	400	510	669	1·71	1·81	1·90	1·47	1·52	1·45
50-4	428	525	743	1·70	1·82	2·12	1·46	1·51	1·37
45-9	435	568	693	1·74	1·88	2·24	1·41	1·43	1·39
40-4	443	588	689	1·82	1·90	2·36	1·35	1·43	1·34
35-9	474	572	746	1·84	1·98	2·34	1·34	1·44	1·43
30-4	499	621	749	1·91	2·07	2·34	1·34	1·40	1·34
25-9	501	650	764	2.00	2·23	2·70	1·32	1·37	1·27
20-4	482	674	777	2·08	2·42	2·98	1·28	1·32	1·26
15-9	433	692	782	2·47	2·87	2·97	1·25	1·26	1·28
All Ages[3]	446	620	736	1·83	2·22	2·51	1·38	1·37	1·32

Columns 1-3 show how many officers per 1,000 actually took uncertified sick leave of any length. Notice that less than half the men, less than two-thirds of the single women and less than three-quarters of the married women did so. More interesting still, the percentage that did so *declined* as age (and therefore, in most cases, length of service) increased. The one exception is the slight increase in the percentage of men until a peak is reached in the 25-9 age-group, after which it declines like the women's percentage. Columns 4-6 shows how many

[1] An analysis of the sick leave of 939 Postmen (Higher Grade) in 1947 and 1950 was, however, carried out by the Post Office, who separated them into groups with roughly mean equal ages, but with different lengths of service. It was found that while their certified sick leave showed no definite trend as length of service increased, their mean days of uncertified absence *decreased*, just as it does with age in the 3 per cent. sample.

[2] The staff groups covered include not only the desk classes, but also the inspectorate, messengers, professional scientific and technical civil servants, and supervisory and manipulative grades in the Post Office.

[3] Higher age-groups are not shown, because of the selective effect of retirement, but are included in the rates for 'all ages'.

absences, on average, were taken by each absentee; this is highest in the teens, and thereafter goes steadily down, for both sexes. The only consistent increases are found in Columns 7-9, which show the mean length of each absence; and the most likely explanation of this is simply that with increasing age one takes a little longer to recover from even short-term illnesses such as colds. The *decreases* in Columns 1-6 are the opposite of what we should expect on the uncharitable hypothesis. The explanation of the decrease is no doubt that as age increases the percentage of illnesses for which uncertified absence is sufficient becomes less; in other words, they turn into certified sick leave, which, as we shall see, *increases* with age.

Married Women. In the tables dealing with uncertified sick leave it is clear that single women make more use of it than men, and that married women make even more use of it than single women. These differences are of course found in the sick-leave statistics for practically all occupations, not only in uncertified but also in certified sick leave. Table 6.03 shows that the same difference is found among the women respondents to my questionnaire from the desk grades of the two Ministries. A large percentage of women's short-term absence—absences, that is, of one or two consecutive days—is no doubt attributable to minor menstrual disorder. The difference, however, between the short absences of single and married women, though it is also a feature of most occupations,[1] is harder to explain as a purely physiological phenomenon. A much higher percentage (73.6 per cent.) of married women of all ages than of single women (62.0 per cent.) incurred absences, and the married women who did incur them averaged 2.51 absences each compared with the single women's 2.22.[2] What is more, whereas the average number of absences for each single woman absentee declined steadily—and if anything more steeply than the men's absences—the married women's absences, after an initial decline, stayed at about 2.35 throughout the thirties and early forties—more or less the fifteen years when they may be expected to have young families to care for. Even more interesting is the fact that while more married women than single incurred absences, and incurred more each, their absences were actually *shorter*, not longer as we should expect if their health were really under greater strain. These frequent but short absences—most of them of one day only—are what one would expect if one thinks of the sudden demands made upon married women by unexpected domestic crises, such as the illness of a child. For the first

---

[1] See, for example, *Health in Industry* (Butterworth, 1956), by the Medical Officers of the London Transport Executive, which contains sick-leave figures for male, single female and married female clerical staff that are interesting to compare with those of the civil service.

[2] Since these are means based on several thousand absences, the difference is more significant than it looks.

day of the crisis she has to cope with it herself, but by the second she has usually managed to make some arrangement with a relative or neighbour that will let her get back to work. Most Departments are willing to grant a day or two's special leave with pay in cases of urgent domestic trouble. No doubt many married women do make use of this concession. But special leave calls for more explanations than uncertified sick leave, and so tends to be regarded as a last resort, to be used only when other kinds of leave have been exhausted.

To sum up the evidence for any widespread abuse of uncertified sick leave among the desk grades: there is only one point—the greater amount of uncertified absence among grades with less annual leave—at which it is consistent with this hypothesis; and this difference is much more likely to be due to the greater risk of respiratory infection among these grades. On the other hand, the statistics for married women are not easy to explain on any other hypothesis. With these exceptions, the evidence that I have been able to collect is against any prevalence of abuse among any of the desk grades. This is not of course to say that there are no individuals, or even small groups here and there, who abuse this concession. But it does not seem to be sufficiently common to have any real effect on the statistics.

As for the possibility that married women are using the concession in the way I have suggested, is it one about which we should be very concerned? The point is not, of course, what moral attitude we should take towards such a practice (although if it were we should no doubt have less condemnation for the married woman who takes a day off to look after a sick child than for the man who does so in order to attend a football match). The question is whether the practice is a symptom of a state of affairs that we should want to remedy. It is certainly not a sign of dissatisfaction with conditions of work, or of any pathological attitude towards the job. It is merely a symptom of being a married woman in employment. Whether it is convenient for her employer or not, her first loyalty is almost always to her family responsibilities. If it is very inconvenient to him, the most he can do is to avoid taking on married women; a less drastic alternative is to place those with records of frequent and sudden absences in posts where these will not cause too much disorganisation.

Job-satisfaction. As I have already pointed out, however, we must distinguish between conscious abuse of this concession and the possibility that the amount of sick leave which one takes is influenced by one's interest in and enjoyment of one's work. As everyone knows, if you enjoy your work it takes a more severe attack of flu to make you stay away than if you dislike what you have to do. To what extent, if any, does this affect uncertified sick leave in the service? Here again the respondents to my questionnaire provided the best obtainable evidence. Table 6.05 divides them, according to their replies to Question 60, into

TABLE 6.05

Uncertified Sick Leave and Job-satisfaction

This table shows the days of uncertified sick leave taken by civil service respondents[3] to Questionnaire GG 59, analysed into three groups, according to their replies to the question on job-satisfaction. Actual and expected percentages (in parentheses) are shown. Expected percentages are calculated from the distribution of the three job-satisfaction groups among the grades, and from the different sick leave experience of each grade. Note how close the actual and expected percentages are for those who are neither particularly satisfied nor particularly dissatisfied, and how different they are for the two extreme groups.

Job-Satisfaction Group	N	Days of Uncertified Sick Leave in Twelve Months		
		0	1-3	4-7
		%	%	%
Satisfied	264	59·1 (53·6)	32·9 (36·9)	8·0 (9.5)
In between	675	51·8 (52·3)	38·7 (38·2)	9·5 (9·5)
Dissatisfied	139	41·0 (49·8)	45·3 (39·8)	13·7 (10·4)

three groups—the 25 per cent. whose replies showed a high degree of satisfaction with their jobs, the 13 per cent. who evidently had little enthusiasm for their work, and the 62 per cent. who fell between these extremes.[1] It shows that the tendency to take uncertified sick leave is very much stronger among those who have little liking for their jobs. Not only do more of these people take uncertified sick leave, but when they do they take more days of it. On the other hand, there was no sign of a tendency among them to bunch towards the seven-day limit; the most that could be said is that they showed a tendency (which the others did not) to take two days rather than one,[2] thus

Days: 0 1 2 3 4 5 6 7

% 41·0 12·2 21·6 11·5 7·9 2·2 2·2 1·4

In other words, while their lack of enjoyment of their jobs is clearly linked with the amount of their uncertified sick leave, there is no convincing evidence that they are consciously regulating the amount according to the permissible maximum.

[1] For a discussion of the job-satisfaction scale which was used, and of the distribution of replies, see Chapter 8.
[2] Not necessarily consecutively, although no doubt this was frequently so.
[3] No sick leave information about the Companies' respondents was available.

It was therefore encouraging to find confirmation of these tendencies in the way in which respondents to the questionnaire ranked the attractions of their jobs. One potential attraction which they were asked to rank was 'interest of the work'. Out of non-takers of uncertified sick leave, 38·8 per cent. ranked this first or second out of ten places; out of takers, only 24·2 per cent. did so, and out of takers of 4 to 7 days, only 15·3 per cent. did so. There seems, therefore, to be a very strong relationship of some sort between interest in one's work and uncertified sick leave, at least so far as the desk grades are concerned.[1]

Efficiency. As we saw in Chapter 4, the two most important components of the rather confused concept called 'morale' are job-satisfaction and efficiency. We have just seen that there is a relationship between the former of these and uncertified sick leave. Is uncertified sick leave also related to efficiency? Here again the best obtainable evidence is based on the response to my questionnaire. I was able (as I shall explain in Chapter 8) to divide the respondents, according to certain ratings in the annual reports on them by their superiors, into four groups: those who were outstandingly above average in the performance of their duties, those who were above average, those who were just below average, and those who were well below. The table below shows how these were distributed according to their uncertified sick leave:

TABLE 6.06

Distribution of Civil Service Respondents to Questionnaire GG 59 according to their Efficiency Rating[2] and Uncertified Sick Leave

Efficiency Rating[2]	Days of Uncertified Sick Leave in 12 Months							
	(N)	0	1	2	3	4	5	6	7
		%	%	%	%	%	%	%	%
1 (highest)	(30)	56·6	16·7	13·3	6·7	6·7	—	—	—
2	(456)	50·0	19·0	14·0	8·8	3·3	2·2	1·8	0·9
3	(462)	48·8	14·1	15·0	8·9	7·4	3·5	1·9	0·4
4 (lowest in actual use)	(42)	52·4	11·9	19·0	9·5	2·4	2·4	—	2·4
5	(0)	—	—	—	—	—	—	—	—

Unfortunately, the numbers of respondents who were rated either very high or very low were so small that it is hard to be sure which differences between these groups are due to chance, and which are significant. If ratings 1 and 2 (i.e. the more efficient half of the respondents) and

---

[1] Curiously, however, as we shall see, the connection between the interest of the work and *certified* sick leave was of the opposite kind.

[2] As awarded by their superior officer in his annual report: see Chapter 8.2.

ratings 3 and 4 (the less efficient half) are combined, the result is that there is practically no difference between the percentages of non-takers of uncertified sick leave, which are 50·4 per cent. for the more efficient half, and 49·0 per cent. for the others. The only significant difference is to be found in the percentages who take 4 to 7 days: 8·0 per cent. for the more efficient, 12·7 for the less efficient.[1] On the other hand, this pattern—practically equal percentages of non-takers, and higher percentages of takers of 4 to 7 days, persists even when we break down the respondents into separate groups for each Ministry and each sex so that it is most unlikely to be due to chance.

At first sight it is surprising that there is not a stronger connection between uncertified sick leave and efficiency, if there is such a definite relationship between it and job-satisfaction. But we shall see in Chapter 8 that the relationship between efficiency and job-satisfaction is by no means what one would imagine.

I also examined the replies to the questionnaire to see whether takers of uncertified sick leave showed any greater tendency than non-takers to believe

(i) that their work had 'a bad effect on their health', 'physically' or 'mentally';
(ii) that they were more hardworked in comparison with 'most other people in their office at their level'.

There were no really significant tendencies of this kind. Indeed, there was a slight tendency for takers of 4 to 7 days to include a *smaller* percentage of those who thought themselves hardworked (29 *v.* 36 per cent.), but the probability of this difference occurring by chance was rather too high—slightly greater than 1 in 10.

To sum up what has been established so far. Uncertified sick leave is fairly certainly an index of something more than the mere incidence of respiratory infections and other minor disorders among the desk grades. This is not to deny that most of it is due to this cause. But there is clearly an association between it and the interest and enjoyment which the civil servant finds in his work. We cannot, of course, be completely certain that it is the interest and enjoyment that influences his sick leave; it is after all possible that people whose health makes more short absences necessary are also people who find their work less interesting and enjoyable. Only an experiment in which officers with a high rate of uncertified sick leave were transferred to work that seemed likely to be more interesting to them, and officers with low rates were transferred to less interesting posts, would remove the uncertainty; and it is an experiment which it would not be difficult for Departments to carry out, in view of the very great frequency with which civil servants are moved from post to post.

[1] The probability of obtaining such a difference by chance is about 1 in 50.

Certified Sick Leave

We must now turn to the more intricate subject of certified sick leave. To judge by the 3 per cent. sample, the average male civil servant takes 11·6 days off with a doctor's certificate in every twelve months (and 1·1 days without one). The average single woman in the service takes 12·6 days with a certificate (1·9 without one); and the married woman takes 18·8 (2·45 without one).[1]

In the section on uncertified sick leave I have already commented on the position of married women. Like their short absences, their longer ones exceed in days per woman-year those of single women and still more those of men. They form an increasing percentage (27 per cent. by 1958) of all the women in the service, who in turn make up some 26 per cent. of all established non-industrial civil servants (and 30 per cent. of all non-industrial civil servants, including those who are unestablished). But having made the suggestion that their short-term sick leave is strongly influenced by their family crises, I do not think that much is to be gained by continuing to include references to their sick-leave behaviour in the rest of this chapter. The medical vicissitudes of married women are complicated by confinements and menopausal disorders which have little to do with the conditions of their work, and will merely distract us from the question we are considering, which is the extent to which certified sick leave is a symptom of attitudes to work. In this section, therefore, 'women' means single women,[2] unless anything is said to the contrary.

As in other occupations, the average number of days of sick leave

---

[1] For comparison with the rates of other office workers, I cannot find anything better than the figures for technical and clerical workers in the London Transport Executive which are published in *Health in Industry*. These cover the years 1950-52 (i.e. towards the end of the period of the 3 per cent. sample). The staff concerned had to produce medical certificates for absences of more than three days; and they were limited to 13 weeks on full pay and 13 weeks on half pay in any twelve months. The average number of days absence per man-year for male technical and clerical staff was about 9·6 (compared with the male civil servant's total of 12·7): for unmarried female clerical staff it was 11·5 (compared with 14·5 in the civil service); and for married female clerical staff it was 17·5 compared with 21·2 in the civil service). Part of the explanation may lie in differences in average age; it is likely that the L.T.E. women had a lower average age than women in the civil service; but the men's average age was just over forty-four, which—if we may judge by the Ministries who took part in my questionnaire—cannot be much below the average for male civil servants. It is also possible that medical standards for entrants to the L.T.E.'s employment were higher; they certainly involved a medical examination for all entrants. Against this possibility must be set the fact that many of the civil servants were employed in healthier localities than London, which has a very high degree of air-pollution. We cannot, I am afraid, exclude a strong probability that the civil service's more generous allowance of sick leave on full and half pay is an important contributory factor.

[2] Including widows and divorcées who have not remarried.

TABLE 6.07

Age and Total[1] Sick Leave of Established Non-Industrial Civil Servants

(Based on the 3 per cent. sample)

Age-group	Mean Days per Man-year	
	Men	Single Women
75-9[2]	106·00[3]	64·00[3]
70-4[2]	16·46[3]	21·06[3]
65-9[2]	17·95	21·02[3]
60-4	18·69	23·49
55-9	17·42	19·71
50-4	15·30	17·56
45-9	13·24	15·29
40-4	10·81	13·32
35-9	10·17	12·61
30-4	9·54	12·71
25-9	8·55	13·50
20-4	9·05	15·25
15-9	9·50	12·58
All ages . . .	12·74	14·49
Total number of sample	69,640	22,608

increases with age, as Table 6.07 demonstrates. This table has only two interesting features. One is the way in which the sick leave of men *declines* in the twenties, before beginning the steady upward climb which is normal.[4] This may be due to the intake of fit young men in their early twenties—for example, fresh from National Service; or, as someone suggested to me, the explanation may be that in their teens they are more likely to be subject to maternal discipline and care, which makes them take days off for minor complaints. A third possibility is that it takes them a year or two to acquire maximum resistance to the respiratory infections which are so common among office workers. The other anomaly in Table 6·07 is the tendency of women in their twenties to do just the opposite; their sick leave *increases* in their twenties, and falls again almost to the level of their teens, and it is not until their late thirties that it begins its upward climb. There is a similar hump in the London Transport Executive's figures for the sick leave of female

---

[1] i.e. certified and uncertified.
[2] In these age-groups the retirement of the less fit has, of course, a selective effect upon sick leave.
[3] The sample totals less than 50 for these groups.
[4] There is no anomaly of this kind in the London Transport Executives figures for male clerical and technical staff in *Health in Industry*.

clerical staff. Unfortunately separate figures for the different categories of disorder were not available from the 3 per cent. sample for the civil service; but the London Transport Executive's publication includes tables for the commoner disorders, and shows that as far as women are concerned a hump in the twenties appears in the curves for the common cold, bronchitis, 'diseases of women'[1] and functional nervous disorders.

On the other hand, this hump does not seem to be a feature of morbidity in the female working population as a whole. The Ministry of Pensions and National Insurance allowed me to consult their tables showing days of incapacity per thousand of the population at risk, analysed by sexes, age-groups and diagnoses. These showed that while there was a sharp increase in days of incapacity as women passed from their teens into the early twenties (6·1 per woman in the teens, 9·6 for the age group 20-4), the rate continued to increase, instead of falling again. By far the largest single contributor to the 9·6 days was respiratory tuberculosis, which alone accounted for 1·2 days. Although the rate for this continued to increase among the higher age-groups, this was due not to an increasing attack-rate but to the cumulative effect of the long and recurrent absences from work which are associated with this disorder. Men's absences with this diagnosis amounted to only 0·6 days per person in the same age-group—less than half the women's rate. The Ministry's tables also confirmed that minor respiratory disorders, such as the common cold, and acute tonsillitis and pharyngitis, together with the anaemias (a 'disease of women') showed massive humps that did not appear among the men. It seems unnecessary to look further for an explanation. Part of the hump in women's twenties seems to be attributable to minor respiratory disorders and gynaecological complaints, the rest to tuberculosis. The explanation of the *decrease* that follows may well be that women with long absences due to tuberculosis would be the very ones who would disappear from the later age-groups, having died or been retired on medical grounds.

A much more interesting feature of the tables from the 3 per cent. sample was the marked differences between the rate for the different staff groups, of which the most important are given in Table 6.08. There is no tendency here for grades with the more responsible jobs to take more sick leave. On the contrary, the higher the grade the lower the number of days of sick leave per man-year.[2] But before we jump from this observation to the conclusion that the responsibility and interest of the work of the Administrative and other higher grades preserves them from some of the ills that afflict the lower grades, we must consider several other possibilities.

[1] i.e. International Code Numbers 620-89.
[2] Women administrators cannot be regarded as an exception to this generalisation since the sample in their case was too small.

TABLE 6.08

Relationship between Staff Group and Total Sick Leave among Non-industrial Civil Servants

(Based on the 3 per cent. sample)

Staff Group[1]	Mean Days per Man-year	
	Men	Single Women
Administrative	7·89	18·18[2]
General Executive	9·58	10·87
General Clerical	12·12	13·88
Sub-clerical	17·28	16·39
Typing	32·88[2]	15·66
Inspectorate	7·20	11·21
Messengers, etc.	15·90	18·55
Professional, Scientific and Technical (Grade I)	6·01	7·95
Scientific and Technical (II)	9·14	11·96
Ancillary Technical	11·00	16·52

For example, if medical standards for entry into the lower staff groups were less exacting, members of these groups might be expected to fall ill more often or more severely. But what I learned from the Civil Service Commission seemed to rule this out as an important factor. The only classes for which they deliberately demand a higher standard of health are those whose members will probably have to serve abroad—for example, the Foreign and Colonial Services. Otherwise the standard is the same for all grades. The civil servants in the 3 per cent. sample who had been recruited between the wars would all have undergone a medical examination. Those who had entered as temporary civil servants during the 1939-45 war, and had later been admitted to 'established' status, would have had their records for the previous year or two examined to see whether they had incurred any long periods of sick leave: those who had were medically examined. This seemed quite as stringent a test as an automatic medical examination. The current system by which would-be Clerical Assistants, Clerical Officers or Executive Officers simply fill in a 'health declaration' denying or admitting that they have suffered from certain disorders, and are examined by a doctor only if their history seems to call for it, was not introduced until after the period covered by the 3 per cent. sample (1946-53). The only grade which was likely to be a bigger 'health risk' was the Messenger's, which included a large number of disabled ex-servicemen from both wars; but it is worth noting that the male Messenger's rate was not quite as high as that of the male sub-clerical.

[1] Certain staff groups, such as the Departmental Executive and Clerical Classes, are omitted in order to simplify the table, to which they are not essential for our present purpose.

[2] The sample numbers less than 50 for these groups.

We must also consider the extent to which the lower grades, with their lower incomes, may have suffered from lower standards of medical care, and of living generally. As far as medical care is concerned, the vast majority of those represented in Table 6.08 must have made use of the National Health Service from 1949 (if not 1948) onwards; and the figures for these years of the 3 per cent. sample show the same differences between the staff groups. The effect of lower standards of nutrition and housing can only be guessed at, not measured; I can only say that I doubt whether they account for differences between staff groups with salaries so close as were those, for example, of the Executive and Administrative Classes during this period.

But at least two other possibilities have to be considered. One is that differences in the age composition of the various groups are wholly or partly responsible: we have seen that the sick rate increases very substantially with age, at least after the twenties. The other possibility is that the conditions under which the lower grades work expose them more frequently to respiratory infections. We have already seen how important a part the common cold and other minor infections play in the sick leave of young women. But few people realise that over one-quarter of all sick leave in the service is due to colds, influenza and other *minor* infections of the nose, throat and lungs.

It seemed to me, however, that there was a way in which the 3 per cent. sample could be used to test the effect of age composition and varying risk of respiratory infection; and as the point was an important one I persuaded the Treasury to devote some of the time of their extremely busy Hollerith machines and staff to this task. We selected three consecutive years (1949, 1950 and 1951) during which the National Health Service was in operation, but before the Great Smog of 1953 (which so sharply increased the incidence of bronchitis and other respiratory complaints). From the 3 per cent. sample we took all the cards that represented an absence for a minor respiratory disorder, and found the total number of such absences and their average duration for each separate ten-year age-group of each separate staff group. This enabled me to standardise the average duration of each absence in such a way as to eliminate the effect of the different age compositions of the staff groups. In addition, since we had selected only cards that represented absences for minor respiratory disorders, we were dealing only with cases of officers who had in fact been infected; in other words, whatever the chances of their being infected had been, these were the absences of those whom chance *had* selected.

It may be asked why I chose minor respiratory disorders and did not simply study the figures for some other non-infective disorder. In the first place, no other group of disorders was nearly as frequent; the respiratory disorders gave me the best chance of securing a substantial number of representatives of each staff group (as it was, there were too few women administrators). In the second place, this group of disorders is one from which, as a rule, people recover, and recover quickly: and what I wanted to see was how long they took to *return to work*. If the interest and responsibility of the work helped to determine the amount of certified sick leave, this should show itself in the time which different grades took to get back to their desks, particularly after a type of illness which is usually not very severe or alarming.

The result, as Table 6.09 shows, was very interesting indeed. The pattern of Table 6.08, with its steady decrease of sick leave as one ascended the staff groups, had completely disappeared. Instead, most of the staff groups were very close to the means for the non-industrial civil service as a whole. In other words, whatever a civil servant's grade when he gets influenza or bronchitis, he takes roughly the same number of days to get back to work. The only striking observation was that women take, on average, a day *less*, although, as we have seen, their annual quota of certified sick leave is greater than the men's.

TABLE 6.09

Mean Duration of Absences for Minor Respiratory Disorders occurring in 1949, 1950 and 1951 in the different Staff Groups of the Established Non-industrial Civil Service
(Based on the 3 per cent. sample, and standardised for age)

Staff Groups	Mean Duration of Absence in Days (number of absences in parenthesis)	
	Men	Women
Administrative	13·5 (28)	—
General Executive	14·2 (509)	13·8 (146)
General Clerical	13·4 (1,152)	13·0 (633)
Sub-clerical	15·4 (153)	12·0 (535)
Typing	—	12·2 (395)
Inspectorate	13·4 (33)	19·9 (9)
Messengers	15·5 (383)	19·7 (12)
Professional, Scientific and Technical (Grade I)	13·2 (218)	12·7 (6)
Scientific and Technical II	13·4 (416)	13·5 (44)
Ancillary Technical	13·3 (203)	12·0 (139)
Post Office Supervisory and Manipulative	13·3 (3,287)	12·3 (987)
Departmental Executive	12·4 (458)	14·3 (52)
Departmental Clerical	13·7 (467)	12·7 (193)
All groups	13·6 (7,307)	12·7 (3,151)

The uniformity is not quite complete. We ought probably to disregard the apparently long absences of the women inspectors, messengers and professional and scientific staff; for their numbers in this sample are small. Probably the only figure for women that is significantly above the mean is that for women in the General Executive Class, who take 1·2 days more than the typical woman civil servant to come back to work. Their male colleagues, too, take a little longer, but only 0·6 days more than the mean. Among the men, the long absences were found among the sub-clericals and messengers; and the latter, as we have seen, are likely to have a lower standard of health because they include so many disabled ex-servicemen. On the whole, however, it is remarkable how little deviation there is from the means. Table 6·09 demonstrates the deceptiveness of Table 6.08 for our purpose.

In different Ministries. It seemed possible, however, that although there was little difference between the staff groups there might be differences between Ministries. The Acton Society Trust, for example (*loc. cit.*), claimed to have found differences between the sickness absences of shop assistants and factory staff which were related to the size of the organisation; and although, as I have argued, it is not possible, on the evidence as published, to be sure that the differences are not geographical and connected with variations in the degree of local air-pollution, this was obviously a possibility that must be investigated.

A table had been compiled from the 3 per cent. sample which showed separately for a large number of Ministries their mean days of total sick leave per man-year for each of the eight years of the sample. There were two rather unfortunate deficiencies in these tables. One was that they did not distinguish uncertified from certified sick leave; it would have been very interesting to see whether uncertified sick leave varied with the Ministry. The other pity was that in compiling the 3 per cent. sample no steps had been taken to make sure that the very small Departments—those with less than 2,000 staff each—had been properly represented.[1] Perhaps for this reason these had been lumped together as one group in the tables; but even if they could have been separated the numbers in the sample for Departments of only a few hundred staff would have been far too small (the whole sample for Departments with less than 2,000 staff was less than 50 for each of the eight years).

I also decided that I must exclude Ministries in which either

(i) a large percentage of the staff are engaged on out-of-door work which is likely to raise their standard of health above that of the sedentary office-worker;

or (ii) a large percentage were stationed outside London, where the high degree of air-pollution is associated with a high rate of respiratory disorders. No doubt staff in Newcastle-on-Tyne, for example, were not free from the effects of air-pollution, but differences of degree (or of climate) might very well reduce the effect of this upon their health.

---

[1] For the purpose for which the sample had been taken, there was no point in designing it for a thorough separate analysis of the sick leave of all the numerous small Departments.

TURNOVER AND SICK LEAVE

I therefore excluded

> The County Courts Department, whose officers are scattered throughout the county towns of England;
>
> the Ministry of National Insurance (as it then was), which had large blocks of staff at Newcastle-on-Tyne and Blackpool;
>
> the Forestry Commission, many of whose staff live a hardy sylvan life;
>
> the Ordnance Survey, many of whose staff are tramping the contour-lines of Britain;

I also excluded the Post Office because its sick rates had already been found to have some unusual features; this was of course by far the largest of all the Departments, with some 350,000 staff.

Even so, I was still left with twenty Ministries, ranging from those with just over 2,000 non-industrial staff to one with 50,000. Their sick rates varied considerably: the highest for both sexes, 14·14 days, was about 66 per cent. above the lowest, 8·49, and the range among the men was even wider. Inspection suggested that there was some slight tendency for the larger Departments to have a higher rate, but calculation showed that the relationship was negligible.[1]

So far, there was no confirmation of any relationship between size and sick leave.[2] But we have been dealing with the sizes of organisations 'on paper'. These sizes are not like the sizes of staffs in shops or factories which are all located on one site. It was quite possible that while the 'size of formal organisation' (as I shall call it)[3] has nothing to do with sick leave, the latter might be related to size in one or both of two other senses. It might be related, as the Acton Society's Trust observations suggested, to the total numbers of staff working at the same location; I shall call this the 'size of office'.[3] Or it might be related to the size of the much smaller groups in which individuals actually did their work —for example, to the size of a Branch or Division in a Ministry; I shall call this 'size of working unit'.[3] After all, if numbers of staff did have some mysterious effect upon sick rates, this was probably mediated in some way by the staff's consciousness of size. If so, someone who belonged to a Ministry that was small in total size, but which was wholly located in one large building, would probably have a stronger feeling of the enormousness of the unit to which he belonged than a member of a really large Ministry who worked with a few other staff in

---

[1] For men, $r=0.05$; for women, $r=0.03$, which are not significant.

[2] Nor could I see any other factor with which the differences between Ministries seemed to be linked. I even considered whether the age of the Ministry might have anything to do with it; but found low rates among Ministries with a long history—such as the Admiralty and Home Office—as well as among recent creations, such as DSIR!

[3] As I cannot find these clearly distinguished anywhere else, I am afraid that I must coin my own terms for them.

a small detached office. What impressed the C.O.s in Records Branch at Benton was not the enormous size of their Ministry but the enormous size of their Branch. Here the 3 per cent. sample could not help. As for the large and the small Ministries which provided the respondents to my questionnaire, comparison of their certified sick leave showed a remarkable similarity rather than any difference. It was only their uncertified sick leave that showed any sign of being more frequent in the large Ministry, as we have already seen.

The Post Office, however, were interested in this point. Not only have they taken an interest in the sick leave of their staff for longer than almost any other organisation in this country (their sickness records go well back into the nineteenth century); they also believed that their sick rates for units such as Head-Postmasters' Offices showed this relationship with size. Unfortunately these rates were open to two objections. First, they were rates for a varied assortment of grades and occupations, of which the proportions varied from one office to another; and we have seen how differing exposure to infection can affect sick rates. Secondly, like the Acton Society Trust's units, these offices were scattered throughout Britain, some in areas with high air-pollution, and some—usually the smaller offices—in rural areas with less air-pollution.[1]

The Post Office were very helpful, however, and allowed me to select and examine sick-leave returns from those rendered by all their different units in London. By limiting my selection to London I was doing my best to eliminate differences in the degree of air-pollution and other environmental conditions that might affect health. Another principle of my selection was to take only those offices where all or practically all of the total staff shown on the return actually worked at one address. From these I selected only those where members of the desk grades were to be found. It was slightly unfortunate that the returns treated clerical, executive and administrative staff as one group; but mindful of the way in which I had reduced the sick rates for minor respiratory disorders among the staff groups to a uniform level, I realised that I could probably reduce to a negligible level any differences due to differing proportions of different grades by calculating what I call 'the sick rate for the sick'. To obtain this, the total days of sickness for the group are divided not by the total number of members at risk (this would give the ordinary sick rate) but by the number of those who actually incurred sickness. I could not, I am afraid, eliminate the possible—but presumably not very large—effects of different age compositions among the desk grades in my selected offices; but it seemed

---

[1] Indeed, in an effort to eliminate the effect of differing risks of infection I calculated the sick rate for the sick alone—i.e. the mean days of total sickness per head *for those who incurred sickness*, and made the odd discovery that while the women's rate increased with size of formal organisation, the men's actually *decreased*!

reasonable to expect that chance would do this. This process of selection left me with the twelve offices shown in Table 6.10, ranging in size from one employing 90 staff of various grades to the giant office with 6,410 staff. The clerical, executive and higher staff employed at them amounted to 3,461. In size and range, therefore, the sample was very satisfactory; and I think that my method of selection went further towards eliminating unwanted factors than any previous test of this hypothesis.

It was therefore interesting to find that there was a definite relationship between the total size of the staff at each office ('size of office') and the 'sick rate for the sick'. The larger the staff, the higher tended to be the mean days of sickness per annum taken by the sick of both sexes although as Table 6.10 shows there were exceptions.[1] At first sight it also suggested that there might be a close relationship between the sick rates for the sick and the numbers of clerical and higher staff; in other words, that their sick rates were related to the number of their colleagues in the desk grades working in the same building. But the connection here was very slight.[2] On the other hand, the ordinary sick rates for both men and women (i.e. days of sickness divided by staff at risk) also showed a strong relationship to size of total staff, although not quite as strong as did the sick rate for the sick. In other words, Table 6.10 seems to demonstrate that in some way the size of the total number of staff working in the same building is positively related both to the mean number of days of sickness per desk worker per annum and to the number of days of sickness per sick desk worker per annum. The first of these relationships might conceivably be explained by the greater risk of infections of various kinds among larger blocks of staff; but the second can hardly be.

I would very much have liked to be able to see whether this relationship held good not only for total sickness but also for uncertified sickness. But uncertified sickness was not shown separately on the returns, and to ask for this information to be specially rendered for some 3,400 men and women would have caused a great deal of work. We saw that respondents to my questionnaire from the Large Ministry's headquarters took significantly more uncertified sick leave than those from the Small Ministry, and that there seemed to be no obvious explanation of this. On the basis of only two Ministries, together with the connection between certified sick leave and size in the Post Office units, it seems distinctly possible that this is another example of the 'size effect'.

I should perhaps emphasise that what Table 6.10 does *not* show is

---

[1] The correlations between numbers of all staff and the sick rates for the sick were
for men, $r = 0.60$,
for women, $r = 0.63$.
Both correlations are too large to be attributed to chance.

[2] $r = 0.08$ for men.

TABLE 6.10

Relationship between Staff Complements and Sick Rate for the Sick in twelve Post Office units in Greater London

Unit	Postal District	Average No. of *all* Staff			Clerical, Executive and Higher Staff					
					Men			Women		
		Men	Women	Both	Employed	Taking Sick Leave	Sick Rate of Sick[1] (days)	Employed	Taking Sick Leave	Sick Rate of Sick[1] (days)
A	E.C. 1	47	43	90	40	28	8·2	31	24	12·3
B	N.W. 1	80	20	100	26	13	14·4	8	7	15·6
C	W.C. 2	75	39	114	61	34	10·4	26	18	10·2
D	E.C. 4	214	121	335	195	118	8·2	93	69	18·4
E	N.W. 2	361	4	365	6	5	5·0	4	2	4·5
F	E.C. 1	464	71	535	287	164	12·6	28	16	21·7
G	N.W. 2	840	60	900	17	14	12·1	17	14	14·9
H	N. 1	898	199	1,097[2]	143	97	20·7	62	50	10·8
I	E.C. 1	881	422	1,303	704	393	12·5	275	188	14·1
J	N. 7	548	1,369	1,917	478	387	15·0	736	593	19·3
K	S.W. 1	2,750	569	3,319	69	38	23·9	42	37	17·8
L	E.C. 1	6,296	114	6,410[2]	92	61	17·5	21	17	25·5

[1] I.e., mean days of certified and uncertified sickness absence in 1958 per officer taking sick leave.

[2] Some of the staff of each of these units worked in separate buildings near the main one. Their sickness absences could not be distinguished from those of the other staff, but if their numbers are deducted from the totals of staff the correlation coefficients are slightly higher.

whether there is a relationship between sick rates and size of working unit. This would be even more difficult to test than the hypothesis which we have just confirmed, and in my discussions with different Departments I could come across no situations which seemed to lend themselves to a test of this sort. I do think, however, that the hypothesis becomes rather less probable in the light of Table 6.10. For it would lead us to expect that sick rates would be fairly closely related to numbers of staff *of the same grade* working at the same location, although this is not necessarily the same thing as the size of the immediate group of which the individual feels himself part (and in large offices is almost certainly not the same thing). But as we have just seen, this relationship is not at all close. Indeed, since the larger offices usually (but not invariably, as the Table demonstrates) have greater numbers of clerical and higher staff, the relationship is no more than one would expect simply as a reflection of a relationship with total staff.[1]

All that I have managed so far, however, is to demonstrate the connection between size of office and certified sick leave among desk grades in the civil service under conditions which are open to less question than any other demonstration of which I know. We do not yet know why there should be this connection. The Acton Society Trust found that both variables were associated with higher rates of voluntary absenteeism, which is often a sign of low job-satisfaction.[2] But what information the Post Office were able to give me did not suggest that there were any of the signs of low job-satisfaction in the larger of these twelve offices. There was no history of frequent complaints or grievances among the staff; there had been no dismissals and only five compulsory retirements among the lot in 1958. There had been only 33 voluntary resignations (of which at least a quarter were on marriage), and these were scattered fairly evenly among the twelve offices. The only interesting feature was the requests for transfer to other work. At the end of 1958 there were 258 of these which had not been met, and 227 were from the Unit J, where there were large numbers of C.O.s engaged on repetitive and uniform tasks, very much like those I have described at Newcastle. But the sick rates in this office, though somewhat above the mean, were certainly not the highest. Was there any other evidence of a connection between certified sick leave and job-satisfaction among civil servants?

Job-satisfaction, etc. We saw that among the respondents to my questionnaire *uncertified* sick leave was related to their job-satisfaction and to the place which they accorded to the interest of their work as an attraction of their jobs. But there was no really definite relationship

---

[1] Viteles (*loc. cit.*, p. 138) quotes studies showing that industrial workers prefer to work in small groups. But this does *not* make it likely that their total sick leave will be less if they do so.

[2] They did not attempt to measure job-satisfaction: this is my gloss.

between *certified* sick leave and job-satisfaction: and the relationship between it and the place given to the interest of the work was surprising. There was actually a tendency[1] for those who had taken *more* sick leave in the twelvemonth to give it a higher place:

TABLE 6.11

Staff taking	Number	Percentage placing 'interest of the work' first or second
0 days	709	10·8
1-10 ,,	146	11·7
11-20 ,,	92	15·2
21-30 ,,	51	17·6
31-41 ,,	26	23·0
42+ ,,	26	36·0
All staff .	1,049	12·6

It is a pleasant exercise to speculate why this should be so. Do those who find their work so absorbing devote themselves to it with such energy that they impair their health? Or are those with poorer health less able to find energy or interest for other pursuits? Does illness breed insincerity, or a desire to give what will be thought 'the right answer'?

The relationship between certified sick leave and efficiency was very much what you would expect:

TABLE 6.12

Staff taking	Performance Ratings	
	1 & 2	3 & 4
0 days	71·0	62·2
1-10 ,,	14·5	14·4
11-20 ,,	8·8	9·7
21-30 ,,	4·4	6·1
31-41 ,,	1·3	3·8
42+ ,,	1·0	3·8

There was a slight, but significant,[1] tendency for more of the staff with the lower ratings to take certified sick leave, and, in addition, to take more than 10 days of it. One would expect substantial amounts of sick leave to produce this effect upon one's performance rating in three ways. It would interfere with the continuity of one's work; and in trying to pick up the threads after absence there is always the odd thread that has crossed one's path without one's knowing. Illness is

[1] The probability of its occurring by chance is less than 1 in 100.

sometimes debilitating enough to sap one's energy for work for some time afterwards. Thirdly, superiors who have to render annual reports, though they may do their best to make allowances for these factors, may not be able to help forming a lower opinion of the man who is often away when he is needed. There is certainly nothing mysterious about this relationship.

There was no discernible connection between the very prevalent tendency to think that one was more hard-worked than one's colleagues (about 35 per cent. of all civil service respondents) and the amount of certified sick leave. On the other hand, there was a slight tendency among the takers of a lot of certified sick leave to include a higher percentage of those who believed that their work had a bad effect on their health. Question 14 was based on the assumption that it was in reality exceedingly unlikely that desk work of the type performed by the vast majority of the respondents would be such as to do genuine harm to their physical or mental health; it was thus a rough and ready way of estimating the percentage of those whose attitude to their work was slightly—or more than slightly—hypochondriac. In Table 6.14 overleaf is the result for the Ministries and the firms. The uniformity of the percentages is strong confirmation of the assumption that the replies reflect a characteristic of personality rather than a state of affairs. The replies in effect divide the respondents into three main groups. Those who said 'No'—over three-quarters of all respondents—were the least hypochondriac. Those who chose one of the affirmative answers—about 7 per cent.—were the most hypochondriac; and those who were 'uncertain'—about 15 per cent.—can be regarded as intermediate cases, although they must have included a substantial number of people who simply could not be bothered to make up their minds. The interesting thing, of course, is the extent to which the percentage of affirmative answers[1] remains steady through all the groups.

The choice of one or other of the affirmative replies showed a slight but definite association with the number of days of certified sick leave among the civil servants:

TABLE 6.13

Days taken	N	'Yes, physically'	'Yes, mentally'
0 days	721	1·8	3·9
1-10 ,,	153	1·3	3·9
11-20 ,,	96	3·1	6·3
21-30 ,,	52	9·6	7·7
31-41 ,,	26	—	3·8
42+ ,,	25	—	12·0
All staff	1,073	2·1	4·5

[1] i.e. 'Yes, physically' *plus* 'Yes, mentally'.

This association was particularly marked among the 'Yes, mentally' replies. It is, of course, very probable that someone who has suffered a good deal of ill-health will attribute it to the nature or conditions of his work, although in most such cases it is very likely that he would have suffered the same disorders in other occupations (we are of course concerned here with desk work and not with jobs where there is a genuinely high risk of occupational disease). Since desk work is 'brain work', it is understandable that it should be blamed for some of the mental ill-health of office staff. Incidentally, I had expected to find that staff at higher levels, with more responsibility and presumably more harassing demands on their time, would yield a higher percentage of 'Yes, mentally'; but it is only in the firms that this was so: the higher civil servants (including the professionals) plumped instead for 'Yes, physically'!

In most cases, those who said 'yes' chose mental in preference to physical harm: this was particularly striking in the firms where a relatively high percentage of the men made this choice. So did quite high percentages of men in the junior Executive grades and female C.O.s and C.A.s in the Ministries. Women were less inclined to say 'yes' than men, except among the C.O.s and C.A.s, where there was an unexpected little group of 6·7 per cent. who said 'Yes, mentally'.

Do any of these relationships help to explain the connection between sick rates and size of office? It is hard to see how. A great deal more investigation will be needed before we can have any clear idea of the factors that are at work. In particular, it will be necessary to exclude one very obvious and prosaic possibility—that the larger the office the harder it is to exercise control over certified sick leave. It may not merely be a question of the extent to which Welfare Officers are able to call upon frequent invalids; it is possible that in the larger offices, where staff at the numerous and junior levels are more likely to be working at subdivisions of uniform tasks, it is easier for Smith's work to be split up between Brown and Jones, so that there are not so many tender enquiries as to when Smith will be feeling able to return. But this is nothing but speculation; only a thorough survey of these or similar offices would provide a basis for firmer inferences.

Conclusion

This examination of sick leave in the service was prompted by the hope of finding an index that would serve as an indirect measure of 'morale'—or, more precisely, of job-satisfaction and efficiency. One thing that it has certainly illustrated is how easy it is to draw fallacious conclusions and how many covert factors are at work; the best example is probably the apparent effect of grade upon sick rate, which practically disappeared in the case of respiratory disorders when we extracted the duration of absences. Another moral that can be drawn from this

TABLE 6.14

Beliefs about the Effect of Office Work on One's Health among the Respondents to Questionnaire GG 59

(See Chapter 8)

Question 14: 'Does your work have a bad effect on your health?'		N[1]	'No'	'Yes, physically'	'Yes, mentally'	'Uncertain'
			%	%	%	%
Large Ministry		780	76·1	2·9	4·0	17·0
Small Ministry		310	81·8	2·3	3·6	12·3
Civil servants in both		1090	77·6	2·7	3·9	15·8
Both firms' staffs		650	78·0	1·8	6·4	13·8
North Firm		340	74·0	2·3	7·5	16·2
South Firm		310	83·0	0·9	5·1	11·0
Civil Service grades	Administrative*	90	78·1	4·6	1·1	16·2
	Executive above H.E.O.*	90	76·6	3·2	1·1	19·1
	H.E.O. and E.O.:					
	men	310	70·8	2·9	6·4	19·9
	women	130	76·2	2·4	1·6	19·8
	C.O., C.O. (Sec.) and C.A.:					
	men	230	82·5	2·2	3·5	11·8
	women	150	82·7	1·3	6·7	9·3
	Professional*:					
	Large Ministry	60	78·1	3·1	1·6	17·2
	Small Ministry	20	85·7	9·5	—	4·8
Firms' levels	Upper level	60	81·1	1·7	8·6	8·6
	Middle level:					
	men	200	77·0	2·0	8·5	12·5
	women	40	82·0	—	2·6	15·4
	Lower level:					
	men	140	74·6	1·3	6·0	18·1
	women	210	80·6	1·8	4·6	13·0

examination is that we still know very little about the health of civil servants. There are Departments—such as the Post Office and the Health Ministries—that keep and study careful records of their staff's morbidity; in contrast, the Ministry of Pensions and National Insurance, though well equipped to keep fully mechanised records, do not do so. Even the magnificent 3 per cent. sample has not been analysed to anything like its full extent; for example, rates for different groups of illnesses have not yet been extracted. Other heavy demands on the time of the Treasury's staff and machines are largely to blame for this;

[1] Ns are approximate to nearest 10: they exclude 'spoilt' answers, the numbers of which vary slightly from one question to another. They also exclude a few women in the civil service grades marked *, so that the Ns for the grades do not equal the total N for the civil servants.

but I hope that more information of this kind will be extracted before the period of the sample becomes something of mere historical interest.

But this is by the way. Have we found any aspect of 'morale' of which sick leave, certified or uncertified, is a useful index? Certified sick leave, as we have just seen, is not related in a very interesting way to many of the things in which we are interested. Its connection with efficiency is very much what we should expect. Its connection with job-satisfaction appears to be practically nil. Its relationship to the value which staff attach to the interest of their work is curious rather than edifying. Its relationship to grade is almost certainly to be explained by differences in risks of infection. The only interesting characteristic which we have been able to observe is its connection with size of office; and so far this serves only to raise the question 'Why?'

Uncertified sick leave is rather more interesting from our point of view. As we have seen, it is definitely related both to job-satisfaction and to the place which staff accord to the interest of their work. Its relationship to grade is probably no more than the phenomenon which we have explained away in the case of certified sick leave. With the possible exception of married women, we have found no large category of desk staff who seem to be abusing this privilege; and in the case of married women the 'abuse', if it exists, is venial and probably preferable to any alternative.

On the whole, however, this chapter has illustrated the danger of applying to the study of large organisations hypotheses which are based on the behaviour of individuals. Because there is an undoubted need for an index of attitudes to the job which is more sensitive than crude signs of extreme dissatisfaction such as strikes or resignations, and because we know that illness so often has contributory causes in the psychological state of the individual, investigators have been tempted to assume that the sickness rates of a whole organisation or group within an organisation will meet this need. We have seen that the civil service sick-leave rules provide conditions for testing this assumption which could hardly be bettered; and that some of the variations in sickness rates probably have psychological explanations. But with these exceptions, the statistics, considered as an index, are disappointing. In all but the occasional case, sick leave seems to indicate simply that the civil servant is sick.

7

TWO MINISTRIES AND TWO COMPANIES: ARRANGING A QUESTIONNAIRE

In the previous chapter I discussed the extent to which quantifiable behaviour of office staffs—and in particular sick leave—could serve as an indirect measure of their attitudes to their work; and we saw how limited were the possibilities of this. In any case, no indirect measure, however sensitive, could be a complete substitute for direct, first-hand information from the office workers themselves. It was just this kind of information, however, that seemed to be almost entirely lacking. A great many books have been written about the British civil servant, some of them by authors with experience of being one. Most of them, of course, are concerned not so much with his personality, attitudes and feelings as with his function and official relationship to his Minister, the public and Parliament. He is spoken of as the 'instrument of his Minister', very much as if Ministers had one civil servant each; he is an abstraction, possessing, like the geometer's point, position but no magnitude. Even authors who try to hang flesh and clothes on this point—usually by describing 'a day in the life of a typical civil servant' succeeded in giving him only one or two dimensions. Almost always the typical civil servant turns out to be an Assistant Secretary or Principal who arrives in his office at 10 a.m., drafts an answer to a Parliamentary Question and lunches in his club, afterwards presiding at a meeting, and finding his way over to the House to sit in the box all evening. For every Assistant Secretary who really lives like this there must be a hundred civil servants in lower ranks—and many Assistant Secretaries too—who don't.[1]

What I needed was information about the attitudes of civil servants, obtained at first hand from the civil servants themselves. One way of obtaining it would have been interviews of the kind I conducted at Newcastle: but they would have had to be very long to cover all the ground I wanted to, and very numerous to cover an adequate sample. Even a team of skilled interviewers takes a long time to recruit and brief for the job.

---

[1] One of the very few writers who make it clear that the administrator is only a fraction of the civil service—the conspicuous top of the iceberg—is Mr. F. Dunnill, whose book *The Civil Service: Some Human Aspects* (1956) attempts—with a great deal of success—to bring on to the stage the members of the Executive and Clerical classes. Anyone who wants some insight into the factors that underlie the outward behaviour of the service should read this book.

The obvious method was a postal questionnaire. Civil servants are used to devising articulate answers on paper to questions however ingenious or silly, and the filling-in of a questionnaire should not be as formidable a task to them as it is to some manual workers. More important still, if a large enough number of civil servants could be induced to answer a questionnaire this would get round the difficulties which arose from the differences between such factors as the nature of their tasks, the personalities of their superiors and colleagues, and their own backgrounds and histories. The larger the number who replied, the greater would be the chances that they would include most of the typical tasks, situations and personalities of Whitehall.

I considered whether this questionnaire should be distributed to a random sample of officers in the various Departments of the service and the several regions of Britain, but there were both practical and theoretical objections to this. I should need the assistance of their Departments in distributing the questionnaire and in obtaining the necessary information about those to whom it was distributed; and I should have to have the agreement of the staff sides of the Whitley Councils to the issue of the questionnaire if I wanted a favourable response from every grade. To arrange this with every Department, or even with all the large ones, would have been an immense undertaking, since it would be necessary to discuss such a proposal with the Establishment Divisions of each Ministry. Even if this had been possible, I should have been faced with information about civil servants in such widely scattered locations, types of work and other circumstances of such variety that the information would have had to be analysed in almost unthinkable detail to make sense of it.

I decided to concentrate, therefore, upon officers of desk grades working in two Ministries in or close to Whitehall itself. I would try to arrange it that one should be large and the other small enough to test the hypothesis that attitudes vary with the size of the organisation. In case some of the responses might be affected by differences in physical environment I would try to ensure that the recipients of the questionnaire would be drawn from as few office-buildings as possible. For example, complaints about 'the canteen' would be more interesting if I knew that they were about the same canteen. What I wanted to know was not so much whether Mr. A had a better canteen than Miss X, as whether Mr. A complained more about the same one than she did.

It also seemed to me that the value of the civil servants' answers to my questionnaire would be greater if I could compare them with answers from office workers outside the service. I decided to try to find a large firm that employed enough office workers in a large building in Central London to be comparable with my smallish Ministry; there was of course no hope of finding one with an office staff of anything like the size of one of the large Departments.

Finding Ministries and Firms

The task of finding Ministries that were both suitable and cooperative was surprisingly easy. The first smallish Ministry which I approached reacted with a helpful interest. I was not surprised when they stipulated that I should keep their identity a secret, and I shall therefore refer to this Ministry as the 'Small Ministry'; although perhaps 'medium-sized' would convey a fairer impression, since it was one of the half-dozen or so whose staffs number between 2,000 and 5,000. It is concerned with an important aspect of social policy in this country, and its activities are not infrequently the subject of controversy in Parliament. Its headquarters, as you would expect of such a Ministry, were in a stately building within a mile of Westminster Abbey, and although many of its staff were housed in other buildings in the Greater London area, we agreed to confine the survey to this building.

Finding a large Ministry was not quite so easy. Of the four to which I wrote one proved to have too many of its staff in the provinces; another could not give me one particular piece of information about its staffs in the form in which I wanted it; and a third simply replied, 'I regret that we do not feel able to collaborate in this research'—a response which was certainly free from the verbosity and ambiguity of which the service is sometimes accused. The fourth however, was interested in the idea, and proved suitable, although it was impossible to confine the survey to the staff of a single building, and in order to secure enough of the higher grades some staff in other buildings not far away had to be included. The majority came from a group of three modern office buildings, not far apart in Central London. This Ministry was one of the large ones, with a staff of well over 12,000. Its activities, which brought its officers into contact with several sectors of industry, had nothing to do with social policy, and were, at least at this time, less frequently debated in Parliament than those of the smaller Ministry.

Finding a firm that was willing to co-operate was by far the most troublesome task. Fortunately I had sought the help of the Institute of Personnel Management, whose Information and Publications Officer, Miss Harris, made untiring efforts to interest large firms in my proposal. Two declined it without wasting any of my time or theirs. One was genuinely interested, but eventually came to the conclusion that it would coincide too closely with a reorganisation of staff which it was preparing, and would be mistaken by the staff for a part of this reorganisation.

The fourth firm was also interested. Its Chief Personnel Officer obviously had his own views about the practical value of this kind of research, but thought that its findings about his firm might be of interest to him and his Directors. After some discussion his Directors agreed, and from that stage onward I was able to rely on the fullest co-operation. Indeed, I was now almost embarrassed by my success, because the organisation consisted of a number of associated firms, of which two employed large blocks of office workers in large buildings in the same part of Central London. It was part of my agreement with the Directors that I should survey both of these firms, in the hope that some interesting differences might emerge. Since it was also part of my understanding with them that the names of the firms should be kept secret, I can describe them only by saying that both of them manufactured goods for the home and overseas market, but that one, which I shall call 'the South Firm', was chiefly concerned with articles for household use, while the North Firm's products were of a more specialised and technical nature, of value to industry and certain Government Departments.

The Procedure

The arrangements for issuing and returning the questionnaire required a good deal of thought and discussion. It was obviously necessary to have a certain amount of factual information about the respondents to compare with their replies to the 'attitude' questions. Some of this information, such as their sex, age, and previous careers, could be supplied by the respondent himself. But it was also desirable to know two other things—the amount of sick leave he had taken over the last twelve months (or the most recent twelve months convenient to the Ministry), and how good he was at his work. For the first we could not trust the respondent's memory; and for the second we had to rely on the annual reports which are filled in by the immediate superior of every Senior Executive Officer or officer of lower grade.[1] Each report includes a verdict on the subject's 'overall performance of his duties'. Unless the report is very unfavourable, this verdict is not disclosed to the subject although the superior officer is encouraged to give his subordinates his general impression of their performance; so that the overall performance rating, like the sick-leave figures, would have to be supplied by the Ministries' Establishment Divisions.

With the North and South Firms the problem was slightly different. Their sick-leave conditions were quite unlike those of the civil service. Until January 1959, any continuation of payment during sickness absences had been at the discretion of the management, and although the continuation of pay in almost all cases had been encouraged, there had been considerable variation in practice. Nor did the firms use annual reports or overall performance ratings. Employees were, as a

[1] The justification for dispensing with annual reports for higher ranks is presumably that in most Ministries they are so few that the officers concerned come under the personal observation of those who will decide whether to promote them. But in the Large Ministry there were so many Principals that they too were the subjects of annual reports.

ARRANGING A QUESTIONNAIRE 147

rule, interviewed once a year by their immediate superior, and given a short verdict on their performance, culminating with the information that they would or would not receive an increment for the next year. We could not therefore expect any useful information from the firms under those two heads. On the other hand, whereas the civil servants could fill in their own grades, the firms' employees could not, since these grades were closely linked to their salary scales, of which they did not know the exact limits. As in the majority of private firms, the employees' exact salary and his standing with the firm were closely guarded secrets between him and the firm.

Yet it was obviously important to be able to tell, for example, whether a respondent from one of the firms belonged to the same or a different level from another respondent whose views were different, or who came from the other firm; and even more important, although clearly more difficult, to tell whether he should be regarded as the equivalent of an administrator, one of the Executive grades, or a clerical officer or clerical assistant in the civil service. The firms therefore agreed to tell me, in very strict confidence, the salary group to which the employee belonged (but not his actual salary). I cannot say very much about these salary groups without betraying the firms' confidence. It would have been difficult, and fallacious, to equate them closely with any grade in the civil service; and in any case the numbers in any one grade or salary group would be too small for statistical purposes. But the information enabled me to divide the firms' respondents into three levels, which I shall call simply the 'upper', 'middle' and 'lower' levels. It seemed to me that the positions which the upper level occupied in the firms corresponded to those which the Assistant Secretaries, Principals, Assistant Principals and Executive Officers of the rank of Senior Executive Officer and above occupied in the Ministries; while the middle level corresponded to the Executive and Higher Executive Officers. The lower level I took to be the equivalent of the Clerical Class; and in this case I was able to distinguish, I thought, those who corresponded to Clerical Assistants from those who did work more like that of Clerical Officers: but as will be seen from the Table at the end of this chapter both recipients and respondents at this level were actually less numerous than the level above, and the replies from them were not sufficient in number to be treated separately for statistical purposes.

This meant that I had to be able to link up information about sick leave, performance rating or (in the firms' case) salary group with the right questionnaire. On the other hand everyone agreed that respondents would fill up the questionnaire more willingly if they could be assured that their names were not being disclosed to the investigators. The solution eventually worked out was this. The questionnaire would be given in bulk to the Establishment Divisions of the two Ministries, together with a pre-paid 'business reply' envelope, addressed to me, for each questionnaire. Each Establishment Division would draw up a list of the recipients of the questionnaire, and give each recipient a serial number; the list would also show the amount of certified and uncertified sick leave he had taken in the most recent period of twelve months that could conveniently be examined in their records, and the overall performance rating in a form that will be discussed in the next Chapter (in the case of the firms it would show only the salary group). A questionnaire would be numbered with the recipient's serial number, and addressed to him, together with one of the pre-paid reply envelopes and a covering note from his Establishment Division to assure him that there was no objection to his answering the questionnaire. If he decided to do so, his instructions were to fill it in without signing it, seal it up in the envelope, and post it. His Establishment Division would supply me with the list of serial numbers, which would contain the information about sick leave and performance rating, but would not include the recipients' names.

This achieved several important objectives. It made it possible to assure the recipients that the investigators would not know their names, while the Ministry would never see their answers. It enabled us to identify those who had not sent in questionnaires by a certain date, and to send them reminders. There was also a minor advantage. Because of a rather crowded layout on page 2 of the questionnaire quite a few respondents missed the question asking for their sex; and one or two failed to mark their age-group. The system made it possible to get this information from their Establishment Division, and I considered that by doing so we should not be violating the undertaking not to reveal their answers to their Ministry.

A great deal of credit not only for working out this idea but also for executing it smoothly must go to the Establishment Divisions of the two Ministries. One of the difficulties of making all these arrangements was that while the two Ministries knew each other's identity the Ministries did not know who the firms were, and the firms did not know who the Ministries were. I had therefore to conduct two sets of discussions in parallel, instead of being able to collect the representatives of all four organisation round one table. Fortunately the Personnel Officers of the two firms were willing to fall in with the arrangements agreed with the Ministries, and in the event their Personnel Departments carried them out with great efficiency. I am sorry that the anonymity of the four organisations prevents me from thanking by name all those who undertook the main burden of the work.

The Staff Associations

There was one more fence to be crossed. This was the sort of survey about which the staff associations of the civil servants concerned would obviously have to be consulted. The office workers of the two firms were not organised into associations (although of course their industrial workers were); so that no consultation with them was possible. But among the civil servants the first reaction of many recipients would be to wonder whether their staff associations had been consulted; and if we could reassure them on this point their response was much more likely to be favourable.

In the event these consultations gave the Ministries much less trouble than I had feared. The associations concerned were the First Division Association (representing the Administrators), the Society of Civil Servants (representing the Executive Class) the Civil Service Clerical Association (representing the Clerical and Sub-clerical Class) and the Institution of Professional Civil Servants (representing the few professional staff whom we agreed to include for comparison). In the Small Ministry the proposal was received with interest and welcomed, and several useful comments were made on the draft questionnaire, of which copies had been supplied so that the representatives could have an idea of the sort of questions that it would contain.

In the Large Ministry its reception was a little more cautious. Questions were asked about the possibility that the results would be published and would contain comments on one grade or another that would be the subject of unfavourable publicity. This was an understandable point and I gave an undertaking that if the question of publication should arise the national headquarters would first be shown what I proposed to say about their respective members. With this the representatives were content. Like the staff side of the Small Ministry, they took an interest in the survey, and put forward some constructive suggestions. Indeed, it is possible that the higher response from the Large Ministry was due to their helpfulness.

Drafting the Questionnaire

The process of finding Ministries and firms, of reaching agreement on the arrangements and of obtaining the consent of the staff sides took three months. Meanwhile I was preparing the questionnaire. The final version of this will be found in Appendix B. But the butterfly went through many strange shapes before it emerged in all its glory.

In the first place, the questions had to be devised so that the answers to each would fall into a definite and not too large number of categories. 'Free' answers, that is, answers for which the respondent chooses his own words, and which may therefore consist of a phrase, a sentence or a short essay, make interesting reading but are very hard to classify or quantify. As many of the questions as possible, therefore, were given 'multiple-choice answers', among which the respondent could choose the one that suited his attitude best. Because there were so many respondents the answers had to be in a form that could be punched on to cards (in this case Hollerith 80-column cards); that is, each possible answer had to be distinguishable by a number. It would have been possible for someone to go through each filled-in questionnaire numbering each answer so that the card-puncher could copy the numbers; but this was avoided in all but a few answers by 'pre-coding'; that is, by numbering each possible answer so that the card-puncher had merely to look for the number which had been ticked by the respondent. There was a slight risk that these numbers would influence the answers themselves; for example, that respondents might mistakenly think that the numbers showed the value that was attached to each answer, and might avoid answers with what they thought were low values. To avoid this I explained these numbers on the front page of the questionnaire, and also arranged several questions so that the apparent 'values' were obviously inconsistent. In devising the coding and layout of the questionnaire I received extremely helpful advice from Mr. P. G. Gray of the Social Survey Division of the Central Office of Information, and from Dr. Rollett of the Oxford Computer Laboratory.[1]

I had hoped to find that similar questionnaires had been devised for other occupations and would provide me with ready-made questions. This hope was not wholly inspired by laziness, because bitter experience has shown that if a number of questions are devised by one man, or even a team of men, and then incorporated in a questionnaire, a certain percentage of them will be found to be useless. Some of them will be misunderstood because the author is using words in a different way from the respondent. Often the author is being too educated and precise and the respondent fails to appreciate his distributions. On the other hand, it sometimes happens that the respondents have a more precise usage for certain terms, of which the author is unaware. Being a civil servant of thirteen years' standing I thought I knew the language of Whitehall; but as soon as I began to try out my questions on members of grades whose background was rather different from mine I found that I was making mistakes of idiom (and other mistakes to which I will come in a minute). For example, when I asked questions about a man's 'job' I meant him to understand his present duties; but quite a few people thought that I meant their whole career as civil servants. On the other hand, while 'your present duties' seemed to convey what I meant to civil servants, it did not quite ring the bell with the private firms'

[1] There were clearly some questions to which the respondents must be allowed to compose their own answers. As in most questionnaires of this kind it seemed a good idea to end with a section in which the respondent could insert any comment or complaint of his own which he felt that the questionnaire had not given him a chance to express, or which previous questions might have suggested to him; and as it turned out this question (No. 62) received quite a lot of interesting answers. Spaces were also provided beside some of the multiple-choice answers in which respondents were invited to inset anything they wished to add; questions 11 and 47, for example, drew quite a few additions of this kind.

employees; and I had to add the gloss 'your present post'. Again, a mistake which I did not find out until too late was to refer to a man's 'superiors' when I meant his 'superior officer'; one or two civil servants corrected the questionnaire at this point, and it seems possible that some people's susceptibilities were offended by my use of the word 'superior'.

Another kind of mistake is to ask questions to which everyone gives the same answer. If you ask, 'Do you like most of your colleagues?' 99 respondents in every 100 will say 'Yes'. Either their feelings about their colleagues really consist of some degree of liking, or they do not care to admit to any other sort of feeling. But you may induce them to admit to different feelings if you divide up the possible answers by offering phrases that express several different degrees of liking; for example

'Most of my colleagues are
    very likeable....................
    likeable........................
    all right.......................'

Indeed, you may even get a few respondents to agree to the phrase 'not very likeable', if you arrange the question so that this phrase is not the worst that is offered; for example, by offering the phrase 'most unlikeable'. This phrase is so strong that very few people will actually use it, but it will allow some people to feel free to agree to 'not very likeable'. This is what I call 'adding a false bottom'.

It was this sort of question which I hoped to be able to borrow, ready-made and tested, from questionnaires that had been used by other research workers. I could not, however, find any that had been applied to office workers as such. Dr. Barbara Aalto, of the Counselling Center at the University of California, had used a questionnaire to measure the attitudes of people in the U.S.A. towards 'working for the Government'; but this had been devised primarily to assist in vocational guidance and selection of potential civil servants. Its questions were too wide and naïve to be of much assistance in distinguishing the attitudes of people already employed in the civil service. I found more useful material in questionnaires issued to British factory workers by such investigators as M. Argyle, G. Gardner and F. Cioffi, 'Social Factors in Productivity'—an unpublished report submitted to the Department of Scientific and Industrial Research in 1956) and John Handyside of the National Institute of Industrial Psychology. I was, for example, able to borrow from the latter's questionnaires the Hoppock job-satisfaction scale, with a modification made by Handyside: the result will be found in Question 60.

But with this exception it was ideas rather than ready-made questions that I was able to get from these sources; almost all their questions had to be modified before they were suitable for office workers. In drafting questions of this kind it is usually found—or assumed—that the wording must be as simple and colloquial as possible. But this seems to repel rather than attract the civil servant; the reason may be that he is trained to use his words with precision, and resents being 'talked down to'.

Having collected some ideas for questions, and put rough drafts on paper, I proceeded to try them out on people. Apart from the experts themselves, whom I plagued with drafts, I was fortunate to find some ex-civil servants at Ruskin College. These were men and women from different grades and Ministries fairly far removed from my own experience. They were interested and intelligent, and the result of these discussions was to alter the questions and their form considerably.

The second draft was tried out in a less informal fashion. I was giving lectures to a week-end school run by the W.E.A. for clerical officers and similar grades in the civil service, and I invited the students to fill in the questionnaire. They did so with a good deal of enjoyment, and the results were discussed at a final session. This led on to criticisms of the drafting of the questions, and a great many mistakes of layout and wording were corrected. In particular, what is now Question 56 was considerably altered. This question was a device of my own to attempt to see what variations there were in people's ideas of the status of their own job, and whether they thought that the other members of their community agreed with their valuation of it. Since it was the first time, to the best of my knowledge, that a question of this form had been used, I was anxious to improve it as much as possible. As we shall see when we come to consider the results of the questionnaire, it was a question which irritated some respondents and puzzled others; but it was not wholly unsuccessful, and some of the credit for improving it must go to the W.E.A. students.

I could not collect a symposium of other grades in this way, but I persuaded friends of mine in different Departments to offer the second draft to acquaintances of theirs who could answer it without my knowing who they were and without their answers being seen by the intermediary. In this way I was able to try it out on a few civil servants at different levels.

There are always a few people who fill in questionnaires so carelessly, frivolously or maliciously that their replies do not really indicate their attitudes. In the hope of detecting some of these—I could not expect to detect them all—I repeated Question 23 in the form of Question 50. In the event, ten men and one woman claimed in one answer that they had too much responsibility, but in their other answer said that they wanted more. This represented 0·6 per cent. of the respondents, and the percentage was the same among the civil servants and the staff of the private firms. Among the civil servants all but one of the men were in the Executive class in the large Ministry. Nobody who claimed

ARRANGING A QUESTIONNAIRE

to have too little responsibility wanted less. None of these replies were from people who had received reminders; this is a little surprising, since a reminder might be expected to make some recipients fill in their questionnaires hastily and carelessly. The questionnaires of these eleven respondents were eliminated from the tabulation of replies.

Suspicions of the Questionnaire

By this stage, however, time was pressing. The Ministries and the firms were practically ready. It was February, and if the results were to be examined before the end of my sabbatical year the issue of the questionnaire could not be delayed much longer. Two unfortunate things, however, happened in February. An influenza epidemic attacked office staffs in Central London, and Mr. Colin Hurry became a national figure as a result of his house-to-house survey of opinion on the nationalisation of the steel industry in marginal constituencies. One of the allegations made about this survey was that the opinions of individuals who were interviewed would be disclosed to a political party organisation; and Mr. Hurry's statements might not have reassured everyone on this point.

I was afraid that the influenza would reduce the number of people who would be at their desks to answer my questionnaire, and might produce artificially dissatisfied replies from those who were suffering from 'post-influenzal depression'. I cannot exclude the possibility of the latter, but in actual numbers the response was satisfactory. I was also afraid that the publicity given to Mr. Hurry's methods might lead recipients of my questionnaire to suspect me of being in league with 'the management' or of some even more sinister rôle. The use of a serial number on the questionnaires in the Argyle-Gardner-Cioffi survey (*loc. cit.*) had aroused suspicions of this kind of collusion among the factory workers who received them; some of the serial numbers were torn off before the questionnaires were returned, and the total response—37 per cent.—was disappointingly low. But in this survey the investigators tried to make the serial number unobtrusive by placing it on a bottom corner of the last page, so that when it was noticed it was quite likely to look suspicious. I hoped that if I put my serial numbers on the front page and explained the method of issue with a frank reference to the serial number if would forestall suspicions of this kind. I also made it clear in paragraph 5 of the introduction that my report would not make it possible to identify the answers of any individual.

Suspicions were voiced in one or two questionnaires, and, as it turned out, one or two people in the private firm were not completely reassured: when reminders were issued by the firms to owners of serials for which I had not received replies, more suspicions were aroused. By explaining the method more fully to those who voiced these suspicions the Personnel Officers were able to deal with them, but the moral for future surveys of this kind is 'Be as frank about the arrangements as you can'. It would have enlarged an already long introduction to go more fully into the mechanics, but it would probably have been worth it. In the Ministries, perhaps because the mechanics had been discussed fully with the staff associations' representatives, no suspicions were voiced either in the questionnaires or to the Establishment Divisions, although one respondent deleted his serial number before replying. Not even the most suspicious respondent, however, actually referred to Mr. Hurry; and it is quite possible that he had nothing to do with these suspicions.

At all events, we decided not to defer the issue of the questionnaire. The date chosen was the 20th February: by issuing on a Friday we hoped to give people too little time to discuss the questionnaire with each other before taking it home for the week-end; and we hoped that many would fill it in and post it before returning to work on Monday. It was important to prevent as much discussion as possible before people filled it in, because experience and experiments have shown that people's judgments tend to alter in the direction of the norm if they discuss them with each other.

The choice of a Friday was the idea of one of the firms' Personnel Officers, and though it is impossible to know how successful it was, it was clearly a very good suggestion. About 44 per cent. of the civil servants' questionnaires and 31 per cent. of the firms' were posted on or before Monday the 23rd, and it is safe to assume that there was little chance for these respondents to discuss the questions in detail.

Among later questionnaires there were one or two signs of collaboration or discussion. One piece of evidence was the receipt of a single envelope containing two questionnaires, belonging to a male and a female office worker and bearing slight traces of a meal. It is not difficult to picture them filling the questions in together in the canteen; but on examination they proved to have agreed to differ on a few of their replies.

I had felt that it was essential to make it clear in the introduction to the questionnaire (as well as in the reminders) that the recipients were not under any compulsion to reply. I added that 'every person who refuses—or forgets—to do so slightly reduces the value of the survey'. These two points were repeated in the reminders. The covering notes from the recipient's Establishment Officer of Personnel Officer did not attempt any strong persuasion.

The Response

In spite of all these snags and doubts, the percentage of forms returned was very satisfactory. As I have already mentioned, 44 per cent. of the civil servants and 31 per cent. of the firms' employees posted their replies on or before the Monday after issue. A week later the per-

ARRANGING A QUESTIONNAIRE

centages were up to 60 and 48. At this point I asked the Ministries and firms to issue the reminders. These went out in the last two working days of the week, and on or by the third Tuesday after issue the firms' percentage was 59, and the civil servants' 70. Experience with other postal questionnaires suggested that little more would be gained by a second reminder, and the Establishment and Personnel Officers felt that this would merely irritate without stimulating. Instead, they agreed to put up a notice which gave their staffs some information about the response to the questionnaire, and repeated in even stronger terms the assurances about its confidentiality. By 20th March, four weeks after the day of issue, the percentages of response were:

Large Ministry	79
Small Ministry	64
North Firm	63
South Firm	65
All four organisations	70

This response compared very well with the response to other postal questionnaires dealing with attitudes to work. The Argyle-Gardner-Cioffi survey received back only 37 per cent. of its questionnaires. The National Institute of Industrial Psychology 'get, on average, 70 per cent. returned, and a range so far, in different organisations, of 60 per cent. to 75 per cent. But we give these out personally to the people at their work-place, and collect them twenty-four hours later in the same way, which encourages a higher response than one could anticipate with postal methods.'[1]

It is possible that the response would have been even higher if the questionnaire had been shorter. Certainly with 10 pages and 62 questions it was a formidable document. But my experience with the 'pilot' draft at the W.E.A. course had shown that clerical officers actually enjoy answering questions about their job and their attitudes to it. The final version was longer than the draft, but I had every hope that it was not too long. As it turned out, though there were plenty of criticisms of the questions, very few people indeed complained that there were too many of them. Out of 1,758 usable questionnaires, one came back with the words 'too busy' scrawled across it, and one respondent wrote 'too many questions' in answer to Question 62. It therefore seems unlikely that length had much to do with the response. With every questionnaire there is a hard core of people who will not reply however often they are reminded or approached.

Meanwhile I had been trying to make the arrangements for having the Hollerith cards punched and sorted. The Institute of Statistics at Oxford, though intended to provide services of this kind, were handi-

[1] From a personal communication from Mr. John Handyside.

capped by shortage of staff and antiquated equipment. The late Dr. Burchardt, however, and, following his death, Mr. K. J. C. Knowles, who acted as Director for the interregnum, were very anxious to be helpful. I was eventually able to secure the part-time services of one of their trained card-punchers, Mrs. Smith, who punched 1,100 cards with such accuracy that though she occasionally discovered a mistake I myself never succeeded in doing so. The cards for the firms' replies were punched by some of the staff of the Usher Institute in Edinburgh, working outside their regular hours; I should like to record my appreciation of their helpfulness, efficiency and accuracy.

It was clear, however, that the nearest Hollerith sorting equipment, which was said to be the doyen of its type in England, would take an unthinkable time to handle the cards when they were punched. People who heard of my plight began to bring me rumours of Hollerith machines that would sort the results electronically instead of mechanically, and I eventually managed to locate one of these machines at Harwell near by. When I approached Dr. J. Howlett and Mr. J. E. Hailstone of the Theoretical Physics Division of the Atomic Energy Research Authority about the possibility of using one of their Hollerith Electronic Calculators they were not only willing to discuss it but were extremely interested in my questionnaire. Without very much ado they agreed that their Hollerith 555 Calculator should do all the tabulations that were at all likely to be interesting.

The use of the calculator greatly increased the number of tables that could be compiled in a given number of man-hours. The calculator was programmed so that every time my 1,758 questionnaire cards were put through it, it issued a new set of cards; each of which represented a row of the desired matrix, and showed the totals in each cell of this row. These cards were then put through a Hollerith tabulator, which printed the table; in this way, three or four tables could be compiled with one through-put of my cards. Anyone familiar with the process of compiling tables by mechanical sorting will know how greatly this increased the number of tables that could be contemplated. In the event, some 500 tables were compiled in this way.[1]

How Representative were the Replies?

The main results of the questionnaire are described in the next chapter. Anyone who is seriously interested in them, however, is bound to ask the question, 'How safe is it to assume that the replies fairly represent the attitudes of the employees in the four organisations?'

[1] Even so, both the programming of the Calculator and the handling of the cards involved a great deal of thought and painstaking work on the part of Mr. J. E. Hailstone and Mr. C. W. Jackson, to whom I owe a very great debt. Mr. Hailstone's advice on the statistical problems raised by the results was another piece of help without which I should have been in great difficulties.

I have already described the steps which I took to ensure that the questionnaire asked the right questions in the right way; and we shall see that while some of the questions did not elicit very interesting answers, most of them did. The extent to which the respondents felt safe in replying frankly is of course difficult to gauge without interviewing a large percentage of them; a step which would have been contrary to the anonymity which we had promised them. But enough of the replies were extremely critical to make it unlikely that fear of their being traced to their authors was an important factor; for example, 11·5 per cent. of the firms' employees said that 'the men at the top' were 'not quite competent enough' or 'incompetent' and the percentage among the civil servants was not much lower (10·7 per cent.).

I have also made it clear that while the recipients were not an ideally distributed sample of all Whitehall civil servants or of Central London office workers, they were, as nearly as possible, one hundred per cent. of the grades in which I was interested who worked in the headquarters buildings of the two Ministries and the two firms, and that nothing interfered very seriously with the issue or return of the questionnaire.

The questionnaires were returned by roughly two-thirds of the recipients in the Small Ministry and the North and South Firms, and by more than three-quarters of the recipients in the Large Ministry. It is always possible, of course, that the third or quarter which did not reply differed from those who did in the very attitudes in which I was interested; for example, that those who were most efficient and contented with their jobs did not bother to fill in questions about them. It is so difficult to find ways of interviewing non-respondents in surveys of this kind that no reliable evidence on this possibility has yet been published. But recent investigations by the National Institute of Industrial Psychology suggest that if there is a tendency of this kind it is for the non-respondents to consist of those who are neither very satisfied nor very dissatisfied.[1]

I myself compared the scores on the job-satisfaction scale (Qn. 60) of those respondents who had received reminders with those of respondents who had replied without being reminded, on the assumption that if non-respondents differed much from respondents on this scale, those who needed reminding should show a difference in the same direction, although perhaps less marked. Certainly the firms' employees who had needed reminders showed an even greater tendency than the others to choose the most popular of the 11 phrases, and this was consistent with the N.I.I.P.'s results: but the civil servants showed no significant difference. The most that can be said is that neither the N.I.I.P.'s results nor mine supported any suggestion that more respondents tend to be drawn from the satisfied than from the dissatisfied recipients, or vice versa. If anything, more may be drawn from both

[1] From a personal communication from Mr. John Handyside in June 1959.

ends of the range than from the middle. Since it is the ends of the range which are most interesting to the investigator, this hypothesis is obviously the least damaging of the three. In any case, the higher the response the less must be any difference between respondents and non-respondents.

My comparison, however, of respondents who needed reminding with those who did not disclosed one interesting tendency: the older the respondent, the more likely he was to have needed a reminder, as the table below shows:

TABLE 7.01

Percentage of each Age-group which returned Questionnaires after Reminders

Age-group	Civil Servants	Firms' Staffs
Under 20	—	14·0
20-29	15·3	18·2
30-39	12·7	19·7
40-49	13·8	26·0
50-59	23·0	31·0
60 or over	24·2	38·5

This tendency was even more marked among the private firms' staffs than among the civil servants, and when we remember that it was the firms from which the poorest response came, this suggests the possibility that a disproportionately high percentage of non-respondents would have been found to belong to the older age-groups; in other words, that the respondents had a tendency to represent the younger age-groups. The other possibility is simply that the older men and women were more deliberate about filling in and posting this formidable document: but the N.I.I.P.'s investigations support the first hypothesis.

Table 7.02 shows the distribution of the recipients and the respondents at different levels. The lowest response was from members of the clerical grades (or their equivalents in the firms), but even this was above 50 per cent. Fortunately the higher officers, who were less numerous, responded best; otherwise their replies might not have been numerous enough to be reliable.

As it was, the percentages of women in the higher grades of the two Ministries was too small to allow any conclusions to be drawn from any differences between their answers and those of their male colleagues; and in the upper level of the two firms there were no women at all. But among the Clerical and lower Executive grades (i.e. H.E.O. and E.O.) and their rough equivalents in the firms there were enough women to allow their replies to be analysed separately where this seemed likely to yield something interesting.

With these minor distortions, therefore, the results described in the next chapter can safely be treated as reflecting some interesting differ-

TABLE 7.02

Recipients and Respondents—Distribution of Recipients, Respondents and Women at various levels in the Ministries and Firms
(all figures are percentages)

Civil Service Grades[2]	RECIPIENTS[1]					RESPONDENTS						
	Ministries		Firms		Both sexes				Women as % of grades			
	Large	Small	North	South	Ministries		Firms		Ministries		Firms	
					Large	Small	North	South				
Administrative	7.5%	8.0%	8.5%	4.5%	7.8%	10.0%	12.1%	4.8%	5.4%		none	
Executive above H.E.O.	10.4	2.7			10.6	3.3			4.1			
H.E.O. and E.O.	36.3	40.5	57.4	52.9	38.1	45.7	59.9	57.1	28.7		16.6	
Clerical Officers and C.O. Secretaries	31.0	37.5	32.4	39.4	30.5	30.3	26.9	35.2	37.1		59.5	
Clerical Assistants	6.1	3.3	1.7	3.2	4.7	3.6	1.1	2.9	60.4			
Professional grades	8.7	8.0	—	—	8.3	7.1	—	—	2.2		—	
All levels	100	100	100	100	100	100	100	100	26.3		38.7	

[1] These figures do not necessarily of course indicate the percentages of staff at these levels in the organisation as a whole; the recipients were confined to headquarter buildings.

[2] For the reasons given in the text it was not easy to distinguish the firms' staffs into levels exactly equivalent to the civil service grades; for example, professional grades in the firms were not clearly distinguished from the higher management.

ences, either between the two ministries or between the two firms, or between different levels of staff or in some cases between the civil servants and the other office workers. To step from this to the assumption that these differences are typical of all Ministries or all private offices would of course be risky. In the case of the two Companies it would be unjustifiable, since there is no agency like the Treasury to promote uniformity in the personnel policy of private firms. The most that I can say of them is, 'This is what Companies' headquarter offices *can* be like.' On the other hand, the probability that the civil service respondents are representative of their counterparts in the desk classes of other Departments is somewhat greater.[1] Not only are conditions of service homogeneous, but also I find it difficult to think of any important respect in which the Large or Small Ministry were freaks. The civil servant who, reading the next chapter, is convinced that his Department is not like these should ask himself what his grounds for this conviction are. He will find that they are the things which his subordinates, colleagues and superiors allow themselves to say or do in his presence, interpreted according to his own pre-conceptions about people. The next chapter shows what my respondents allowed themselves to say to someone outside the Ministry by whom they could not be identified. It cannot, I am afraid, be entirely free of my own preconceptions and interpretations, but I hope that these are distinguishable from the facts.

[1] The professional civil servants, of course, must be an exception to this statement.

8

TWO MINISTRIES AND TWO COMPANIES: RESULTS OF THE QUESTIONNAIRE

Since the whole aim of the questionnaire was to provide something more than subjective impressions, its results must be allowed to speak for themselves, with the minimum of interpretation. This chapter therefore contains more tables and other statistics than do its predecessors. But it will save tiresome repetitions, and may make the reader's task easier, if I make the following points here and now:

(i) with very few exceptions, all figures are percentages. Unless the contrary is stated they are percentages of the number (N) of respondents who gave a meaningful answer to that question;

(ii) as many of the tables as possible are in a standard form, showing the Ministries, Companies and their grades and levels in a standard order, and giving in the first column the number (N) to which the percentages relate;

(iii) except where the contrary is expressly stated, any difference between percentages which is referred to in the text is significant at least at the ·05 level (and in most cases at the ·02 or ·01 levels); that is, the probability of their being due to pure chance is less than 1 in 20, and in most cases less than 1 in 50 or 100;

(iv) in one or two cases the giving of a definite percentage for a certain subdivision would make it possible for people within one of the Ministries or firms to draw an inference about an individual respondent. To prevent this I have sometimes had to combine two subdivisions in an apparently illogical way, or otherwise be slightly vaguer than I should like;

(v) the results described in this chapter are only a selection from the 500 or so tables which the Hollerith installation at Harwell produced. These in turn were only a selection from the 5,000 or so which it could have produced in theory (I am counting only two-dimensional tables). Both the other demands on the Calculator and on its staff, and the fact that a single human being had to examine the tables it produced, made it necessary to limit the tables to those that seemed likely to yield interesting associations or to test preconceived ideas about connections (e.g. between efficiency and enjoyment of one's job). Unlikely associations—for example, between the sex of one's superior officer and the time taken to travel between office and home—have not been examined; nor, on the other hand, have some which were likely but uninteresting (for example, between marital status and participation in office clubs);

(vi) the reader who is allergic to tables of figures should be able to follow the argument in the text without consulting them.

8.1. SOME FACTS ABOUT THE RESPONDENTS

Before examining the attitudes which were disclosed by the questionnaires, we must get a clear picture of what the respondents were. How old were they? How many of them were women? What sort of careers had they had?[1]

Sex and Age (Qns. 3, 2)

At all levels, except the firms' lower level, men outnumbered women. 26 per cent. of the Ministries' respondents and 38 per cent. of the firms' were women. There were no women among the firms' upper level, but about a fifth of the middle level were women. About a third of the H.E.O.s and E.O.s in the Ministries were women, and the senior Executive grades and administrators contained smaller percentages. There were very few women among the professional civil servants who responded. In case there were any marked differences between the attitudes of men and women, it seemed best to tabulate the replies of the sexes separately where there were enough women to justify this, but to exclude the replies of the women where there were not; so that the tabulated replies for the Administrative, senior Executive and professional civil servants, like those of the upper level respondents in the firms, are exclusively male. But women in these groups who responded should not feel that their replies are wasted: they are included in the figures for each Ministry as a whole, and for the civil servants, and were studied for their spontaneous comments.[2]

There were some striking differences in the age distribution of the men and women at the different levels in the Ministries and firms.[3] The mean age of all the civil servants was very much greater than that of the firms' staffs (43·6 v. 33·4 years). The bulk of the lower levels in the firms were in their twenties, while the peaks of the clerical grades in the Ministries were in the thirties. The age distribution of the middle levels in the firms and the E.O. and H.E.O. grades in the civil service was not very different, either for men or for women. The administrators

[1] Other facts about them have already been discussed in earlier chapters (their sick leave in Chapter 6, and their use of the Welfare Officers in Chapter 2).
[2] q.v., in Section 8.3 of this chapter.
[3] This table is likely to be a *slightly* distorted picture because of the tendency, mentioned in the previous chapter, for older people to yield a lower percentage of respondents. But it is most unlikely that this distortion has shifted any peaks from one age-group to another, or falsified any comparisons between grades.

RESULTS OF THE QUESTIONNAIRE

tended to be younger and the higher Executive grades to be older than the upper level in the firms. In the Small Ministry the complete absence of professionals under forty (at least among these respondents) was noticeable, and of the Large Ministry's professionals only 3·1 per cent were in their thirties.

TABLE 8.01

Ages

		N[1]	Age-groups					
			Under 20	20-29	30-39	40-49	50-59	60 & over
	Large Ministry	780	0·8	11·7	28·0	27·7	26·0	5·8
	Small Ministry	310	1·6	10·4	30·2	27·9	23·7	6·2
	Civil servants in both	1090	1·0	11·3	28·6	27·8	25·4	5·9
	Both firms' staffs	650	8·6	35·7	26·9	18·0	8·8	2·0
	North Firm	340	7·5	36·2	30·2	16·7	8·0	1·4
	South Firm	310	9·9	35·1	23·3	19·5	9·6	2·6
Civil Service grades	Administrative*	90	—	6·9	34·5	43·6	13·8	1·2
	Executive above H.E.O.*	90	—	—	17·2	31·2	49·5	2·1
	H.E.O. and E.O.: men	310	1·0	19·6	35·9	22·4	16·9	4·2
	women	130	2·4	15·1	34·1	31·7	15·1	1·6
	C.O., C.O. (Sec.) and C.A.: men	230	1·8	6·2	33·6	20·4	25·6	12·4
	women	150	0·7	15·2	21·2	25·2	28·4	9·3
	Professional*: Large Ministry	60	—	—	3·1	46·9	45·3	4·7
	Small Ministry	20	—	—	—	35·0	60·0	5·0
Firms' levels	Upper level	60	—	3·5	26·3	42·1	26·3	1·8
	Middle level: men	200	—	21·0	44·5	26·0	7·5	1·0
	women	40	—	18·0	30·7	33·3	18·0	—
	Lower level: men	140	8·8	56·0	16·9	6·1	6·8	5·4
	women	210	20·2	47·0	17·1	9·7	5·1	0·9

Careers of Respondents (Qns. 1, 5, 6, 7, 9)

Table 8.02 shows:

(i) The percentages of respondents who had worked in some other office before entering their present Ministry or Company.

---

[1] Numbers are approximate to nearest 10: they exclude 'spoilt' answers, the numbers of which vary slightly from one question to another. They also exclude a few women in the civil service grades marked *, so that the numbers for the grades do not equal the total number for the civil servants.

TABLE 8.02

Respondents' Careers

	N[1]	Question 5: 'Before entering your present Company or Ministry had you been an office worker in any other kind of office?'						Question 6: 'How long have you been in your present Company or Ministry?' (Count 6 months or more as 1 year, 5 months or less as 0.) Years						Question 9: 'How many years have you been in your present post?' (Count 6 months or more as 1 year, 5 or less as 0.) Years				Question 7: 'Since you have been in your present Company or Ministry how often has your job been changed (including promotions, but not minor changes in part of your duties)?' Times					
		No	Yes, in the civil service	Yes, in a private office	Yes, in nationalised industry	Yes, in local government	Yes, in some kind of office	0	1-10	11-20	21-30	31-40	Over 40	0	1-4	5-8	Over 8	0	1	2	3	4	5 or more
		%	%	%	%	%	%	%	%	%	%	%	%	%	%	%	%	%	%	%	%	%	%
Large Ministry	780	34·3	23·3	30·9	1·1	2·0	8·4	0·4	42·3	48·3	7·5	1·0	0·5	7·4	62·2	17·3	13·1	9·4	12·1	13·4	18·8	13·1	33·2
Small Ministry	310	32·6	30·6	20·9	0·3	6·5	9·1	2·3	40·5	40·6	7·1	8·8	0·7	9·2	58·8	16·0	16·0	15·5	17·4	15·5	15·8	11·5	24·3
Civil servants in both	1090	33·8	25·3	28·1	0·9	3·3	8·6	0·8	41·8	46·2	7·4	3·2	0·6	7·9	61·4	16·8	13·9	11·2	13·6	13·9	18·0	12·8	30·5
Both firms' staffs	650	31·9	3·6	47·0	2·5	1·6	13·4	6·5	73·4	11·1	7·3	1·7	—	8·6	63·2	15·1	13·1	48·9	20·5	11·7	8·2	4·5	6·2
North Firm	340	34·2	4·5	44·2	2·1	1·2	13·8	6·3	71·7	12·7	7·2	2·1	—	10·1	62·7	13·9	13·3	47·7	18·7	12·2	8·6	5·8	7·0
South Firm	310	29·4	2·7	50·1	3·0	2·0	12·8	6·7	75·2	9·4	7·4	1·3	—	6·8	63·9	16·4	12·9	50·3	22·5	11·1	7·7	3·0	5·4

[1] Numbers are approximate to nearest 10: they exclude 'spoilt' answers, the numbers of which vary slightly from one question to another.

Nearly half the firms' employees had been in another private firm's office, but very few had been civil servants. On the other hand, while over a quarter of civil servants had been in another Ministry, even more had been in a private office. A handful had worked in local government or nationalised industry. Comparison of their attitudes towards their present Ministry or Company showed remarkably little difference between those who had experience of other organisations and those who had not (see the section 'Attitudes to their own Organisation').

(ii) The lengths of time for which percentages of respondents had
   (a) been with their present organisation;
   (b) been in their present posts.

Here again there were striking differences between the Companies' respondents and the Ministries. The former had been with the Companies for an average of 6·6 years, of which they had spent the last 3·9 in their present posts, while the civil servants had served an average of 13·1 years in their Ministries, of which they had spent, on average, the last 4·1 years in their present posts.

(iii) The numbers of changes of job experienced by percentages of respondents in their present organisation. The frequency with which civil servants are moved from one post to another is one of the features of the service which outsiders find hard to understand, and inconvenient in their dealings with it. We shall discuss its possible effects on attitudes to work later. In the meantime, Table 8.02 allows us to make a rough comparison between the civil servant and the other office workers in this respect. Since 73 per cent. of the latter had been in their firms from 1 to 10 years, and since 49 per cent. had suffered no change of job, and a further 20 per cent. had suffered only one, we can see how small are the chances of more than one change of job in these firms; and this one change may well be the result of a promotion (which the respondents were asked to include in their estimates). Of the civil servants, on the other hand, 88 per cent. had been in their Ministries between 1 and 20 years, and 75 per cent. of all had experienced two or more changes—31 per cent. of them more than four. Even allowing for promotions, this confirms that the rate of change is much higher. It seems to have been particularly high in the Large Ministry, one-third of whose respondents had experienced five or more changes in spite of the fact that a smaller percentage than in the Small Ministry had been more than 20 years in the organisation. (Differences between the firms were insignificant.)

166   MORALE IN THE CIVIL SERVICE

Promotion (Qn. 1)

The civil service respondents had been asked in Question 1 to mark their original grade as well as their present grade, so that in their case it was possible to compare the two and see what percentage of the main groups had their origins in the various lower grades. The table below shows the result for the desk grades (there would have been little point in including the professional grades in this tabulation):

TABLE 8.03

Present Grades	Original Grades					
	Administrative	Executive above H.E.O.	H.E.O. & E.O.	C.O.	C.A.	Others
Administrative .	% 46·7	% 1·1	% 15·2	% 16·3	% —	% 20·7
Executive above H.E.O. .	—	2·1	16·5	36·1	5·2	40·1
H.E.O. & E.O. .	—	—	22·1	29·4	20·5	28·0
C.O. or T.C. II .	—	0·3[1]	—	0·6[1]	32·3	30·7	36·1
C.A. or T.C. III	—	—	—	12·5[1]	68·8	18·7

The table shows the considerable extent to which the higher grades are open to promotion from the lower ones. 33 per cent. of the administrators had entered the service through the Executive or Clerical grades (although none appeared to have done so as Clerical Assistants). 41 per cent. of the senior Executive grades had entered as Clerical Officers or Clerical Assistants and, less surprisingly, 50 per cent. of the junior Executive grades had done so. The other striking fact was that substantial percentages of all these groups had had their origins in a large number of other miscellaneous grades in the service. Quite a number had begun their careers in the Post Office as postmen or telegraph operators. Others had begun as boy messengers and a very substantial number had been technicians of one sort or another in various Departments. This table emphasises even more strongly than Mr. Frank Dunnill's book[2] the fallacy of picturing the desk classes of the civil service as consisting almost entirely of a homogeneous group of recruits through the three main channels of entry. For example, only 47 per cent. of the administrators had begun their careers as such.

[1] The original grade is occasionally higher than the present grade in the case of officers who have become established after serving in a temporary capacity (e.g. a Temporary Clerk Grade II, though the equivalent of a C.O., might become established as a C.A.) and of officers who have been re-employed in a lower grade after reaching retiring age.

[2] *The Civil Service; Some Human Aspects.*

RESULTS OF THE QUESTIONNAIRE

All these, and no doubt some of the Executives, would be university graduates: the rest would probably not be.

Spare-time Work and Other Activities (Qns. 12, 13, 16, 17, 18)

Respondents were asked about the frequency with which they did official work after regular hours, or took it home; and Table 8.04 shows their estimates. Allowances must be made here for two things. Working after regular hours, either at the office or at home, is a practice that varies very much with the level of the employee, certainly in the civil service and probably in the firms. In the case of the clerical grades in headquarters offices, for example, the decision whether they shall work after regular hours involves the payment of overtime, and is taken not by them but by their superiors. As for taking work home, much of it is not as portable as the brief-case of the senior Executive or administrator. Both in the Ministries and the firms, therefore, most of the respondents who claimed to work after hours on 2, 3 or more nights a week, or to take work home, came from the higher levels, and the differing proportions between the levels in the different organisations makes it difficult to compare their estimates with any confidence. The most that can be said is that even allowing for this effect the estimates of the North Firm suggest a strikingly high level of activity after hours. The other factor that has to be taken into account is that among the higher levels of office worker to work for longer hours than most of one's colleagues is to acquire merit, and even some sort of moral advantage over them. We shall see (in the section 'Some aspects of the work itself') how strangely high is the percentage of office workers who consider themselves more hardworked than their colleagues at the same level. So that respondents' estimates on this subject are probably generous to themselves; but no doubt the generosity of the civil servant and the firms' employee is about equal.

Table 8.04 also shows how many respondents disclosed that they did office work for some other organisation in their spare time. A handful did so in order to supplement their income; but in the civil service quite a substantial 13 per cent. did so out of interest. These include, no doubt, those who like to fill some of their leisure by acting as secretaries or treasurers of charitable organisations, staff associations, golf clubs, and so forth. This practice is significantly more common among the civil servants than among the firms' staffs.

Office Clubs and Societies (Qns. 17, 18)

The formation of clubs or societies within offices to assist staff to pursue some of their recreations and leisure interests together is usually regarded as good for 'morale', and as we saw in Chapter 2 is something in which Welfare Officers in the civil service are supposed to take an

TABLE 8.04

After Working Hours

	N	Question 12: 'On how many nights a week, on the average, do you do official work after regular hours?' Nights each Week					Question 13: 'How often do you take official work home?'				Question 16: 'Do you do any office work for some other organisation in your spare time? (You need not answer if you prefer.)'			Questions 17-18: 'In your office, is there a club or society for any of your spare-time interests?'				Question 10: 'How many minutes does it take you to travel from your office to your home each evening, by the most direct route, from door to door?' Minutes						
		0	1	2	3	4 or more	Never	Hardly ever	Sometimes	Frequently	No	Yes, out of interest	Yes, to supplement my income	No	Not sure	Yes	Taking part in its activities	Under 15	15 to 30	30 to 45	45 to 60	60 to 75	75 to 90	Over 90
		%	%	%	%	%	%	%	%	%	%	%	%	%	%	%	(% of N)	%	%	%	%	%	%	%
Large Ministry	780	66·8	15·7	8·4	4·1	5·0	46·8	31·8	17·8	3·6	83·8	13·4	2·8	13·9	3·1	83·0	18·4	0·9	7·6	14·7	31·7	27·7	11·3	6·1
Small Ministry	310	71·7	12·4	6·5	5·2	4·2	48·5	29·0	17·6	4·9	87·6	10·8	1·6	6·2	2·0	91·8	36·9	1·0	11·1	16·9	31·9	20·2	8·1	10·8
Civil servants in both	1090	68·2	14·7	7·9	4·4	4·8	47·4	31·0	17·7	3·9	84·8	12·7	2·5	11·7	2·8	85·5	23·6	0·9	8·6	15·3	31·7	25·7	10·4	7·4
Both firms' staffs	650	60·1	16·3	10·4	6·1	7·1	49·2	21·7	21·6	7·5	90·3	5·8	3·9	4·6	0·8	94·6	39·2	1·4	9·7	21·7	30·9	22·6	9·1	4·6
North Firm	340	53·0	16·7	12·0	7·8	10·5	46·5	19·0	24·0	10·5	88·6	6·7	4·7	3·2	0·6	96·2	46·5	2·0	9·2	22·5	27·5	20·7	11·5	6·6
South Firm	310	68·0	15·7	8·7	4·3	3·3	52·0	24·8	19·0	4·2	92·2	4·9	2·9	6·1	1·0	92·9	29·7	0·6	10·3	20·8	34·7	24·7	6·7	2·2

[1] Numbers are approximate to nearest 10: they exclude 'spoilt' answers, the numbers of which vary slightly from one question to another.

interest.[1] It was therefore interesting to see (Table 8.04) that either through official encouragement or the spontaneous efforts of the staff themselves, well over 90 per cent. of respondents found that at least one of their interests was catered for by an office club. The exception to this happy announcement is the Large Ministry, where the percentage was only 83 per cent. Here the explanation may well be that, unlike the other respondents, theirs were drawn not only from the main headquarters buildings, but also from two others, which were not catered for by clubs within the buildings themselves. In any case, I do not think that the Large Ministry need feel that this reveals a serious deficiency, since Question 18, by contrast, showed how very much smaller was the percentage of staff who took part in the activities of these clubs. For example, although 92 per cent. of the Small Ministry's staff said that there was a club or society which catered for one of their interests, only 37 per cent. took any part in its activities. By far the highest percentage—47 per cent. in the North Firm—is still quite low in comparison with the 96 per cent. of their respondents who felt that there was a club which met one of their needs.

One of the factors that must discourage a great many from participating is the time which they take to reach their homes again at the end of the day. The next section deals with this.

Travel to Work (Qn. 10)

At the request of the firms I had included a question to find out roughly how much travelling their office staffs had to do in order to get to work. To avoid giving any impression that we were concerned with punctuality in arriving at work I made the questions refer to the journey back to home. This proved to be a question to which almost everyone knew the answer: only one respondent from each organisation failed to complete it. Table 8.04 shows some difference between the four organisations, most easily seen by comparing the percentages who took more than an hour from door to door:

South Firm	33·6
North Firm	38·8
Small Ministry	39·1
Large Ministry	45·1

The civil servants on the whole live further away from their work.

8.2. JOB-SATISFACTION AND EFFICIENCY

In Chapter 4, where we considered what the term 'morale' meant, we saw that it was really no more than a field of study, and that instead

---

[1] While so far as possible arranging matters so that the clubs and societies 'run themselves'.

of asking 'What is the morale of Mr. X like?' we must ask a number of separate questions. The most important of these from the employer's point of view is 'How efficient is Mr. X?'; the most important from the employee's point of view is 'How much does he enjoy his work?' The questionnaire was designed to provide some sort of answer to both questions, and we must discuss the results of these before we can properly appraise the respondents' replies to other attitude-questions.

Job-satisfaction (Qn. 60)

My attempt to measure respondents' enjoyment of their job consisted of a question which was deliberately placed on the last page of the questionnaire, so that by the time they came to answer it they would have considered all the aspects of their job which were covered by the preceding fifty questions, and would feel that they were summing-up their attitude to it. The question itself begins '*All things considered*, how do you feel about your present job?' Respondents had a choice of 11 replies, ranging from 'I love it' to 'I hate it'. These phrases were based on the job-satisfaction scale developed by R. Hoppock, with an addition inserted by John Handyside, of the National Institute of Industrial Psychology, who had used it in his researches among factory workers in this country.[1] This scale is a very well-tried measuring instrument, and by using it I was enabled to compare my respondents with those of other surveys.

The distribution of the replies is shown in Table 8.05. There is the usual peak at 'I like it on the whole', and the usual dips interrupting the curve at 'I like it a good deal'[2] and 'I am indifferent to it'. In order to make it easier to compare the distributions of the various grades with each other, and civil servants' replies with those from the firms, as well as to study their relationship with replies to other questions, I decided to divide the replies into three groups, which can be seen in Table 8.05. I would call replies 0, 1 and 2 the 'satisfied' group; replies

---

[1] His insertion, 'I like it a good deal', was intended to increase the discriminatory power of the scale at the usual peak, where so many respondents (usually well over one-third) choose 'On the whole I like it'. It is not a complete success, since the normal distribution is now broken by a sharp dip at this point: either because the scale is otherwise an equal-interval one, or because the phrase chosen is not one that respondents would naturally use, or perhaps for both reasons. But since this was the form in which the scale has been used most often in this country, there were obvious advantages in adopting Handyside's version.

This insertion, and also the slight effect obtained by presenting the scale upside down, and other points, are discussed in N.I.I.P.'s Interim Research Note No. 1, of January 1959.

[2] See the footnote to the previous paragraph. The dip of 'I am indifferent to it' may be due simply to respondents' preference for some phrase which indicates a definite attitude of liking or disliking.

6, 7, 8, 9 and x the 'dissatisfied' group; and 3, 4 and 5 the 'in-between' group. This division is not quite arbitrary, for it ensures that the peak group falls in the centre of the 'in-betweens' and also includes one set of replies on each side of this group. The 'in-between' includes 61 per cent. of the civil servants, and 46 per cent. of the firms' staff. This leaves, however, a substantial 11-13 per cent. in the long low tail formed by replies 6-x, and an even more substantial 25-46 per cent. to form the 'satisfied' group. It is important to remember, however, that when I refer in this chapter to 'satisfied' or 'dissatisfied' respondents, I am using the terms to denote groups defined in this way.

The difference between the distributions of the civil servants' and of the firms' replies is striking. There is not much difference between the size of the dissatisfied tail (12·9% v. 10·8%), but 43·1 per cent. of the firms' staffs gave satisfied replies compared with only 23·5 per cent. of the civil servants. Comparison with the replies of office workers from three other firms who completed the job-satisfaction question in a questionnaire issued by the National Institute of Industrial Psychology showed that in distribution these resembled the replies of the civil servants rather than those of the North and South firms. But the high satisfaction of the latter is very largely due to the replies from the middle and upper levels, which, as we shall see from Table 8.06, were remarkably satisfied. The replies from the higher levels of the Ministries also contained higher percentages of satisfied ones, but the difference was not nearly so marked.

The Passage of Time. Time, the great healer, certainly seemed to have a therapeutic effect of some sort upon dissatisfaction with one's work. The older the respondent, the more likely he was to enjoy it. This phenomenon had been observed in studies of manual workers—for example, by Wyatt and Marriott in their survey of three British factories.[1] But several possibilities had to be considered. In the first place, the explanation might simply be that the more dissatisfied employees resigned from their jobs, so that the older workers who remained tended to be those who did not dislike their work. In the factories studied by Wyatt and Marriott, labour turnover was high, so that they could not rule out this possibility. In the civil service, on the other hand, as we saw in Chapter 3, resignations are much less frequent, and the two Ministries were no exception; so that this explanation would not serve. But there were other complications. The older the respondent, the longer he was likely to have belonged to his Ministry or Company.

---

[1] *A Study of Attitudes to Factory Work*, by S. Wyatt and R. Marriott: Medical Research Council Special Report No. 292, published by H.M.S.O., 1956. It should be noted that this survey made use of a much cruder measure of job-satisfaction than the Hoppock scale. Other studies by the National Institute of Industrial Psychology also show an age-effect, according to a personal communication from Mr. John Handyside.

TABLE 8.05
Job-satisfaction
(Ministries and Companies)

Question 60: 'All things considered, how do you feel about your present job?'	N[1]	(0) 'I love it'	(1) 'I am enthusiastic about it'	(2) 'I like it very much'	(3) 'I like it a good deal'	(4) 'I like it on the whole'	(5) 'I like it fairly well'	(6) 'I like it a little'	(7) 'I am indifferent to it'	(8) 'On the whole, I don't like it'	(9) 'I dislike it'	(x) 'I hate it'	Satisfied (i.e. choices 0–2)	In between (i.e. choices 3–5)	Dissatisfied (i.e. choices 6–x)
		%	%	%	%	%	%	%	%	%	%	%	%	%	%
Large Ministry	780	3·0	3·1	19·2	13·9	31·7	15·8	4·3	2·8	4·6	1·1	0·5	25·3	61·4	13·3
Small Ministry	310	2·6	4·3	18·3	15·4	33·9	13·7	3·3	3·3	2·9	1·3	1·0	25·2	63·0	11·8
Civil servants in both	1090	2·9	3·4	19·0	14·4	32·1	15·3	4·0	2·9	4·2	1·2	0·6	25·3	61·8	12·9
Both firms' staffs	650	7·6	14·0	21·5	11·3	25·4	9·4	3·0	2·6	4·3	0·6	0·3	43·1	46·1	10·8
North Firm	340	5·8	14·5	19·8	10·8	25·8	10·8	3·5	2·6	5·8	0·6	—	40·1	47·4	12·5
South Firm	310	9·5	13·5	23·3	11·9	24·8	8·0	2·5	2·5	2·8	0·6	0·6	46·3	44·7	9·0

[1] Numbers are approximate to nearest 10: they exclude 'spoilt' answers, the numbers of which vary slightly from one question to another.

RESULTS OF THE QUESTIONNAIRE

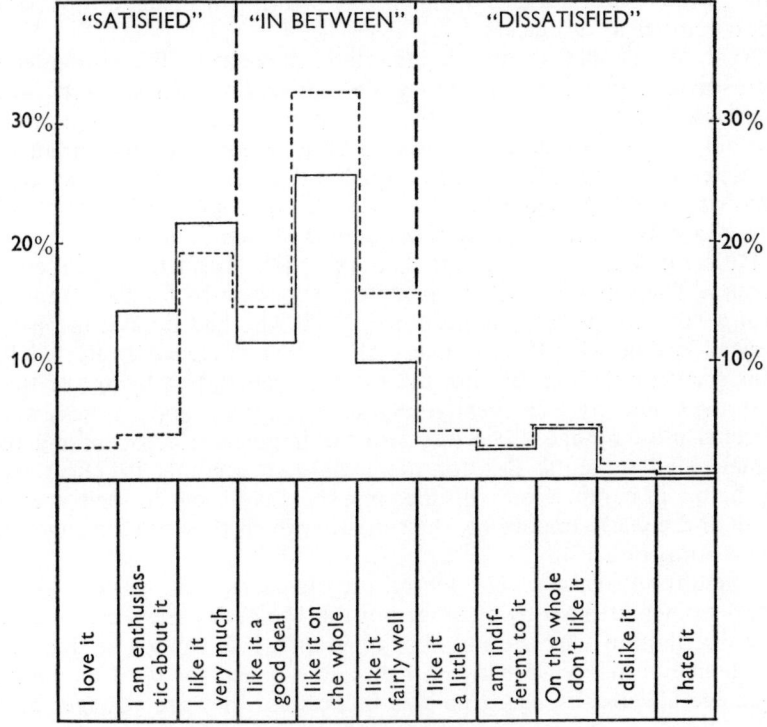

FIGURE 8.01

Job satisfaction of Civil Servants (------)
and Firms' Staffs (———)

Perhaps it was really time spent in the same organisation that increased job-satisfaction? Wyatt and Marriott found that this was not so in their factories, but manual workers are not desk workers. Moreover, yet another time-factor might be operative. The longer a respondent had been with his organisation, the longer he was likely to have been doing the work he was now engaged on.[1] Factory workers do not usually change their tasks without changing employers, so that there is little hope of distinguishing the effects of time on the job and time in the factory. But among office workers, especially civil servants, changes of post within the organisation are more frequent, and it was not only possible but also very desirable to isolate the influences which age,

[1] Strictly speaking, there were more than three time-factors—for example, time spent in the civil service or in private office work. But in most cases this would not differ from time spent in the Ministry or Company: we have seen that most of the civil servants had not served in another Ministry.

time in the organisation and time in the post might or might not have upon enjoyment of one's work.

Analysis[1] revealed a complex and interesting picture. The respondents were divided into four groups—male and female civil servants, and male and female Company staff. The civil servants, on average, were not only ten years older, but had also been longer with their organisations; and although there was not much difference between the average time which they had spent in their present posts the civil servants had had about five times as many changes of post (see Table 8.02).

Different time-factors appeared to affect job-satisfaction in different groups. The women in the Companies, who were by far the youngest group—two-thirds being under thirty—and who had on average spent very little time with the Company or on their jobs, were affected by time spent on the job, but not to any significant extent by age or time with the Company.[2] The next youngest group, the Company men, were affected most by age.[2] Age was also the important factor among the female civil servants. But for the male civil servants its effect was negligible in comparison with the time they had spent in their present jobs, and equally important, the time for which they had belonged to their Ministries.

These results raise several tantalising questions. Why are the Ministries' women affected by age, but not the Ministries' men, although in age distribution they are not very different? This cannot be due to a fundamental difference between men and women, for the Companies' men *are* affected by age. Can this be because they are younger men,

---

[1] By Mr. J. E. Hailstone, using a multiple regression technique. Assuming the job-satisfaction scale to be an equal-interval one, so that scores on it could be treated numerically (e.g. 'I love it'$=0$; 'I hate it'$=11$); and assuming the distribution of scores on it to be roughly normal (in fact they are slightly skewed towards '0'), he arrived at the following linear equations:

Where $j=$ the job-satisfaction score, and a, p and m indicate the value of 'z' in the expression

$$z = \frac{\sigma j}{\sigma y}(y - \bar{y})$$

in the case of age (a), years in the post (p) and years in the Ministry or Company (m) respectively, for

men in the Ministries: $j - \bar{j} = -0.0038a - \underline{0.0716p} - \underline{0.0880m}$

women in the Ministries: $j - \bar{j} = -\underline{0.1602a} - 0.0812p - 0.0566m$

men in the Companies: $j - \bar{j} = -\underline{0.1929a} - 0.1942p + 0.0265m$

women in the Companies: $j - \bar{j} = -0.0909a - \underline{0.1953p} + 0.0130m$

(The underlined values are the only ones which are significant at the ·01 level: but for men in the Companies, p was significant at the ·05 level.)

[2] There was even a slight indication that time spent in the Companies actually *lowered* the job-satisfaction of both the men and the women: but the effect was so very slight that there is no evidence that it is due to anything but chance.

who have not been so long in their organisations? If so, why are the youngest group of all, the Companies' women, affected by time in the post and hardly at all by age?[1] The theory that could answer all these questions would have to be elaborate and speculative indeed.

What we can say is that in certain circumstances the job-satisfaction of both male and female desk workers can be independently increased by two separate factors—age and time in the post.[2] This is of much more than academic interest. Time in the job is one of the factors that can be readily manipulated by the employer; and later in this chapter I shall be discussing the present approach of the civil service to this notorious problem.

The confirmation of the effect of age, on the other hand, is interesting for the very reason that it is a factor that cannot be manipulated. It demonstrates that one's enjoyment of one's work can increase through some process that is quite beyond anybody's control. Whether the process is one of constitutional change, or whether we simply learn, like Solon, that the ideal job is unobtainable this side of the grave, is still an open question.

Level in the Hierarchy. Another factor with which job-satisfaction was clearly linked in some way was the respondent's level in the hierarchy. Table 8.07 shows how, broadly speaking, the higher ranks contained higher percentages of satisfied and lower percentages of dissatisfied desk workers than did the lower levels.[3]

Among the civil servants, the most dissatisfied are the male C.O.s and C.A.s—a fact which is consistent with the high rate of wastage among young male C.O.s which we noticed in Chapters 3 and 6; while the Administrators were the most satisfied of the desk workers proper. In passing, however, the remarkably high job-satisfaction of the Small Ministry's professionals should be noted: they really seem to derive pleasure from their work (of which I can say no more than that it gives them scope for a certain amount of design and other creative activities). In the Companies, the highest satisfaction is shown by the upper-level

[1] We must not overlook the possibility that the association between time in the job and satisfaction with it is an illusion caused by the tendency of those who dislike the job to ask for a transfer to another one. In the Companies, this might be the explanation of the apparent effect of time in the job upon the young women. But in the Ministries, as in the civil service generally, transfers from post to post usually take place when the needs of the organisation and not the wishes of the individual call for them; and I do not think that this explanation will account for the association in the case of the Ministries' men.

[2] And probably even by time in the Ministry, for 796 male civil servants, 500 of them C.O.s, E.O.s or H.E.O.s, are a very satisfactory sample.

[3] The possibility that this was an illusory effect, due to higher percentages of older respondents, or respondents who had been longer in their present posts, among the higher levels, was of course considered; but a partial association test showed that the relationship between job-satisfaction and grade had little to do with the time-factors.

men and by the middle-level women; the latter have achieved the highest positions which women can hope for in these firms. In contrast, the dissatisfaction of the lower levels is marked; some though not all of it is explained by the fact that these grades contain a high percentage of young men and women who have been only a short time in their jobs, so that neither age nor adjustment to the work has yet affected their attitude to their work.

TABLE 8.06

Job-satisfaction
(Grades or Levels)

Level (or Staff Group)	(N)[1]	Job-satisfaction Category		
		Satisfied	In between	Dissatisfied
		%	%	%
Civil Servants:	(1090)	25	62	13
Administrative*	(90)	32	59	9
Executive above H.E.O.*	(90)	28	67	5
H.E.O. & E.O.:				
men	(310)	20	67	13
women	(130)	21	64	15
C.O., C.O. (Sec.) & C.A.:				
men	(230)	20	62	18
women	(150)	29	55	15
Professionals*:				
Large Ministry	(60)	27	69	5
Small Ministry	(20)	60	35	5
Firms' Staffs:	(650)	43	46	11
Upper level	(60)	65	28	7
Middle level:				
men	(200)	53	43	4
women	(40)	67	31	3
Lower level:				
men	(140)	31	49	21
women	(210)	28	59	14

Estimate of One's Own Abilities. This table disposes of the comfortable assumption that office workers at the lower levels enjoy their jobs as much as those nearer the top, because the work of each level is more or less suited to its abilities. Certainly, as the following table shows, there was a strong tendency in both Ministries and Companies for those who felt that the work was below their capabilities to be dissatisfied with it:

[1] Numbers are approximate to nearest 10: they exclude 'spoilt' answers, the numbers of which vary slightly from one question to another. They also exclude a few women in the civil service grades marked *.

TABLE 8.07

Job-satisfaction Category	(N)	Question 32: 'I feel that my duties are			
		Well below	A little below	More or less suited to my capabilities'	A little beyond	Well beyond[1]

		%	%	%	%
Civil Servants:					
Satisfied	(263)	21	33	45	0·4
In between	(680)	23	39	37	1
Dissatisfied	(143)	45	31	22	2
Firms' Staffs:					
Satisfied	(272)	13	35	50	2
In between	(310)	22	38	38	2
Dissatisfied	(72)	58	31	10	1

But as we shall see, the lower the grade or level of the respondents, the higher the percentage who regarded their duties as well below their capabilities.

We are faced, therefore, with the question why grade or level in the hierarchy should be associated with job-satisfaction in this way. At first sight the answer is in the preceding paragraph: 'because the work of those in the lower grades is below their capabilities'. But this begs a lot of other questions. In the first place, all we know is that more of the dissatisfied *regard* their jobs as below their capabilities: we do not know that this attitude reflects the facts. Indeed, two pieces of evidence suggest that it does not. We shall see in the section on 'Individual Efficiency' that this bears little relationship to respondents' own estimates of their ability, and that its relationship to the respondents' grades is the opposite of what we should expect if the work of the lower grades were really more below their capabilities than that of the higher grades. In the second place, of course, all we have here is evidence of an association, and not evidence of the direction or nature of the causal link. For all we know, it is low job-satisfaction that causes people to regard the work as too easy for them, and not vice versa; nor must we forget the possibility that some third factor is causing both. It is only when we are faced by an association between job-satisfaction and something that could not possibly be affected in this way—such as age— that we are justified, without further evidence, in dismissing these hypotheses. What is more, we shall find that job-satisfaction is associated with many other attitudes.

It may be argued, however, that in the case of grade we *are* dealing with something which, like age, cannot very well be affected by job-satisfaction, so that it must be grade or something that varies with grade

[1] Very few indeed chose this reply.

which is influencing job-satisfaction. But before we can pursue this line of thought we must consider first the possibility that job-satisfaction *does* influence grade, by hastening promotion. After all, another common assumption is that the more you enjoy your work the better you are at it. What is the relationship between job-satisfaction and individual efficiency? This is one of the most important questions for any study of morale.

Efficiency

It was, of course, impossible to attempt to measure and compare the efficiency of the Ministries and firms as organisations, for the reason I have outlined in Chapter 5. But in the case of most of the civil servants it was possible to obtain a rough estimate of each individual's efficiency by using the part of his annual report in which his immediate superior sums up what is called his 'performance of duties'. This is not entirely the unsupported verdict of one fallible human being, for the report must be countersigned by the officer immediately above the one who signs it; and the rating given under this head must be consistent with the general trend of the answers to a great many other detailed questions. If it appeared inconsistent with these, or with the trend of previous annual reports by the same or other superiors, it would be questioned by the Establishment Division.

On the Large Ministry's form of annual report the individual's 'performance of duties' was summed up by marking one of five possible choices. In the Small Ministry's form this was not provided for, so that for my purpose the Establishment Division had to sum up the ratings given under the other detailed headings, instead of simply giving me the marking awarded by the superior himself; but it was arranged that they too would use a five-choice scale.[1] As Table 8.08 shows, the distribution of ratings was slightly different in the two Ministries; the Large Ministry tended to make more use of ratings 3 and 4 and less of 1 and 2 than the Small Ministry; and the explanation may lie in the differences I have just described.[2] But in both cases the distribution of the ratings was sufficiently symmetrical to make me confident that I had here a rough but serviceable way of classifying my respondents according to their efficiency at their work.

The most striking thing about the ratings in both Ministries is of course the complete absence of the lowest rating, 5. It is the rule of the Service that a reporting officer who awards this rating must tell the

---

[1] Another, less important, difference was that in the Large Ministry but not in the Small Ministry Principals and Assistant Principals were the subject of annual reports.
[2] Although one respondent did allege that senior staff in the Small Ministry 'disliked giving adverse reports' (see 'Discipline').

subordinate that he is doing so; and this alone is enough to ensure that it is used very rarely.[1] I was told by the Small Ministry that in the last year there had in fact been one or two cases in which it had been awarded (and acted upon): but these individuals must either have been in parts of the Ministry that had not received my questionnaire or have been among the recipients who did not respond. Indeed, it is possible that the extremely inefficient are less likely to respond. Even so, the absence of the lowest rating is striking.

TABLE 8.08
Individual Efficiency
(Civil Service Respondents only)

	N	Superior Officers' Ratings for 'performance of duties'				
		1	2	3	4	5
		%	%	%	%	%
Large Ministry	740	1·2	44·4	49·0	5·4	—
Small Ministry	260	8·1	49·2	41·9	0·8	—
Civil servants in both	1000	3·0	45·7	47·3	4·0	—
Age-groups—[2]						
20-9 years	120	5·0	42·5	50·8	1·7	—
30-9 ,,	290	4·5	61·1	32·3	2·1	—
40-9 ,,	260	2·7	45·8	47·3	4·2	—
50-9 ,,	250	1·6	34·8	55·5	8·1	—
60 or more	70	—	29·0	66·7	4·3	—

This means that in practice the least efficient of my respondents were the 4 per cent. who were rated '4'; and even these were very few. It is not until we reach '3' that we find any substantial number. It is almost universally accepted in the service that to award this rating is to damn a man with faint praise. Table 8.08 bears this out, for it shows that the ratings are distributed so symmetrically on either side of a line drawn *between* '2' and '3' that to award '3' to someone is to place him in the *lower half* of the Ministry so far as his performance of his duties are concerned. In other words, if we want a rough but reliable division between the sheep and the goats from the point of view of efficiency we can group together '1' and '2', and be sure that they are the better half, and '3' and '4' and be sure that they are the worse half.

[1] The same tendency to avoid the lowest rating is found in the Civil Service in the U.S.A., where, according to P. M. Blau (Appendix A), officers have to be told of their rating whatever it is.

[2] Omitting respondents under twenty, very few of whom had been in post long enough to be the subject of an ordinary annual report.

Table 8.08 also shows the distributions of the ratings in the different age-groups (omitting the teenagers, very few of whom had been in their posts long enough to be the subject of an ordinary annual report). It is interesting to see how the percentage of the lower ratings increases after the thirties, the age-group which has the biggest share of the two above-average ratings. The percentage of the worst rating, '4', increases steadily with age, until we reach the sixties, in which the weeding-out process of retirement has probably helped to reduce it: in any case, the numbers in this age-group are rather small.

Another fact which emerged from a comparison of the ratings awarded to the different grades was that the higher the grade, the higher the percentage of its members who obtained one of the two higher ratings:

	(N)	Ratings	
		1 & 2	3 & 4
		%	%
Principals,[1] Assistant Principals and S.E.O.s . .	(118)	61	39
H.E.O.s and E.O.s	(432)	53	47
C.O., C.O. (sec.) and C.A.	(373)	45	55

The Concomitants of Efficiency. Any organisation which is interested in efficiency must wonder whether, in its individual form, it is associated with attitudes that can either be measured and used as means of distinguishing the less from the more efficient, or manipulated and used as a means of raising efficiency. There were several subjects on which the respondents' replies might be worth comparing with their efficiency. It was hardly surprising to find that the more efficient half showed a stronger tendency than the rest to regard the system of promotion as working fairly, since they had benefited more from it: this merely reassured me that I was probably succeeding in measuring something. But some other results were more surprising.

'*The Value of Your Work.*' As we saw in Chapter 4, several of the definitions of 'morale' stressed the importance of a sense of purpose, presumably on the assumption that this is associated with efficiency. I use the word 'assumption' deliberately, since I have found no record of any attempt to test the hypothesis, or even to formulate it clearly. It may be true of situations among military groups—such as that described by Paterson[2]—but it did not seem to be true of my civil

[1] Since Principals and Assistant Principals in the Small Ministry were not the subject of formal annual reports (see a previous footnote) all the Principals and Assistant Principals in this group come from the Large Ministry. But since the ratings in the Large Ministry tend to be lower than in the Small Ministry, this again ought to *lower* the ratings of these grades, not raise them!

[2] *Loc. cit.* in Chapter 4.

servants, although my measuring instruments may have been too crude. I compared their efficiency ratings with their replies to Question 28 on the 'value of their work', and the result was unexpected:

Efficiency Rating	(N)	'Essential to the community'	'Useful but not essential	'Neither useful nor essential
		%	%	%
1	(28)	53·6	35·7	10·7
2	(452)	56·0	39·8	4·2
3	(466)	60·4	36·4	3·2
4	(40)	65·0	35·0	—

Although a healthy 58 per cent. believed their work was essential, there was if anything a slight tendency for the percentages to be higher among the less and not the more efficient, I say 'if anything' because the difference was not really large enough to be accepted as statistically significant. The point is, however, that there was certainly no tendency for belief in the value of one's work to be *positively* associated with individual efficiency.

Esprit de corps. On the other hand in the replies to Question 44 there was a small but significant tendency for more of the more efficient (36 per cent. of ratings 1 and 2) than of the less efficient (30 per cent. of ratings 3 and 4) to regard their own Ministry as 'much better' or 'slightly better' than others. This was interesting, because the study of the Prudential Insurance Company described in Appendix A found that 'pride in the work group' was connected in some way with higher collective efficiency. What I was trying to measure was pride in the organisation, not in the small working group; and individual, not collective, efficiency; but the similarity is interesting.

Attractions of the Job. Question 47 invited respondents to assign an order of value to ten features of their job which seemed likely to be attractions. The result is discussed in section 8.3 of this chapter, but I must anticipate that discussion here to show how little difference there was between the more and the less efficient. Table 8.09 demonstrates this. There were a few significant tendencies: more of those with rating 2 than of those with rating 3 ranked the 'interest of the work' at or near the top of their list, and fewer put pensions first; but in both these cases those with the highest possible rating were more cynically materialistic. It was pleasant to see how little store the most efficient set by hours of work, until I saw that the least efficient did the same. It was equally tempting to moralise over the high percentage of the least efficient who valued holidays above most other things: but an even higher percentage of the most efficient did the same. Three of the outstanding civil servants put 'physical conditions of work' at the head of their list or second, although this may simply have been to show their disillusionment, which, as we shall see, also manifested itself in their attitude to the civil service as a career.

TABLE 8.09

Attractions of the Job and Individual Efficiency

This table shows percentages of respondents assigning very high places (1 or 2) to ten potentially 'attractive features' of their job, with percentages in parentheses of those assigning very low places (9 or 10) to them. To simplify the table, intermediate places are omitted.

Feature of the Job	Performance Rating				All Civil Servants [1]	Firms' Staffs
	1	2	3	4		
Hours of work	3% (13)	12% (7)	16% (6)	5% (3)	13 (8)	13 (15)
Pension rights	40 (—)	32 (2)	40 (2)	38 (3)	34 (2)	16 (15)
Security of job	67 (—)	64 (0·2)	68 (0·7)	65 (—)	63 (0·5)	40 (3)
Promotion prospects	3 (23)	10 (24)	4 (33)	3 (30)	7 (28)	21 (27)
Pay	14 (10)	20 (6)	21 (7)	26 (5)	21 (7)	39 (4)
Interest of the work	23 (10)	32 (5)	23 (8)	34 (3)	32 (6)	50 (6)
Holidays	37 (—)	27 (2)	25 (2)	33 (5)	26 (2)	3 (16)
Status in community	3 (57)	3 (55)	2 (49)	3 (46)	3 (50)	5 (41)
Physical conditions of work	10 (30)	3 (29)	4 (29)	— (24)	4 (29)	12 (19)
Social life with colleagues	— (57)	2 (67)	1 (63)	— (82)	2 (65)	8 (50)
N[2]	30	445	450	40	1090	650

Estimates of One's Own Abilities. It was interesting to compare the efficiency ratings with respondents' own estimates of the extent to which their jobs were suited to their capabilities. The table opposite shows the response of the different grades to Question 32 on this subject.

[1] Including those with no performance ratings.
[2] Since a small but variable number of respondents with ratings 2, 3 or 4 omitted to give places to some of the features, these figures are approximate.

Very few respondents indeed would confess to finding their work even a little beyond them: so that except for a handful of very modest or very discouraged people the reply chosen by those who were least confident of their capabilities was that the work was 'more or less suited to them'. Even so, this left room for considerable variation. It was noticeable, for example, that the men in the firms' upper levels were less confident than the administrators or senior Executive grades in the civil service, although the difference may have been a chance effect. There was, however, an unmistakable tendency both in the firms and in the Ministries for the lower grades to contain a higher percentage who felt that their work was well below their abilities. The sharpest difference is between the C.O.s and the grades above them in the civil service. Note how the percentage of 'well belows' is about 19 per cent. for the Administrative and Executive grades but jumps to twice that among the Clerical grades.

TABLE 8.10

	N[1]	Question 32: 'I feel that my duties are			
		Well below	A little below	More or less suited to my capabilities'	A "little" or "well" beyond
		%	%	%	%
Civil Servants:					
Administrative . .	90	17·4	35·9	45·6	1·1
Executive above H.E.O.	100	19·6	35·1	45·3	—
H.E.O. and E.O. .	440	19·2	41·0	38·5	1·3
C.O., C.O. (Sec.) and C.A. . . .	380	39·2	32·4	28·1	0·3
Professional:					
Large Ministry .	60	16·9	40·0	43·1	—
Small Ministry .	20	19·0	19·0	57·2	4·8
Firms' Staffs:					
Upper level . .	60	10·5	47·4	38·6	3·5
Middle Level . .	240	15·5	38·5	43·5	2·5
Lower level . .	350	28·5	32·6	37·8	1·1

It is striking to compare this with the distribution of efficiency ratings for the various civil service grades which was discussed earlier in this section. There we saw that the lower the grade the smaller the percentage who were rated as above average in efficiency (i.e. ratings 1 or 2). Here, we find that the lower the grade, the greater the percentage who rate their own capabilities high. We have already seen how the percentage of people who feel that their duties are well below their capabilities is highest among the group with low job-satisfaction. It

[1] Ns are approximate to the nearest 10: they exclude 'spoilt' answers, the numbers of which vary slightly from one question to another.

may well be that this divergence between the respondents' own estimates of their capabilities and their superiors' estimates is important to an understanding of the dissatisfaction of office workers at the lower levels, and particularly of male Clerical officers.

However this may be, a comparison between the respondent's own estimate and his superior's estimate is interesting in itself:

TABLE 8.11

Efficiency Rating	(N)	Question 32: 'I feel that my duties are			
		Well below	A little below	More or less suited to my capabilities'	A "little" or "well" beyond
		%	%	%	%
1	(29)	28	31	38	3
2	(453)	29	39	32	0·4
3	(468)	26	35	38	0·6
4	(40)	28	28	41	3

Notice how some of those who feel that their duties are below their capabilities are considered by their superiors to be suffering from quite the opposite misfortune, while half of those who are modest enough to consider their jobs beyond them are rated above average, one of them as exceptionally good.

There was a slight tendency for the more efficient half of the respondents to be more confident of their ability to do the job of their immediate superior (Qn. 49): 82 per cent. of them were fairly sure that they could. But as 76 per cent. of the less efficient half were also quite confident of this, the difference—though significant—is less striking than one would hope!

Job-satisfaction and Efficiency

One of the most important comparisons was between job-satisfaction and efficiency: most people assume that those who like their jobs most are also best at them. But the table below shows that the relationship is certainly not so Utopian:

TABLE 8.12

Efficiency Rating	(N)	Satisfied	In between	Dissatisfied
		%	%	%
1	(30)	30·0	50·0	20·0
2	(451)	22·4	65·9	11·7
3	(465)	21·7	64·5	13·8
4	(42)	28·6	52·3	19·1

If you compare the more efficient half with the less, there is apparently no association at all between efficiency and job-satisfaction. This is not the first time that this observation has been made; indeed Kristy, whose study of Post Office counter clerks is summarised in Appendix A, found that the more efficient ones were the most dissatisfied. But the table above simply demonstrates an absence of association between efficiency and job-satisfaction so far as the desk grades are concerned, with one interesting exception. If you look at the percentages for the very efficient and the very inefficient, you will see that in both cases they yield higher percentages of 'satisfieds' and 'dissatisfieds'.[1] In other words, if you are one of the 93 per cent. who are regarded as either just above or just below the average in the performance of your job, this seems to have no connection with your enjoyment of it; but if you are regarded as very good or very bad, you are more likely to have strong feelings of liking or dislike for it. Moreover, you may be very good at it and dislike it, or very bad at it and enjoy it.

Advice on Careers (Qn. 54). On the other hand, there was quite a close relationship, as one might expect, between job-satisfaction and the sort of advice which respondents said they would give to a friend who was thinking of entering their career in the same way as they had, and this was related in a rather unexpected way to efficiency, as Table 8.13 shows. A surprising number of those who expressed satisfaction with their jobs would have advised against following their careers (19.8 per cent. of civil service respondents), and it was still more remarkable that the Clerical class, which had the highest percentage of dissatisfied, were not more opposed to the service as a career. Generally speaking, however, the more satisfied with the job the more likely they were to advise in favour. It was therefore striking to find that the more efficient half of the respondents included a higher percentage of those who were against following their own careers. This is not altogether inexplicable; the better workers may have believed that had they chosen another career they would have done better for themselves. Indeed, some of them may have felt that if they had been able to enter the civil service 'on a higher floor' they would have got further; Table 8.13 shows that a very high percentage (55.4 per cent.) of the senior Executive grades were against following their own careers, which is just what we should expect on this hypothesis. Here again the replies of the very inefficient are more like those of the very efficient than are those of the intermediate categories. Somewhat the same pattern appeared in the replies to Questions 22 and 29 (Variety and Scope for Initiative): there was not much difference between those who were just above or just below average in efficiency, but the outstandingly efficient showed a stronger tendency to feel that they had plenty of scope for initiative (45 per cent. compared with 28 per cent. for rating 2, 24 per cent. for rating 3, and

[1] The probability of this difference occurring by chance is just over 1 in 50.

30 per cent. for rating 4), and on the other hand a very strong tendency to complain of lack of variety (69 per cent. compared with 22 per cent., 24 per cent. and 30 per cent. for ratings 2, 3 and 4). Here again there was a slight tendency for the worst ones also to show this tendency more strongly than the middle ratings (2 and 3); it was not by itself significant, but its appearance in four sets of replies, all dealing with attitudes to aspects of the work itself, suggests that it is due to more than chance. It *may* be an indication that those rated as very inefficient by their superiors include a few who are potentially well above average but are misfits in their present posts, or in the civil service.

TABLE 8.13

Advice to Potential Entrants

Advice which respondents would have given to a friend thinking of entering their career in the same way and with the same qualifications (Qn. 58).

	AGAINST		IMPARTIAL	IN FAVOUR	
	Strongly	Rather		On the whole	Strongly
	%	%	%	%	%
Job-satisfaction:					
Satisfied	7·2	12·6	21·3	44·5	14·4
In-between	13·2	27·8	29·4	27·5	2·1
Dissatisfied	37·8	30·0	18·9	12·6	0·7
Efficiency Rating:					
1	16·7	30·0	33·3	16·7	3·3
2	17·1	27·0	24·0	28·8	3·1
3	14·0	20·3	29·5	31·0	5·2
4	23·8	33·3	14·3	23·8	4·8
Grades[1]:					
Administrative[1]	7·7	32·9	22·0	29·7	7·7
Executive[1] above H.E.O.	18·1	37·3	15·9	26·6	2·1
H.E.O. and E.O.	14·8	27·2	25·6	29·0	3·4
C.O., C.O. (Sec.) and C.A.	16·9	18·0	28·3	31·5	5·3
Professional:					
Large Ministry	15·6	18·8	34·4	25·0	6·2
Small Ministry	10·0	5·0	25·0	35·0	25·0
Levels in the Firms[1]:					
Upper[1]	3·5	19·3	7·0	50·9	19·3
Middle	3·8	10·1	26·2	47·7	12·2
Lower	8·4	10·4	28·3	43·4	9·5

[1] These include both men and women: but there were no women in the upper levels of the firms, and very few among the administrative and senior Executive grades in the civil service.

So far, then, as I was able to measure respondents' efficiency, its associations with facts about them and their attitudes were interesting by reason more of their weakness or a complete absence rather than their strength. Some were simply weak versions of what I had expected; for example, its links with age, or with views on one's ability to do the job of one's superior, or on the promotion system. In some cases even the expected was lacking, as we have seen in the case of the aspects of their jobs which respondents' found most attractive. Its only really interesting connections were with the tendency to be disappointed in the service as a career (Qn. 54); with a certain amount of *esprit de corps*; and with level in the hierarchy.

Estimated Status. As far as job-satisfaction is concerned, we have now disposed of the possibility that it is associated with higher grades because it goes with greater efficiency and so hastens promotion.[1] This means that we can consider other explanations of why it should be associated with grade.

One thing that was bound to be closely connected with the respondents' actual grade or level in the hierarchy was his 'estimated status'. We know both from experience and other studies that many people set a great deal of store by what can loosely be called their 'importance'. This seems to make them pursue otherwise inexplicable ends, such as the acquisition of a house or car that is too large for their needs or means, or attendance at ceremonies which they do not enjoy. Was it possible to measure office workers' feelings on this subject?

It was necessary to distinguish between three meanings of 'importance.' In the first place, it might be possible to assign an objective 'importance' to respondents, at least in relation to each other and the organisation, by seeing where they stood in the hierarchy. This is what I have roughly achieved by grouping them in grades and levels. In the second place there was 'importance' in the sense of the respondent's own estimate of his importance. So far as his relative position within the organisation was concerned this was not likely to differ in any very interesting way from his objective position as determined by his grade or level.[2] But there was also his feeling about the importance of being, say, a Departmental Manager in a Company, or a Chief Executive Officer in the civil service, in relation to other occupations in the community. This might vary in a more interesting way. It would of course, be stupid to ask 'how important do you think you are?' even if some measuring scale could be devised for the respondent's reply. That

[1] At least in the civil service; I cannot be so definite about the Companies.
[2] I am not forgetting the possibility that in some Companies Mr. X may be on a lower *scale* of salary than Mr. Y, although he may be in a post that is obviously more 'important' than Mr. Y. Indeed, the classical form of this allegation is that Mr. X may unwittingly be receiving less than Mr. Z, *who is one of his subordinates*. Sometimes the explanation is not so horrific after all; Mr. Z may have spent longer on an overlapping salary scale than the newly appointed Mr. X.

would arouse almost as defensive a reaction as 'How conceited are you?' But there were ways round the difficulties.

I approached this rather awkward subject in three of my questions. I included 'status in the community' in the list of 'Attractions of the job'. Next to 'social life with colleagues' it was the least popular of the attractions. Either the respondents did not value this much or they did not want to admit to doing so. I also asked, in Question 28, whether respondents regarded their job as essential to the community, useful but not essential, or neither. Fifty-nine per cent. of civil servants: and 41 per cent. of the firms' respondents chose 'essential'. A mere 3 per cent. of both groups (chiefly at the lower levels) took such a poor view of their work that they saw it as neither useful nor essential. The firms' percentages were very close to each other, but fewer of the Small Ministry's respondents than of the Large Ministry's regarded their jobs as essential (53% v. 61%). The levels and grades did not differ very much, with the exception of the administrative and senior executive grades in the Ministries. The former took a more cynical view of their jobs, as the following figures show:

	Essential %	Useful %	Neither %
Administrative	59	38	3
Executive above H.E.O.	73	27	–

Thirdly, I devised a question which I hoped would induce respondents to indicate their estimate of their job's importance and value to the community in such a way that their estimates could be readily compared. Question 56 is the result. Respondents were asked to assign a place to their own job in a list of nine occupations, which included several that are frequently entered by women. More important, the range of occupations was intended to include some that were exalted enough to make the upper levels think twice before putting their own jobs at the head of the list, and at least one—taxi-driver—that was sufficiently humble to make the most junior desk worker hesitate before ranking his or her job below it. It was just this sort of question that I would have liked to test on a fairly large scale beforehand; and while the small number of draft questionnaires that I tried out on civil servants did enable me to improve it, the replies summarised in Table 8.14 show that it could be improved still further. For example, the percentages who placed their job first distinguish sharply between the upper level in the firms (11 per cent.) and the middle and lower levels (2-3 per cent.); and similarly between the administrators (16 per cent.) and the other desk grades (2-5 per cent.) in the civil service.[1] What has happened is

[1] But note the very high places which the Small Ministry's professionals assign to their jobs: 35 per cent. in first place, 29 per cent. in second or third, and none below fifth. Even the very small number of this sample does not prevent this from being remarkable. It was this group that showed such high job-satisfaction.

RESULTS OF THE QUESTIONNAIRE

that there is one occupation—Member of Parliament—which, as I had expected, most respondents placed at the top of their lists, but which substantial percentages of the administrators and upper level employees in the firms ranked after their own jobs. This in itself is informative; but I should like to have included some other occupation which might have succeeded in splitting up these levels still further. Perhaps 'Minister of the Crown' would have thinned out the respondents who placed their own jobs at the top.

TABLE 8.14

Status

		N^1	Place assigned by respondents to their own job in ranking nine occupations in order of importance and value to the community (Q. 56)				
			1	2 or 3	4 or 5	6 or 7	8 or 9
			%	%	%	%	%
Civil servants in both		1090	4·2	22·7	47·6	19·8	5·7
Both firms' staffs		650	3·5	8·2	39·5	32·8	15·9
Civil Service grades	Administrative*	90	16	48	33	4	—
	Executive above H.E.O.*	90	2	42	44	10	1
	H.E.O. and E.O.:						
	men	310	2	20	55	17	5
	women	130	—	17	57	21	5
	C.O., C.O. (Sec.) and C.A.:						
	men	230	3	16	45	26	11
	women	150	5	14	40	32	9
	Professional:						
	Large Ministry	60	7	24	46	22	2
	Small Ministry	20	35	29	35	—	—
Firms' levels	Upper level	60	11	21	51	13	4
	Middle level:						
	men	200	3	12	49	27	9
	women	40	3	9	40	37	11
	Lower level:						
	men	140	2	7	38	37	17
	women	210	3	2	28	40	27

Nevertheless, the question was not unsuccessful. It showed, for example, what a sharp difference there was between the upper level and the rest of the employees of the firms, and between the administrators and the senior Executive grades in the Ministries; note how few of the

[1] Numbers are approximate to nearest 10: they exclude 'spoilt' answers, the numbers of which vary slightly from one question to another. They also exclude a few women in the civil service grades marked *, so that the numbers for the grades do not equal the total number for the civil servants.

latter choose first place, and even when we compare the first three places their 44 per cent. is well below the administrators' 64 per cent. One, either in joke or self-abasement, places his job in last or second last place. Except in the Clerical grade of the civil service, women are more modest about their jobs than men. Allowing for this, the percentages show, as one would expect, that the lower the respondent's place in the official hierarchy the lower the value he assigns to his job. They show too that the civil servant tends to assign more importance and value to his job in relation to the others listed than does the firms' employee, not only at the higher levels but even among the most junior clerical staff. It is interesting, however, to see how widely members of the same level range. There is a good deal of variation in the nature of the tasks performed by the Clerical class in the civil service, but not enough to explain how some of its respondents ranked their jobs first, others last or second last.

These wide variations—so much wider than the facts seemed to justify—occurred among all the levels, and suggested that something was affecting either the actual judgments of respondents or the judgments they decided to profess. Modesty (either sincere or assumed) or facetious self-disparagement might account for the occasional upper level member of the firms' staffs, or the senior Executive or professional civil servant who ranked their jobs below that of shop assistant or taxi-driver. Facetiousness might also be responsible for some respondents at the other extreme. But even if we dismiss the extremes as insincere, we have still to explain a considerable width of range. It seemed possible that this was connected in some way with respondents' feelings about their work. The obvious test of this hypothesis was to see whether it varied with job-satisfaction,[1] and sure enough it did:

TABLE 8.15

Category of Job-satisfaction	Place assigned by civil servants, with firms' percentages in parentheses, in Qn. 56				
	1	2-3	4-5	6-7	8-9
	%	%	%	%	%
'Satisfied'	36 (62)	34 (61)	22 (49)	15 (32)	15 (26)
'In between'	61 (33)	58 (33)	68 (44)	65 (58)	43 (44)
'Dissatisfied'	2 (5)	9 (6)	10 (7)	19 (10)	41 (30)

Either the higher you rank your job the more you like it, or vice versa. In fact, job-satisfaction seemed to be associated with estimated status

[1] It would obviously have been possible to see how many other attitudes the variation in job-ranking was associated with, but there was a limit both to the tables that could be considered and to the inferences that could be drawn from them.

more closely than with actual grade, and the two associations were independent.[1] In other words, your chances of enjoying your job seem to be greater if you *either* occupy a high place in the hierarchy *or* have a high estimate of your status in the community (even if you do not occupy a high place in the hierarchy); and the latter possibility seems to increase your chances more than does the former.

There was another aspect of feelings about status that I wanted to get some information about. This was the extent to which respondents thought that others' estimates of the status of the respondents' jobs corresponded with the respondents' own estimates. Experience suggested that this too was something that mattered to people: 'status-symbols' such as huge cars or a large secretariat are intended to alter others' estimates as well as one's own. How many respondents thought that others did not consider their jobs as important as they themselves did? Question 56 therefore asked respondents to rank the same list of occupations in the order which they thought their friends and acquaintances (outside the respondents' organisation) would give them.

Respondents had coped very well with the first part of Question 56; only 5 per cent. of the civil servants and 10 per cent. of the firms' staffs had baulked at it. But this second part was too much for another 11 per cent. of civil servants and another 20 per cent. of the firms' staffs. Either they did not see the point of this task or they saw it and did not like it. At all events, the result was that the whole question was completed by only about 84 per cent. of civil service respondents and 70 per cent. of the firms. Nevertheless, 906 civil servants and 462 firms' employees formed a substantial sample.

Of these, 65 per cent. of civil servants and 44 per cent. of firms' office workers seemed to think that their friends and acquaintances would give the respondents' jobs a *lower* place in the list than would the respondents themselves. Another 15 per cent. of civil servants and 25 per cent. of firms' employees thought their jobs would be ranked *higher* by their friends than they themselves would rank them. The remainder (20 per cent. and 32 per cent.), who made their friends give their jobs the same place as they themselves did, no doubt included a certain number who did not see how there could be any difference; but this only emphasises how few of the respondents felt that their estimate corresponded to that of others. The distribution was as shown in Table 8.16.

It is striking to see how widely the difference ranges—from the man who thinks that others are deceived into overestimating the importance of his job to the man who clearly feels that this is greatly underestimated. The latter of these feelings is one to which the civil servants

[1] This was determined by a partial association test performed on civil service replies only.

seem much more prone than the firms' employees, who show a greater tendency towards the other reaction.[1]

TABLE 8.16

	(N)	Respondents' estimate of place assigned by others, compared with own estimate					
		Higher	Equal	Lower by			
				1	2	3	4 or more
				places			places
Civil Servants	(906)	% 15	% 20	% 20	% 22	% 11	% 12
Firms' staffs	(462)	25	32	23	13	4	3

What does all this suggest? It confirms that nearly all the respondents were considerably 'status-conscious', and it shows that their estimates of their own status was linked to their position in the hierarchy but by no means limited by this; respondents quite low in the hierarchy could have quite a high estimate, and vice versa. If they had both a high actual grade and a high estimate, they were extremely likely to be people who enjoyed their work. If they had *either* a high actual grade *or* a high estimate, they were also very likely to enjoy their job, but *more* likely if they had a high *estimate*. Since it is easier to have a high estimate if you have a high actual grade, it is distinctly possible that the direction of causation is from grade to estimate of status, and from that to job-satisfaction; in other words, that one reason why many of these respondents liked their jobs was that their position in the hierarchy encouraged them to regard themselves as important to the community.

'*Words for the Work*'. But can we dismiss so summarily the other possibility[2] that high job-satisfaction *produces* a high estimate of status? This leaves the connection between job-satisfaction and grade still to be explained; but there are other ways of doing this. For example, respondents were also asked (in Qn. 59) to pick, from two lists of five adjectives each, those which they would apply to their work when they were 'fed up with it', and those they would apply when they were enjoying it. Table 8.17 shows that among fed-up respondents—both in

[1] It was not practicable to test whether these feelings were associated with attitudes such as job-satisfaction, since the higher the place assigned to his job by the respondent himself the more room he had to assign it a lower place in his friends' list (and the less room to assign it a higher place). In fact, the result was to produce an apparently paradoxical association: the more one's friends underestimated one's job, the more one enjoyed it!

[2] The third possibility, that estimated status influences grade by hastening promotion, seems academic.

the Ministries and in the firms—the most popular adjective was 'frustrating' (38-35 per cent.). Next for the civil servants was 'thankless'; but for the firms' respondents their work was not so much thankless as 'tiring'. 'Pointlessness' was the criticism that was made least often by both groups.

TABLE 8.17

Words for the Work
(Question 59)

Respondents	(N)	'When you are fed up with your work, what would you call it?'				
		Frustrating	Pointless	Worrying	Thankless	Tiring
		%	%	%	%	%
Civil Servants:						
Satisfied	(255)	33	3	14	25	25
In between	(674)	39	8	12	26	15
Dissatisfied	(143)	38	23	8	25	6
All	(1072)	38	9	12	26	16
Firms' Staffs:						
Satisfied	(261)	33	5	19	11	32
In between	(299)	34	11	12	20	23
Dissatisfied	(72)	40	28	6	21	6
All	(632)	35	10	14	16	25
		'When you are enjoying it, what would you call it?'				
		Popular	Responsible	Useful	Interesting	Creative
		%	%	%	%	%
Civil servants:						
Satisfied	(263)	1	24	20	51	5
In between	(676)	1	22	30	46	1
Dissatisfied	(136)	4	18	49	29	1
All	(1075)	1	22	30	45	2
Firms' Staffs:						
Satisfied	(270)	0·4	21	9	56	14
In between	(303)	2	15	26	52	5
Dissatisfied	(64)	6	8	47	30	9
All	(637)	2	17	21	51	9

When they were enjoying their work, both civil servants and firms' respondents tended strongly to call it 'interesting' (45-51 per cent.), with 'useful' next. Very few regarded their work as 'creative' and fewer still as 'popular': most of the former were probably professionals in the Small Ministry.

The most interesting difference, however, was between the different job-satisfaction groups. The preference of the satisfied respondents for certain adjectives was not the preference of the dissatisfied. 'Pointless', for example, was chosen by only a few of the satisfied (3-5 per cent.), but by about 1 in 4 of the dissatisfied (23-28 per cent.): conversely, 'tiring' and 'worrying' were chosen by much smaller percentages of the dissatisfied. There were similar differences in the other list of adjectives. 'Interesting' becomes rarer and 'useful' commoner as we descend the job-satisfaction groups.

The close link between job-satisfaction and the interest of the work was emphasised by the order in which the satisfied and the dissatisfied ranked the attractions of their job (Qn. 47). By far the most striking difference in their lists was the place assigned to this attraction:

TABLE 8.18

Job-satisfaction Category	(N)	Percentage assigning high or low place to 'interest of the work'	
		1st or 2nd place	9th or 10th place
		%	%
Satisfied	(263)	55	1
In between	(669)	28	5
Dissatisfied	(126)	2	22

In comparison, differences in the places assigned to other 'attractions' were unremarkable. The dissatisfied were less impressed by the more positive attractions, such as promotion prospects, and voted more heavily for such things as hours of work, pensions and, to a marked extent, security of job (68 per cent. of them gave it 1st or 2nd place, compared with 54 per cent. of the satisfied). The places assigned to pay by both groups were much the same.

A marked difference in the place assigned to the interest of the work was also noticeable among the replies of the different grades (Table 8.19).

Notice how close the pattern is to that of job-satisfaction. The Small Ministry's professionals, who seemed to enjoy their work most, also place its interest highest. The male C.O.s and C.A.s, who were the most dissatisfied, seem to find little interest in it. The Large Ministry's professionals and the senior Executive grades, whose job-satisfaction was practically the same, are equal here too.

RESULTS OF THE QUESTIONNAIRE

TABLE 8.19

Grades or Levels	Percentage assigning 1st or 2nd place to 'interest of the work' (Qn. 47)
	%
Civil Service:	
Administrative (men only)	77
Executive above H.E.O. (men only)	48
H.E.O. and E.O. :	
men	26
women	27
C.O., C.O. (Sec.) and C.A. :	
men	15
women	16
Professional:	
Large Ministry	48
Small Ministry	81
Firms' Staffs:	
Upper level (men only)	77
Middle level:	
men	65
women	63
Lower level:	
men	33
women	36

Other Attitudes

To sum up: there were close associations between five pairs of things:

> job-satisfaction and grade,
> job-satisfaction and estimated status,
> job-satisfaction and the interest of the work,
> grade and estimated status,
> grade and interest of the work.

These seem quite sufficient to explain why the higher grades get more satisfaction out of their work. There is, however, a complication to be noticed. Job-satisfaction was also connected with attitudes to several other aspects of the job—discipline, colleagues, physical environment, the promotion system, methods of supervision, the variety and responsibility of the work, respondents' estimates of how hard-worked they were, and of whether their Ministry or Company was better or worse than others. For example, pride in one's own organisation was more closely linked with enjoyment of one's work than with efficiency, although both the associations were significant. Generally, however, these associations were not as marked as the ones we have been examining. Where they took some interesting form I shall mention this in the section of 8.3 which deals with the subject; here I shall merely say that the replies of the dissatisfied tended to be more critical in one way or another—and sometimes in both ways!—than those of the satisfied. There are so many of these slight associations that they are almost certainly effects rather than causes of low job-satisfaction. But this raises the question how we can be sure that the association between job-satisfaction and interest, and between job-satisfaction and estimated status, are not of the same nature as these other associations. Perhaps the explanation here too is simply that the dissatisfied are more critical? Perhaps the only things that really influence job-satisfaction are what we rather vaguely call 'temperaments'? Perhaps all other associations are merely the effect of more critical or favourable attitudes?

We must certainly recognise the importance of 'adjustment' in determining whether people like, dislike or are indifferent to their work; and the time-effect we have noticed emphasises that to a certain extent job-satisfaction depends on processes beyond anyone's control. But the closeness of its connection with actual level in the hierarchy—a connection which is independent of age or efficiency—is another firm fact. Grade by itself cannot increase one's enjoyment of one's job: but it is easy to see how higher estimated status and more interesting work could do so.

We have still to explain, of course, why the work of the higher grades should be more interesting. This may appear to be questioning the obvious: but sometimes the answer is not so simple after all. At least one of my respondents found that 'I have recently come on promotion from a job which I found extremely interesting to one which gives very little scope for the talents that earned my promotion'. In other words, it is not inevitable that the work of a higher grade should be more interesting than the work of a lower grade. I shall return to this point later.

8.3. ATTITUDES

The replies summarised in the section that follows are not reports of objective facts about the respondents—such as their age, or the time they have spent in their jobs—but reflection of attitudes. Some of the questions made it quite plain that it was an attitude they were concerned with: for example, 'Do you approve of this? (the organisation's policy with incompetents)' (Qn. 42). Other questions had to appear to be asking for reports of objective facts; for example, 'How does the system of promotion work at your level . . .?' (Qn. 54), but were really eliciting an expression of attitude. It is true that in some cases the respondents' attitudes are attitudes toward slightly different situations: the promotion system may work differently for different staff groups. In such cases too much weight should not be placed on differences between groups; but it is still extremely informative to study the variation between members of the same group. Anyone who doubts whether Question 54 ('How does the promotion system work at your level?') is really concerned with attitude rather than fact should look at the replies to it from the Large Ministry's 64 professional respondents; 'As fairly as possible'—15·6 per cent.; 'fairly on the whole'—40·6 per cent.; 'a little unfairly'—21·9 per cent.; 'very unfairly'—21·9 per cent. They can't all be reporting objective fact.

Moreover, what I have said in 8.2 of this chapter makes it clear how inevitable are critical attitudes among a certain percentage of any group that is not selected for its high job-satisfaction. These reflections may prevent the reader from being too alarmed or elated (according to his own attitude to civil servants or private office workers) by the attitudes revealed in the sections that follow. He should certainly not fall into the error of those investigators who diagnose a grave disorder in the spiritual health of an organisation on the strength of a percentage of complaints which they have not compared with those from a normal control. They are like the medical student who can find something wrong with anyone because he has never examined a healthy body. If the present survey had confined itself to one organisation, we should mistake a great many of the criticisms in the following sections for symptoms of diseased morale. In fact, many of them are just symptoms of being an office worker, under the stresses that this entails, or even symptoms of being human. It is not the extreme attitudes of some individuals that should alert our attention, but differences between groups, whether they are the sexes, the grades and levels, the two Companies or the two kinds of office worker.

On the other hand, this does not mean that because these replies reflect attitudes rather than objective facts they can be dismissed as unimportant. If the employees of one organisation differ significantly from those of another in their attitude to some aspect of their job, and if this is not accounted for by some real difference in circumstances, then this is something to think about. It may be due to misunderstanding—a failure of communication between management and employee. It may be due to a defect in personal relations. Or it may simply be that nobody responsible has thought about this subject.

Spontaneous Comments (Qn. 62)

Useful light was thrown on the replies to the attitude questions by the spontaneous comments which respondents were given the opportunity to make here and there, and particularly in Question 62. This asked 'Is there anything you would like to add about your work, your Company (or Ministry), the building where you work, your colleagues, this questionnaire, etc.?' Most of the comments were about the questionnaire itself: 201 criticised either the drafting or the entire conception, 61 expressed approval and interest and 2 were ambiguous.[1] Since the

---

[1] 'I am more interested in your job than mine' (a woman).

'I think this questionnaire should have been illustrated by Ronald Searle' (an administrator).

TABLE 8.20

Attractions of the Job

(As ranked by respondents in replies to Question 45)

Percentage of respondents (to nearest whole number) assigning 1st or 2nd and 9th, or 10th place to the ten potential attractions. (Separate percentages for each Ministry or Firm are given only when the probability of the differences occurring by chance is 1 in 20 or less.)

	N[1]	Hours of Work		Pension Rights		Security of Job		Promotion Prospects		Pay		Interest of the Work		Holidays		Status in Community		Physical conditions of Work		Social life with Colleagues		Place assigned
		1 or 2	9 or 10	1 or 2	9 or 10	1 or 2	9 or 10	1 or 2	9 or 10	1 or 2	9 or 10	1 or 2	9 or 10	1 or 2	9 or 10	1 or 2	9 or 10	1 or 2	9 or 10	1 or 2	9 or 10	
Large Ministry[2]	780								26								53					66
Small Ministry[2]	310								32								43					60
Civil Servants in both	1090	13	8	2		63	0·4	7	28	21	7	32	6	26	2	3	50	4	29	2		65
Both firms' staffs	650	13	15	16	15	40	3	21	27	39	4	50	6	3	16	5	41	12	19	8		50
North Firm[2]	340																	15				47
South Firm[2]	310																	8				54

[1] Numbers are approximate to nearest 10: they exclude 'spoilt' answers, the numbers of which vary slightly from one question to another. They also exclude a few women in the civil service grades marked *, so that the numbers for the grades do not equal the total number for the civil servants.

[2] Separate percentages for Ministries or Companies are given only when there is a significant difference.

comments on other subjects also included far more complaint than compliment, this reaction to the questionnaire was not wholly discouraging.

As for the other comments, it was interesting to see that almost all of them dealt with subjects on which the respondents had already answered a question; and they thus served to emphasise and illuminate the points on which respondents felt so strongly that they burst into prose. These comments were very useful in clarifying both critical and favourable attitudes, and where they can be quoted without betraying the authors I have included some of the most pointed in the sections that follow.[1]

Attractions of the Job (Qn. 47)

Respondents were invited to rank ten features of their jobs in order of attractiveness. An adequate impression of the value which civil servants and firms' staffs attached to these ten items can be got from the percentages who assigned one of the top two places or one of the bottom two places to each, and this is what I have shown in Table 8.20. The order in which most civil servants ranked these attractions, and for comparison the order in which most firms' employees ranked them were:

Civil servants' order		Firms' order
1	Security of job	2
2	Pension rights	5
3	Interest of the work	1
4	Holidays	10
5	Pay	3
6	Hours of work	6=
7	Promotion prospects	4
8	Physical conditions of work	6=
9	Status in the community	9
10	Social life with colleagues	8

The similarities in these orders are more striking than the differences. The lower places assigned by the firms' staffs to pension rights and holidays were not hard to explain: in both cases they were less fortunate

[1] A few of them mentioned topics which I had not thought of, but should have. These were:

London as a place to live or work in (18 unfavourable comments from all four organisations);

Too little staff training (both Ministries and the South Firm);

Lack of opportunities for advancement for women (both Companies, but not the Ministries).

O

than the civil service, and in any case their pension scheme had only recently been introduced, and may not have been well known to the younger employees. However this may be, the result was that other items achieve a higher place on their list than on the civil servants' list. Both civil servants and firms' employees, however, place security of job very high; and interest of the work is given a high place, though the firms' staffs place it first, and the civil servants third—after security and pensions. As we should expect, there was very little difference between the preferences of the two Ministries or between the two firms, whose conditions of service were as similar as those of the Ministries. A larger percentage of the Small Ministry's staff seemed pessimistic about promotion prospects, and higher percentages of the Large Ministry's staff gave very low places to 'status in the community' and 'social life with colleagues'. This last item was also rated very low by respondents from the South Firm. But the chief difference between the firms was in the percentage who regarded physical conditions of work as one of the leading attractions; this was of course due to the new building into which the North Firm had recently moved (see the section on 'Physical Environment').

It is interesting to compare the civil servants' order with the replies elicited by Miss Box's survey of attitudes to the civil service as a career. In the summer of 1946 her team interviewed some 2,600 professional, technical and clerical workers, schoolboys, schoolgirls and their parents, whose replies were classified under headings very similar to mine.[1] Were there any important differences between my respondents, who were actual civil servants, and Miss Box's, who were either *potential* civil servants or *parents of potential* civil servants?

All her groups—parents, children and workers—regarded security of job as the chief attraction, with pensions next. They disagreed about the order in which pay, promotion prospects, working hours and holidays should be ranked. To the professional and technical workers the civil service holidays seemed the biggest and promotion prospects the least of these attractions; while women clerical workers and mothers of school-children put promotion prospects first. 'Good social standing' was mentioned quite often—by 10 per cent. of the parents and 5 per cent. of the other groups; physical conditions of work and social life with colleagues do not seem to have been mentioned often enough to achieve a separate place in Miss Box's report.

But the striking difference is that while my civil servants ranked interest of the work very high on their list of attractions, Miss Box's respondents not only did not mention it as an attraction, but even gave 'uninteresting' or 'dull' or 'routine' work as one of the chief *disadvantages*. I think it is fair to say that to the outsider the tasks of bureau-

[1] *Recruitment to the Civil Service: an Inquiry made by the Social Survey for H.M. Treasury*, 1946.

cracy seem far less interesting than they do to the bureaucrat himself. This may be true of most office work: after all, the civil servant who reads this chapter must find it hard to understand how my Company respondents could possibly regard the interest of their work as its chief attraction. When we recall how the job-satisfaction of male civil servants, which was closely associated with interest in the work, increased with the time spent in the job, this observation strongly suggests that 'interest' is not always an intrinsic quality of some kinds of work but may be something which work begins to assume after one has been doing it for some time.

Question 47 also asked 'Is there anything which you would mark above any of these (items)?' and while not many respondents could think of something to put before security, pensions and the interest of their work, those who did were interesting. Here are the Large Ministry's attractions:

'Complete freedom to exercise personal discretion.' (a male H.E.O.)

'The democratic discussions between colleagues on proposed actions (with regard to work) and our self-criticisms.' (a male E.O.)

'The possibility of changing one's job fairly frequently within the organisation.' (a female H.E.O.)

'Opportunity to serve community. New equality of career opportunity for women (which does not seem to be so in business).' (a female S.E.O.)

'Tradition of civilised behaviour and self-discipline, as opposed to more competitive organisations where the individual may be more blatantly engaged in self-advertisement and on the make.' (a male administrator)

The Small Ministry's list was:

'Not having to "keep up with the Joneses" in matters of fashion, entertainment, etc.' (a female E.O.)

'Yes—relations with colleagues. These are pleasant and free of the pettiness and jealousies common to commercial and business offices.' (a female C.O.)

'Satisfaction in working for the State rather than a private individual or firm.' (a male H.E.O.)

'As a civil servant one is serving the community.' (a male professional)

and two rather nice ones to conclude the list:

'Power.' (a young female C.O.)

'Yes, happiness in doing a job one really and truly loves, as I do.' (a femal

The firms' respondents had rather different ideas. The North Firms' list was:

'Most attractive of all, the opportunity of practising and improving in one's profession with the help of experienced and very capable superiors and colleagues.' (a middle-aged man)

'Yes, the pleasure derived from companions and work itself.'
(a middle-aged woman on clerical duties)

'Being considered as an individual and treated as such. Atmosphere happy.'
(a female secretary)

'Interest of the manager in the staff for their welfare, etc.' (a woman)

'Pride in being a responsible member of a successful team.'
(a middle-aged man on management duties)

'Opportunity to use initiative without interference.'
(a middle-aged man on management duties)

'Satisfaction in being of some service . . .' (a man from the upper level)

'The helpfulness and patience of people superior to me.' (a young girl)

'I feel that I just "belong"—I am happy and content just daily doing my best—always appreciating my good fortune in being part of such a good organisation.'
(a woman in a fairly senior position)

'A job worth doing in a new and rapidly expanding field gives satisfaction.'
(a man in the upper level)

and from the South Firm:

'Sense of loyalty to an excellent employer.' (a man from the upper level)

'Freedom to sell ideas to others in an advisory capacity.'
(a man from a fairly high level)

'Freedom, within limits of company policy, to act on my own initiative. The challenge of responsibility.' (a man from the middle level)

'Real enjoyment in one's work.'
(a middle-aged woman in a fairly responsible job)

'A free hand to make decisions, etc., provided that the results are justified.'
(a man on management duties)

Disadvantages of the Job (Qn. 48)

Respondents were asked here to do the opposite of what they had done in Question 47—to rank a list of potential disadvantages by assigning '1' to the least satisfactory, and so on. Some of the items on the list—hours of work, promotion prospects, pay—were identical with items in the list of attractions. Here the replies for the most part simply confirmed the impression conveyed by Table 8.20. In the case of promotion for example, 48 per cent. of civil servants (52 per cent. in the Small Ministry, 46 per cent. in the Large Ministry) ranked it as the most or second most unsatisfactory thing about their jobs, compared with 36 per cent. of the firms' respondents (38 per cent. in the North Firm, 34 per cent. in the South Firm).

One new item, however, 'the attitude of the public to your work', came a close second to promotion, and I shall discuss this in its place (see 'The Public and the Press'). Apart from this, the most interesting replies were those that responded to the final query, 'Is there anything else which seems to you even less satisfactory than any of these?'

The Large Ministry's bugbears were:

'The feeling that the job probably isn't necessary at all—that I (and others) are just carrying out Parkinson's Law.'[1]
(a member of the Executive class in the Large Ministry)

'The number of meetings to be attended; the mass of paper of negligible value to be circulated.' (another)

'Yes, the solid pyramidal organisation structure which involves so many people in most actions leading to a decision. . . .' (another)

'Overall lack of efficiency and good organisation, and lack of means to do anything effective except in a very limited sphere.' (another)

'The impersonal nature of one's work and one's place in the Ministry.'
(a female C.O. from the Large Ministry)

'Lack of contact with Head of Branch and lack of sense of personal loyalty.' (another)

'The quantity of the work, which claims too much of one's mental energy.'
(an administrator)

The Small Ministry's were:

'Being treated as though I am an imbecile; unable to think for myself.'
(a middle-aged woman on clerical duties)

'Having to do a variety of things without being given any reason for them.'
(a member of the Executive class)

'Lack of knowledge among branches of each other's work.' (another)

'Limited mental capacity and education of vast majority of people here.' (another)

The firms' grievances were rather different. First the North Firm's:

'By far the most unsatisfactory: shortage of qualified staff results in work that is intricate and highly technical being given far less thought than it deserves.'
(a middle-aged man)

'Lack of management planning of career lines.' (a man at a fairly high level)

'Inability to use technical knowledge and to gain further knowledge.'
(a man in the middle level)

'I think — days' holiday a year is terrible, and after you've given the firm — years service you are generously given 1 extra day.' (a young woman)

'Anti-feminine bias in filling salaried position.[2] Not long enough annual holiday after — continuous years of service. . . .' (a middle-aged woman)

And from the South Firm:

'Frustration due to lack of co-ordination.' (a man at a fairly high level)

'Not lack of responsibility but of certainty that my decisions will be upheld.'
(a man)

---

[1] One male H.E.O. in the same Ministry, however, made the rather original point that 'It is possible for work created by Parkinsonism to be both interesting and pointless'.
[2] See 'Promotion'.

Other quotations from both civil servants and firms' employees will be found under headings such as 'Promotion', 'The Men at the Top', etc.

Promotion (Qns. 54, 55, 47)

In view of the importance of status to office workers, it was to be expected that the possibility of promotion to higher grades or levels would be of great concern to them.

As we have just seen, promotion prospects were not regarded by civil servants as one of the attractive aspects of their careers; only 7 per cent. placed this item first or second, while as many as 48 per cent. placed it last or second last. The same percentage of firms' employees ranked this item very low, but 21 per cent. gave it first or second place.

In both Ministries the principles and procedure for promotions were very much the same. Their object was to promote the best among those with a certain amount of seniority. The seniority principle, which is so often misunderstood outside the service, is regarded as a safeguard against the promotion of a man who is lucky enough to please a particular superior, or to be in a spectacular post at the right time. It is observed to a greater or lesser extent in most hierarchical organisations with a long history, such as the armed services. It does not mean that the senior man in the grade below is invariably considered, far less chosen, for promotion. At every level in the service there are a number of very senior men and women who are no longer considered for any promotion, but are 'passed over' each time one has to be made. What is more, the higher the level of the promotion, the more stringent is the standard of fitness for it.

For promotions to all but the highest grades in my sample—i.e. Assistant Secretary, Principal and Senior Chief Executive Officer—the procedure was broadly as follows. When vacancies were foreseen—and in some cases it was the policy to select for the foreseeable vacancies of the next twelve months—officers who had served a certain minimum number of years in the grade below and who had not already been passed over were interviewed by a 'promotion board' of senior officers of their own Department, with a member of the Establishment Division in the chair.[1] The Board arrived at its choice on the basis of the candidates' records, including their annual reports, and the interview itself. Candidates who had not been called for interview in spite of having sufficient seniority, or who had been called but not chosen, could appeal in writing. In the Small Ministry their appeal was considered by the Permanent Secretary in person, whose decision was given to them in writing. In the Large Ministry a candidate whose appeal seemed to have some substance was interviewed again by a similar board.

[1] For some senior executive posts in the Small Ministry interviews were not with a promotion board proper, but with a small panel of senior officers.

In practice, the minimum seniority which makes an officer eligible for consideration varies from one Ministry to another according to the relationship between the numbers and age-structure of contiguous grades. In the case of the two Ministries we are considering there was only one grade in which the effect was very different. In the Large Ministry, C.O.s with 9 to 10 years' seniority were considered for promotion; whereas in the Small Ministry they had to have been C.O.s for 12 to 13 years. In both Ministries, E.O.s were considered for promotion to H.E.O. after 8 years as E.O.s, H.E.O.s for promotion to S.E.O. after 7 to 8 years in the Small Ministry and about a year longer in the Large Ministry. Assistant Principals were considered for promotion to Principal at the age of about 28 or 29 in both Ministries. As for promotions from Principal to Assistant Secretary, the officers actually promoted in recent years in the Small Ministry tended to be around the age of forty; in the Large Ministry their ages ranged more widely, from the mid-thirties to the mid-fifties.

Promotion in the Companies

In the two Companies, promotion seemed to be a much less systematic affair. In the first place, it could take two forms. A man or woman might be moved up from one salary scale to a higher one without any change of duties. The other form of promotion was of course the appointment of the man or woman to a different post (though usually in the same Department or Section) with more authority and a higher salary scale. In the second place, my impression was that both kinds of 'promotion' took place sometimes on the initiative of the management, sometimes as the result of a request by the employee himself. Some of the respondents' comments suggested that they had made requests for such transfers unsuccessfully; and some respondents seemed to feel that by doing so they might endanger their present jobs. In the third place, if a vacancy occurred, it was by no means certain that it would be filled by promotion; it was quite possible that an 'outsider' would be brought in. (In civil service Departments this occasionally occurs at the highest levels, and sometimes at lower levels when promotion in one Department is abnormally fast; otherwise it is most exceptional.)[1] Thus no employee entering the firms at any level could count on being considered for promotion at certain stages of his or her career. Posts were filled by taking what appeared to be the best man within sight, and there did not seem to be any modification of this principle to console employees.

As Table 8.21 shows, fully two-thirds of the civil servants thought their system worked 'fairly on the whole' or even 'as fairly as possible'.

[1] I am, of course, excepting the appointment of new C.O.s, E.O.s and A.P.s as a result of competitive examinations.

TABLE 8.21

Promotion

		Question 54: 'How does the system of promotion work at your level?'				Question 55: 'Tick the *two* things which seem to you to count most for promotion at your level in your office. Please tick *two*.' Percentages, which are of N, are rounded to nearest whole number							
	N[1]	As fairly as possible	Fairly on the whole	A little unfairly	Very unfairly	Seniority	Ability	Hard Work	General Education	Experience	Being in the right place at the right time	Good relations with superiors	Management of subordinates
Large Ministry	780	% 20·8	% 46·9	% 23·0	% 9·3	% 48	% 51	% 5	% 8	% 25	% 33	% 28	% 1
Small Ministry	310	15·9	44·3	28·2	11·6	60	46	3	10	11	41	27	1
Civil servants in both	1090	19·4	46·3	24·4	9·9	51	50	5	8	21	35	28	1
Both firms' staffs	650	28·7	47·4	18·8	5·1	18	59	15	10	37	27	27	2
North Firm	340	25·3	47·8	21·3	5·6	15	58	15	10	37	29	29	2
South Firm	310	32·5	46·9	16·1	4·5	22	60	15	10	38	24	25	2
Civil Service grades													
Administrative*	90	35·2	48·9	13·6	2·3	62	77	8	2	11	22	18	—
Executive above H.E.O.*	90	19·4	57·0	17·2	6·4	22	72	9	4	25	42	24	—
H.E.O. and E.O.:													
men	310	17·3	52·9	21·2	8·6	53	53	3	8	24	32	26	1
women	130	11·9	54·0	33·3	0·8	49	54	—	10	17	47	22	2
C.O., C.O. (Sec.) and C.A.:													
men	230	18·2	33·6	33·6	14·6	60	34	5	13	22	33	32	0·4
women	150	22·9	38·2	33·6	15·3	56	38	7	11	23	36	28	1
Professional*:													
Large Ministry	60	15·6	40·6	21·9	21·9	54	36	—	3	20	39	47	—
Small Ministry	20	22·2	38·9	27·8	11·1	22	50	6	—	22	39	61	—
Firms' levels													
Upper level	60	30·9	41·8	25·5	1·8	9	76	14	13	31	25	29	3
Middle level:													
men	200	21·2	55·0	21·2	2·6	14	62	11	10	35	33	32	2
women	40	48·5	42·4	6·1	3·0	9	75	18	15	48	21	15	—
Lower level:													
men	140	24·1	44·5	22·6	8·8	25	49	11	9	33	36	34	3
women	210	35·4	44·3	14·1	6·2	23	60	22	10	46	17	21	1

[1] Numbers are approximate to nearest 10: they exclude 'spoilt' answers, the numbers of which vary slightly from one question to another. They also exclude a few women in the civil service grades marked *, so that the numbers for the grades do not equal the total number for the civil servants.

The administrators were the most approving (84%), and next were the senior Executive grades (76%), almost all of whose members had achieved several promotions. Least enthusiastic were the male C.O.s and C.A.s (52%), who had to wait 9 to 13 years to be considered for promotion; and it is noticeable that the Small Ministry, where the C.O.s had to wait longest of all, were the more critical of the system (40% *v.* 32%). But the professionals in the Large Ministry were also more critical (44%) than average (32%): from their spontaneous comments it was clear that several felt that they should be considered for appointment to Administrative or senior Executive grades. Women in the clerical grades were less critical than their male colleagues, and in the junior Executive grades, although more women than men regarded the system as working a little unfairly, only one (compared with 27 men) condemned it as *very* unfair.

Although the firms' methods of promotion seemed much less calculated to impress employees with their fairness, their respondents were on the whole much less critical of them. Only 5 per cent. regarded them as very unfair (*v.* 10% of the civil servants), and fully three-quarters recorded either complete or modified approval. Although the men at the lowest level—like their counterparts in the Ministries—were more critical than their superiors, the difference was not nearly so great (31% *v.* 27%). But it was interesting to see that the upper level men, usually much more enthusiastic than the administrators in the civil service about their conditions of employment, were in this case less so.

The attitudes of the women were interesting. It would be hard to find any other office organisation in Britain in which women's opportunities for promotion are so nearly equal to men's as they are in the desk classes of the civil service; a fact that was mentioned by some of the civil service women. Two Permanent Heads of Departments are women, and several have reached grades just below this. The two Ministries seemed to be no exception; there were several women among the respondents in the administrative and senior Executive grades. In contrast, it was very difficult for women in the firms to attain positions of real responsibility, and several complained of this in their spontaneous comments.

The few women in the firms who had reached the middle levels were extremely enthusiastic about the system of promotion; so were the handful of women in the administrative and senior Executive grades in the Ministries. At the clerical levels, women seemed more content with the system than men, although the percentage of female C.O.s who condemned it as very unfair was as large as among the men. Women in the junior Executive grades, on the other hand, did not, with one exception, take this extreme attitude; nor did as many express enthusiasm; they were inclined to faint praise or condemnation.

As we saw in Section 8.2, job-satisfaction is associated both with actual level in the hierarchy and with estimated status. It was therefore no surprise to find that it was also associated with attitudes to the system of promotion, even when allowance was made for the differences between grades and levels in job-satisfaction and attitudes to the system of promotion.[1]

The list of factors which might, in the respondents' view, count for promotion had been revised as a result of the pilot test, and was fairly satisfactory, if we can judge by the comments which respondents added. Two of the factors ('being in the right place at the right time' and 'good relations with superiors') were deliberately cynical, and it can be assumed that most of the 34 per cent. of civil servants and the 24 per cent. of other office workers who regarded the system as unfair in some degree marked one or other of these items.[2]

Since the principles on which both Ministries made their promotions were supposed to be well known to the staff, and no secret was made of the minimum seniority required for consideration, it was to be expected that a large number of civil servants would mark seniority as one of the two factors that counted most. Indeed, it was surprising that the percentages that did so were not higher; 62 per cent. was the highest for any staff group. The higher the grade the greater the tendency to mark 'ability' as the other important factor (77 per cent. among the administrators and only 34-38 per cent. among the C.O.s).

Since most civil servants knew that seniority was an important factor, and most firms' employees knew that in their case it was not, more of the latter had to distribute their choices among the other seven items, with the result that they appear for example to attach more weight to 'hard work' than civil servants; but comparisons of this sort are fallacious in the case of this table. Between themselves the firms were remarkably similar. Their most popular choice was of course 'ability', with 'experience' a definite second. The lower levels showed more tendency to think that seniority counted a lot, and the lower level men were more cynically inclined to vote for 'being in the right place at the right time' instead of for 'ability'.

The comments which were added by respondents, either here or at the end of the questionnaire, made their views on the promotion system even plainer. Some civil servants in the clerical and junior Executive

[1] For example, only 26 per cent. of satisfied civil servants were critical of it, although the expected *percentage* (calculated from the distribution of 'satisfieds' among the grades and the percentages of the grades who were critical) was 34 per cent. The corresponding percentages for the firms were 15 per cent. (actual) and 23 per cent. (expected).

[2] It will be seen from Table 8.21 that 63 per cent. of civil servants and 54 per cent. of firms' staffs did so. Since each respondent was asked to mark *two* items, this is fairly consistent with this assumption. Note too that it is the most critical grades who mark these items most frequently.

grades felt that it was not so much ability at work as ability to impress a Promotion Board that really helped. The impression is that 'people who can talk easily come off best' (a middle-aged E.O.), and that 'they judge you it seems on your knowledge of *The Times*, not on your ability to do a job' (a young C.O.). Some would prefer a board of trained interviewers, instead of officers from their own Ministry. The young civil servants chafed at the years which they had to spend before they were eligible for promotion; 'if Einstein were doing my job he would be required to do it for seven years before he would be considered for promotion'. The older ones, on the other hand, complained that their age was a bar to promotion, which was being given to the young. But there was the occasional word of praise: 'promotion in the civil service is in my view much more fair than anywhere outside, even if not perfect' (a member of the Executive class with several promotions behind him). One Higher Executive Officer had found that promotion had removed him 'from a job which I found extremely interesting to one which gives very little scope for the particular talents which earned my promotion'.

In the firms, the most frequent criticisms were that often posts were not filled by promotion at all, but by bringing in men from outside; and that it was 'not what you know but who you know that matters'. Women complained that they had little chance of promotion—a complaint unheard of in the Ministries. One or two seemed to feel that there was a risk involved: 'if I were single I would try for promotion'.

I suggested in Chapter 6 that the heavy wastage among young male C.O.s in the smaller Ministries might be connected with the length of time for which they had to wait before being considered eligible for promotion. The wastage rates for these two Ministries were consistent with this explanation. In 1957, when the average resignation-rate of male C.O.s throughout the service was just over 13 per thousand, it was 11 per thousand in the Large Ministry: but in the Small Ministry, where the C.O.s had to wait about three years longer, it was as high as 34 per thousand.

Pay (Qns. 47, 24)

In contrast to promotion prospects, their pay was placed high among the attractions of their job by quite a number of civil servants (21 per cent.) and even more of the firms' staffs (39 per cent). 70 per cent. of the civil servants and 82 per cent. of the firms' employees said that they were 'fairly paid'.

The easiest way to compare the grades and levels is to look at the 'underpaid' column in Table 8.22. If the women (who are much more satisfied with their pay) are disregarded, the percentage among the men in the firms is very even (23 or 24 per cent.). In the Ministries, about 30 per cent. of the men in the desk grades claim to be underpaid; the

TABLE 8.22

Pay

	N¹	Question 24		
		'Overpaid'	'Fairly paid'	'Underpaid'
		%	%	%
Large Ministry	780	2·7	70·0	27·3
Small Ministry	310	3·2	69·0	27·8
Civil servants in both	1090	2·8	69·8	27·4
Both firms' staffs	650	1·7	81·9	16·4
North Firm	340	2·6	77·0	20·4
South Firm	310	0·6	87·6	11·8
Civil Service grades				
Administrative*	90	2·3	65·1	32·6
Executive above H.E.O.*	90	2·2	52·1	45·7
H.E.O. and E.O.:				
men	310	1·3	66·7	32·0
women	130	5·6	86·4	8·0
C.O., C.O. (Sec.) and C.A.:				
men	230	2·7	67·8	29·5
women	150	4·0	87·3	8·7
Professional*:				
Large Ministry	60	3·1	56·3	40·6
Small Ministry	20	5·0	45·0	50·0
Firms' levels				
Upper level	60	—	76·9	23·1
Middle level:				
men	200	—	76·9	23·1
women	40	5·1	92·3	2·6
Lower level:				
men	140	0·7	75·0	24·3
women	210	3·7	90·8	5·5
Replies to job-satisfaction (Question 62)				
All Civil Servants — Satisfied (replies 0–2)	260	1·5	70·7	27·8
In between (,, 3–5)	680	2·2	70·3	27·5
Dissatisfied (,, 6–x)	140	8·4	65·0	26·6
All Firms' Staffs — Satisfied (replies 0–2)	270	—	84·1	15·9
In between (,, 3–5)	310	1·6	83·5	14·9
Dissatisfied (,, 6–x)	70	8·3	66·7	25·0

¹ Numbers are approximate to nearest 10: they exclude 'spoilt' answers, the numbers of which vary slightly from one question to another. They also exclude a few women in the civil service grades marked *, so that the numbers for the grades do not equal the total number for the civil servants.

exceptions are the senior executive grades (46 per cent.) and the professionals (40-50 per cent.). Even these exceptions do not prevent the uniformity of the percentages from being remarkable, when we consider the differences between the pay of the various grades and levels.[1] It suggests that in any group of office workers there is a substantial element that will regard itself as underpaid whether its pay is near the bottom or near the top of the range for the occupation. The only sub-groups which seem to need special explanations are the professionals and the senior members of the Executive class in the civil service. It is at least possible that in both cases the percentage of those dissatisfied with their pay is higher because it is easier for them to find another group with which to draw comparisons. In the case of most staff groups in the non-industrial civil service the difficulty of finding similar outside occupations, with which to compare their pay is notorious, and led the Priestley Commission to recommend the setting up of the Pay Research Unit. But professional civil servants who can compare their salaries with those paid to men with similar qualifications in jobs outside the service have no such difficulty. Will the same explanation account for the senior executive grades' dissatisfaction? In their case it is very possible that the comparison which they are drawing is with the salaries of the administrative grade. In neither case, of course, am I entering into the question whether these comparisons are justified; and in both cases this suggestion is no more than speculation.

Attitudes to pay had remarkably little connection with job-satisfaction. Among 'attractions of the job' it was ranked 1st or 2nd by 20 per cent. of the satisfied and 23 per cent. of the dissatisfied—an insignificant difference. There was a slight tendency for the dissatisfied employees of the firms to regard themselves as underpaid, but it could well have been due to chance. The only observation about which it was possible to be sure was that both in the Ministries and the firms the handful who said they were 'overpaid' tended to be those who were dissatisfied with their jobs. One administrator said that his pay was 'too much for what I do, too little for what I could do'.

Physical Working Environment (Table 8.23: Qn. 11)

The office-buildings which housed the Ministries and firms were quite diverse. A substantial number of the Large Ministry's respondents worked in a large building, originally built between the wars for a big Company; but many worked in post-war buildings of fairly modern

[1] It was unfortunate that just before the issue of the questionnaire in February 1959 the Clerical grades had just been conceded a pay increase, which may have temporarily reduced the percentage of C.O.s among my respondents who regarded themselves as underpaid. But my pilot test of the questionnaire among the handful of C.O.s took place during the pay negotiations, and disclosed a surprisingly high percentage who said 'fairly paid'.

TABLE 8.23

Physical Working Environment

Question 11: 'If you think that any of the things listed here ought to be improved in the office where you work, please tick them (tick as many as you like)'	N[1]	No Suggestions	Noise	Dirt	Ventilation	Lighting	Draughts	Heating	Canteen	Room to work	Decoration and Furniture	Lavatories	Other Suggestions	Suggestions per Respondent
		%	%	%	%	%	%	%	%	%	%	%	%	
Large Ministry	790	7.7	33.4	34.5	27.6	23.8	18.6	11.8	36.9	28.3	33.4	27.2	9.6	2.84
Small Ministry	310	5.3	36.6	42.8	33.6	39.9	28.3	13.0	36.9	27.6	43.2	41.3	19.0	3.55
Civil servants in both	1100	7.0	34.1	36.4	29.1	27.4	21.2	12.0	36.9	28.0	35.9	30.8	12.3	3.03
Both firms' staffs	660	18.5	14.4	17.4	31.9	9.4	20.4	8.8	32.1	22.8	16.6	5.2	5.8	1.85
North Firm	350	22.7	12.1	11.2	35.3	5.7	15.2	12.1	30.8	19.5	16.4	2.3	6.3	1.67
South Firm	310	13.7	16.9	24.3	28.1	13.4	26.2	5.1	33.6	26.5	16.9	8.6	5.1	2.05
Civil Servants: men	810	8.2	34.1	31.6	27.7	24.8	16.7	11.8	35.4	27.0	37.0	24.8	12.5	2.84
women	290	3.8	34.0	50.0	33.0	34.7	33.7	12.9	40.3	30.5	32.6	47.5	11.1	3.59
Firms' Staffs: men	400	21.5	17.5	18.5	32.0	6.2	12.1	6.9	31.4	23.7	19.0	4.4	5.7	1.78
women	260	13.7	9.4	14.7	31.7	14.5	33.4	11.8	33.3	21.6	12.9	6.7	5.9	1.97

[1] Numbers are approximate to nearest 10: they exclude 'spoilt' answers, the numbers of which vary slightly from one question to another.

design. The Small Ministry's building was much older: it had been designed at the turn of the century and resembled many of the Whitehall Ministries in having large, high rooms, cavernous corridors and wide, dignified staircases. Modern equipment, such as lifts and boilers, had been installed by improvisations amounting almost to violence; and rooms intended to provide an excessive amount of space for one nineteenth-century official had to accommodate half a dozen clerical officers.

The South Firm worked in an inter-war office building, which to the visitor at least seemed to compare quite well with others of the same age and size. The North Firm, however, had quite recently moved into a brand new building, designed for their requirements, and presenting a striking contrast to the well-used appearance of the two inter-war offices and the aged stateliness of the Small Ministry.

These differences were of course reflected in the replies to Question 11 (and Question 47, on the attractions of the job). The firms' staffs produced fewer suggestions for improvements than the civil servants; the North Firm produced the fewest and the Small Ministry the most. Table 8.23 shows how uniform are the percentages of complaints on certain items. It may comfort those who run the canteens both in those offices and elsewhere to see that about one in three office workers seem to be critical of their canteens. Women, as might perhaps be expected, had more criticisms, especially of canteens, draughts and the lavatories; but rather surprisingly men complained more about decoration and furniture.

Respondents were given an opportunity to add items of their own to the list in the question, and many did. Several of the North Firm's staff here expressed their appreciation of their new building (others did so in reply to Question 62). The civil servants in both Ministries made many requests for improvements in office machinery (including telephones) and typing (including secretarial) services. Several in the Small Ministry complained that members of the same branch were often separated from each other by 'miles of corridors'. The firms' criticisms were fewer and more miscellaneous.

Colleagues (Qn. 27)

Although two-thirds of the civil servants and half of the private firms' staffs attached practically no value to social life with their colleagues (see 'Attractions of the job'), very few would admit that their colleagues were anything but likeable, and the verdict 'All right' was the nearest to condemnation that any substantial number would use. Men were slightly readier to use it than women (except in the clerical and sub-clerical grades of the civil service), and the firms' men were somewhat readier to use it than the Ministries'.[1] In the civil service it

---

[1] Because they had not been together so long?

TABLE 8.24

Personal Relations

		Question 27: Most of my colleagues are			Question 40: Relations between employees at different levels are			Question 37: Discipline is—					Question 39: Respondents who regarded their organisation as	
	N^1	'Very likeable' or 'likeable'	'All right'	'Not very likeable' or 'Most unlikeable'	'Too democratic'	'About right'	'Not democratic enough'	'Unnecessarily strict'	'Strict but necessary'	'Just enough'	'A little easygoing'	'Much too lax'	'Friendly'	'Impersonal'
		%	%	%	%	%	%	%	%	%	%	%	%	%
Large Ministry	780	88·4	10·9	0·7	2·0	79·7	18·3	0·9	5·5	60·5	30·5	2·6	41·2	58·8
Small Ministry	310							1·3	1·6	49·5	41·4	6·2	45·8	54·2
Civil servants in both	1090	85·1	13·5	1·4	5·7	82·4	11·9	1·0	4·4	57·4	33·6	3·6	42·5	57·5
Both firms' staffs	650							3·8	5·0	52·4	35·6	3·2	79·0	21·0
North Firm	340							2·9	2·6	50·5	41·4	2·6	79·4	20·6
South Firm	310							4·8	7·7	54·5	29·1	3·9	78·4	21·6
Civil Service grades														
Administrative*	90	92·0	6·9	1·1	1·2	86·0	12·8	—	—	48·2	48·2	3·6		
Executive above H.E.O.*	90	95·7	4·3	—	4·3	88·2	7·5	—	4·3	55·8	37·7	2·2		
H.E.O. and E.O.: men	310	86·3	13·1	0·6	2·2	77·7	20·1	0·6	3·2	53·4	38·3	4·5		
women	130	92·1	7·9	—	1·6	73·6	24·8	—	2·4	54·4	38·4	4·8		
C.O., C.O. (Sec.) and C.A.: men	230	86·8	12·3	0·9	0·4	78·7	20·9	0·9	8·0	60·6	28·7	1·8		
women	150	84·9	13·1	2·0	3·4	78·2	18·4	2·7	8·1	64·2	21·6	3·4		
Professional*: Large Ministry	60	85·9	14·1	—	3·2	80·9	15·9	1·6	1·6	60·2	31·8	4·8		
Small Ministry	20	95·0	5·0	—	—	85·0	15·0	10·0	—	75·0	10·0	5·0		
Firms' levels														
Upper level	60	87·7	8·8	3·5	5·3	84·2	10·5	—	1·8	40·3	56·1	1·8		
Middle level: men	200	87·0	12·5	0·5	4·5	85·5	10·0	1·5	3·5	53·8	37·2	4·0		
women	40	89·7	10·3	—	2·7	81·1	16·2	2·7	—	54·1	43·2	—		
Lower level: men	140	78·4	19·6	2·0	10·5	72·0	17·5	4·8	2·7	49·7	36·7	6·1		
women	210	86·6	12·0	1·4	4·4	86·3	9·3	6·6	9·9	55·8	26·3	1·4		

[1] Numbers are approximate to nearest 10: they exclude 'spoilt' answers, the numbers of which vary slightly from one question to another. They also exclude a few women in the civil service grades marked *, so that the numbers for the grades do not equal the total number for the civil servants.

was noticeable that members of the less numerous grades were less ready to use any but a favourable phrase about their colleagues, a larger percentage of whom they probably knew personally. In the firms, however, this did not seem to be so: members of the upper level showed the greatest tendency of all groups (3·5 per cent.) to choose 'Not very likeable' or worse.

Some of the spontaneous comments at the end of the questionnaire confirmed that the firms' staffs found relations less happy than they would wish. 'Like all large companies it is full of petty hatred' (a young woman). '... There is no personal contact except on senior levels.... The tendency of survival of the fittest is very much in evidence, and it is generally recognised on certain levels that one has colleagues in business but not friends' (a middle-aged man). But most of the comments on this subject came from women, and expressed liking for their colleagues: '... the feeling generally is one of friendliness, and I always find my colleagues anxious to co-operate in every way' (a woman with some responsibility, in her fifties).

Among the civil servants both critical and enthusiastic comments like these were much rarer. 'Colleagues nearly all a fine crowd' (an elderly professional). One woman C.O. placed 'relations with colleagues' above all other 'attractions of the job' (q.v.), and said 'they are pleasant and free of the pettiness and jealousies common to commercial and business offices'. The only criticism I could find came from a married woman in her fifties in a clerical job, 'I object to lazy, dirty and untidy colleagues who do not pull their weight'.

Inter-level Relations (Qn. 40)

Table 8.24 also shows respondents' opinions of the relations between employees at different levels. In practice, distinctions between grades and levels were sharper in some of the organisations than in others. In the Companies, a few amenities—such as a special canteen or washroom—were reserved for certain of the higher levels. In one of the Companies certain levels were brought coffee on a tray in the middle of the morning, while the rest received tea from a trolley. Most of the staff addressed each other as 'Mr. Smith' and 'Miss Jones'; Christian names were used only where they were on terms of genuine friendship; and as we have seen this was rare. 'Sir', on the other hand, was not often used, unless by a junior employee addressing a director. On the whole, relations between different levels of staff were neither servile nor informal, but 'correct'.

Practice in the civil service is no longer as uniform as it was. The Small Ministry was probably quite a good example of the modern development of traditional usage. There were no special lavatories, canteens or even separate tables for senior officers. In addressing each other members of the same staff group—Administrative, Executive or

Clerical—usually called each other by their plain surnames: 'Mr.' or 'Miss' was reserved for addressing someone in a superior grade, or a member of the opposite sex, and Christian names were more frequent than in the Companies. A senior officer might call his Personal Assistant 'Betty' without fear of comment, though she would call him 'Mr. Jones'. Even the Permanent Secretary of a Ministry is 'Smith' to most of his administrative colleagues, although the practice of addressing him as 'Secretary' is now commoner. The most formal gulf is between civil servants and Ministers, who are called 'Minister' or 'Sir' and seldom use the civil servants' canteen.

In the Large Ministry, however, the atmosphere was rather different. There was a 'Senior Officers' Mess', and lavatories reserved for the men at the top. Modes of address were not very different from those of the small Ministry, but my impression was that there was slightly more formality even between members of the informal Administrative class. These differences may have had several causes—the enormous size of the organisation, the association between the Ministry and other kinds of organisation in which such distinctions were usual, and even the layout of the headquarters' building itself.

In both Ministries and Companies, leisure activities were usually shared only by personal friends, or by members of the same office clubs: and as we have seen more office workers participate in these on paper than in practice. Nor was there any custom whereby senior officers invited their immediate subordinates to their houses at least once a year. Office parties were organised at Christmas among the middle and lower levels of the Ministries, but in the Companies the only occasion of this kind was the more formal office dance.

Most of the respondents seemed to accept the atmosphere in their own organisation as normal: nearly 80 per cent. in all four organisations described inter-level relations as 'about right'. Rather surprisingly, in view of the differences between the Ministries which I have described, there was little difference between their respondents' verdicts. On the other hand, the civil servants as a whole showed a significantly greater tendency to label their relations as 'not democratic enough.' This feeling seemed to be strongest among the clerical and junior executive grades, but least common among the senior executive staff, who had instead a slightly stronger tendency to choose 'too democratic'.

In the firms the criticism 'not democratic enough' was less frequent; women in the middle levels and men in the lower levels were most prone to voice it. A small percentage of most grades—and oddly enough a substantial 10·5 per cent. of the lower male office workers—thought relations were too democratic, a feeling that was slightly commoner in the firms than in the Ministries. Between the two Ministries and between the two firms the differences were insignificant.

One or two of the critics made their attitudes clearer at the end of the questionnaire. Some of those in the firms who thought relations *too* democratic made it clear that what they had in mind was discipline (q.v.). In the civil service, one of the Executive class in the Small Ministry said 'there are many who consider it bad policy to have any social interests or activities with the people they work with'. On the whole, however, it was hard to be sure exactly what the critics had in mind.

Discipline (Qn. 37)

There were marked differences between Ministries and between firms in respondents' views on discipline (Table 8.24). Very few civil servants, and only slightly more firms' employees[1] thought that it was unnecessarily strict, although as much as 5 to 7 per cent. of men and women in the firms' lower levels chose this reply. Even the verdict 'strict but necessary' was not much used, except by men and women in the clerical and sub-clerical grades in the Ministries. What was striking was the percentage who chose 'a little easy-going' or 'much too lax'. Nearly 48 per cent. of the Small Ministry (compared with 33 per cent. of the Large Ministry) and 44 per cent. of the North Firm (compared with 33 per cent. of the South Firm) chose one or other of these criticisms.

Quite apart from these dissimilarities between the organisations, however, it is interesting to see how many office workers would apparently approve of somewhat stricter discipline. Although this is more marked in the higher levels, it is surprisingly prevalent among those who are 'at the receiving end' so far as discipline is concerned; at least a quarter of men and women at the lower levels of the Ministries and the firms felt this. (Note, too, the 6·1 per cent. of lower level men in the Companies who firmly said 'much too lax'; and remember that it was among these lower level men that the surprisingly high 10 per cent. thought inter-level relations were too democratic.)

Some examples of lax discipline were given at the end of the questionnaire. 'Superiors have too easy a conscience about working hours in their own cases. They should set a good example to their staff before deciding conditions and rules for them. . . .' (a C.O. from the Small Ministry). This puts its finger on an old sore spot. Junior civil servants who are supposed to be at their desks at 9 a.m. see their seniors arriving at hours varying from 9.30 to 10 a.m. The juniors' lunch-breaks are of specified length; the seniors are given more latitude (another subject of comment). What the juniors do not see is the seniors working after the juniors leave at 5.30 p.m., and taking work home; but what they do

[1] This criticism seemed to be associated with low job-satisfaction (see the section 'Job-satisfaction'). Respondents with high job-satisfaction who thought discipline was strict tended to choose 'strict but necessary'. This was more marked, however, among the firms' respondents.

notice is the occasional case in which the senior arrives late and leaves at the same time as they do.

Other points made by the Small Ministry's respondents were that the 'general attitude tends to be friendly rather than business-like. Higher grades dislike giving adverse reports—generally bad for youngsters starting a career' (a middle-aged male C.O.); and that 'more work would be done if the Ministry were run on the lines of an efficient outside business house (e.g. more formal arrangement of seating to encourage less private conversation, institution of the check-card system for all ranks of employees, and stronger disciplinary action taken against the few who do not do an honest day's work' (a female C.O.). Once more, the striking feature of these criticisms is that they come from the grades that are at the receiving end of discipline, and not from the seniors.

In the Companies there were far fewer differences in time-keeping habits between the levels. Not only the juniors but also the most senior staff were supposed to be at their desks at 9 a.m., and I was assured that this rule was strictly observed. It is possible that at the other end of the day many of the seniors also left at half-past five like their juniors; but in the North Firm there is no doubt that a sizeable group at the top stayed behind for at least another hour or so. Nevertheless, the firms' staffs had one or two criticisms of slack discipline. In the North Firm 'the women are far too noisy and loud but are rarely told off by the boss' (a man). In the South Firm 'one feels that the Company is over-democratised, and that a small amount of ruthlessness, particularly in regard to punctuality, would not come amiss. Top management is too lax.' (a man). On the other hand, a woman in the same firm felt that people were 'too hot on time, and very unfair about it. The girls who have done long service do not get told off about it, but the new girls get reprimanded.' This was the only comment, from any of the four organisations, that came near to a complaint that discipline was too strict; and even this one contrives to imply that except for newcomers discipline is lax.

It was therefore interesting to find, among the comments of one of the men at a higher level, the sentence 'I wish I were a little harder, particularly with other and older members of the staff—it would make my job easier.'

The Immediate Superior (Qns. 25, 31, 49, 51, 52)

Respondents were asked to say whether their immediate superior was male or female and older, younger or the same age as themselves (Qn. 31); whether in their jobs they had too much, enough or too little 'supervision and guidance' (Qn. 25); whether they could do their superior's job (Qn. 49); and whether they were 'usually' or 'hardly ever' told when they made mistakes or did 'a particularly good job' (Qns.

51, 52). These questions were scattered so as to minimise any impression that they were passing judgment on their immediate superior (you will recall how the C.O.s at Newcastle shied at this).

Over 80 per cent. of both civil servants and firms' staffs seemed satisfied with the amount of supervision and guidance they received; the South Firm were slightly more critical than the rest. In the civil service men who were critical usually complained of 'too much' (11·1 per cent.): only 5·7 per cent. chose 'too little'. Their women colleagues tended to do just the opposite: 11·0 per cent. said 'too little', and only 6·8 per cent. 'too much'. There was little difference between the reactions of the grades, with the exception that the Large Ministry's professionals contained a very high percentage (23·1 per cent.) who thought they suffered from an excess of supervision.

In the firms the pattern was different. The women were less critical than the men, and the latter, at least at the middle and lower levels, complained more often (about 12 per cent.) of 'too little supervision'. The largest single block of critics, however, was the 15·5 per cent. of men at the lower level who complained of too much supervision.

Several spontaneous comments revealed the nature of respondents' criticisms of the way in which they were supervised:

'Insufficient encouragement is given to using initiative and being creative, and to working together as a team, which leads to frustration and lack of interest in what could otherwise be a satisfying job.' (a female E.O.)

'I am prevented from getting to see the whole picture, but am bogged down with detail. . . .' (another)

'(The chief disadvantage of the job is) lack of contact with the Head of Branch, and lack of sense of personal loyalty.' (another)

'One tends to adopt a "couldn't care less" attitude because there is no one superior (or boss) to work for, but a never-ending chain of people to whom work has to be shown and is frequently amended.' (another)

'(The chief disadvantage of the job is) having to do a variety of things without being given any reason for them.' (another)

'The job is unimaginative and the attitude of my immediate—though not only—superior is negative and slow.' (another)

'I find that work of an interesting nature is hogged by superiors, leaving the rest to me without any possibility of passing it on. . . .' (a professional)

For some reason, all but one of the quotable and concrete comments from the civil service on this subject came from female E.O.s.

Here are some comments from the firms:

'The work is interesting; the only thing is the staff is not properly handled: relations between Section Supervisors and the staff are hopeless. Rude and sarcastic remarks are passed often. There is nothing wrong with the Company—it is excellent.'
(a man from the North Firm)

'My immediate superior's ... interest in other people leaves a lot to be desired. No job is properly done unless he does it himself. (This) ... imposes more work ... and generates lack of confidence in his juniors.' (another, at a fairly senior level)

'... there seems to be a tendency for immediate superiors to add extra rules and regulations to general ones.' (a woman in the North Firm)

'... but in spite of this there is no personal contact except on senior levels. The "small cogs" are not aware of the operation of the whole.'
(a fairly senior man in the South Firm)

'(I would like) more variations and responsibility; to have my word believed and not doubted because I am a woman. Can hardly move without permission. I like to sign my own letters.
In short, I like to be treated as a grown-up (a competent one) and *not* like a school-girl.' (from the South Firm)

'My main problems—
 (i) lack of clear division of responsibilities on my level;
 (ii) overworked high-power superior ... who cannot afford time to discuss problems properly or even to see people on my level often when some policy matter needs urgent settlement.' (from the South Firm)

'My immediate boss seems incompetent in office management.'
(from the South Firm)

'... Suggestions should always be passed on to the immediate superior of the person receiving the suggestion, as quite often the wrong person receives credit for suggesting; and also at least two people should examine the suggestion before it is turned down.' (from the South Firm)

As for the question whether they could do the job of their immediate superior, it was evidently one about which both civil servants and firms' staffs had already thought; for the percentage who were 'not sure' was remarkably small (about 3 per cent. and 10 per cent.) in comparison with the numbers who hedged in replies to some other questions. The lower their grade or level, the higher the percentage who thought they could; but women were less confident than men, and the women in the firms much less confident than their civil service sisters. Indeed, the civil servants as a whole were more confident than the firms' staffs. The most confident of all were the Large Ministry's professionals.

I thought it would be interesting to see whether the sex or age of the superior had anything to do either with the subordinate's feeling that he could do the job above him or with any feeling that he was suffering from an excess or lack of supervision. In the civil service there was no sign of any association of these kinds. I did, however, find that among the 204 civil servants working under women there was a very significantly higher percentage who *wanted a move* either 'very soon' or 'before long' (47·1% *v.* 36·3%). This increase was even more evident among the 80 *women* who were working under *women* (51·2% *v.* 33·3%); and these also showed a significant difference in general job-satisfaction (24·1% being dissatisfied compared with 12·6% among the 207 *women* working for *men*).

In the firms practically all the employees who were working under women were themselves women (50 out of 55), and they showed a slight tendency not only to enjoy their jobs less and to want a move more than the other women, but also a greater tendency to say that they were too much supervised (14·3% v. 7·0%) and to be confident that they could do the job of the woman they were working under (62·0% v. 22·4%).

In other words, both men and women enjoy their jobs more if their immediate superior is a man; and this reaction is particularly marked among women. The women in the civil service did not carry it to the length of allowing it to affect their judgment as to whether they could do the job of the woman over them, or whether she was supervising them too closely; but it is at least probable that this is what the firm's women were doing.

This evidence of a reaction of women to working under someone of their own sex—and the similar though less strong reaction of men to working for women—will be no surprise to anyone who has worked in an office; indeed it may strengthen his suspicion that the function of statistics is to demonstrate what one knows already. But it is pleasant, and what is more it inspires confidence in the reliability of questionnaires, when they confirm what is common knowledge. This is also a good example of a result that I should probably have failed to get if I had simply asked respondents some such question as 'How do you like working for a woman?'[1] Respondents' answers to that sort of question are distorted by feelings of what their attitude ought to be; and another thing that everyone knows nowadays is that one ought not to mind working under a woman. As I have pointed out, the civil service today probably offers women at all levels the nearest thing to equality of opportunity with men for promotion and for responsible and interesting work[2] that they are likely to find in any non-professional career in this country. But it seems that irrational feelings die hard.

Respondents were also asked 'Are you told when you make a mistake?' (Qn. 51), and 'Are you told when you have done a particularly good job?' (Qn. 52), and allowed to choose between the replies 'Usually' and 'Hardly ever'. Over 85 per cent. of both civil servants and firms' staffs said that they were usually told when they made mistakes: there was no significant difference between the two kinds of office workers

---

[1] One man commented at the end of the questionnaire on
'The general objection by males to female supervision of which there seems to be such a preponderance.'
and one woman said
'I don't enjoy working to a female supervisor.' But that was all.
[2] It already, of course, offers equal pay.

or between Ministries, or between firms. But the replies to the second of these questions showed differences, best seen by comparing those who said that they were hardly ever told when they had done a particularly good job:

	%
Large Ministry	50·2
Small Ministry	56·1
Civil Servants in both	51·8
Both firms' staffs	41·4
North Firm	37·0
South Firm	45·4

The difference between the Ministries is not quite large enough to pass our standards of significance: the probability of its being a chance effect is about 1 in 10. The difference between the firms is probably due to the larger proportion in the South Firm of lower-level men, whose replies, as we have already seen, are usually more critical. But the difference between civil servants and firms' staffs is very significant.[1]

When the answers to these two questions were compared with scores on the job-satisfaction scale, I found that the percentage (13·5) of all respondents who felt that they were hardly ever told of their mistakes did not vary much between those who were satisfied and those who were dissatisfied with their jobs. But when it came to being told of one's successes, the difference was very significant[2]:

	Satisfied	In between	Dissatisfied
	%	%	%
'Hardly ever'	40·0	53·9	59·4

Clearly this grievance has some connection with low job-satisfaction.

Consultation about Changes (Qn. 57)

This question asked 'Are you consulted about changes in the way in which work is organised or the conditions under which you work?' I wanted to see whether there was any difference between the four organisations in respondents' feelings that they were or were not consulted about such things. Since the Ministries had the Whitley machine while the office staffs of the firms had no corresponding organisation which the management could use to sound the views of the staff on contemplated changes, I had expected that the Ministry's respondents would show signs of feeling that they were consulted more often. Not a bit of it:

---

[1] The probability of its being due to chance is under 1 in 1,000.
[2] Again the probability of its being due to chance was less than 1 in 1,000.

TABLE 8.25

Respondents from	Replies to 'are you consulted (etc.)?'		
	'Always' or 'Usually'	'Sometimes'	'Not usually' or 'Never'
	%	%	%
Large Ministry . . .	46	31	24
Small Ministry . . .	42	29	29
North Firm . . .	51	27	22
South Firm	49	28	23

The firms' respondents seem to report more frequent consultation than the Ministries' and the percentage in the small Ministry who replied 'Not usually' or 'Never' is significantly higher than in the other three organisations. It may be that the effect of having a staff association is to reduce the feeling that one is consulted personally. I must emphasise, however, that the question does not show whether, for example, the Small Ministry's respondents were particularly dissatisfied with the extent to which they were consulted; they may have been quite content with whatever consultations took place with their associations. Certainly not one of the spontaneous comments from this (or the other) Ministry made any complaint on this subject.[1] If I had been concerned with relations between staff and their associations it would have been possible to ask several more precise questions; but I leave this interesting subject to someone else.[2]

The 'Men at the Top' (Qn. 36)

Respondents were asked for their impression of the competence of the 'men at the top', a phrase which was chosen with deliberate vagueness. To some civil servants it would mean the Minister and his Parliamentary Secretary; to some, the permanent head of the Ministry and his immediate deputies; to others, a mixture of the two. To the firms' staffs there was also the possibility that it would mean the directors, the senior executives or both. I could have been less ambiguous without difficulty; but what I wanted was the respondent's attitude to whatever people he regarded as running his Ministry or firm. Only 23 civil servants and 27 of the firms' respondents baulked at the question, either because it was ambiguous or because it was delicate.

If we can judge from the spontaneously offered comments at the end

[1] There was one complaint from an employee of one of the firms that he was not consulted about changes affecting him.
[2] Miss B. V. Humphrey's book *Clerical Unions in the Civil Service* (1958) does not deal with it either.

of the questionnaire, most civil servants were thinking of the administrators when they answered this question:[1]

'The men at the top appear to feel no personal responsibility towards those below them. Consequently the junior and middle ranks feel for the most part that nobody at the top really cares whether they are there or not. There is thus little sense of loyalty to an organisation.' (a member of the Executive class)

'The people at the top seem to have little idea of the difficulties experienced in the work of the lower grades. They are theory men, always proposing schemes which do not work out well in practice. In proposing these schemes they do not consult the people who will have to work them. . . .' (another)

'Insufficient trouble is taken by those at Assistant Secretary level and above to get to know the staff.' (another)

'The lack of interest by the "top men" in the feelings of their subordinates on matters generally." (another)

All these—and one or two others—came from the Large Ministry's respondents; there was nothing comparable from those in the Small Ministry.

By far the most uncomplimentary group were the professional civil servants in both Ministries, over 30 per cent. of whom regarded the men at the top as not quite competent enough or, worse still, incompetent. Only a fairly uniform 9 per cent. of the other groups of civil servants made these choices. The critical attitude of their professional colleagues is probably a symptom of the feeling that the decisions taken by the laymen who are either their administrative colleagues or their Ministers pay too little regard to the technical advice or needs of the professionals; this is part of the problem of relations between the desk grades and the scientific and professional grades, which has already begun to interest the Treasury's Training and Education Division.[2] It would have been interesting to see what the desk grades thought of the professionals.

In contrast was the very high opinion which the administrators and senior Executive grades expressed of their chiefs; 48 and 40 per cent. respectively used the phrase 'really able', and only about 10 per cent. used one of the derogatory labels: one respondent in these two groups said 'incompetent'. The lower grades were less inclined to use the superlative, but no more inclined to cast doubts on the competence of the men at the top. Women in the clerical grades were, for once, rather more enthusiastic than their male colleagues.

Although this was a respect in which the Ministries might well have differed, they were remarkably similar. The firms, on the other hand,

[1] Not one respondent referred to his Minister in any part of the questionnaire. This may have been the effect of piety. It is quite as likely, however, that as with the C.O.s in Newcastle, the Minister was to most of the respondents too remote a figure.

[2] See the article 'Scientists versus Administrators' by Z. M. T. Tarkowski and Avice V. Turnbull in *Public Administration* for autumn 1959.

TABLE 8.26

The Men at the Top

		N^1	Question 36: The men at the top are			
			Really able	Competent	Not quite competent enough	Incompetent
			%	%	%	%
Large Ministry		780	30	58	10	1
Small Ministry		310	34	57	8	1
Civil servants in both		1090	31	58	10	1
Both firms' staffs		650	39	49	10	2
North Firm		340	43	50	6	2
South Firm		310	35	49	14	2
Civil Service grades	Administrative*	90	48	42	9	–
	Executive above H.E.O.*	90	40	48	11	1
	H.E.O. and E.O.:					
	men	310	32	58	9	1
	women	130	26	66	7	1
	C.O., C.O. (Sec.) and C.A.:					
	men	230	26	66	7	2
	women	150	37	57	6	–
	Professional*:					
	Large Ministry	60	16	54	25	5
	Small Ministry	20	20	45	30	5
Firms' levels	Upper level	60	47	42	11	–
	Middle level:					
	men	200	40	48	12	–
	women	40	49	46	6	–
	Lower level:					
	men	140	29	51	14	5
	women	210	42	52	6	2

[1] Numbers are approximate to nearest 10: they exclude 'spoilt' answers, the numbers of which vary slightly from one question to another. They also exclude a few women in the civil service grades marked *, so that the numbers for the grades do not equal the total number for the civil servants.

showed some very interesting dissimilarities. The men at the upper levels were more complimentary and those in the lower levels more uncomplimentary than their counterparts in the Ministries (women showed the same tendency to be more enthusiastic which we noticed in the C.O.s and C.A.s). Most striking, however, was the way in which the South Firm's staff were more critical of its top men than the North Firm's were of theirs. In case this should be due to a difference in the representation of the more critical groups (i.e. the lower-level men), I made a separate analysis of the levels in each firm, but found that at all levels (except among women of the middle level) the South Firm's staff had a lower opinion of their management.

Several of the South Firm's respondents made their feelings about top management a little clearer in their spontaneous comments at the end of the questionnaire:

> 'The company I work for is controlled by an autocratic ... organisation. Amongst many people there is a feeling that more co-operation could be achieved if a lead were given by top management. . . .'
>
> 'Lack of interest shown by the ... men at the top in the company's activities apart from work. . . .'
>
> '. . . . an overworked (member of top management) who cannot afford time to discuss problems properly or even to see managers ... often when some policy matter needs urgent settlement.'[1]
>
> 'Lack of foresight by management: lack of information to staff of what is planned.'
>
> 'Management stupidity.'

These comments are from different levels, some of them by no means junior.

This is a good example of the importance of distinguishing attitude from fact. A good example of a comment that reflected attitude rather than fact was

> 'The people at the top are sometimes not good enough and are often worn out. Also the people at the bottom are on the whole very bad indeed: typists, clerks, etc.'
> (a person in the middle)

With the possible exception of the professional civil servants, the most uncomplimentary office workers were those whose jobs brought them into least contact with the men at the top, and who were probably least able to form an accurate opinion of their competence. What the replies draw attention to is not necessarily a difference in quality between 'the

---

[1] It must not be assumed that the South Firm had nothing but criticisms of their top men. Here is a contrast:
 'The fact that everybody in this Department appears to be happy is undoubtedly due to a large extent to the Head of the Department. . . . He treats the office-boy with as much consideration as he does the Managing Director. . . . His reputation for this goes throughout the Company and outside it.'

men at the top' in the two firms, but a difference in attitude towards them, which seems to exist at all levels.

Subordinates (Qn. 57)

Let us now look at respondents' attitudes to those who worked under them. At the lower levels, of course, many did not have subordinates; and as Table 8.27 shows, this meant that—especially in the firms—quite a large percentage could not reply to Question 57. Indeed, the fact that more civil servants did so is probably an indication that the structure of their organisations is more hierarchical than that of the companies. Fortunately, the respondents at the lower levels were numerous, so that enough of them did reply to enable comparisons to be made.

The replies between which they could choose all dealt with the most important question which can be asked about a subordinate—'How much can you safely leave to his judgment?' The choice of replies ranged from fairly high praise to expressions of considerable lack of confidence:

5. Their judgment is pretty well as good as mine, and I leave them to carry on.
4. They can be trusted to come to me when the need arises.
2. They can be trusted with the easier decisions.
0. They need close supervision to prevent mistakes.

Three other replies, not necessarily incompatible with all of these four were thrown in to see how many people marked them:

6. I would like to keep a closer eye on them, but am too busy.
1. They could be trusted with more responsibility, but under the present system they must consult me.
3. They consult me about trivial things when they don't have to.

Quite a number of respondents did mark more than one of the replies.[1]

The replies yielded several interesting comparisons. The Large Ministry showed less preference than the other three organisations for the really critical verdict 'They need close supervision to prevent mistakes'. The North Firm, where so many respondents had claimed to be working long hours (Qns. 12 and 13) had the highest percentage who replied that they would like to keep a closer eye on their subordinates but were too busy. But otherwise the differences were between the civil service and the firms' staffs, or between different levels. Fully 12 per cent of the civil servants thought that the people under them could be trusted with more responsibility if only the system permitted it. The lower the level of the respondent, the more likely he was

---

[1] They were presented in the random order indicated by the numerals, since the order in the text above would have revealed to respondents the fact that some answers were considered 'better' than others.

TABLE 8.27

Subordinates' Capabilities

Question 57: 'Here are some ways of describing the capabilities of those working under you. Which of them comes closest to describing your own subordinates?'—

(Percentages in these columns are percentages of the totals of these seven kinds of replies: several respondents marked more than one)

		N[1]	Percentage of N who replied to this question (rest having no subordinates?)	'They need close supervision to prevent mistakes'	'They could be trusted with more responsibility, but under the present system they must consult me'	'They can be trusted with the easier decisions'	'They consult me about trivial things when they don't have to'	'They can be trusted to come to one when the need arises'	'Their judgment is pretty well as good as mine, and I leave them to carry on'	'I would like to keep a closer eye on them, but am too busy'
			%	%	%	%	%	%	%	%
	Large Ministry	780		9·5		23·0	4·1	39·9	6·3	3·5
	Small Ministry	310		14·8		19·7	4·4	42·3	6·8	3·1
	Civil servants in both	1090	74	10·9	12·3					5·1
	Both firms' staffs	650	59	16·1	7·5					1·1
	North Firm	340								
	South Firm	310								
Civil Service grades	Administrative*	90	96	3·4	4·5	19·3	3·4	60·3	6·8	2·3
	Executive above H.E.O.*	90	98	5·9	10·9	15·9	2·0	59·5	4·9	0·9
	H.E.O. and E.O.: men	310	89	9·3	15·8	17·6	4·0	42·1	5·9	5·3
	women	130	92	8·9	10·4	23·7	1·5	40·7	8·9	5·9
	C.O., C.O. (Sec.) and C.A.: men	230	25	17·5	7·0	7·0	12·3	35·1	19·3	1·8
	women	150	33	16·7	—	20·8	8·3	37·5	4·2	12·5
	Professional*: Large Ministry	60	59	7·7	9·6	23·1	1·9	51·9	5·8	—
	Small Ministry	20	55	16·7	16·7	16·7	8·3	41·6	—	—
Firm's levels	Upper level	60	97	6·9	3·5	12·0	1·7	65·5	6·9	3·5
	Middle level: men	200	80	13·9	4·6	18·6	4·1	48·0	4·6	6·2
	women	40	42	5·6	5·6	5·6	11·1	66·5	—	5·6
	Lower level: men	140	37	20·3	8·7	20·3	7·2	21·8	15·9	5·8
	women	210	7	19·6	2·2	6·5	15·2	36·9	13·1	6·5

[1] Numbers are approximate to nearest 10: they exclude 'spoilt' answers, the numbers of which vary slightly from one question to another. They also exclude a few women in the civil service grades marked *, so that the numbers for the grades do not equal the total number for the civil servants.

to feel that he could not rely on his subordinates: so far as the civil servants were concerned this was consistent with the lower efficiency ratings which tended to be given to the lower grades.

In view of the signs that respondents did not enjoy working under women, was there any difference between men and women in their attitude towards their subordinates? Women were not quite as ready as men to use the most approving verdict of all (except apparently in the junior Executive grades). Except for the female clerical officers, they did not show any great tendency to claim that they were too busy to keep as close an eye on their subordinates as they would like. The percentages who chose the most critical remark—'They need close supervision to prevent mistakes'—were very much the same as among their male colleagues. On the whole they did what women sometimes seem to do in answering questionnaires—they chose moderate rather than extreme replies. Several of the apparent differences in Table 8·27 between men and women civil servants are reversed in the firms. There is no evidence in these replies that women are more 'difficult' to work under.

Some Aspects of the Work Itself (Qns. 15, 22, 23)

Since the nature of respondent's work varied considerably, even among men and women at the same level, the questions that could be sensibly asked about it were limited to aspects such as its variety, the amount of responsibility it involved, whether it seemed to him essential, how hardworked he was, and what his relations with the outside public were like.

On the subject of variety, the replies were very much what might have been expected. The higher the level, the less frequent the complaints of too little variety; indeed, there was a slight increase in the complaints of too much! Women complained just as much as their male colleagues on this score. There was a barely significant tendency for the firms' staffs to complain more frequently of lack of variety; this was one of the few instances in which they were more critical.

On the subject of responsibility, too, there was the same tendency for the lower levels to complain more about the lack of it: hardly anyone complained of having too much. The highest percentage of complaints came from the men at the lower levels of both the civil service and the firms. The least critical were the women in the firms' middle levels; and women on the whole missed responsibility less. There were no significant differences between the two firms, the two Ministries, or the two kinds of office worker. Over a third of them all felt that they could do with more responsibility, and perhaps the most interesting feature of these figures is that this fraction is no higher among the civil servants than among the firms' staffs.

TABLE 8.28

The Work

	N[1]	Question 15: Compared with most other people in your office at your level, are you					Question 22: Variety			Question 23: Responsibility		
		Much less hard-worked	Slightly less hard-worked	About the same	Slightly more hard-worked	Much more hard-worked	Too much	Enough	Too little	Too much	Enough	Too little
Large Ministry	780	% 1	% 4	% 59	% 31	% 6	% 3	% 76	% 21	% 1	% 60	% 39
Small Ministry	310	2	7	59	27	6	1	76	23	1	63	36
Civil servants in both	1090	1	5	59	29	6	2	76	22	1	61	38
Both firms' staffs	650	2	5	59	26	8	2	72	26	1	62	37
North Firm	340	3	6	56	26	9	1	74	24	1	59	40
South Firm	310	1	4	63	26	6	3	69	28	1	66	33
Civil Service grades												
Administrative*	90	—	15	51	27	7	5	86	9	1	70	29
Executive above H.E.O.*	90	2	4	62	26	6	3	94	3	1	76	23
H.E.O. and E.O.:												
men	310	1	5	58	30	7	2	79	19	1	65	34
women	130	2	5	60	31	2	2	78	20	2	68	30
C.O., C.O. (Sec.) and C.A.:												
men	230	0.4	2	60	29	9	2	66	32	1	45	54
women	150	1	4	57	32	5	1	66	34	1	58	41
Professional*:												
Large Ministry	60	—	2	67	30	2	2	83	16	—	58	42
Small Ministry	20	—	5	65	30	—	5	75	20	—	60	40
Firms' levels												
Upper level	60	—	7	47	33	12	11	81	9	—	63	37
Middle level:												
men	200	2	4	55	28	13	2	88	11	—	67	33
women	40	3	5	47	40	5	3	87	10	1	90	10
Lower level:												
men	140	3	3	62	26	5	1	59	40	—	49	51
women	210	2	6	67	21	4	1	60	39	2	62	36

[1] Numbers are approximate to nearest 10: they exclude 'spoilt' answers, the numbers of which vary slightly from one question to another. They also exclude a few women in the civil service grades marked *, so that the numbers for the grades do not equal the total number for the civil servants.

Even more remarkable—and illuminating—is the uniformity of the replies to the question which asked respondents how hard-worked they were. Very few indeed (6-7 per cent.) said that they were less hard-worked than their colleagues; it was noticeable that secretaries in the firms often complained of too little to do: other staff who felt less hard-worked showed a tendency[1] to be dissatisfied with their jobs. In other words, like the claim to be *over*paid, it is often a sign of dissatisfaction, although this was not so in the case of the secretaries. What was quite astonishing, however, was the percentage who claimed to be slightly or much more hard-worked. More than 1 in 3 of all the respondents made this claim, whether they were in the civil service or the private firms. The highest percentage of claims came from the upper-level men and middle-level women (45 per cent.), the lowest from the lower-level women (25 per cent.), in the firms. The civil service was more uniform, ranging from 30 per cent. among the Small Ministry's professionals to 38 per cent. among male C.O.s.

The percentage of those who claimed to be '*much* more hard-worked' was also very uniform—6 per cent. in all the organisations except the North Firm, where it was 9 per cent. This is consistent with the exceptional percentage of employees in that firm who claimed that they worked after regular hours or at home (see 'After Working Hours').

With this possible exception, the conclusion that most certainly should not be drawn from these percentages is that they are anything like a true reflection of the state of affairs. As I said when discussing the subject of working after regular hours, to work long hours is to acquire merit, and even a moral advantage over one's colleagues: it is the office-worker's prayer-wheel. To be more hard-working in this or other ways confers similar advantages, particularly if work—like justice —is not only done but seen to be done. There are cases, too, in which the belief that one is doing more than one's share is a chronic grievance, and sometimes the justification for it is so scanty that it amounts to an occupational neurosis. But not a neurosis of the dissatisfied; the claim to be *more* hard-worked than one's neighbour is if anything a little commoner among those who enjoy their work. What is almost certain is that it is made by so many of the respondents that it cannot be true in every case.

The Public and the Press (Qns. 48, 19, 20, 21, 38)

One of the most striking things about the civil servants' lists of the disadvantages of their job (q.v.) was the high percentage (38 per cent.) who ranked the attitude of the public to their work as one of the two most unsatisfactory features of it; it was second only to promotion

---

[1] Significant at the ·01 level.

TABLE 8.29

Public and Press

	N	Question 19: How much of your time is spent in face-to-face or telephone conversations with the public, with customers or with outside organisations?					Question 20: Would you like more contacts of this kind, or not?			Question 21: How does the public (etc.) react, on the whole, to what you have to do?			Question 38: Press criticism of the Company (or Ministry) is				
		Almost all	Most of it	About half	Not very much	Practically none	'Much' or 'A bit' more	No change	'A bit' or 'much' less	In a (very or fairly) friendly way	In a tolerant way	In a (slightly or very) unfriendly way	Occasional and usually fair	Occasional and usually unfair	Frequent and usually fair	Frequent and usually unfair	Very rare or I wouldn't notice any
Large Ministry	780	3	3	24	51	20	% 45	% 52	% 4	% 80	% 19	% 1	% 30	% 33	% 6	% 16	% 16
Small Ministry	310	—	1	16	59	24	48	50	2	75	19	7	36	23	14	9	19
Civil servants in both	1090	2	2	21	53	21	46	51	3	78	19	3	31	30	9	14	17
Both firms' staffs	650	3	6	30	31	29	44	51	5	85	14	1	18	3	4	0·2	76
North Firm	340	3	7	35	33	22	48	46	5	88	11	1	18	5	5	0·3	71
South Firm	310	2	6	26	29	37	40	56	4	81	16	2	17	0·3	2	—	81

[1] Numbers are approximate to nearest 10: they exclude 'spoilt' answers, the numbers of which vary slightly from one question to another.

prospects. The percentages among the middle and higher grades of the service was even higher:

	%[1]
Administrators	41
Executives above H.E.O.	47
H.E.O.s and E.O.s	45
C.O.s and C.A.s	29
Large Ministry's professionals	26
Small Ministry's professionals	6

But the reason may simply have been that the clerical officers and professionals felt more strongly about other grievances. Unlike most other complaints, this was much more strongly voiced by the *satisfied* civil servants:

	%
Satisfied	42
In between	41
Dissatisfied	17

The dissatisfied respondents did not seem to be as interested in the public's attitude.

In other questions (19-21) respondents were asked how much of their time was spent in conversation with the public in some form or other, whether they would like more such contacts, and how the public reacted to what the respondents had to do. They were also asked how frequent and how fair Press criticism of their organisation was. A great deal of the work of civil servants involves the control and restriction, by fiscal or other means, of the activities of other organisations or private individuals, and even when it involves positive assistance it is usually criticised for being too little or too late. I wanted to see what impression this made upon the Ministries' respondents (Table 8.30).

As Table 8.30 shows, the civil servants spent on the whole much less of their time in contact with people outside than did the firms' staffs: 74 per cent. compared with 60 per cent. among the firms' staffs said 'not very much' or 'practically none'. Only 4 per cent. of the civil servants spent most or almost all of their time in outside contact, and practically all of these were either professionals in the Large Ministry, or junior Executives. There seemed to be some connection between this aspect of their work and job-satisfaction, but the connection appeared stronger among the firms' employees:

A very large percentage of both types of respondent (44-46 per cent.) wanted more such contacts: those who expressed this desire most frequently were the Clerical grades in the civil service (58 per cent. of the men and 52 per cent. of the women), and the lower level staff in

[1] All groups include women.

the firms (56 per cent. for men and 50 per cent. for women). Since women are usually supposed to have a stronger liking than men for work involving personal contacts, it was surprising to find that if anything[1] the men expressed this desire more frequently than the women. The dissatisfied in both the Ministries and the firms tended to want *either* more *or* less contacts; but even among the satisfied respondents one-third wanted more.

TABLE 8.30

Job-satisfaction group	N	Time spent in conversation with public				
		Almost all	Most of it	About half	Not very much	Practically none
		%	%	%	%	%
Civil Servants:						
Satisfied	258	3	3	25	52	17
In between	678	2	2	22	54	20
Dissatisfied	143	1	1	15	52	31
Firms' Staffs:						
Satisfied	271	5	9	37	29	20
In between	303	1	4	27	34	35
Dissatisfied	69	1	3	23	30	42

Very few of the respondents in the two firms and the Large Ministry seemed to have encountered real antagonism on the part of the outside world—if we may judge from the replies to Question 21. In the Small Ministry, however, a significantly larger percentage (7 per cent.) did report this. The nature of their work may have been responsible; certainly the Small Ministry had more dealings with the private individual, who is often more emotional than public bodies in his transactions with the civil service. But on the whole the civil servants did not differ from the firms' staffs to the extent which I should have expected.

As for Press criticism, the firms had naturally encountered less of it than the Ministries, so that a good three-quarters either did not answer Question 38 or said 'I wouldn't notice any.' Indeed, I wondered what the 4 or 5 per cent. of their staffs who had noticed 'frequent' Press criticism really meant by 'frequent'. The Ministries' replies were more interesting. Where the Press was concerned, it was the Large and not the Small Ministry which complained of unfair criticism: 49 per cent. replied either 'occasional and usually unfair' or 'frequent and usually unfair', compared with only 32 per cent. in the Small Ministry. Here again the explanation may lie in the nature of the Small Ministry's work.

[1] The difference, however, might well have been due to chance: what is certain is that the women's percentage did not exceed the men's.

Several civil servants (but none of the firms' respondents) felt strongly enough about the attitude of the public or the Press to mention it spontaneously:
As one of the chief disadvantages of the job (Question 48):

'General public opinion towards civil servants.' (a male S.E.O.)

'The periodical unfair criticism by the Press of the Civil Service in General.'
(a male E.O.)

'However unfair public criticism is a civil servant may never answer back.'
(a professional from the Small Ministry)

And as a final comment in Question 62:

'Popular denigration of the public service inhibits the satisfaction that would otherwise accrue from work which is generally varied, responsible and challenging. It has also the practical effect of discouraging recruits of the right quality.'
(a male S.E.O.)

'When my Ministry or the Civil Service as a whole is subject to unjustified criticism (usually by critics who are ignorant of the facts and the peculiar difficulties that face public employees) little attempt seems to be made to answer them.'
(a male C.O.)

All but one of these comments came from the Large Ministry.

Changes of Job

In the two Companies, a transfer from one post to another—unless it meant some sort of promotion to greater authority or pay—was rare. What is more, it was regarded with suspicion by the transferee, who seemed to feel that his position was in some way threatened by it: perhaps moves of this kind were looked upon as ways of disposing of employees who did not 'fit in'. There was no recognised practice of giving promising employees experience of different subdivisions of the office; and indeed this was a complaint that was voiced by one or two of the men in the middle and upper levels.

In contrast, one of the features of the civil service which outsiders find it hardest to understand is the frequency with which the civil servant is moved compulsorily from one desk to another. He is rarely moved to another Ministry, and then usually with his consent; but he is liable to be taken at short notice from work on which he has been engaged for several years and posted to another part of his Department where the work is different both in its subject-matter and in the technique which it requires. Sometimes this transfer merely moves him a few yards down a corridor; but in other cases he finds himself posted to another part of Britain. Even when promoting a man his Establishment Division usually try to arrange that his new post shall not be in the same subdivision of his Department.

Several justifications of this practice are usually offered. In Ministries of all sizes there is a constant incidence of vacancies from deaths, retirements and promotions. Some of these can be filled by new entrants to the service, but in the senior Executive and Administrative grades this is clearly impossible. To promote the man (or woman) immediately below the vacancy would ensure that the new occupant of the post knew something about part at least of its tasks; but might mean promoting someone who was both junior to and less efficient than others in the grade. Moreover, many people believe that he will find it harder to act as the superior officer of people with whom he has only recently been working as a colleague.

Many transfers, however, are not the result, direct or indirect, of a vacancy. There is a feeling in the service that it is undesirable for a man to specialise too long in any one kind of work. Not only may this make it more difficult for him to adapt himself to another kind of work when it becomes necessary to transfer him; but he may also become less efficient at his present task, through developing views, not to say prejudices, which may hinder changes of policy or method. A more positive argument is that he may learn ideas from one kind of work which he can put to good use in another. The chances that he may be unable to unlearn inappropriate ideas are presumably less, because his new colleagues and superiors can be relied upon to be critical.

It is not only 'the management' who advocate the practice of constant transfer. In many Ministries the staff themselves, through their associations, have sought this. At almost all levels except the very highest, there are jobs in all Departments that are regarded as more 'interesting' than others; and there are also posts that are regarded as giving their occupants a better chance than others of 'showing their good points': remember how the C.O.s at Newcastle sought transfers into the smaller Branches, where their tasks would be more individual, for this same reason. Many Establishment Officers have therefore agreed with their staff sides upon a time-limit—such as five years—for keeping officers in the Executive and Clerical grades in any one post, irrespective of the wishes of the officer himself. There is usually a reservation in favour of the elderly officer, nearing retirement, who would find it very hard to adapt himself to a change of duties.

But there are great disadvantages in the practice. Outsiders who have become used to dealing with one officer, and have begun to trust his ability to grasp their point of view and the technicalities of the subject, are understandably disconcerted when he is replaced by someone who has to confess quite frankly that he is learning all about it 'from scratch'. Even more important is the loss of ordinary individual efficiency that follows any transfers. The new occupant of the post may eventually contribute new approaches and new ideas to it, and may be, in the end, better at doing the job than his predecessor. But for months, perhaps years, his lack of knowledge of the previous history of his subjects will compel him to take longer over any problem than he would do if his experience had been continuous. No filing system, however efficient and complete, is as good as the human memory at throwing up the relevant and discarding the irrelevant. Moreover, it must be harder for the civil servant to 'identify himself' with his job when this involves such frequent changes of identity, or to take a pride in being an expert on any subject when the system seems designed to emphasise his laymanship.

What light did my surveys throw on this notorious problem? In Chapter 5 we saw how the *collective* efficiency of the Ledger Sections seemed to be higher among those whose C.O.s had been left longer together. It was unfortunately impossible to tell whether there was any association between the *individual* efficiency of the Ministries' respondents and the number of changes of job they had experienced.[1] We have already seen (in 8.2) that one of the time-factors with which the job-satisfaction of the men in the Ministries was associated was the length of time for which they had been left in their jobs. But since there seems to be no association between job-satisfaction and individual efficiency nothing can be inferred about the effect of frequent transfers upon the latter.

The most interesting feature of the replies to Question 30 was that the desire for a transfer seemed to be more frequent in the organisations where transfers were in fact more frequent. 55 per cent. of the firms' staffs wanted to stay where they were, although these respondents can have had very few changes of job: but in the Ministries, where 62 per cent. of respondents had had 3 or more changes of job, only 44 per cent. wanted to stay where they were. Since the Ministries' respondents were on average a decade older, and since a desire for change is supposed to be a symptom of youth,[2] the difference is very striking. It was also observable between the Ministries and firms themselves; those with the highest rate of change were also those with the most respondents who expressed a desire for a change. One member of the Executive class in the Large Ministry even placed 'the possibility of changing one's job fairly frequently within the organisation' at the head of her list of 'attractions of the job' (q.v.). In the Small Ministry,

---

[1] Since the more efficient presumably tended to have achieved more promotions, and therefore more 'changes of job' as defined in Question 7. In fact, the tabulation did show a tendency in this direction, with the reservation that the very inefficient (i.e. rated '4') showed a slight tendency to have more changes of job than one would expect. This is not surprising, since they were probably moved about either to get them out of jobs where they were doing harm or in the hope of finding some task at which they were efficient.

[2] A supposition which seemed so certain that it was hardly worth testing. Certainly the desire for a move was most frequent in the levels with higher percentages of staff in their teens and twenties, both in the Ministries and in the Companies.

on the other hand, where changes were less frequent, a respondent of the same grade and sex gave as the chief *disadvantage* 'continued liability to transfer from one type of work to another without any regard for the officer's preference, length of service, etc.'. It seems to be a case of *l'appétit vient en mangeant*; the more frequent the changes are in your career or the careers of your colleagues, the more you feel a need for a change.[1]

Another civil servant, again of the same sex and grade, drew attention to the effect of frequent changes upon the subordinates (and superiors) of the transferees:

'I'm awfully sick of doing all the donkey-work for an endless string of new people put in senior positions over me. In (less than 10) years the 3 posts above mine have been filled by (i) 5 men, (ii) 5 men, (iii) 4 men in succession—14 in all. I have also had 5 (juniors) in succession, 3 without previous experience of this kind of work: yet the work goes on. No promotion for me—I'm over 40.'

Attitudes to their Own Organisation (Qns. 33, 34, 35, 39, 44)

Page 6 of the questionnaire contained a number of questions about the respondents' Ministry or Company. Most of these dealt with topics which have been discussed in other sections; examples are discipline, inter-personal relations, and the men at the top. But one or two remain to be dealt with.

The most important of these is Question 44, which asks the respondent to sum up his impression of his own organisation by saying whether, 'all things considered', it is better or worse than other Ministries or Companies. This is a good example of a question which could be mistaken as an attempt to compare the Ministries or Companies themselves, but is really comparing nothing more than the attitudes of their respondents. As I have already said, there was remarkably little difference between the verdicts on this point of those who had and those who had not worked in some other office before entering their present one[2]; and this emphasises that we are dealing here not with objective comparisons but with differences between attitudes.

This was of course what the question was intended to do. I wanted to see whether there were any significant differences between the employees of the four organisations in what can loosely be called *esprit de corps*. The question was placed at the end of a number dealing with

---

[1] See J. C. Flugel's *Studies in Feeling and Desire* (1957) for other examples of this phenomenon.

[2] One of the Large Ministry's professionals, however, said at the end of the questionnaire, 'Having worked in two private firms and one Government Ministry my experience is that the Ministry is the better employer. There is far more attention to the welfare of the employee and staff are not at the "mercy" of a bad-tempered or spiteful employer. Sickness is treated in a really human manner and staff are looked on as personalities and not chattels.'

RESULTS OF THE QUESTIONNAIRE

many aspects of his organisation, so that respondents would have had their minds directed towards all these before answering this one.

As Table 8.31 shows, there were quite marked differences between the civil servants and the other office workers. The latter showed a strong tendency to choose the reply 'much better' (32% v. 7%), and a great reluctance to say that their organisation was in any degree worse (2 per cent.). The civil servants, on the other hand, included a substantial 11 per cent. who thought that their Ministry compared badly with others, and only 34 per cent. (compared with the firms' 70 per cent.) who regarded it as to any extent better. The firms did not differ significantly from each other, but the Small Ministry received more praise from its respondents than the Large.

The differences between the grades in the civil service were small. The administrators differed from all the other desk grades by showing a strong tendency to choose either 'slightly better' (38 per cent.) or 'slightly worse' (19 per cent.) instead of sitting on the fence of 'about the same' (only 35 per cent., compared with 55 per cent. for the service as a whole). In the firms, favourable comparisons became less frequent as the levels descended. With the exception of the small number of women in the firms' middle levels, who were very enthusiastic, women did *not* show more *esprit de corps* than men: if they are more loyal, as is sometimes said, it must be to small groups or to individuals.

There was a strong tendency for those who thought their Ministry better, to be satisfied with their jobs and a slight but significant tendency for them to come from the more efficient half of the respondents.

Table 8.31 also summarises the replies to a few minor questions about the organisations. On the adequacy of staffing, there was great similarity between all four organisations, except at one point: the Large Ministry was regarded as 'overstaffed' by an unusually large percentage of its respondents (35 per cent. compared with 23-28 per cent. for the other three organisations). This was reflected in some of the spontaneous comments at the end of the questionnaire. It may have been an impression created by the sheer size of the Large Ministry: for a much larger percentage of its respondents than of the Small Ministry's regarded it as 'well organised' (40% v. 28%) and 'up to date' (65% v. 35%). On both these aspects the firms' staffs were much less critical of their organisations than were the civil servants, and showed very few differences: more of the North Firm's staff thought it 'very up to date' (45% v. 26%), but otherwise the percentages were remarkably similar.

Respondents' spontaneous comments (Qn. 62) included both praise and disapproval of their organisations:

'I work in a . . . Ministry, which I believe to be less pedestrian and hamstrung by tradition and precedent than (others) . . .'
(an administrator in the Large Ministry)

'The Ministry's organisation is poor.'   (an E.O. from the Small Ministry)

TABLE 8.31

Their own Ministry or Company

Here are some things which are often said by people about the organisation in which they work. Please tick the phrase in each group which seems to you most applicable to your own Company or Ministry.

	N	Question 33:				Question 35:				Question 39:			Question 44: All things considered, in comparison with other Companies (or Ministries) this one seems to me—				
		Very up-to-date	Quite up-to-date	Slightly old-fashioned	Very old-fashioned	Well organ-ised	Hard to say	Badly organ-ised		Under-staffed	About right	Over-staffed	Much better	Slightly better	About the same	Slightly worse	Much worse
		%	%	%	%	%	%	%		%	%	%	%	%	%	%	%
Large Ministry	780	5	60	32	4	40	42	18		9	56	35	6.4	25.2	56.5	9.9	2.0
Small Ministry	310	1	34	57	8	28	50	22		10	63	27	7.7	33.3	51.3	7.0	0.7
Civil servants in both	1090	4	53	39	5	37	44	19		9	58	33	6.7	27.5	55.1	9.1	1.6
Both firms' staffs	650	36	59	5	—	60	30	10		10	65	26	31.6	33.1	28.2	1.8	0.3
North Firm	340	45	51	4	—	61	30	9		12	61	28	34.5	39.7	23.7	1.8	0.3
South Firm	310	26	68	6	—	59	30	11		8	69	23	28.2	35.4	33.3	1.8	0.3

'. . . . I have always enjoyed my work and consider I am fairly treated by the Ministry.' (an H.E.O. from the Small Ministry)

'In comparison with many other Companies of which I have had experience I think that this Company is by far the most modern and go-ahead, but is subject to internal politics which tend to distract day-to-day procedure.'
(a man in the North Firm)

'My Company is one of the most up to date in the industry. . . . It is inclined to become impersonal as it expands, but that too has its own advantages.'
(a woman in the North Firm)

'A very go-ahead company.' (a man in the South Firm)

'This Company is a very good one to work for.' (a woman in the South Firm)

'All things considered I think, I work for one of the best organisations in the country.' (a woman in the South Firm)

The unfortunate Personnel or Establishment Departments of all four organisations were the targets for allegations of inhumanity or lack of a consistent policy. They can console themselves with the reflection that the uniformity of this criticism suggests that it is inescapable; and there were also one or two appreciative comments, all concerning the way in which the respondent had been treated while ill.

8.4. SUMMARY

As this chapter has demonstrated, the questionnaire yielded a great deal of information, some of it confirming, some of it discrediting, common hypotheses about civil servants or private office staffs, and some of it suggesting new ideas. A summary in such circumstances is bound to be a mixture of omissions and over-simplifications, but I shall set down here the observations which are most likely to interest the general reader.

Men and Women

Women were unheard of in the Companies' upper levels, and were outnumbered by men at all other levels except the most junior ones in the Companies. Some of the Companies' women resented their lack of opportunities for promotion. In the Ministries, where there were a few women at all levels, and equal pay had practically been achieved,[1] there was no feeling of this kind.

Desk workers of either sex who had women as supervisors showed a certain dissatisfaction with their jobs, though only one or two expressed dislike of working for women. Since there was no evidence that women were less willing to trust their subordinates, this feeling is probably irrational: it may be connected with the importance of

[1] The process of increasing women's salaries so as to equal men's, which began in 1954, was completed in January 1961.

estimated status for the desk worker, for to work under a woman makes it more probable that the job will be regarded as comparatively unimportant.

In attitudes, women did not differ from men as much as I had expected. At the lower levels they showed a little less dissatisfaction with their jobs, but this difference was not observable among the Executives in the Ministries. They were somewhat less critical of the system of promotion, even in the Companies, and they showed much less tendency to regard themselves as underpaid; but since most of them were single, and most of the men married, this difference is not surprising. They were more critical of draughts, dirt and lavatories; but men were more critical of decoration and furniture, perhaps because these were status-symbols. In the Companies and the clerical grades of the Ministries, women showed more respect for the competence of the men at the top. They complained less about lack of responsibility, but just as much about lack of variety. On subjects such as discipline, their colleagues, loyalty to the organisation, whether they worked harder than their colleagues, and whether they would like more personal contact with outsiders, it was not possible to find any significant differences.

Ministries compared with Companies

The Ministries' desk workers were on average much older, with more women at the higher levels but fewer in the junior posts. Transfers from job to job were more frequent in the Ministries and more popular with their staffs. More of the civil servants did voluntary office work out of interest in their spare time; and they tended to live further from their office. Perhaps for these reasons, they were not so keen on taking an active part in office clubs and societies.

Their job-satisfaction was lower at most levels than that of the firms' staffs. The civil servants were also much more inclined to advise against following their own careers. But their estimates of their status were higher. 'Frustrating' was the favourite word with which both kinds of desk worker condemned their work, but the civil servants' second choice was 'thankless' and the firms' was 'tiring'. Both kinds of office worker ranked the interest of the work high among its attractions, but the civil servants put security first and pensions second. For the civil servants the attitude of the public to their work was one of its chief disadvantages, and they had encountered much more criticism from the Press, which many regarded as unfair, although about a third labelled it fair.

Although the promotion systems in the Ministries were much more systematic, and there was much less tendency to fill vacancies by appointing outsiders, their respondents were more critical of the fairness of the system: promotion boards were the target for a lot of spontaneous criticism. Comparison between levels with roughly equal salary scales showed that more of the civil servants claimed to be underpaid.

The civil servants were less inclined to label their organisations 'friendly', and more inclined to choose 'impersonal'; they were also more inclined to regard inter-level relations as not sufficiently democratic, although it was difficult to see what basis there was for these differences. In spite of the active Whitley machinery for consultation on matters affecting staff, they seemed to feel that they were less often consulted than the firms' employees, perhaps because of the very fact that in the firms, where there were no staff associations, any consultation had to be direct with individuals. The summing-up of the civil servants on their own Ministries was much less complimentary: they were more prone to describe them as old fashioned and badly organised, and less ready to claim that they were better than other organisations of the same kind.

The Large compared with the Small Ministry

Perhaps because of its very size, the Large Ministry was regarded by fully a third of its respondents as over-staffed, and they were on the whole more lukewarm about its merits in comparison with other Ministries. Its respondents, however, seemed particularly conscious of the unfairness of Press criticism, which in the Small Ministry was more often accepted as fair. A high percentage of its staff lived more than an hour's journey from their work, and participation in office clubs was very infrequent. Changes of job were much more usual, but no less welcome, than in the Small Ministry. Its promotion system was regarded as fair by more of its respondents, and more of them gave it credit for according due weight to ability and experience.

In the Small Ministry, where the Clerical Officers had to wait longer before they were considered for promotion, the system was subjected to more criticism, and there was a greater tendency to allege that 'being in the right place at the right time' was important. The Small Ministry's respondents were the most inclined to feel that they were not personally consulted about changes in the organisation or conditions of their work. A high percentage regarded discipline as too easy-going, or even as much too lax; time-keeping and talking at work seemed to be what most critics had in mind. The Small Ministry's staff were also the most dissatisfied with their physical working conditions, and especially with the dirt, the draughts, the lavatories, the furniture and decorations, and the long distances that separated members of the same sub-unit.

The Civil Service Grades

The typical[1] administrator was a man in his forties, as often as not promoted from the Executive or Clerical classes or from some other

[1] i.e., modal. It must be remembered, of course, that the recipients of my questionnaire did not include any above the rank of Assistant Secretary.

job inside or outside the service. Where his efficiency rating was recorded, it was usually above average, and he enjoyed his job more than most members of the other desk grades. For him, one of its chief attractions was its interest, and like his colleagues in the senior executive grades he was less inclined to regard it as below his capabilities. His estimate of its status was higher not only than that of the other civil service respondents, but also than that of the upper level men in the Companies. He was very critical of discipline, which he regarded as too easy-going, but like his senior executive colleagues he was very willing to trust his subordinates, and he was especially apt to regard his colleagues as likeable. He had a high opinion of 'the men at the top', whom he had the best chance of seeing at work. In comparing his Ministry with others, he was less inclined to sit on the fence than his juniors were, and more inclined to say that it was better or worse.

The typical Chief or Senior Executive Officer was in his fifties, with a long career in the service behind him, usually beginning in the Clerical Officer grade. His efficiency was high, but his enjoyment of his work was only moderate, and he was inclined to advise others against following his own career. He did not regard his job as below his capabilities, but he did feel that he was underpaid, perhaps in comparison with his administrative colleagues. He found his work less interesting than did the administrators, but more than his juniors. He was not anxious for more democratic relations between the grades. He had less complaints than any other civil servant about aspects of his work such as variety or responsibility, and was as willing as the administrator to trust his subordinates.

The typical Executive or Higher Executive Officer was in his thirties, although nearly a third of the women were in their forties. Half of them had begun their careers as C.O.s or C.A.s. Their efficiency ratings were more or less evenly divided between the better pair and the worse; but they showed more tendency than their seniors to regard their jobs as slightly below their capabilities. Their enjoyment of their jobs was neither very high nor very low, but a substantial percentage were inclined to advise against following their careers. They found their work less interesting than did their seniors, and estimated its status as middling. They were more critical of the promotion system, but *less* dissatisfied with their pay than their seniors; the female junior executives, like the female clerical staff in both the Ministries and the Companies, were more satisfied with their pay than any other group, and indeed contained a handful who said they were overpaid. Many men and women in the junior executive and clerical grades regarded inter-level relations as not democratic enough; but there were also substantial percentages in these groups who thought discipline too easy-going, although the clerical staff at any rate were more likely to be subject to it than to exercise it.

The C.O.s and C.A.s were distributed fairly evenly through the thirties, forties and fifties, but a substantial 12 per cent. of the men and 9 per cent. of the women were over sixty. Quite a number had begun their careers in other grades of the civil service, especially the manipulative grades of the Post Office. Their efficiency ratings tended to be 3 or 4, but fully 70 per cent. thought their jobs a little or more than a little below their capabilities. The men's job-satisfaction but not the women's was lower than expectation, but only about a third were inclined to advise against their own careers. They did not greatly value the status or interest of their jobs and they were particularly conscious of the lack of variety and responsibility. A high percentage regarded the promotion system as unfair; it was the clerical staff who had to wait longest before they could be considered for promotion. Unlike their counterparts in the Companies, they were not markedly more critical of the men at the top than their seniors were, but they were much less inclined to trust their subordinates (if any). In comparing their Ministry with others they tended to sit on the fence and to say 'about the same'. The male clerical staff (who had recently been conceded a rise in pay) were not more dissatisfied with their pay than the administrators, and less so than the senior Executives.

There is little point in generalising about the professional civil servants who responded. They represented only three of the many professions in the service, and they were in any case included only to serve as one kind of control with which to compare the desk workers (the other controls were of course the Companies' desk workers). But one or two things are perhaps worth mentioning. In the first place, almost all of them were over forty. In the second place, the job-satisfaction of the Small Ministry's professionals, whose work was to some extent creative, was remarkably high; but among the Large Ministry's professionals, whose work was not very different from that of the Executive Class in some other Ministries, the pattern of job-satisfaction was very like that of the senior Executives. The Small Ministry's professionals were very much inclined to advise in favour of following their own careers; their estimates of their status were much higher than those of any other group, and four out of five of them placed the interest of their work first or second on their list of attractions of the job. This did not prevent them, however, from being very dissatisfied with their pay and with the promotion system, although the Large Ministry's professionals, who thought they should have a chance of promotion into the Administrative or senior Executive grades, were even more critical of the system. Both Ministries' professionals showed very little confidence in the ability of the men at the top, by which they almost certainly meant the administrators; but the Small Ministry's professionals showed a marked tendency to compare their own Ministry favourably with others.

Efficiency

Individual efficiency, so far as it could be measured among the civil servants by their superiors' ratings, showed remarkably few associations with other factors. It had no connection with the officer's own opinion of his capabilities, although it was associated with age: it seemed to reach a peak in the thirties, and thereafter to decline. Apart from a tendency for the most and the least efficient to like or dislike their jobs more strongly than the rest, there was no association between it and enjoyment of one's work. There were some other odd similarities between the attitudes of the most and the least efficient: both, for example, complained more about lack of variety in their work. We have already seen in Chapter 6 that the more efficient took less certified and uncertified sick leave; but it is not easy to be sure which is cause and which is effect, if indeed the relationship is as simple as that. It was encouraging to find that the more efficient attached more value to the interest of their work, but discouraging to see that if anything more of the less efficient believed in its usefulness. A heartening difference was the higher percentage of the more efficient who believed that their own Ministry was better than others; rather less heartening was their tendency to advise against following their own careers in the service. All this creates the impression of the more successful desk worker in the service as no more idealistic than his brethren, but if anything a little more hard-headed, realistic and disillusioned.

Job-satisfaction

We saw in Chapter 6 that lack of enjoyment of one's job is related to a higher rate of uncertified sick leave, although not to an extent that suggested conscious malingering. In this chapter we have seen that, in various circumstances, it can be associated with age, time spent in the job, and even time spent in the Ministry. The association with age suggests that job-satisfaction is to some extent determined by 'temperament'.

The striking association, however, between it and level in the hierarchy could not be explained in this way. Two other factors strongly linked both to level and job-satisfaction were 'estimated status' and 'interest of the work'; and it seemed likely that these factors really did influence it, rather than the converse. Promotion, however, does not necessarily lead to more interesting work, and we need to know more about the quality called 'interest'. While it is no doubt associated to some extent with 'variety', 'responsibility' and personal contact with people outside the office, there are indications that it may not depend so much as we imagine on the nature of the task, but may be affected by time-factors and perhaps other influences.

Although job-satisfaction was associated with attitudes to many aspects of the work, and probably coloured respondents' replies on these subjects, it had surprisingly little relationship to attitudes towards pay, except in the case of the few dissatisfied ones who said that they were 'overpaid'.

Uniformities

So much for the differences: in some cases the absence of any was quite as interesting. The job-satisfaction of the civil servants, their consciousness of lack of variety and responsibility in their work, their respect for the ability of the men at the top, the extent to which they were willing to trust subordinates, their feeling that the attitude of the public to their work was one of its chief drawbacks, and at the same time their desire for more contacts with the public, were very much the same in the two Ministries, although the grades diverged to some extent. But even the grades were remarkably similar in some ways: about one in three male administrators, junior Executives and clerical staff felt underpaid, although their pay was very different; and practically all the grades agreed on the main attractions of their jobs.

Indeed there were several respects in which even the Ministries and the Companies' staffs were very similar. One in three of them all felt that they were more hard-worked than their colleagues. One in three complained about the canteens and the ventilation; food and air are close to everyone's heart. More than one in three regarded office discipline as too easy-going, whether they were at the administering or the receiving end.

One of the lessons to be learnt from these uniformities is the fallacy of diagnosing 'low morale' in an organisation without comparing its symptoms with those of other organisations. Quite apart from the doubtful utility of the whole concept of 'morale', comparison of this kind might well show that what seemed to be pathological symptoms were in fact equally frequent in all offices of the same kind, and even—as we have seen here—in offices of another kind.

This is not to deny that my questionnaire did reveal some symptoms among the civil servants—or, in other cases, the firms' staffs—which should attract concern; and I shall discuss these in my final chapter. The point is that it is only by comparisons and the study of differences that we can distinguish the apparently from the genuinely pathological.

9
SOME REFLECTIONS

The investigations I have been describing in the previous chapters provided a good deal of information about the desk worker in the British Civil Service, in a form which was as free as I could manage from what I have called 'impressionism'.[1] This information did not, of course, answer all my queries; indeed, we have seen that it sometimes raised new ones. Perhaps the most interesting examples of the unanswered questions were:

(i) *What makes work interesting?* In the first place, is 'interest' a simple or—like 'morale'—a composite notion; and, if the latter, is it a useful or misleading one? If useful, is it measurable? And, if measurable, is it associated with any other measurable factors, such as variety, time in post, aptitude for the nature of the task, time spent in contact with other human beings, or the number of other workers known to be doing similar tasks?

(ii) *Why do young male clerical officers resign in such large numbers?* Is this a temporary phenomenon, confined to ex-National Servicemen? Is it characteristic of all young male office workers? Is it related to promotion prospects, or to the nature of the tasks allotted to them? Is it eliminating the better or the worse recruits?

(iii) *Why does the sick rate for the sick increase with the number of workers in the office building?* Is control less strict in the larger units? Or does the worker feel less indispensable?

(iv) *What sort of training (if any) makes office workers better at managing subordinates?* How can it be administered to as large a percentage of the desk classes as possible? Can 'leadership' be instilled into very senior civil servants, or is it an incommunicable gift? Is individual efficiency related to leadership or the ability to manage subordinates?

These are all questions with an obvious relevance to the day-to-day management of any large office organisation. The answers to them may seem obvious, but they are not. They are the sort of questions which nobody can answer simply by drawing on his own experience, or even on the experience of Whitley Councils or working parties, however

[1] See Chapter 1.

SOME REFLECTIONS

unanimous. What seems to be required is the systematic collection and study of facts about a very large number of desk workers.

While the civil service itself has not so far taken any initiative in this direction—possibly for the reasons I have suggested in Chapter 1—I must not give the impression that it is wholly opposed to research of this kind. It is worth pointing out that all the facts in this book—except for the very few which had already been published—were either provided by the Treasury and other Departments or obtained with the co-operation of Departments, staff associations and individual civil servants; and that these same Departments then gave me permission to publish them. This is an indication of the extent to which the service is prepared to submit to investigations of this kind and face the results.

Nor are the results wholly unfavourable. In a survey of this kind one's attention is inevitably attracted to the imperfections rather than to the excellences; the eye comes to rest on the blemishes. It is therefore worth looking for a moment at the ways in which the service seems to have been successful in tackling the problems of morale.

One factor which can seriously reduce individual efficiency at work is domestic difficulties; and a very effective means of dealing with this has been evolved in the form of the Departmental Welfare Officer.[1] It is of course impossible in the nature of things to find out what percentage of remediable difficulties is brought to the Welfare Officer; but Table 2.01 showed that a substantial fraction not only of the lower desk grades but also of senior executives and administrators made use of him, and that a very satisfactory percentage of these regarded the result as helpful. There seemed to be only two dangers. One was that the Welfare Officer's duties in connection with visits to the sick might be carried out in such a way that he came to be regarded—however unjustly—as a spy of the Establishment Division. The other was that the method of appointing Welfare Officers, usually from the General Executive Class in the same Ministry, might deprive the service of the benefit of the trained professional social worker, and might also make staff less likely to bring their private troubles to him because he was merely 'one of themselves'. But on the whole the Departmental Welfare Officer seemed to me to be a very effective instrument for keeping to a minimum the effects of domestic troubles upon efficiency at work.

We have seen, too, that although job-satisfaction in the desk grades of the Large and Small Ministries was not as high as it seemed to be among the North and South Firms' respondents, the desk grades of the civil service did not, on the whole, exhibit the known symptoms of very low job-satisfaction. Labour turnover in general was small: it was only among young male Clerical Officers that it had reached a strikingly high level, and for all we know this may be a general characteristic of young male office workers at the lower levels. Absenteeism was rare and strikes

[1] See Chapter 2.1.

unheard-of; but since both these symptoms were counter to the discipline and traditional conduct of the consciously middle-class office worker, they were not reliable indices, and it seemed necessary to look instead at sick leave, particularly in its uncertified form, which is the salaried worker's opportunity for absenteeism.[1]

Although the generosity of the civil service's sick leave conditions is such that the employee who dislikes his work, or work in general, would have little difficulty in staying away for at least seven days in a twelve-month, and in prolonging certified absences for minor disorders such as colds and influenza, the evidence was against any widespread abuse of this kind. It seemed likely that the sick leave of married women was at least partly determined by family crises as well as by their own state of health; and a sample of otherwise unsatisfactory Post Office employees at the lower levels had shown suspiciously high sickness rates. But with these exceptions genuine, conscious abuse of the system was not frequent enough to show up in the statistics for any separate staff group in the desk grades, either in the eight-year sample from all Departments or in the one-year records for all the respondents from the Large and Small Ministries. The worst that could be said was that there was a tendency for those with low job-satisfaction to take a little more uncertified sick leave; and this is by no means the same thing as conscious malingering.[1]

At Benton, where sixteen hundred Clerical Officers in teams of equal size performed the same tasks week after week, month after month, for anything up to ten or eleven years, what was most interesting was the extent to which they had adjusted themselves to this situation. It is true that most of those who found it impossible to do so had no doubt obtained a transfer or, in extreme cases, resigned. But resignations were infrequent—more infrequent than among London Clerical Officers—and transfers were hard to get: so that the great majority must be assumed to have adjusted themselves to the work. It is also true that the members of the Executive Class who ran Benton were very conscious of the problems of man-management which it presented, and must receive a good deal of credit for their efforts to overcome them. Nevertheless, the extent to which the C.O.s accepted the prospect of long periods of repetitive paper-work was remarkable.[2]

Even my questionnaire to the Large and Small Ministries, which like all such documents tended to bring out the worst in people, did not reveal any full-sized skeletons. Indeed, the spontaneous comments by respondents, although containing as usual more criticism than compliment, still included a great deal of praise for many features of the service. These included the generosity of the sick-leave scheme, the fairness of the promotion system, the absence of rivalry and jealousy, the feeling that one was serving the community, and occasionally the

[1] Chapter 6.   [2] Chapter 5.

interest of the work. Those who are determined to find fault with the service may argue that not all of these are entirely healthy symptoms; that a sick-leave scheme which is so generous as to arouse enthusiasm is too generous, and that too little rivalry means a lack of drive. But many of the spontaneous compliments quoted in Chapter 8 could not be interpreted in this way.

Several civil servants said that their Ministries were free from the favouritism and jealousy that was to be found in private companies. Some of these respondents must have been relying on hearsay, but others had first-hand experience; and there were one or two comments from the two companies which supported this point of view. As for women, there is no doubt that the civil service offers them the nearest thing to complete equality with men that they are likely to find in any kind of office work in this country—or in most others. Complete equality of pay has now been achieved. Promotion prospects have long been completely equal in theory, and almost so in practice; in the firms, nobody even pretended that there was any such principle. As we saw, there was a tendency among office workers of both sexes to dislike working under women, but no evidence that women were in fact less willing to delegate. Moreover, the scarcity of important differences between the attitudes of men and women in the civil service suggests that where women are treated as the equivalent of men they are less apt to think differently than is commonly supposed.

Comparison with the firms' respondents showed that, while there were important differences in attitudes, many responses from the civil servants that would otherwise have seemed to be evidence of gravely diseased morale were in fact very much the same as the responses of the other office workers. Examples were their complaints of too little variety or responsibility; the feeling of many that they were more hard worked than their colleagues; or their views on the capabilities of men at the top: but there were many other similarities. If they were symptoms of anything, it was of being office workers, or even of being human.

Even where there were differences between the civil servants and the private firms' staffs—for example, in the leniency towards the inefficient which they attributed to their organisation—they were differences of degree and not of kind; the belief that the inefficient were allowed 'to get away with it' was not confined to the two Ministries, although it was less common in the two Companies.

I am not of course arguing that the prevalence of symptoms, or the fact that they are to be found outside as well as inside the civil service, is a reason for accepting them as signs of health, any more than I would argue that bronchitis should be accepted in the inhabitants of industrial towns simply because it is endemic there. What seems to follow, however, is that in speculating about the causes of such symptoms we must look at the common background as well as the individual settings of our civil servants. It would be superficial to suggest that the percentage of civil servants or Company employees who thought that discipline was too easy-going consisted entirely of those who worked in sub-units where it actually was more lax. Of course, this is part of the answer; one of the Ministries and one of the Companies yielded particularly high percentages of such criticisms. But even in the other two organisations not less than one-third of the respondents felt the same; and, as I have already pointed out, a substantial number came from grades which are at the 'receiving end' of discipline, and would have had their freedom curtailed by any tightening up. We must look for causes not only in the situation of individual civil servants but also in the situation of the British civil servant in general.[1] This is, of course, the point at which we are no longer observing facts, or even interpreting them, but merely speculating. There are, however, a few things about civil servants—and even about people in general—which we can allow ourselves to know without insisting on rigorous observations; and if these are to be linked to what we have observed a little latitude is needed.

The situation of the desk workers in our civil service is illustrated in a simple, clear and not too extreme way by the predicament of the clerical staff in Records Branch at Benton. The society to which they belong has determined that certain services shall be performed for it, among which are the payment of allowances to its members who have paid contributions and are now unable to earn through illness, childbearing or unemployment. Since one condition of payment is past contributions, records of these have to be kept and used to check claims. The necessary operations are repetitive, and while they call for logic and the ability to select and apply complex rules, these are skills which are possessed by machines as well as by human beings.[2] But for technical reasons[3] the task is beyond the capacity of present-day machines, and must therefore be done by men and women. Because the job is a secure one, with reasonable pay and working conditions and a generous pension at the end of it, it is possible to recruit and retain enough of them to perform the task at a level of efficiency which is

[1] To some extent it may also be the situation of the bureaucrat in most modern democracies; but I distrust international generalisations even more than those which I am allowing myself to make about the desk classes in the British Civil Service.

[2] It may be argued that all office work that is not creative can be reduced to these two skills, and could therefore in theory be performed by a machine. This would be so if the rules governing the office's decisions and other procedures could be expressed in the form of a finite set of instructions. This is more or less the case in Records Branch, where the rules have in fact been codified on paper, and the same is true of much clerical work inside and outside the civil service. But at some level in the hierarchy in most organisations it ceases to be possible to envisage, far less to devise, a finite collection of instructions covering all possible situations; and it is at this point that human beings are needed not only in practice but in theory. The trouble is that so many of them behave as if the finite set of rules is still sufficient.

[3] See page 70.

apparently acceptable to the society that required it to be performed. But however satisfactory the material conditions of their work, the operators find the work itself too machine-like to be satisfying.

They cannot modify the rules so as to alter the conditions of eligibility to accord with their own sympathies, for this would mean making a payment to a mother-to-be in Birkenhead which was being denied by the man at the next desk to a woman in identical circumstances in Margate, and sooner or later chance or the Sunday press would bring this to light. Even their procedures for carrying out the task in accordance with the rules cannot be varied to suit their own temperaments, for this would probably disorganise the team. The only human beings with which they come into official contact are engaged on tasks of the same kind, most of them of exactly the same kind; their only communication with the men and women who are affected by their work is by means of a contribution card or some other stereotyped form. After a few months or at most a year or so of this they are as proficient at their tasks as their physical and mental constitution allows. Some are capable of work at a higher level, but cannot be given it without promotion, for which they cannot be considered until their turn comes. They cannot console themselves with the reflection that comfortless though the task itself may be they have the esteem and gratitude of the public whom they serve. This consolation is reserved for the followers of more spectacular careers, such as surgeons, politicians or members of fire brigades. To society the civil servant is not the man who is conscientiously performing the rather dull job which it created, but the man who refuses concessions to its less fortunate members, and occasionally has the effrontery to demand higher pay for doing so. Both at Benton and in the two Ministries the civil servants were impressed with the 'thanklessness' of their job, and the public's unfortunate attitude towards it.

The civil servant is popularly supposed to be insensitive to criticism from outside. There is no doubt that both the conditions under which his work is done and the way in which he is trained to think tend to insulate him from the reactions of the man in the street. Few of those whom we have been considering come into direct contact with the people affected by their decisions; this is especially true of headquarters offices whose dealings with the individual are usually carried on by local offices or by professional inspectors of one kind or another. In any case, one of the first lessons with which the desk classes are inculcated is that they must think of the effect of their decisions upon the situation as a whole, and not of the dismay or joy that they will bring to the individual. If they lost any sleep over the individuals whom they were compelled to frustrate, they would be condemned to eternal insomnia. The civil servant must therefore develop a detachment from the emotional pressure that people and organisations bring to bear on him, while making it plain that he is aware of the strength of their arguments and feelings. It is easier to achieve the former than both of these feats, and since it is the former that is essential he will often acquire an unsympathetic *persona*, both on paper and in face-to-face transactions.

There are many civil servants who manage, in spite of disparagement by the Press and the public, to cling to their own belief that what they are doing is valuable and interesting. But it is the exceptional man or woman who is quite uninfluenced by the considerations I have been describing, and the service is too numerous to be composed of the exceptional. It would not be surprising if the average civil servant were influenced by the doubts cast upon the necessity for what he is doing, or if his pride in the service or in his own Department were shaken by the popular estimate of their efficiency. In a money-conscious, status-seeking society it is natural that he should think of this month's pay, next year's promotion and the eventual pension; and if circumstances make it hard for him to be motivated by more exalted considerations he is quite likely to become obsessed by these tangible ones. We saw how uniform were the percentages at each level who regarded themselves as underpaid; how security and pension seemed to most the chief attractions of their jobs; and how strongly the lower grades felt about their prospects and methods of promotion. Promotion meant, of course, higher pay, but it also meant higher status, and the society in which the civil servant works—and lives outside his work—is status-seeking as well as money-conscious.

Like all desk workers, your non-industrial, non-professional civil servant belongs to the middle class.[1] Some have chosen this career because of their middle-class origins, some because they have seen it as an escape from the working class. The difference is not entirely one of income-level, for the skilled manual worker usually earns more than the clerical officer. So far as material things are concerned, it is a distinction between ways of spending one's pay-packet, between styles of dress and, most characteristic of all, between choices of residential area. If the distance at which one lives from one's work in Central London is an index of one's 'middle-classness', the civil servants in the two Ministries were even more middle-class than the desk workers in the Companies. But the difference between them and the manual worker—speaking still from the point of view of the external observer—is also a difference between codes of behaviour. Absenteeism and strikes are practically unheard of among civil servants and other desk workers; and even absenteeism disguised as sick leave seems to be rare.

How is the difference seen by the civil servants themselves? Certainly most of them would point to the security of their jobs, and to the prospect of a pension for themselves or their widows at the end of it. We have seen how high these aspects ranked in their estimation—much

[1] See David Lockwood's *The Black-coated Worker* (1958).

higher than in the estimation of the Companies' staff.[1] But another aspect of their job that seemed to be important to them was its status, which was closely linked with their enjoyment of their work, and which many of them felt to be undervalued by their friends outside the service. The fact that they refused to place this item high in the list of attractions of the job probably confirms that they felt they had not achieved the status they wanted, and not that they did not value it. This desire for status distinguishes the middle (and the upper) classes from the working class, and is not confined to office workers. The young girl in the clerical grade who said she valued 'power' is no more status-conscious than the politician-don who called his autobiography *Power and Influence*.

It is probably the office worker, however, who has been most ridiculed for this desire. He is laughed at for wearing bowler hats and pin-striped trousers—so much so that he now leaves the former to the Brigade of Guards and the latter to stockbrokers; or for aspiring to a carpet and a secretary.[2] The reaction of a status-minded society to the office worker's special form of status-seeking has been so sharp that he has become very self-conscious about it. There are fashions in the kind of satisfactions, physical or spiritual, that can be openly pursued, and at the moment the pursuit of status has to be disguised as carefully as the hunt for more sensual gratifications.

In the civil servant's case his need for recognition of his status is in conflict not only with his self-consciousness about it, but also with many of the restrictions under which he works. His 'power and influence' may be considerable, but their more spectacular manifestations are announced by Ministers, and such actions as he takes on his own are anonymous. If he guides a Committee to a coherent conclusion and writes their report for them, he is thanked on the last page, but it is known by the name of his Chairman. If he makes a public speech at a dinner or a conference, he must not say anything new, or if he does he must attribute it to his Minister. If in spite of this he achieves some favourable publicity, he is regarded by his colleagues with the same mixture of distrust and envy as a co-respondent in a divorce case.

---

[1] The latter's pension scheme, of course, was not so generous, and the security of their jobs may well have been less at the higher levels, if the figures quoted in Chapter 3 for dismissals in another large industrial concern are typical.

[2] Everyone knows nowadays that carpets, large desks and personal secretaries are status-symbols. To be exact, they are positive status-symbols. My own experience drew my attention to the existence of negative status-symbols when I began to use a portable typewriter for minutes and drafts that did not require a professional typist. I found it difficult to understand the rather embarrassed amusement of my colleagues, until I realised that the typewriter was a symbol of a lower level in the hierarchy. I have no doubt that the same is true of most highly organised and stratified offices; but it is not true, for example, of universities, where few dons nowadays would be comfortable without their Remingtons or Underwoods.

The rule of anonymity is usually justified on the grounds of Ministerial responsibility; the politician must take both the credit for success and the blame for failure. At the level of important decisions this is unexceptionable, even when a Minister who has just assumed office receives the credit for years of planning or research. But what was a Parliamentary convention has led to a public misconception. For example, Ministers are sometimes credited with their Department's successes while their civil servants are blamed for the mistakes. Some of these mistakes are undoubtedly the fault of unimaginative or overworked officers; but others are the inevitable result of a structure and system for which the civil servants themselves are not to blame. A good example is the popular impression that the time taken by Ministries over major and minor transactions is always due to the procrastination of bureaucrats. Most delays are caused by consultation, and 'Government by consultation' means consulting not only other Divisions and Departments, but often also the representatives of the very people who attribute the resulting delay to the idleness of civil servants. Occasionally (it must be said) the delays or ambiguities of the bureaucrats are in fact due to the hesitation or vagueness of the Minister, however decisive and clear-minded his public utterances may be.

Even when there has been no miscarriage and no delay, the mere fact that most Departments function as a control upon the activities of individuals and organisations means that their response to most requests or proposals has to be negative. However reasonable or inured the recipient may be, every negative reply must slightly worsen his opinion of the Department. There have been Ministers who were so conscious of this that they did not want letters to begin with such phrases as 'I am directed by the Minister . . .' Most recipients, however, regard these words as a mere fiction behind which the bureaucrat shelters himself, and feel that if their requests had really reached the Minister himself they would have been more sympathetically received —an impression which is encouraged by the fact that by writing to their M.P. they can get a reply signed by the Minister himself. Since these replies must convince not only the civil servant who drafts them but also the Minister who signs them, and must pass through the hands of many senior officers, they are prepared with more care than the letter which merely passes between the official and the citizen. This is understandable, if not pardonable: but the result is the impression that the Minister is human, the bureaucrats not.

These conflicts are probably more rather than less acute among the junior grades of the service. Their anonymity is more nearly absolute; in some Divisions no correspondence can be signed by officers below the rank of Executive. The C.O.s in Records Branch at Benton, who saw little of their superiors and nothing of their Minister or the public, suffered noticeably from a feeling that their work was not valued. Even where the job includes interviewing members of the public the junior officers' freedom to adjust the operations of the system is closely circumscribed. One out of three in the two Ministries regarded the job as *slightly* below their capabilities and another one out of three regarded it as *well* below them. But even here there was a conflict, for many of the junior staff who felt this were regarded as rather below standard by the superior officers who report on them. This may be a symptom of an ageing corps: it is the elderly who tend to detect a decline in the qualities of the younger generations. However that may be, the lower the grade of the officer, the less willing his superior officer was to delegate responsibility to him, but the more likely he himself was to feel that he had too little responsibility.

The service lays great emphasis upon the possibility of promotion— much more than do private firms. Table 8.03 showed that this is no empty promise. But the very permeability of the ranks of the service stimulates ambition and impatience. The young C.O. who is both ambitious and educationally bright has a good chance of promotion to Executive Officer through the competitive examination; but otherwise he must wait twelve years or more to be considered for normal promotion—longer than any other desk officer.

This means that the conflict between his own and his superior officer's estimate of what he can be trusted with is of great importance; indeed it is probably the central problem of the clerical class. The question is not who is in the right, but whether the gap between the two sides can be reduced. In theory, more trusting superiors and more trustworthy subordinates could be secured both by selection and by training: in practice, even if techniques of selection were perfect, there is not enough scope for choice to be effective. This leaves training, which for this purpose can take three forms. There are the two methods of teaching the job itself. Formal training of subordinates away from their day-to-day jobs is becoming more common in the service: the C.O.s began their careers in the Records Branch at Benton with several weeks of pure instruction. Training at the desk involves both subordinates and superiors, and if it is properly done increases not only the efficiency of the trainee but also his superior's confidence in him. It is, however, harder to do properly, and demands time, patience and intelligence from the superior.

The third instrument is training in delegation. Two factors make the civil servant a bad exponent of this skill. One is the theory of Ministerial responsibility, which means that he must constantly ask himself whether any conceivable mishandling of a problem could embarrass his Minister. He will probably follow the principle 'If in doubt, do it yourself'. Secondly, the traditional rule of the service is that the civil servant must answer to his Minister or to his superiors for anything that is done by those under his authority, unless it was done in defiance or neglect of his injunctions: in consequence, he has every reason to circumscribe his subordinate's actions by precise instructions, and to leave as little as possible to chance or errors of judgment.

The result in some Ministries is a very close adherence to the hierarchical system in handling work. Let us suppose, for example, that applications from the public for some kind of facility are normally dealt with by a section run by a Higher Executive Officer, which is part of a Branch under a Principal, which in turn is part of a Division under an Assistant Secretary: the Division belongs to a group of which an Under-Secretary has charge.[1] The Under-Secretary may express a desire for information about the way in which these applications are handled; and the man who really knows may be the Higher Executive Officer. In some Ministries the latter's answer, whether written or oral, would be filtered to the Under-Secretary through the Principal and Assistant Secretary, each of whom would feel obliged to master the details lest he be unable to answer his superior's questions and so be regarded as not having a thorough grasp of his job. There are Ministries, however, where this strict adherence to the chain of responsibility is not considered necessary unless each link in the chain is actually able to contribute information or advice; and the Higher Executive Officer's answer would be given directly to the Under-Secretary; the intervening officers would be told that this was happening and would be able to join in any discussion if they wanted to. 'Leap-frogging' of this kind has several advantages. From the point of view of organisation, it minimises the duplication of work—and the delay—which takes place when each officer in the hierarchy has to master a topic before the papers can be passed up to his superior. To the subordinate who is allowed to make direct contact with the officer who is likely to take the final decision it means not only that he has a better chance of understanding the reasons for the decision, but also an enhanced feeling of the value of his work.

Such departures from strictly hierarchical procedure are of course initiated in the interests of efficiency—usually at times when the organisation is pressed hard for time—and not with an eye to the estimated status of junior officers. Since the Baratarian experiment recorded by W. S. Gilbert,[2] no one has suggested that promotion should be used solely in order to increase job-satisfaction. The civil service, however, leans backwards in its determination to avoid this mistake. The titles which it applies to its desk grades are notoriously misleading. There is a tale of a Company director who wanted to speak on the telephone to the official responsible for his current grievance; on being offered the Under-Secretary he exclaimed ' I don't deal with Under-Secretaries—give me the Higher Executive Officer.' It is true that the newer the grade the less degrading its title; Directors and Controllers are now becoming

[1] See p. 13.
[2] In 'The Gondoliers, or The King of Barataria', 1889, Act II.

common in the newer Ministries. Another minor concession to Baratarianism is the use of the word 'officer': Anthony Trollope's 'Three Clerks' would nowadays be 'Three Clerical Officers'. But this does not rid the grade of the menial associations which 'clerking' has somehow acquired.

Civil servants themselves are of course seldom misled by their own titles, and in any case are much less rank-conscious in their dealings with each other than, for example, soldiers or sailors are. The civil service, however, does resemble the armed services in grouping its desk workers into tiers—the Administrative, Executive and Clerical Classes; and this in itself may help to account for the feeling among so many Executive and Clerical Officers that relations between the different levels are not democratic enough.[1] The practical aspects of the distinctions are that they provide direct entry to the desk classes at three different educational levels; that promotion from one to another involves either another examination or a much more formidable selection procedure than promotion within a class; and that the organisation of Departments is based on the assumption that certain duties can be performed only by members of one or other of the three classes. This last principle means that there is considerable overlapping in salary scales and levels of responsibility between the lower Administrative and the upper Executive grades. Branches whose work is regarded as involving certain operations —such as 'policy-making'—are run by Principals, while others, which may be numerically stronger, have Senior Executive Officers as heads; and there are Chief Executive, Senior Chief Executive and Principal Chief Executive Officers in charge of subdivisions—such as Records Branch at Benton—which are larger in size of staff and volume of work than those of many Assistant Secretaries or Under-Secretaries.

As we have seen, class-to-class promotions are so frequent that a large fraction of the Administrative and Executive Classes began their careers in junior classes; and the effect of this upon inter-class relations is of course good. It is in the area of overlap that the distinction is beginning to be questioned. The theoretical justification for it is that by labelling a man an administrator you make it possible for someone without personal knowledge of his capabilities to know that he can safely be placed in a post concerned with legislation or other forms of policy-making. The practical limitations to this argument are that at this level few civil servants are assigned to posts by people without knowledge of what they as individuals can do; and that to be a member of the Administrative Class is no guarantee of competence at *all* the tasks to which members of it are liable to be assigned. Indeed, there are

---

[1] See Table 8.24. This is a difficult topic on which to generalise with confidence, because of the very self-consciousness about status which I have mentioned. This self-consciousness is particularly acute when 'class' is involved, and it is an unhappy coincidence that this is the word used for each of the three main tiers of the service.

advocates of amalgamation of the two—or even of the three—classes who argue that this would allow more and not less freedom to select the right man for the post. A three-level entry system could still be operated; but the ageing Principal who had lost the ability to cope with new ideas could be transferred to a Branch where his capacity for handling staff and organising work could be used, while the young Senior Executive could be tried out on problems of policy-making, without the formalities involved in downgrading and class-to-class promotion. As might be expected, those in favour of fusing the Administrative and Executive Classes belong at the moment to the latter[1]; but it will be interesting to see whether they gain any ground.

A far more serious problem, however, is the relationship between the administrative and executive officers on the one hand and the professional civil servants on the other. We saw one symptom of this in the attitude of the professionals in the two Ministries towards 'the men at the top'. These professionals were of two very different sorts, and my own experience of working in three Departments and dealing with half a dozen others has confirmed that this phenomenon is to be found wherever the two kinds of civil servant have to work closely together. The professionals regard the desk worker as timid or fumbling because he does not put their advice into effect forthwith, preferring to submit it to advisory committees and other forms of consultation. The desk worker retorts that the professionals are incapable of visualising the broader entailments of their advice, and of distinguishing what is politically practicable from what is not. This failure to understand and accept each other's rôles and codes of behaviour is most acute when the professional group is a recent innovation in the Department, or when the individual civil servant is new to his rôle: as I have pointed out, most professionals enter the service after some sort of career outside it. Desk workers, on the other hand, are moved from post to post so often that many do not have time to settle down in harness with their professional 'opposite numbers'; and the permanence of the professional emphasises their own impermanence; it is their opinion and not his which is sought.

Another aspect of estimated status of which civil servants are becoming increasingly conscious is the standing of the civil service as a whole in the eyes of the general public. It is a cliché of leader-writers that we have 'a civil service which is second to none . . .'; but this lip-service is usually the prelude to a sermon on some fresh bureaucratic iniquity. The centenary of the Northcote-Trevelyan reports, as a result of an ironic act of Nemesis, was celebrated by the scandal of Crichel Down. In the popular conception—or 'brand-image', as advertising agencies call it—the typical civil servant is a tea-drinking,

[1] I must not give the impression, however, that this is a declared aim of the Society of Civil Servants.

file-passing incompetent, with more respect for precedent than for human problems. He wears pin-striped trousers and a black jacket, and is pedantic and inhuman in ordinary intercourse; indeed he prefers to deal with the rest of humanity by letter, or at best by telephone. His short-term thoughts are on the clock and his expenses sheet, while his long-term concerns are his pension and his annual leave (supplemented of course by his seven days of uncertified sick leave).

Little is done to correct this picture. Part of the reason is no doubt that the public relations officers of the separate Ministries look upon their subject-matter as being the functions which their Ministries perform. They would argue, I think, that if the public conception of the civil servant is anyone's baby, it lies on the doorstep of the Treasury or the Civil Service Commission; and so perhaps it does.

The brand-image of the bureaucrat, however, is to a large extent the result of innumerable public criticisms of individual Ministries. The deliberately adopted policies of these Ministries are of course for Ministers to defend, mainly in speeches within or without the walls of Parliament. But many public attacks on Departments are concerned with alleged instances of the inefficient, inhumane or unimaginative handling of individual transactions within the framework of established policy. Several of my respondents felt that their Ministries too often made no public defence against attacks on their actions which could easily have been repelled. We must not assume too readily that my respondents knew better than those who made the decision; but the reasons for not issuing a public refutation of some unjustified criticism are not always the best. Sometimes the criticism is not brought to the attention of the right person until too late; sometimes the reply would involve direct reflections on the efficiency of a public authority with whom the Ministry want to remain on good terms; sometimes the full story seems too complex to be squeezed into a paragraph or so. Now and again, it seems, the reason is simply the shunning of the light of publicity which is a conditioned reflex of the civil servant. Information Officers themselves are not exempt from it; many of them are members of the Executive Class, and share the outlook of their executive or administrative colleagues. Sometimes a reply, drafted by many nervous hands, is delivered in such guarded terms that it actually strengthens the impression that something has gone wrong. A soft answer may avert wrath, but attracts suspicion. Whatever the reason, the number of public attacks upon specific actions of individual Ministries greatly exceeds the number of effective replies.

To a greater or lesser extent what I have been describing is the predicament of every desk worker in the civil service, and a good many elsewhere. Many have more contact with outsiders, more variety, more scope for modifying the rules or the procedures, and duties which are more easily distinguishable from those of the man at the next desk, than did the Clerical Officers at Benton. What they all have in common is that for a large part of their time they are performing tasks not because they find them enjoyable in themselves, nor even because they are means to ends which they themselves have chosen to pursue, but simply because they are necessary parts of one of the services provided by the organisation in which they have chosen to make their careers.

At this point I may be asked, 'But don't civil servants enter the service as the result of a free choice, and if it is intolerable aren't they equally free to leave it?' The question in this form mistakes the point, which is not that such a predicament is intolerable, but that on the contrary those in it adjust themselves to it, as we have seen that they did even at Benton, and that some of the most criticised features of the service are the result either of the predicament itself or of their adjustment to it. Nor are the civil servant's alternatives as simple as the question implies. The careers open to members, or would-be members, of the middle class without a professional or teaching qualification is very largely a choice of some kind of office work, and for such choosers the civil service still offers sufficient attractions to enable it to exercise a certain amount of selection. Once the young Clerical Officer, Executive Officer or Assistant Principal has got in, he can get out again, but it takes courage to do so. He soon acquires a wife, a dwelling, children and all sorts of other commodities that have to be paid for; and to change to another occupation usually means a drop in salary which may not be as temporary as he hopes. The gates that he has entered are not the gates of a prison, but they close with a perceptible clang.

So far I have been describing the position of the civil servant as an employee. What is the position of his employers? Since this book is a description of a problem, and not a prescription for a remedy, I shall confine myself to a statement of the facts and the issues as I see them.

In the first place, who are the civil servants' employers? There are three answers to this question. To say 'the Crown' is nowadays to say nothing, except that the civil servant will have great difficulty in bringing any legal action against his employer. To say 'his Minister' is to accept a Parliamentary fiction. The approval of the Minister or in the case of very senior officers the Prime Minister is required in such matters as the dismissal of a civil servant, or the promotion of the senior administrators; and the approval of the Chancellor of the Exchequer is required for any general change in pay or conditions of service. But most Ministers' terms of office are so short that only an absorbing interest in the civil service would enable them to contribute much to decisions of this kind; and while they are Ministers they are naturally absorbed in the responsibilities and not the tools of office. The railway passenger seldom interests himself in the careers of the engine-driver and the guard. Ministers therefore rely on their senior advisors in such matters to an even greater extent than in matters of state. In practice, therefore,

SOME REFLECTIONS 263

the civil servant's employers are other civil servants, and in particular those in the establishment divisions of the Treasury and his own Ministry. In the field of 'morale', what are, or should be, the issues from their point of view?

In Chapter 4 I pointed out that the only two aspects of the subject known as 'morale' which it was sensible to regard as ultimate objectives of a personnel policy were efficiency and job-satisfaction; but that we should be clear whether we are aiming at the latter because it fosters the former or because it can be justified as an end in itself.

The assumption that the more you enjoy your work the better you are at doing it had already become suspect as a result of studies of other kinds of workers, and the result of the survey of the two Ministries discredited it still more. It has still to be seen whether job-satisfaction has any connection with the *collective* efficiency of an organised team of desk workers, of the kind which I studied at Benton; but the balance of probability is against this. There are therefore no grounds for arguing that we should try to increase desk workers' enjoyment of their jobs in order to get better work out of them.

This does not mean, however, that high job-satisfaction has no practical advantage. We saw that it seems to be associated with a lower rate of uncertificated sick leave. This may mean that an increase in job-satisfaction would reduce the civil service version of industrial absenteeism, low as it is. We saw too that the most dissatisfied among the civil servants was the male clerical officer, who also shows the greatest tendency to leave the service in his first few years after entering it. Both these observations may well be linked to the prospect of twelve years of labouring in the paper vineyards of Whitehall before he can expect to be considered for promotion; and until this situation alters it may not be possible to reduce wastage very much. But there is clearly a likelihood that an increase in job-satisfaction would reduce wastage.

Thirdly, we have seen how the civil servants with low job-satisfaction tended to advise against following their own careers, while those who enjoyed their jobs were much more inclined to advise in favour. The civil servant who gets little satisfaction from his job is a poor recruiting sergeant, and discouragement is always more contagious than encouragement. If competition for entry to the desk classes were so keen that the Civil Service Commissioners had no difficulty in finding enough recruits of the right quality, that would not matter; but this has long ceased to be so.

Even if there were not these indirect links between job-satisfaction and efficiency, it would still be arguable that it is part of the modern rôle of 'the good employer' to consider not only how to make his employees more efficient but also how to increase their enjoyment of their work and even of their leisure. The civil service has for many years assumed that its policy must be that of the good employer, partly in the hope of attracting and retaining good recruits, partly in concert with other large employers of office staffs, and partly, no doubt, acting with a genuine eye to the interests of its employees. So that any measures which seem likely to increase their enjoyment of their work without actually lowering efficiency deserve consideration.

Nevertheless, the main concern of the civil servant in his rôle of employer must be with efficiency, both individual and collective. I have, I hope, made clear the difficulty of comparing the collective efficiency of large units in the civil service in any way that would justify the drawing of scientific conclusions; the most I myself could achieve was the study—at Benton—of differences between small working groups whose efficiency under similar conditions seemed to vary. This study emphasised the importance of two things. One was the keeping of the members of the team together for as long as possible, so that they could develop the habit of co-operation, while at the same time weeding-out the men, or more often the women, with whom the other members could not co-operate. This may have a moral for the many Departments in which frequent changes of post are the rule among the desk classes. There are, as we have seen, arguments for and against the practice, and the civil servants in the two Ministries were divided between those who approved and those who disliked it. But their enjoyment of their work seemed to increase the longer they were left to do it; and if, as seems probable, their collective efficiency also increased, the two arguments combine to make a very strong case. The other factor which seemed to be important at Benton was firm supervision. The Clerical Officers welcomed tact and humanity in their Executive Officers, but they felt that the task of getting the best out of the Ledger Sections required authority, and there was no sign that they resented firmness. It is worth recalling here that in the two Ministries and Companies a substantial percentage of respondents at all levels regarded discipline as too easy-going.

As for individual efficiency, we have seen that like job-satisfaction it too alters with age; but unlike it, seems to decline after the thirties. It seems to be quite unrelated to one's own estimate of one's capabilities, and indeed—as I have already pointed out—the lower the officer's grade the greater the divergence between his own and his superior's estimate of what he can do.

The importance of methods of selection and of training in raising individual efficiency is too obvious to need any emphasis from me, even if it had fallen within the scope of my enquiry. But are any other, more mysterious, influences at work? And, if so, are they of a kind which we have any hope of manipulating to serve our practical ends? We have seen that enjoyment of the work seems to have no effect upon individual efficiency. Indeed, the results of my questionnaire pointed to only one attitude that seemed to be associated with it in a useful way—

the feeling that one's Ministry was better than others. If this were an entirely new observation I should hesitate before laying any emphasis on it. It has, however, long been an assumption of military commanders that *esprit de corps* makes good soldiers; and the investigators in the Prudential Insurance Company at New Jersey found that 'pride in the work-group' was associated with *collective* efficiency among their female office workers. None of this, of course, proves conclusively that to raise 'pride in the organisation' will raise individual efficiency; but it is so easy to see how such an attitude may operate to increase the individual's incentive to work well that the possibility cannot be neglected.

Another way in which it is almost certain that efficiency can be influenced has been discussed in Chapter 3, where I set out the evidence that I was able to obtain about rates of dismissal, compulsory retirement and demotion for inefficiency. These rates have been extremely low in recent years, so low in fact that civil servants themselves seem to be critical of the leniency with which incompetents among them are handled. I have argued that any attempt to use 'morale' as a ground of appeal against a higher rate of dismissal and demotion is based upon a misconception of the nature of 'morale', and that there is only one admissible argument against a higher rate—that there would not be enough replacements of better quality.

In fact the reason why the rates are not higher is almost certainly not a rational but an irrational one—what I have called the 'protectiveness' of the civil servant towards his colleagues. This quality has also been illustrated in three other ways. The respondents to my questionnaire were very reluctant to describe their colleagues as anything but likeable, and though the Companies' staffs showed the same tendency it was stronger in the Ministries and strongest among the grades that formed the smallest groups—the administrators and professionals. It was also very strong among the C.O.s at Benton, who had worked together for so many years; they had resisted 'individual counts' of their work, lest the result should penalise their weaker brethren. Although the fact that they were organised into a strong staff association may have helped to make their resistance effective, we should not assume that it was 'trade unionism' which was ultimately responsible for their attitude; the Administrative Class, which is the least 'organised' of the desk classes, seems to show the same sort of protectiveness in its reluctance to dismiss or demote any of its members.

Protectiveness seems to be associated with at least two factors, and probably with others. One is the size of the group, as we have just seen. The less numerous the members of a grade in an organisation, the larger the percentage who will be personally known to each other, and the more reluctant they seem to be either to describe their colleagues as anything but likeable or to make any report on their immediate subordinates that may harm their careers. The second factor is the length of time for which the members of the group have worked together. This is suggested not only by the evidence of the Ledger Sections at Benton but also by the fact that the civil servants in the two Ministries, who had been there longer than the other desk-workers had been in their Companies, were even less inclined to criticise their colleagues, and that the Small Ministry's staff, who had worked together rather longer than the Large Ministry's, gave their subordinates somewhat higher ratings.

A third factor which probably encourages protectiveness is the amount of criticism from outsiders which the organisation has to face. It would not be surprising if the effect of attacks by press and public were to make civil servants close their ranks.

Two things should be noticed, however, about this protectiveness. It did not prevent the civil servants in the two Ministries from being extremely critical of the leniency with which—at least in their view—the incompetent were treated; and they were even more critical than the firms' staffs. Nor did it discourage either type of desk worker from saying quite frankly that discipline was too lax or easy-going. Even those in the lower grades, who were less likely to give than to receive as far as discipline was concerned, seemed to prefer this to seeing their colleagues 'get away with it'. More interesting still was the fact that the more senior civil servants, whose exercise of discipline was regarded as too lenient by their juniors, were themselves critical of the discipline. All this suggests that the senior civil servants were conscious of the need for more stringency, both in important matters such as dismissal or downgrading and in more ordinary matters of discipline, but were inhibited for some reason from translating awareness into action.

Protectiveness was not associated with a high degree of loyalty to the Ministry. The civil servant is able not only to entertain the idea that Press criticism of it may be justified, but also that it is no better than the rest, or even a little worse; in this respect he is less loyal—or more objective—than the desk worker in the Companies. There is a tendency to regard 'protectiveness' as a selfish quality, but to assume that 'loyalty' and *'esprit de corps'* are intrinsically meritorious. Yet when we turn from moral attitudes to the consideration of efficiency, the issue is not so simple. Protectiveness may reduce—even to vanishing point—the number of employees who are dismissed or disciplined for inefficiency; but it may be inseparable from working together in a team. *Esprit de corps* may be associated with efficiency, both in groups and in individuals; and it did not seem to prevent the Small Ministry's respondents from accepting Press criticism as fair or from being very critical of discipline in their own ranks. But it may blind organisations to some of their faults.

More important is the strong probability that protectiveness is connected with a factor that—in some circumstances at least—actively increases collective efficiency. Certainly this was what seemed to be happening in the Ledger Sections at Benton, where the better sections were those in which the C.O.s 'helped each other out'. I have no statistical evidence to prove that it also happens among the higher grades, or even among the clerical staff in the more fragmented sections of Whitehall Ministries: but co-operation between officers at all levels is essential to any Department.

At this point we are as close as we are likely to be in our present state of ignorance to the nodal point of the tangle of factors that is labelled 'morale'. This is the question how to contrive an alliance between the protectiveness of the civil servant, with its good as well as its hampering effects, and the efficiency of the organisation to which he belongs. The team-work, lack of individualism and absence of feuds which are symptoms of this spirit foster collective efficiency. It is tempting, as we have already seen, to argue that what is repugnant to the feelings of its members must damage this efficiency. But this argument is based partly upon an assumption about the nature of morale and partly upon the supposition that the feelings of civil servants would be outraged by a raising of the acceptable level of efficiency and discipline; and such evidence as I have been able to offer suggests that both are mistaken.

I have tried however to describe problems rather than to make facile suggestions for their solution. Where the facts point so obviously in a single direction that it would be wrong-headed to look in any other I may have broken this rule and said so. But with these exceptions I think we are still at the stage where it is a slight advance merely to be able to state the problems in reasonably precise terms. In many cases I am sure that I have done no more than clothe in words and figures what has long been at the back of many civil servants' minds.

APPENDIXES

A. Summaries of some studies of the psychological conditions of office work
   I. in the British Civil Service;
   II. elsewhere.

B. Questionnaire GG 59 (see Chapters 7 and 8).

APPENDIX A

I. IN THE BRITISH CIVIL SERVICE

Typists

(a) 'Typing Pools: a study in satisfactions in work', by R. G. Stansfield,[1] 1948. Unpublished: copy in Treasury O & M file 248/09.

This paper 'reports a study, in certain Ministry of Works Typing Pools, of satisfactions arising out of work and their dependence on the social group and the social situation of the Pool. The method of investigation, based on the "free interview", is described . . . and the "pilot" nature of the present research is stressed. . . . The broad conclusions are: (i) that the idea that there can, and should, be positive satisfactions arising naturally from work hardly enters the daily life of these Typing Pools; (ii) that there is a general lack of vivid positive motives for working. . . .'

The paper contained eight recommendations for remedying this state of affairs.

(b) 'Work Preferences of Typing Pool Staff in the Board of Trade', by E. Anstey,[1] A. H. J. Baines[1] and R. G. Stansfield,[1] 1949. Unpublished: copy in Treasury O & M file 248/09 and Board of Trade file IMG 2546/49.

This is based on another investigation by the Board of Trade's Research Unit, this time in co-operation with the Civil Service Commission's Research Unit. 160 girls of the Typing Pool staff of the Board of Trade completed a special 'form of enquiry', and some of them were interviewed as well.

The main conclusions seem to have been:

'(1) Though the great majority of the girls wished to continue full-time or part-time typing, less than a quarter of them were thoroughly satisfied with Pool work.'

. . . . .

'(5) There were significant variations between the degree of satisfaction in different Pools. Part, but not all, of the variation could be accounted for by the different sizes of the pools. The optimum size for a pool would appear to be about 15. It is suggested that these differences should be followed up with a view to making improvements in the less satisfied pools.'

. . . .

[1] The authors were at the time members of the Research Units of the Board of Trade and the Civil Service Commission.

' (7) The majority of the 67 dissatisfied girls (who ranked pool work as fourth choice or lower) expressed a preference for half-time typing, half-time clerical work, for one officer. The administrative change which would do most to increase satisfaction would thus be an increase in the number of Personal Assistant posts.'

Further investigations were proposed, including not only typing pools, but also C.A.s, Secretaries and C.O.s, for the purpose of comparison.

Post Office Counter-clerks

'Criteria of Occupational Success among Post Office Counter-clerks', by N. F. Kristy, 1952. An unpublished thesis in the library of the University of London.

Since this thesis has not been published, and is therefore not easy of access, I shall make my summary slightly fuller than in the cases of the other studies.

Chapter 1 begins by discussing the problems of establishing a scientific criterion of occupational success. It points out that on the one hand Katz and Hyman's study of morale in U.S. shipyards in the 1939-45 war showed 'morale, including job-satisfaction, to be highly correlated with productivity'; but that on the other hand the Michigan Survey Research centre's study of 'Productivity, Supervision and Morale among Railroad Workers' found that 'more men in low-producing sections than in high, express strong intrinsic job-satisfaction'. Kristy suggests, for investigation, the hypothesis that

(i) expression of satisfaction on the part of the employee and

(ii) supervisor- or employer-rating of proficiency on the job

will not necessarily intercorrelate very highly, but rather will intercorrelate in such a way as to bring forth the essential pattern characteristic of general success in this occupation.'

This hypothesis, he says, 'implies that proficiency and satisfaction do not necessarily have a high correlation with one another, and may indeed be negatively correlated in certain occupations'.

Chapter II describes the work and outlook of P. & T.O.s.[1] Those 'who stated (sc., in an interview) that they were very satisfied with their job were typically less proficient counter-clerks. They had usually come up from sorting-office and postman work, and considered that they had reached a high occupational level as P. & T.O.' The sample studied was 260, which was 1 per cent. of the total in the service; 35 per cent. worked in the Greater London area, 65 per cent. in the rest of the United Kingdom. The techniques used were:

[1] Postal and Telegraph Operators.

(*a*) a 'general information questionnaire';
(*b*) an 'occupational satisfaction questionnaire';
(*c*) a sociometric inventory;
(*d*) tests of intelligence;
(*e*) an interview;
(*f*) personal records;
(*g*) supervisors' ratings of success (one was the service scale, the other an 11-point scale specially devised for their study).

Chapter III gives evidence to show that most vocational guidance experts define occupational success as expressing satisfaction by the employee and a rating of proficiency by the employer. But in the case of P. & T.O.s there is the difficulty that the two show 'almost no correlation' (in some elements of the two descriptions there is actually a negative correlation).

Chapters IV and V are devoted to statistical questions.

Chapter VI deals with adjustment to the job. Five variables were studied in the information about the sample:

(i) expressions of team feeling and pride in the work group;
(ii) attitudes towards remaining in the occupation;
(iii) identification with the organisation (i.e. the Post Office);
(iv) grievances;
(v) the interviewer's overall assessment of adjustment to the job;

There was practically no correlation between (i) and the others; whereas (ii), (iii), (iv) and (v) intercorrelated to a fairly high degree. Kristy says that 'a considerable number of closely-knit semi-hostile in-groups do exist among counter-clerks, and these groups so distort the picture concerning team feeling and pride in work-group that this variable has little relation to proficiency or satisfaction in the occupation'.

Chapters VII and VIII are chiefly concerned with statistical questions, but include the observation that satisfaction among the (P. & T.O.s) appears to break down into several main divisions: (1) the most important aspect of satisfaction appears to be a generally pleasant feeling towards the job. (2) the second most important seems to be self-esteem derived from the job in relation to its present and future conditions. Then (3) comes the counter-clerk's view of what he has to do by way of physical effort and attention to the job, in relation to what he gets, particularly in the form of pay, but also by way of self-esteem and future opportunities. Then come three minor elements: (4) physical and emotional strain due to pressure at the counter; (5) future possibilities of the job in terms of promotion; and (6) the degree of satisfied interest in the daily routine in relation to the need for variety.

SUMMARY. Kristy concludes that 'there is almost no relationship between proficiency and satisfaction, among Post Office counter-clerks.' He says that the bright, capable and efficient ones are thwarted and dissatisfied in their occupation, while the duller, less ambitious and less efficient ones feel a fair level of satisfaction.

Scientists

'Incentives', by Stanley Mayne, Secretary of the Institute of Professional
   Civil Scrvants. Paper No. 14 in *The Direction of Research Estab-
   lishments*—the Proceedings of a Symposium held at the National
   Physical Laboratory in September 1956: H.M.S.O. 1957.

In this paper Mayne makes a number of specific, though not radical, criticisms of the position of scientists in the civil service, based on his impressions and not on a scientific study of a representative sample. He divides civil service scientists into three main groups.

'Junior assistants' (i.e. those recruited from boys and girls with the General Certificate of Education (Ordinary)) suffer from a very high rate of wastage; he cites rates of 20 per cent. in the Meteorological Office, and 18 per cent. in the Department of Scientific and Industrial Research (who in the five years from 1950 to 1954 lost 322 of their 469 recruits in this class). Mayne thinks that the two main causes are the lack of facilities for further education granted by these establishments and the small prospects of promotion to the 'medium grades', because of the significance attached to formal scientific qualifications.

As regards its treatment of 'medium grade scientists' (i.e. those recruited with a Higher National Certificate or the General Certificate of Education (Advanced)) the service can claim to set an example to industry and the universities. Mayne's only criticism here is that so few can subsequently get bursaries to enable them to study their subject further at universities; these bursaries exist in theory, but in 1955 only one of the 3,500 to 4,000 eligible Assistants (Scientific) or Assistant Experimental Officers was awarded one.

Among 'High grade scientists' incentives are bound to be less effective, to the extent that they are 'wholly consumed by their science'. But this description, which was true of most scientists in a past generation, is not true of the much more numerous scientists of today. Mayne considers that they should be more free

   (i) to attend conferences[1];
   (ii) to publish papers;
   (iii) to do their own research. Mayne appreciates that this freedom
      must not interfere with the official work of the laboratory, but

---

[1] It is interesting to note, however, from Stein's paper (later in this Appendix), that attendance at conferences was regarded as important only by the *'less* creative' among the industrial research chemists whom he studied!

points out that if it is not granted the scientist becomes discouraged.[1]

Finally, Mayne compares the financial attractions of a career in the senior ranks of the Scientific Civil Service with those of a career in the Administrative Class. He calculates that 'the average administrative career' will yield a salary total of £77,000, while a scientist with an average career in the Scientific Officer class will get only £59,500.

II. OUTSIDE THE BRITISH CIVIL SERVICE

The Dynamics of Bureaucracy, by Peter M. Blau (University of Chicago Press, 1955).

This is an account of two separate studies of the inter-personal relationships between civil servants in two un-named offices in the U.S.A.

One of these was a 'department' of 24 members, belonging to that part of the public employment agency of an eastern state which served the clothing industry by receiving telephone requests from clothing firms for workers and referring applicants for work to jobs for which they seemed suited. During the period of the investigation a system of statistical records was introduced to check the success of individual officers in making 'placements'. This increased 'productivity', as measured by the number of placements, but led to strain in the relations between some of the civil servants, and between the civil servants and their 'clients'. These strains are studied in detail.

The other office was one of the nine district agencies of a bureau whose task was to ensure the enforcement among certain business establishments of two federal laws. The investigation of each firm's practices involved an audit of its books and records, interviews with the employer or his representative and with a sample of employees, a decision whether there had been a violation of the law, and what action could be appropriate, and negotiations with the employer. Each investigation was carried out by a single agent. The agency contained 18 members. Each agent's work was subject not only to supervision by a supervisor but also to a review by a 'review section'. Agents were expected to complete 8 investigations in a month, to find violations in half of them and to obtain the employer's agreement to make voluntary adjustments in at least two-thirds of these. But agents were expected to achieve fairly good relations with the firms investigated. The resulting interpersonal relationships between agents themselves, agents and their supervisors, agents and the 'reviewers' and agents and employers, were studied in detail.

In both cases the investigator was introduced to the staff by a senior

[1] Here again it is interesting to compare Mayne's suggestions with Stein's study.

official as a sociologist and was given an opportunity to explain that he was interested in studying the interpersonal relationships of civil servants. During the three months of each investigation he was able to accompany officers on their 'field' work, and to participate in their informal social contacts with each other (for example, at lunch).

Although the author is the first to point out that these two studies are too small to form the basis of any generalisations about bureaucrats, Part III consists of a number of such generalisations. It is, however, short.

Productivity, Supervision and Morale in an Office Situation, by Daniel Katz, Nathan Maccoby and Nancy C. Morse, of the Institute for Social Research, University of Michigan (1950, pub. by the Survey Research Center, University of Michigan).

This was the first of a series of studies of the 'fundamental problems of organising human behaviour' for which the Survey Research Center received a contract from the U.S. Office of Naval Research. It was undertaken in the 'home' (i.e. headquarters) office of the Prudential Insurance Company in Newark, N.J., the second largest insurance company in the U.S.A. This office alone employed some 10,000 employees. Conditions of work seem to have been attractive: hours were short (seven a day for a five-day week) jobs were exceptionally secure, lunches were free, holidays frequent, and there were pensions, group insurance and disability payments. As in the British Civil Service, employment, transfers between divisions, dismissals, salaries, etc., were handled by a single Personnel Division. 82 per cent. of the non-supervisory employees were women, 71 per cent. unmarried, 46 per cent. between seventeen and twenty-four years of age. Different divisions handled very similar work, consisting of the processing of policies, keeping records on them and handling correspondence on them: the only difference was the geographical areas from which they originated. It was possible to match twelve pairs of high- and low-productivity divisions, although the difference rarely exceeded 10 per cent.

The study was concerned with the attitudes of supervisors and of employees, and the results contained some expected and some unexpected observations. For example, in 'high productivity' sections, as is usual in American surveys, the supervisors were more democratic, more inclined to treat employees as human beings and less detailed in their supervision. But they were also, according to the employees, less good at explaining the reasons for procedures, and less good at standing up for their employees. The employees, too, were surprising. Those in high-productivity sections showed greater 'pride in their work group', but no more 'intrinsic job-satisfaction', no more 'Company-involvement' and no more 'financial and job-satisfaction'. Indeed, in the low productivity sections, *more* employees participated in company recreational programmes, and in the company's suggestion scheme; and *fewer* were critical of the company's rating system and placement policy.

These attitudes were surveyed by means of free-answer interviews, in which the employee's answers were classified on a questionnaire. The number and sex of the interviewers are not stated.

Scientists

'Superiors and Subordinates in Research' (Paper No. 12 in *The Direction of Research Establishments*—the Proceedings of a Symposium at the National Physical Laboratory in September 1956: H.M.S.O. 1957).

Professor Shepard's ideas are based on studies of industrial research establishments in the U.S.A., but it is interesting to speculate on the extent to which they may be true of research establishments in the British Civil Service; certainly he seemed to think that they were.

Shepard says that engineers and scientists are 'the most dissatisfied workers in industry'. Moreover, they are generally resentful and critical of their superiors in management, most of whom are themselves engineers or scientists. At the same time, most of them aspire to managerial positions themselves; only about 10 per cent. felt that professional achievement in science or engineering constituted 'success'.

He says that 'the concepts of management and supervision in most laboratories appear to be similar to the traditional industrial concepts of management and supervision. . . . Resistance to patterns more in accord with both scientific traditions and new directions of industrial organisation is sometimes encountered. . . .' Yet what objective evidence we have—and it is meagre—concerning the organisational patterns connected with effective research, points towards a new emphasis, which Shepard sums up as follows:

'(1) wide participation in decision-making, rather than centralised decision-making; . . .
(2) the face-to-face group, rather than the individual, as the basic unit of organisation; . . .
(3) mutual confidence, rather than authority, as the integrative force in organisation; . . .
(4) the supervisor as the agent for maintaining intragroup and intergroup communication, rather than the agent of higher authority; . . .
(5) the growth of membership of the organisation to greater responsibility, rather than external control of the members' performance of their tasks . . .'

Shepard also observes that 'research performance depends upon more than the quality of the scientist or his relations with his superiors'.

Relations with colleagues are an important source of stimulation. In research groups whose performance was rated high by members there was a more frequent exchange of 'task-oriented information' among the members than among those groups that were rated low. Also, productivity, creativity and enthusiasm decline with length of association: that is, groups with a frequently changing membership are more highly rated than those whose members have been together a long time. Highly rated scientists spend more time in discussion with scientists from other disciplines than with colleagues in their own specialities. He believes, too, that when the relationship of supervisor to subordinate is perceived as that of boss to worker, morale (a term which he does not define) is low. There is a tendency for high performance to be associated with members' ability to influence the supervisors in matters affecting their work. But this tendency is marked only if the supervisor is correspondingly influential with the laboratory management.

In presenting this paper he commented that in his few weeks at the National Physical Laboratory he had found little of the kind of team-work that was common in the U.S.A. There, 'horizontal' team-work between specialists in different subjects was frequent. In England, there was more often 'vertical' team-work between different levels of the hierarchy. Consultation went on in the National Physical Laboratory at a high level, but not interdependence in the task.

'Creativity and the Scientist', by Morris I. Stein, Associate Professor at Yale University, U.S.A. (Paper No. 3 in *The Direction of Research Establishments*—the Proceedings of a Symposium at the National Physical Laboratory in September 1956: H.M.S.O. 1957.)

Professor Stein prefaces his paper with two reservations. Apart from the psychological study of creativity among scientists, it can also be studied sociologically. For example, the scientist is usually required to play three distinct and sometimes conflicting rôles—'scientist proper', 'member of a profession', and 'employee'. The demands of these rôles are quite often inconsistent, for example, in such matters as the sharing of results, or codes of personal behaviour.

Stein's own study, however, is mainly of the psychological characteristics of the individual. His second reservation is that the material for his study consisted of 46 research chemists from two companies in the U.S.A. and that his results cannot therefore be assumed to be true of other types of scientist, or of the same kind of scientist in other countries.

The 46 chemists were ranked as 'more' or 'less' 'creative' by their superiors, colleagues and subordinates; and then subjected to psychological tests.

One set of tests was directed at their childhood relations with their parents and other adults. The *more* creative scientists had apparently felt 'more distant' in childhood from parents and adults generally; they had 'identified' less with their mothers (and probably also their fathers). They had enjoyed group activities and competitive and co-operative games less, and solitary activities more. Their parents had less formal education, and a lower socio-economic status (='class' in a classless society, N.D.W.) than those of the *less* creative chemists. There was no difference in geographical origins—for example, whether the scientists came from a home on a farm, in a suburb or in a city.

The other set of tests was concerned with the scientists' present characteristics. The *more* creative ones did better on verbal intelligence tests. They had a quicker normal pace in writing, but there was no difference in their peak pace; probably they simply worked nearer to their peak pace. They were less authoritarian, and less submissive to authority; more 'integrative', 'dynamic' and 'autonomous' (these concepts were not defined in the paper). They had a greater tendency to see themselves as different in their attitudes from their work group and the general population. But they did not appear to have any greater 'devotion' to science, although this may, of course, have been due to the difficulty of devising a satisfactory set of questions on this point.

Stein also carried out an interesting test to see what incentives weighed most with the two groups. They were asked to imagine that they had succeeded in 'developing a major product for their company', and were then given a list of possible rewards, which they ranked in their order of choice. The average rank order of both groups combined was:

1. being made assistant to the director of research;
2. being sent to a training course for executives;
3. being given a substantial increase in salary;
4. being given a percentage of the profits from their research;
5. being given administrative experience in other divisions within the company;
6. being permitted to choose their own problems for research;
7. being given more people to carry out their ideas;
8. being made assistant co-ordinator of research, production and sales;
9. being sent to all professional meetings, with expenses paid;
10. being given a flat cash bonus;
11. being given increased laboratory space and increased facilities for purchasing equipment;
12. being guaranteed their job for 5 more years.

Contrary to Stein's expectation (which was based on 'observation of scientists in academic institutions and non-profitmaking research laboratories') the rank orders of the *more* creative chemists did not differ much from that of the others. In general, 'scientific' rewards were ranked lower, and administrative and monetary rewards higher than he had expected. The only real difference between the more and the less creative chemists was that the latter gave a higher place to attendance at professional meetings with expenses paid, while the *more* creative gave a higher place to 'a flat cash bonus'![1]

Clerical Grades in the French Civil Service

Petits Fonctionnaires au Travail: *compte rendu d'une enquête sociologique effectuée dans une grande administration publique parisienne*, by Michel Crozier, Chargé de Recherches au Centre National de la Recherche Scientifique (Centre d'Études Sociologiques), Paris (published in 1955 by the Centre).

This investigation was carried out in a large but anonymous Ministry in Paris among the female staff engaged on typing and duplicating and on routine checking of documents. It took place in the spring of 1954, not long after the strike of French civil servants in August 1953, in which some but not all of the women had taken part. The method of the investigation was a private interview, in which the interviewer, primed with information about the educational level, geographical origin and seniority of the employee, and about the profession of her parents, elicited free answers bearing on:

(*a*) job-satisfaction;
(*b*) liking for public service;
(*c*) reactions to discipline;
(*d*) attitude towards her superiors;
(*e*) opinion of the Ministry;
(*f*) friendliness and sociability;
(*g*) interest in politics;
(*h*) interest in her trade union and the extent to which she took part in the strike;
(*i*) 'elegance';[2]
(*j*) leisure activities and cultural tastes.

[1] It is of course possible that Stein has merely discovered what differentiates the preferred incentives of research chemists in private industry from those in other kinds of research, and has not discovered a general characteristic of research chemists as a whole. In any case, a sample of 46 is very small.

[2] Surely this must be the only survey of this kind in which 'elegance' is measured and tabulated; for example:

		%
Négligées	9 ...	16
Peu élégantes	19 ...	33
Standard moyen parisien	12 ...	21
Élégantes	17 ...	30

It was found that (*a*), (*d*) and (*f*) appeared to have a close relation to the subject's social class, while (*c*) and (*e*) were related, though less markedly, to seniority. Interest in trade unionism was, on the whole, related more closely to seniority than to social class—a somewhat unexpected result.

The numbers involved were extremely small—less than 60—and the value of the survey is correspondingly doubtful. But the results, if confirmed in a large investigation, would be interesting.

APPENDIX B

QUESTIONNAIRE GG 59

The questionnaire was accompanied by a note from the Establishment Division (or Personnel Department, as the case might be), making it clear that, while recipients could choose whether to fill it in or not, it had the support of the Ministry (or Company); and attached to it was a pre-paid business reply envelope.

Question 1 was omitted from the questionnaires issued to the Companies, for obvious reasons. Question 3 was given too little space in the layout on page 2, so that it escaped the attention of several respondents. Question 50 was a deliberate repetition of Question 23, for the reasons given in Chapter 7. Question 61 was a device intended to show whether any question was regarded as quite inappropriate by a large percentage of any group, and seemed to be effective; for example, many junior employees marked Question 53. Question 62 provided enough space for all but one respondent, who attached an appendix of his own. Respondents were asked to use ink partly because this is easier to see when card-punching, but partly also because this makes it harder for the respondent to alter his answer after second thoughts.

1	2, 3, 4, 5	6, 7	8	9	10, 11

FOR OFFICE USE ONLY.

QUESTIONNAIRE GG 59

1. This questionnaire is an important part of a project of research into conditions of work in large offices. It is designed to obtain the opinions of a representative selection of office workers on their own jobs.
2. Your Company or Ministry, as the case may be, have agreed to co-operate in this project. The fact that you have received this questionnaire is *not* an indication that they are contemplating any important changes in the conditions of your work or the way in which it is organised.

APPENDIXES

3. Although your Company or Ministry are helping us by issuing this questionnaire to you and others, you are under *no obligation* to fill it in. But your reply will be completely anonymous—you are asked *not* to sign it—and we hope that you will co-operate by sending it in. Every person who refuses—or forgets—to do so slightly reduces the value and interest of the survey.
4. Your answers will remain confidential because the returned questionnaire can be identified only by serial number: the research workers who read it will not know your name. Only your Personnel Department or Establishment Division, as the case may be, know to whom questionnaires are being sent, *and they will never see your answers*. You are asked to seal the completed questionnaire in the pre-paid, addressed envelope which is attached, and put it in the post.
5. The report on the investigation will simply contain statistical summaries of the answers, from which it will be impossible to identify the answers of any individual. The report will not even disclose the name of your Company or Ministry.
6. Please *don't* discuss the questions with anyone before you answer them: it is *your* opinion we want. But there is no objection to your discussing them afterwards with colleagues who have sent in their own questionnaires.
7. In drafting the questionnaire we have had the advice of office workers of many kinds; but the questions have to cover a wide variety of jobs at different levels, so that some of them may not seem very suitable for your own job. *But please answer them all*, and use the place at the end of the questionnaire for indicating the questions that seemed inappropriate.

How to complete the questionnaire:

Please use ink: it is more easily seen by those tabulating the replies.

Wherever possible, *answer by placing a tick (√) in the bracket opposite the reply that seems to you to fit best*; for example,

'This sheet of paper is

    foolscap   .   .   .   .   (√) 0
    quarto   .   .   .   .   ( ) 1
    octavo   .   .   .   .   ( ) 2'

Pay no attention to the numerals on the right of each bracket; they merely help those tabulating the answers. They do *not* indicate which reply is considered best!

Please send in the questionnaire as soon as you can, if possible within three days.

The questions begin on the back of this page:

1. Place a tick (√) against your present rank or grade. Then place a cross (×) against the rank (or 'grade') in which you originally entered the civil service (whether established or not).

10-13

Assistant Secretary . ( ) 00		( ) 13
Principal . . ( ) 01		( ) 14
Assistant Principal . ( ) 02		( ) 15
Principal Executive		( ) 16
Officer . . ( ) 03	[Certain professional	( ) 17
Senior Chief Execu-	grades were listed here.]	( ) 18
tive Officer . . ( ) 04		( ) 19
Chief Executive		( ) 20
Officer . . ( ) 05		( ) 21
Senior Executive		( ) 22
Officer . . ( ) 06		
Higher Executive		
Officer . . ( ) 07		
Executive Officer . ( ) 08		
Higher Clerical		
Officer . . ( ) 09		
Clerical Officer . ( ) 10		
Clerical Officer (Sec-		
retary) . . ( ) 11		
Clerical Assistant . ( ) 12		

If your present or original grade is *not* in the list above, please enter it in the space below:

Present grade................................ *Original* grade ....

....

2. I am in the age-group   **14**

    15-19 . . . ( ) 0   40-44 . . . ( ) 5
    20-24 . . . ( ) 1   45-49 . . . ( ) 6
    25-29 . . . ( ) 2   50-54 . . . ( ) 7
    30-34 . . . ( ) 3   55-59 . . . ( ) 8
    35-39 . . . ( ) 4   60 or over . . ( ) 9

15

3. I am   MALE   . ( )   FEMALE . . . ( ) 1

4. I am
(If you are divorced, widowed or separated, and have not remarried, please reply 'single').

Single . . . ( ) 2
Married . . . ( ) 3

---

5. Before entering your present Company or Ministry had you been an office worker in any other kind or office?

No . . . . ( ) 4
Yes, in the civil service . ( ) 5
Yes, in a private firm's office . . . ( ) 6
Yes, in nationalised industry . . . ( ) 7
Yes, in local government ( ) 8
Yes, in some other kind of office . . . ( ) 9

16, 17

6. How long have you been in your present Company or Ministry? (Count 6 months or more as 1 year, 5 months or less as 0.)

............................years

18

7. Since you have been in your present Company or Ministry how often has your job been changed (including promotions, but *not* minor changes in part of your duties)?

............................times

---

8. What (very roughly) are your present duties? (You may tick more than one heading if you wish.)

19

Management . . ( ) 0
Technical advice or design . . . ( ) 1
Production . . ( ) 2
Finance or accounting ( ) 3
Personnel (e.g. welfare or establishment) . ( ) 4

Public relations . . ( ) 5
Sales . . . . ( ) 6
Secretarial (at any level) ( ) 7
Paper-handling (e.g. filing, letter despatching and other clerical duties) . ( ) 8
Other duties . . ( ) 9

20, 21

9. How many years have you been in your present post (i.e. doing roughly your present duties)? (Count 6 months or more as 1 year, 5 or less as 0.)

............................years

22

10. How many minutes does it take you to travel from your office to your home each *evening*, by the most direct route, from door to door?

under 15 minutes	. . ( )	0
15-30 ,,	. . ( )	1
30-45 ,,	. . ( )	2
45-60 ,,	. . ( )	3
60-75 ,,	. . ( )	4
75-90 ,,	. . ( )	5
over 90 ,,	. . ( )	6

23, 24

11. If you think that any of the things listed here ought to be improved in the office where you work, please tick them (tick as many as you like).

    Anything else? X

    ....
    ....
    ....
    ....

noise . . . . ( )	0
dirt . . . . ( )	1
ventilation . . ( )	2
lighting . . . ( )	3
draughts . . . ( )	4
heating . . . ( )	5
canteen . . . ( )	6
room to work . . ( )	7
decoration and furniture ( )	8
lavatories . . . ( )	9

25

12. On how many nights a week, on the average, do you do official work after regular hours?

    about .... nights a week

13. How often do you take official work home?

    | Frequently | . . ( ) 6 | Hardly ever | . . ( ) 8 |
    | Sometimes | . . ( ) 7 | Never | . . ( ) 9 |

26

14. Does your work have a bad effect on your health?

    | No | . . . . ( ) | 0 |
    | Yes, physically | . . ( ) | 1 |
    | Yes, mentally | . . ( ) | 2 |
    | Uncertain | . . . ( ) | 3 |

15. Compared with most other people in your office at your level, are you

much less hard-worked? ( )	4
slightly less? . . ( )	5
about the same? . . ( )	6
slightly more hard-worked? . . ( )	7
much more hard-worked? ( )	8

27

16. Do you do any office work for some other organisation in your spare time? (You need not answer if you prefer.)

I prefer not to answer . ( )	0
No . . . . ( )	1
Yes, out of interest . ( )	2
Yes, to supplement my income . . . ( )	3

17. In your office, is there a club or society for any of your spare-time interests?

No . . . . ( )	4
Not sure . . . ( )	5
Yes . . . . ( )	6

18. If so, do you take part in its activities?

No . . . . ( )	7
Yes . . . . ( )	8

28

19. How much of your time is spent in face-to-face or telephone conversation with the public, with customers or with outside organisations?

Almost all . . . ( )	0
Most of it . . . ( )	1
About half . . . ( )	2
Not very much . . ( )	3
Practically none . . ( )	4

20. Would you like more contacts of this kind, or not?

Much more . . . ( )	5
A bit more . . . ( )	6
No change . . . ( )	7
A bit less . . . ( )	8
Much less . . . ( )	9

29

21. How does the public, or customer, or outside organisation react, on the whole, to what you have to do?

In a very friendly way . ( )	0
In a fairly friendly way . ( )	1
In a tolerant way . . ( )	2
In a slightly unfriendly way . . . ( )	3
In a very unfriendly way ( )	4

Here are some phrases which are often applied to jobs. Please tick one in each group which seems to you most applicable to your own duties.

22. *Variety*   **30**
    - Too much . . ( ) 0
    - Enough . . ( ) 1
    - Too little . . ( ) 2

23. *Responsibility*
    - Too much . . ( ) 3
    - Enough . . ( ) 4
    - Too little . . ( ) 5

24. *Pay*
    - Overpaid . . ( ) 6
    - Fairly paid . . ( ) 7
    - Underpaid . . ( ) 8

25. *Supervision and Guidance*   **31**
    - Too much of it . ( ) 0
    - Enough . . ( ) 1
    - Too little of it . ( ) 2

26. *Staffing*
    - Overstaffed . . ( ) 3
    - About right . . ( ) 4
    - Understaffed . ( ) 5

27. *Colleagues*   **32**
    Most of them are
    - Very likeable . . ( ) 0
    - Likeable . . ( ) 1
    - All right . . ( ) 2
    - Not very likeable . ( ) 3
    - Most unlikeable . ( ) 4

28. *Value of my work*
    - Essential to the community . . ( ) 5
    - Useful but not essential . . ( ) 6
    - Neither useful nor essential . . ( ) 7

29. *Initiative*   **33**
    My job provides
    - Plenty of scope for it ( ) 0
    - Some scope for it . ( ) 1
    - Very little scope for it . . . ( ) 2
    - No scope at all for it ( ) 3

30. *Time spent in it*
    - I'd like a move very soon . . ( ) 4
    - I'd like a move before long . . . ( ) 5
    - I don't mind one way or the other . ( ) 6
    - I don't want to be moved yet . . ( ) 7
    - I want to stay as long as possible . ( ) 8

31. *Your Superior*   **34**
    My immediate superior is
    - older than me . ( ) 0
    - younger than me . ( ) 1
    - roughly the same age ( ) 2
    and is
    - male . . . ( ) 3
    - female . . . ( ) 4

32. *Suitability*
    I feel that my duties are
    - well below my capabilities . . ( ) 5
    - a little below them . ( ) 6
    - more or less suited to them . . . ( ) 7
    - a little beyond them ( ) 7
    - well beyond them . ( ) 9

Here are some things which are often said by people about the organisation in which they work. Please tick the phrase in each group which seems to you most applicable to your own Company or Ministry:

35

33. Very up-to-date . ( ) 0
    Quite up-to-date . ( ) 1
    Slightly old-fashioned . ( ) 2
    Very old-fashioned . ( ) 3

34. Friendly . ( ) 4
    Impersonal . ( ) 5

35. Well organised . ( ) 6
    badly organised . ( ) 7
    hard to say . ( ) 8

36

36. The men at the top are
    really able . ( ) 0
    competent . ( ) 1
    not quite competent enough . ( ) 2
    incompetent . ( ) 3

37. Discipline is
    unnecessarily strict . ( ) 4
    strict but necessary . ( ) 5
    just enough . ( ) 6
    a little easy-going . ( ) 7
    much too lax . ( ) 9

37

38. Press criticism of the Company (or Ministry) is
    very rare . ( ) 0
    occasional, and usually fair . ( ) 1
    occasional and usually unfair . ( ) 2
    frequent and usually fair . ( ) 2
    frequent and usually unfair . ( ) 4
    I wouldn't notice any ( ) 5

39. Understaffed . ( ) 6
    Overstaffed . ( ) 7
    About right . ( ) 8

38

40. Relations between employees at different levels are
    too democratic . ( ) 0
    not democratic enough . ( ) 1
    about right . ( ) 2

41. Incompetent people are
    got rid of quickly . ( ) 3
    given a chance, and then got rid of . ( ) 4
    put where they do least harm . ( ) 5
    allowed to stay on wherever they are ( ) 6

42. Do you approve of this?
    yes . ( ) 7
    no . ( ) 8
    hard to say . ( ) 9

39

43. I am in direct contact with the men at the top (i.e. of the whole Company or Ministry)
    frequently . ( ) 0
    sometimes . ( ) 1
    hardly ever . ( ) 2
    never . ( ) 3

44. All things considered, compared with other Companies (or Ministries), this one seems to me
    much better . ( ) 4
    slightly better . ( ) 5
    about the same . ( ) 7
    slightly worse . ( ) 7
    much worse . ( ) 8

45. Have you ever consulted one of the personnel officers ('welfare officers' in the civil service) about a personal problem?

41
No . . . . ( ) 0
Yes, on a problem in my work . . . ( ) 1
Yes, on a private problem ( ) 2

46. If so, was the result helpful?

No . . . . ( ) 3
Hard to say . . ( ) 4
Yes . . . . ( ) 5

47. What seem to you the most attractive features of your job in your organisation? Put '1' against the most attractive, '2' against the next, and so on until you have put '10' against the least attractive.
Is there anything else which you would mark above any of these?

.... X 51

Hours of work . . ( ) 42
Pension rights . . ( ) 43
Security of job . . ( ) 44
Promotion prospects . ( ) 45
Pay . . . . ( ) 46
Interest of the work . ( ) 47
Holidays . . . ( ) 48
Status in community . ( ) 49
Physical conditions of work . . . ( ) 50
Social life with colleagues ( ) 51

....
....

48. What seem to you the least satisfactory features of your job in your organisation? Put '1' against the least satisfactory, '2' against the next, and so on until you have put '10' against the least unsatisfactory.

Is there anything else which seems to you even less satisfactory than any of these?

.... X 61

Monotony . . . ( ) 52
Pay . . . . ( ) 53
Promotion prospects . ( ) 54
Hours of work . . ( ) 55
Nature of the work itself ( ) 56
Your colleagues . . ( ) 57
Strain of the work . ( ) 58
Lack of responsibility . ( ) 59
Your superiors . . ( ) 60
Attitude of the public to your work . . ( ) 61

....
....
....

62

49. Could you do the job of your immediate superior?
  - Easily . . ( ) 0
  - With some effort . ( ) 1
  - Not sure . . ( ) 2
  - Not as well as he/she does it . . ( ) 3
  - No . . ( ) 4

50. In your own job, would you like to be given
  - More responsibility? . ( ) 5
  - Less responsibility? . ( ) 6
  - No change? . . ( ) 7

63

51. Are you told when you make a mistake?
  - Usually . . ( ) 0
  - Hardly ever . ( ) 1

52. Are you told when you have done a particularly good job?
  - Usually . . ( ) 2
  - Hardly ever . ( ) 3

53. Here are some ways of describing the capabilities of those who are working under you. Which of them comes closest to describing your own subordinates?

64

- They need close supervision to prevent mistakes . . ( ) 0
- They could be trusted with more responsibility, but under the present system they must consult me . . . ( ) 1
- They can be trusted with the easier decisions . . . ( ) 2
- They consult me about trivial things when they don't have to ( ) 3
- They can be trusted to come to me when the need arises . ( ) 4
- Their judgment is pretty well as good as mine, and I leave them to carry on . . . . ( ) 5
- I would like to keep a closer eye on them, but am too busy ( ) 6
- I do not have any subordinates . . . . ( ) 7

65

54. How does the system of promotion work at your level?
  - As fairly as possible . ( ) 0
  - Fairly on the whole . ( ) 1
  - A little unfairly . . ( ) 2
  - Very unfairly . . ( ) 3

		66
55. Tick the *two* things which seem to you to count most for promotion at your level in your office. Please tick *two*. Any comments? X	Seniority . . . ( )	0
	Ability . . . ( )	1
	Hard Work . . ( )	3
	General Education . ( )	3
	Experience . . . ( )	4
	Being in the right place at the right time . . ( )	5
	Good relations with superiors . . . ( )	6
	Management of subordinates . . . ( )	7

56. How important and valuable to the community is your job? The list below gives nine jobs, including your own, with spaces in which you can assign them an order of importance by giving '1' to the highest, '2' to the next and so on. In the first column give your own opinion, in the second show the order which you think your friends and acquaintances (outside your organisation) would give them:

67, 68

	Your order	*Your friends' order*	
your own work .	( )	( )	
solicitor . .	( )	( )	S69
taxi-driver . .	( )	( )	
Member of Parliament	( )	( )	
school teacher .	( )	( )	
hospital nurse .	( )	( )	
actor or actress .	( )	( )	
shop assistant .	( )	( )	
journalist . .	( )	( )	

		70
57. Are you consulted about changes in the way in which work is organised or the conditions under which you work?	Always . . . ( )	0
	Usually . . . ( )	1
	Sometimes . . . ( )	2
	Not usually . . ( )	3
	Never . . . ( )	4
58. If a friend of yours with the same qualifications were thinking of entering your career in the same way as you did, what would your advice be?	Strongly against . . ( )	5
	Rather against . . ( )	6
	Impartial . . . ( )	7
	In favour on the whole . ( )	8
	Strongly in favour . ( )	9

			71
59. When you are fed up with your work what would you call it?	Frustrating	( )	0
	Pointless	( )	1
	Worrying	( )	2
	Thankless	( )	3
	Tiring	( )	4
When you are enjoying it, what would you call it?	Popular	( )	5
	Responsible	( )	6
	Useful	( )	7
	Interesting	( )	8
	Creative	( )	9

			72
60. All things considered, how do you feel about your present job?	I love it	( )	0
	I am enthusiastic about it	( )	1
	I like it very much	( )	2
	I like it a good deal	( )	3
	I like it on the whole	( )	4
	I like it fairly well	( )	5
	I like it a little	( )	6
	I am indifferent to it	( )	7
	On the whole, I don't like it	( )	8
	I dislike it	( )	9
	I hate it	( )	x

61. Some of the previous questions may have struck you as quite inappropriate to your own position. If so, please mark them in the list below by placing a tick in the bracket opposite their numbers. You can mark as many as you like. As before, pay no attention to the numbers on the right of each bracket.

									73-77	
Question number		Qn. no.		Qn. no.		Qn. no.		Qn. no.		S78
11 . ( ) 0		21 . ( ) 0		31 . ( ) 0		41 . ( ) 0		51 . ( ) 0		
12 . ( ) 1		22 . ( ) 1		32 . ( ) 1		42 . ( ) 1		52 . ( ) 1		
13 . ( ) 2		23 . ( ) 2		33 . ( ) 2		43 . ( ) 2		53 . ( ) 2		
14 . ( ) 3		24 . ( ) 3		34 . ( ) 3		44 . ( ) 3		54 . ( ) 3		
15 . ( ) 4		25 . ( ) 4		35 . ( ) 4		45 . ( ) 4		55 . ( ) 4		
16 . ( ) 5		26 . ( ) 5		36 . ( ) 5		46 . ( ) 5		56 . ( ) 5		
17 . ( ) 6		27 . ( ) 6		37 . ( ) 6		47 . ( ) 6		57 . ( ) 6		
18 . ( ) 7		28 . ( ) 7		38 . ( ) 7		48 . ( ) 7		58 . ( ) 7		
19 . ( ) 8		29 . ( ) 8		39 . ( ) 8		49 . ( ) 8		59 . ( ) 8		
20 . ( ) 9		30 . ( ) 9		40 . ( ) 9		50 . ( ) 9		60 . ( ) 9		

62. Is there anything you would like to add about your work, your Company (or Ministry), the building where you work, your colleagues, this questionnaire, etc.?

S79, 80

....
....
....
....
....

Now

HAVE YOU ANSWERED EVERY QUESTION? (It is surprising how many people miss out one or more.)

If so,

PLEASE POST THIS BEFORE YOU FORGET. (It is surprising how many people do.)

and

THANK YOU FOR TAKING THE TIME AND TROUBLE TO FILL THIS IN.

INDEX

Aalto, Dr. B., 151
absenteeism, 9, 25, 57, 59, 61, 62, 108, 249, 250, 254, 263
accommodation: living, 20; office, 3-4
Acton Society Trust, 112, 132-3, 137
Admiralty, The, 7
advice to potential entrants, 185-7, 242, 244-5, 246, 263
age: collective efficiency and, 81-4
grade and, 243-5
individual efficiency and, 179-180, 246, 264
job-satisfaction and, 110, 171-6, 246
promotion and, 205
resignation and, 40-1, 109-10
respondents', 158, 162-3
retirement and, 34-8
sick leave and, 120-1, 127-8, 130
supervision and, 99-100, 220-1
age-groups: efficiency ratings and, 178-80, 246, 264
job-satisfaction and, 174-6
promotion and, 205
Air Ministry, The, 7
anonymity, 256
Anstey, E., 11, 271
Argyle, M., 11, 60n, 90, 112, 151, 153, 155
armed forces: morale in, 1, 2, 19, 180
Assheton Committee, 26
Atomic Energy Research Establishment, 156
attitude: questions on, 196-241
to management, 1-2, 9, 31, 88, 101-4, 223-7
to own organisation, 195-6, 238-41, 243, 244-5, 266
attractions of the job: 117-18, 181-2, 199-202
attitudes and, 198, 199-202
efficiency rating and, 181-2
job satisfaction and, 194-5

Baines, A. H. J., 11, 271
baratarianism, 258-9
Bartlett, F. C., 57n

Benton, Newcastle, 10, 19n, 33, 45-107, 111n, 252-3. *See also* Records Branch
Bingham, 9
Blankenship, A. B., 58n
Blau, P. M., 78n, 179n, 275
Box, Miss K., 200
brand-image of civil servant, 260-1
Bridges, Lord, 10,
Brook, Sir Norman, 10, 27
Brown, J. A. C., 5n
buildings, 3-4, 211-13
Burchardt, R., 156
Buzzard, Dr. R., 70

Campbell, C. A., 45n
canteens, 3, 20, 68, 212, 215, 247
capabilities, estimate of:
grade and, 183-4, 192, 244-5, 256-7
efficiency rating and, 182-4, 246
job-satisfaction and, 176-8
careers: advice to entrants, 185-7, 242, 244-5, 246, 263
change of, 40-1, 105-6, 111-12, 262
choice of, 105-6, 200-4, 262
respondents', 163-6
changes of job, 97, 165, 173-4, 235-238, 243
Chieseman, Dr., 10
Cioffi, F., 151, 153, 155
Civil Service: Class structure of, 13, 69-70, 259-60
Clerical Association, 10, 66, 68, 74, 75n, 82, 86, 98, 103-4, 149, 265
Commissioners, 3n, 7, 8n, 11, 109, 129, 261, 263
Pay Research Unit, 5, 211
clubs, 20, 167-9, 243
cohesiveness, 50, 58, 60-1, 62, 90-3, 214-15. *See also* protectiveness
colleagues, attitudes to, 213-15, 244
commissions: Civil Service, 3n, 7, 8n, 11, 109, 129, 261, 263
Forestry, 133
Prison, 7
Royal: Pilkington, 5n, 6n
Priestley, 3, 5, 116, 211
Tomlin, 4n
competitiveness, 9, 94-5

consultation: machinery, 7
  with staff, 222-3, 243
cooperation, 61, 87-8, 91-2, 264, 267
County Courts Department, 133
Crichel Down, 43n, 45, 260
Crowther, J., 11, 30
Crozier, M., 280
Culhane, Miss R., 15

Decoration, 212-3, 242, 243
delegation, 257-8
demotion, *see* reversion
desk classes, 12
dirt, 212, 242, 243
disadvantages of the job, 202-4
discipline, 101-4, 108, 217-18, 242, 243, 244-5, 264, 266, 267
disestablishment, 35
dismissal: 34-56
  attitudes towards dismissal for incompetence, 52-4, 56, 265-6
  difficulties of, 49-51
  efficiency and, 41-3, 52-4, 56, 265-6
  fear of, 105
  lesser penalties, 43, 43n
  limits of, 51-4
  optimum rate of, 51, 56
  possibilities as incentive, 51-2, 54
  probation, 45-7
  rates of, 54-6
  responsibility for, 43-5
  retirement, 35-8
  retirement before normal age, 39-43
  reversion and, 35-6
  uses of, 34-56
  views on uses of, 47-56
Dodds, C. H., 99n
domestic problems, 20-3, 121-2
down-grading, 35-6, 43, 46, 47
draughts, 212-13, 242, 243
Dunnill, F., 143n, 166

Education, Ministry of, 64n
efficiency: age and, 81-4
  as aim, 62, 263
  cohesiveness and, 90-3
  collective, 75, 81-4, 85, 89-90, 181, 237-8, 263-7
  concomitants of, 180-4
  definition of, 64
  dismissal and, 41-3, 52-4, 56, 265-6
  group, *see* 'collective'
  individual, 74-5, 82, 178-84, 246, 264
  interest of the work and, 181-2, 246

  job-satisfaction and, 124, 125, 169-96, 244-5, 246, 263-5, 272-4, 276-7
  management training and, 32
  measurement of, 9-10, 48-50, 64-5
  morale and, 1, 6, 25-6, 56, 62-3, 263
  productivity or, 59-60
  retirement age and, 37-8, 41-3, 47-9, 74n, 265-6
  sex and, 80-1
  sick leave and, 124-5, 138-9, 140, 142, 246
  spirit of competition and, 9
  time spent in group and, 81, 84-5, 88-90, 264
  time spent on job and, 81-4, 165
  value of the work and, 180-1
  variations in, 48
  welfare officers and, 249
efficiency rating: 46-7, 178-9, 272-4
  advice to potential entrants and, 185-7
  age groups and, 179-80, 246, 264
  attractions of the job and, 181-2
  esprit de corps and, 181, 265-6
  estimate of capabilities and, 182-4, 246
  grade and, 180
  promotion and, 180, 182
  value of the work and, 180-1
environment, physical working, 3-4, 211-13. *See also* physical conditions of work
esprit de corps, 60, 181, 187, 238-40, 243, 265, 266
Establishment Divisions, 18-19, 34, 46
Estacode, 20, 25, 36n, 45

Fairbairn, A. S., 114n
First Division Association, 149
Flugel, J. C., 238n
Forestry Commission, 133
furniture, 211-13, 242, 243

Gardner, G., 151, 153, 155
Gilbert, W. S., 258
grade: advice to potential entrants and, 185-7
  age and, 243-5
  attitude to: management, 224-6
    own organisation, 239-40
    subordinates, 227-9
    work, 229-31
  efficiency and, 180

INDEX

estimate of capabilities and, 176-7, 183-4
estimated status and, 187-92, 195-6
interest of the work and, 194-6, 244-5
job-satisfaction and, 175-6, 177-8, 192-6, 246, 247
pay and, 209-11
public's attitude and, 231-3
relations: inter-level, 215-17
  personal, 213-15
retirement and, 37
sick leave and, 118-19, 129-31
status and, 195-6
value of the work and, 188
grades: appointment, 8n-9n
  entry, 259-60
  numbers in, 39n
  promotion within, 258-60
Gray, P. G., 150

Hall, Mr. Glanvil, 42
Hailstone, J. E., 156, 174n
Handyside, J., 11, 30, 31, 32, 33, 151, 155n, 157n, 170-1
Harris, Miss E. M., 145
Hawthorne Experiment, 1-2
health: 10, 39-40, 139-41
heating, 212-13
holidays, 115-17, 181, 182, 198-9, 200
Hoppock job-satisfaction scale, 151, 170, 171n
hostels, 20
hours: of work, 181, 182, 194, 198-9, 200, 217-18; work after, 167-8, 217
Howlett, Dr. J., 156
Humphreys, Miss B. V., 223n
Hurry, C., 153-4
hypochondria, 139-40

Industrial Welfare Society, 15
industry: attitude towards dismissal for incompetence, 52-4
  consultation with staff, 22, 23-4
  dismissal rate in, 54-6
  management training in, 31-2
  pay and status in, 5-6
  selection in, 55
  sick leave in, 112-14, 115n
  studies in morale in, 1-2, 9-10
  welfare work in, 15, 16, 17

Inland Revenue, 27
Institute of Personnel Management, 145

Institute of Statistics, 155
intellectual aspect of the work, 3, 6-7
interest of the work: as an attraction of the job, 199-201, 248, 250
  efficiency and, 181-2, 246
  grade and, 194-6, 244-5
  job-satisfaction and, 194-6, 201, 242, 246
  studied at Benton, 93-4
  sick leave and, 124, 125, 138, 142
inter-level relations, 69-70, 99-104, 215-17, 243, 244, 259, 260
interviews: before appointment, 8n-9n
  as research technique, 14, 60, 85-6, 143
  with promotion boards, 204, 209

Jackson, C. W., 156
job: attractions of the, 117-18, 181-2, 199-202
  changes of, 97, 165, 173-4, 235-8, 243, 262
  disadvantages, of 202-4
  fear of losing, 34
  importance of, 187-92
job-satisfaction: 169-78, 198-202, 234-5, 240, 242, 246-7
  absenteeism and, 61, 108, 263
  advice to potential entrants and, 185-7, 263
  age and 110, 171-6, 246, 264-5
  age groups and, 174-6
  assessment of, 60, 170-1
  attractions of the job and, 194-5
  contact with public and, 234
  discipline and, 217n
  efficiency and, 124, 125, 169-96, 244-5, 246, 263-5, 272-4, 276-7
  efficiency rating and, 244-5, 272-4
  employers and, 62-3
  estimates of capabilities, 176-7, 244-5
  grade and, 175-6, 177-8, 192-6, 246, 247
  Hoppock scale, 151, 170, 171n
  indices of, 108-9
  in industry, 108, 170-1
  interest of the work and, 194-6, 201, 242, 246
  labour turnover and, 61, 62, 108-12, 173-4, 263-4
  measurement of, 60, 170, 171n
  morale and, 60, 247, 249-50, 263-4
  other attitudes and, 195-6

job-satisfaction—*continued*
  pay and, 209-11, 246-7, 273
  Press attitude and, 233
  promotion and, 178, 194, 208, 246, 273
  public's attitude and, 233
  responsibility and, 246-7
  scale, 170-1
  sick leave and, 112, 122-4, 125, 137-8, 246, 250, 263
  status and, 187-92, 195-6, 246, 258-9
  studies of, 271-4
  supervision and, 221-2
  time and, 171-5, 201, 246, 264
  women and, 174-6, 242, 280-1

Katz, D., 61n, 65, 101, 181, 265, 276-7
Kerr, 113n
Knowles, K. J. C., 156
Kristy, N. F., 11, 61n, 185, 272-4

Labour and National Service, Ministry of, 7, 39
Landsberger, H. A., 2n
'Large Ministry', 22-3, 52-4, 119-25, 131-41, 145-265
lavatories, 21, 69n, 212-13, 215, 216, 242, 243
leadership, 8, 10, 27, 29, 32, 248
leave, 4, 19, 116-17. *See also* sick leave
level in the hierarchy, 175-6, 177-8, 192. *See also* grade
lighting, 212-3
Lockwood, D., 254n
London Transport Executive, 121, 126n, 127-8
Long, Dr. C. W., 10

Maccoby, N., 61n, 65, 101, 181, 265, 276-7
management: age and, 99-100
  as a skill, 26, 104-5
  as criterion for promotion, 26, 206
  attitudes to, 1-2, 9, 31, 88, 101-4, 223-7
  grade and, 225
  in industry, 9, 31-2, 101
  rôle of Organisation and Methods Division, 7-8
  sex and, 99-100
  training courses, 26-33, 46:
    effectiveness, 29-35, 248
    methods, 27-9

  results, 30-1
  women and, 224-6
Marriott, R., 171, 173
Mayne, S., 274
Mayo, Elton, 1
mechanisation, 68, 70, 252n
Medical Research Council, 171, 173
men at the top, 157, 223-7, 244-5, 247, 260
Ministry of: Education, 64n
  Labour and National Service, 7, 39
  Pensions and National Insurance, 10, 25, 27, 33, 65-107, 128, 133, 141
  Supply, 7
  Works, 3, 68
misconduct, 39-40, 67, 115
monotony, 93-4, 105, 186
morale: attitude to, 6-14
  concept of, 57-63, 247
  definitions of, 57-8, 61-2
  dismissal and, 265-6
  efficiency and, 1, 6, 25-6, 56, 59, 62-63, 263
  factors in, 59-63, 267
  in armed forces, 1, 2, 9, 57, 180-1
  in industry, 1-2
  job-satisfaction and, 60, 247, 249-250, 263-4
  nature of, 57-9
  need to consider, 1-6
  studies in, 1-2, 8-10, 11
  welfare and, 14-26
Morrison, Lord, 47-8, 56
Morse, Nancy C., 61n, 65, 101, 181, 265, 276-7

National Insurance, Ministry of Pensions and, 10, 27, 33, 65-107, 128, 133, 141
National Institute of Industrial Psychology, 30, 151, 155, 157, 158, 170, 171n
noise, 212-3
'North Firm', 22-3, 52-4, 145-265

Office Management Association, 115n
Ordnance Survey, 133
organisation, attitudes to own, 195-196, 238-41, 243, 244-5, 266
Organisation and Methods Division, 7-8, 10, 11, 64, 271
overtime, 167, 168
overwork, 125, 167, 231

Parkinson's Law, 203n
Paterson, T. T., 57n, 112-3, 180
pay: as an attraction of the job, 182, 242-3
  attitudes to, 105, 198-9, 200, 209-11, 247, 251, 254
  commissions on, 4-5
  forfeit of, 43
  grade and, 209-11
  grievances over, 5-6
  job-satisfaction and, 209-11, 246-7, 273
  Research Unit, 5, 211
  status and, 5-6
  valuing the work and, 5-6
  women and, 241, 244, 251, 261
pension: as an attraction of the job, 182, 194
  attitudes to, 198-9, 200, 254
  efficiency rating and, 182
  loss of, 38-9
  retirement, 40-1, 42
  scale, 35n
Pensions: and National Insurance, Ministry of, 10, 27, 33, 65-107, 128, 133, 141
personal: affairs: and the superior, 19-20
  insulation of, 19
  problems: and the welfare officer, 15, 17, 19-20, 23, 25-6
  types of, 20-3
  relations, 213-15, 275-6
Personnel Management, Institute of, 145
physical conditions of work, 105, 181-2, 198-9, 200, 211-3, 243, 252
Pilkington Commission, 5n, 6n
Post office, 25, 65n, 104, 141, 185, 250, 272-4
Press criticism, 234-5, 243, 254, 261, 266
pressure of work, 94-5, 125, 167
pride in the working group, 60-1, 265, 276
Priestley Commission, 3, 5, 116, 211
Prison Commission, 7
private office workers, 24, 52-5, 115n, 145-265, 276-7
probation, 45-6
productivity: assessment of, 64-5, 77-8, 79, 104
  cohesiveness and, 90-3
  comparing, 74-9
  efficiency or, 59-60

factors in, 79-85
  group, 75, 81, 84-5
  helping out and, 91-3
  individual, 74-5
  job-satisfaction and, 276-7
  personal relations and, 87-8, 89
  pride in the working group and, 61
  rates, 75-7, 91
  time and, 81-5
  women and, 80-1, 84, 85
professional civil service, 149, 224, 245, 260, 274
promotion: age and, 205
  as an attraction of the job, 182
  attitudes to, 198-9, 200, 202, 205-209, 238, 244-5, 250, 254
  boards, 86, 96, 204, 209, 242-5
  criteria for, 206, 208-9
  down-grading in interests of, 36, 37
  efficiency rating and, 180, 182
  job-satisfaction and, 178, 194, 208, 246, 273
  management training and, 26
  prospects, 38, 110-11, 182, 241, 242-3
  reports and, 18-19, 46, 257
  respondents' careers, 166-7
  retirement age and, 38
  system, 4, 18-19, 110-11, 204-6, 257, 259-60
  women and, 74, 199n, 203, 207, 209, 241, 151
protectiveness, 50, 86-9, 265-7. See also cohesiveness
Prudential Insurance Company, 61n, 65, 101, 181, 265, 276-7
psychologists: occupational, 1, 2, 9, 10, 55, 57, 63, 90, 112
  rôle of, 7
  studies carried out by, 11
public: attitude of, 48-9, 202, 231-5, 247, 253-4, 260-2, 266
  attitudes to, 233
  contact with, 233-4, 246, 247, 261-2

Questionnaire: age of respondents, 158, 162-3
  arrangement, 143-60
  careers of respondents, 163-5
  drafting, 149-53
  distribution, 144-6
  form, 282-94
  job satisfaction of respondents, 157-8

questionnaire—*continued*
  participants, 145-6
  procedure, 146-8
  promotion of respondents, 166-7
  reasons for adopting this type of inquiry, 143-4
  response to, 154-60
  results of, 161-247
  sex of respondents, 162-3
  summary of results, 241-7
  suspicions of respondents, 153-4

Records Branch: attitude to work, 93-8, 252-3
  comment on study of, 104-7
  description of, 65-6, 134
  interviews, 85-90
  management, 98-104, 205, 267
  productivity, 74-85
  recruitment, 67
  resignations, 111n, 250
  staff relations, 68-70, 250
  valuing the work, 96-8
recruitment, 3, 7, 51, 105-6, 254, 263-4, 264-5
redundancy, 34n, 39
reforms, 260
Reid, D. D., 114n
relations: inter-level, 69-70, 99-104, 215-17, 243, 244, 259, 260
  personal, 213-5, 275-6
  staff, at Benton, 68-70, 250
  with superior, 206
reports: adverse, 46-7, 178, 218
  annual, 18, 26n, 46, 79, 178
  method of giving, 45-7
  promotion and, 18-19, 46, 257
resignation: age and, 109-10
  compulsory, 41-3
  rates of, 109, 209, 248, 250
  reasons for, 109-112
  voluntary, 40-1
responsibility, 152-3, 229-30, 242, 244-7, 257
retirement: age and, 34-8
  before normal age, 38-47
  compulsory: 41-3, 44, 47, 51-2, 54-5
  efficiency and, 37-8, 41-3, 47-9, 74n, 265-6
  grade and, 37-56
  ill-health and, 10, 24, 39-40, 74n
  misconduct, 39-40
  normal, 35-8
  rates of, 39, 40 ,41, 44, 46, 54-6

  reasons for, 37, 38-9
  redundancy, 34n, 39
  voluntary, 38, 40-1, 52, 55, 98
reversion, 35-6
Rollett, Dr., 150
Ruskin College, 152

Scientific and Industrial Research, Department of, 133n, 151
scientific workers, 11, 112, 224, 274-5, 277-80
Scottish Education Department, 64n
Searle, R., 197n
security of job, 182, 194, 198-9, 200, 252
selection, 8, 26, 55, 264-5
Shephard, Professor H. A., 277
sick leave: abuse of, 24-5, 115-22, 250
  age and, 117n, 120-1, 127-8, 130
  as an index of job-satisfaction, 112, 122-4, 125, 137-42, 246, 250, 263
  attitudes to, 250-1
  certified, 117, 126-42, 246
  conditions of, 114-15, 250
  efficiency and, 124-5, 138-9, 140, 142, 246
  grade and, 118-19, 129-31
  in industry, 112-14, 132-3, 137, 146
  interest of the work and, 124, 125, 138, 142
  in the armed forces, 112-13
  other office workers, 126n, 127-8, 146
  Post Office analysis, 120n, 134-5, 136, 137, 250
  rates of absence from, 118, 119, 120, 129, 136
  records, 25
  rules, 24, 114-15
  scheme, 4
  size and, 132-40, 248, 265-6
  staff groups and, 128-31, 142
  uncertified, 115-25, 142, 246, 250, 263
  welfare officers' concern with, 24-5, 115, 140, 249
  women and, 119, 121-2, 126-31, 250
size: 132-40, 248, 265-6
'Small Ministry', 22-3, 52-4, 119-25, 137-41, 145-265
social life with colleagues, 89, 182, 188, 198-9, 200, 213-5
societies, 167-9

Society of Civil Servants, 65, 98, 149
'South Firm', 22-3, 52-4, 145-265
spare-time activities, 167-9, 242
spontaneous comment on questionnaires, 197-9
staff associations: 34, 39, 68, 85-6, 148, 223, 236
  See also Civil Service Clerical Association; First Division Association; Institution of Professional Civil Servants; Society of Civil Servants
staffing, 239, 240, 243
Stansfield, R. G., 11, 77, 271
Statistics, Institute of, 156
status: as an attraction of the job, 182, 188
  attitudes to, 198-9, 200
  consciousness, 191-2, 259
  estimated, 72, 187-92, 244-5
  grade and, 195-6
  in the community, 198-9, 200, 261
  job satisfaction and, 187-92, 195-6, 246, 258-9
  of desk worker, 48-9, 254
  pay and, 5-6
  symbols, 191, 215-16, 242, 255
Strauss, G. R., 45
Stein, M. I., 278
strikes, 3, 9, 57, 59, 108-9, 249-50, 254
subordinates: attitudes to, 227-9, 241-242, 244-5, 247
  training of, 257
Superannuation Acts, 40, 41, 42
  See also pensions
superior officers: attitudes to, 151, 218-22
  relations with, 206
  women as, 100, 102, 220-1, 241-2, 251
supervision: age and, 99-100, 220-1
  as a skill, 26
  at Records Branch, 98-107
  attitudes to, 31, 88, 101-4
  courses for, 27, 99
  degrees of, 218-20
  in industry, 31-2
  job-satisfaction and, 221-2
  methods, 27-9, 264, 277-8
  studies in, 276-7
  training in, 26-33
  time in charge and, 100
  women and, 100, 102, 220-1, 241-2, 251
Supply, Ministry of, 7

Tarkowski, Z. M. T., 28n, 224n
technical officers, 5
time: in the job, 165, 173-5, 264
  in the organisation, 173-5, 246, 264, 266
  in the working group, 85
  job-satisfaction and, 171-5, 196, 201, 246
  keeping, 103, 217-18, 243
  wasting, 103
timing, 75, 93-5
titles, 258-9
Tomlin Commission, 4n
Trade, Board of, 271
training: and Education Division, 27, 28, 29, 224
  management, 26-33, 257, 264-5
  methods of, 257-8
  of civil servants, 7, 257-8
  supervision, 26-33
transfers, 18, 70, 96n, 97, 235-8, 242, 250
travelling time, 168-9, 243, 254
Treasury, The: 5, 261:
  Central Staff Records Division, 117
  Medical Adviser, 10, 40, 114
  Organisation and Methods Division, 7-8, 271
  Training and Education Division, 27, 28, 29, 224
  Welfare Adviser, 15-16
Turnbull, Miss A., 28n, 29, 224n
turnover of staff *see* wastage
typing pools: 11, 77, 255n, 271-2

Unestablished officers, 35n
unions, 34
universities, 4, 77

Valuing the work, 96-7, 180-1, 188, 244-5, 246, 247, 250-1, 254-7
variety in work, 185-6, 229-30, 242, 261
ventilation, 212-13, 247
Viteles, M. R., 9n, 58n, 112, 137n
vocational guidance, 8

War Office, 7
wastage, 61, 109-12, 171-2, 175, 209, 249
Welfare: Adviser to Treasury, 15-6
  Officers: casework by, 20-3, 249
    consultation with, 22, 23-4
    duties of, 20, 167, 169

Welfare—*continued*
  function of, 15, 19, 25-6
  in the Large and Small Ministries, 20-3
  origin of, 15
  recruitment of, 16, 17, 249
  relation of Establishment Division to, 18-9
  sick leave and, 24-5, 115, 140, 249
  training of, 16-18
  voluntary resignations and, 111
  women as, 16n
Whitley: Rt. Hon. J. H., 7
  Councils, 46n, 223, 243, 248
women: as superior officers, 100, 102, 220-1, 241-2, 251
  as welfare officers, 16n
  at Records Branch, 80-1, 84, 85, 87, 100, 102
  attitude, 87, 89, 224-6, 241-2, 244
    to management, 224-6
    to own organisation, 239-40
    to pay, 244
    to subordinates, 228-9, 241-2
    to work, 229-30
  compared with men, 80-1, 102, 241-2, 251
  consultation with welfare officers 22-3
  equal pay for, 241, 251, 261
  importance of the job and, 189-90
  job-satisfaction and, 174-6, 242, 280-1
  pay of, 244
  promotion prospects of, 74, 199n, 203, 207, 209, 241, 251
  sick leave: of married, 121-2, 126-131, 250
    of single, 119, 121, 126-7, 128, 131
  talkativeness of, 73-4
  voluntary resignation rate, 109
work: attitudes to, 93-6, 229-31
  importance of the, 187-90
  pressure of, 94-5, 125, 167
  valuing the, 96-7, 180-1, 188, 244-245, 246, 247, 250-1, 254-7
  volume of, 230-1
  words for the, 192-6
Workers Educational Association, 152, 155
Works, Ministry of, 3, 68
Wouk, H., 58
Wyatt, S., 171, 173

Augsburg College
George Sverdrup Library
Minneapolis, Minnesota 55404